FLEMISH MUSIC AND SOCIETY IN THE FIFTEENTH AND SIXTEENTH CENTURIES

FLEMISH MUSIC

AND SOCIETY IN THE FIFTEENTH AND SIXTEENTH CENTURIES
by Robert Wangermée

ENGLISH VERSION BY ROBERT ERICH WOLF

FREDERICK A. PRAEGER, *Publishers*
New York · Washington · London

FREDERICK A. PRAEGER, *Publishers*

111 Fourth Avenue, New York, N.Y. 10003, U.S.A.

5, Cromwell Place, London S.W. 7, England

Published in the United States of America in 1968
by Frederick A. Praeger, Inc., Publishers

© 1968 by Editions Arcade, Brussels

Library of Congress Catalog Card Number : 6826792

Printed in Belgium

1. Concert in the Country.
Tapestry in wool with linen thread.

Preface

It was an enormous – indeed, I do not hesitate to say grandiose – undertaking to set out to show in both their broad scope and their fine detail those two centuries, the fifteenth and sixteenth, which can rightly be termed the Golden Age of music in the Low Countries. True, it could have been done by ladling out generous doses of praise right and left with, here and there, splendid verbal apotheoses, all this in a purple prose more rich in external brillance than in grasp of things as they truly were.

But such is not the approach of M. Wangermée. A historian in the general sense of the word, but specializing in the history of music, which he teaches with rare competence at the University of Brussels, he is not among those who can be content with a brilliant outward show to the neglect of the true bases of things, of the inner life which gives them vitality and of the relationships which link them to what precedes them and to what surrounds them.

His conception of music history is not at all that of what we might call the specializing specialist, completely absorbed in the heaping up of bits of facts which, granted, are useful but which in themselves scarcely serve to bring out in relief the fundamental aspects of the subject being set forth and explained.

From this can be gathered the importance that M. Wangermée attributes to music as a social phenomenon whose manifestations are infinitely diversified at different times and in different places. The entire first part of his book is taken up with a singularly penetrating study of the role played by the ars musica in the daily spiritual life of human groups, in terms both of the effects this had upon the various forms of music and of how men of past times thought about those forms from the standpoint of their use as well as from that of their aesthetics. One cannot insist too much on the originality and high worth of those chapters in which the development of the art of music is examined in close connection with a given social situation, whether religious or secular. Nothing is more apt than such a method to help us understand to the fullest music of past ages without the obstacles of classroom dreariness or irksome pedantry.

It is not without regret that one finishes reading such a book, packed as it is with broad notions both rich in meaning and firmly based on facts. And it is also not without a certain melancholy that we come to the end of this long apprenticeship, to the twilight which, at the end of the seventeenth century, closed in relentlessly on the immense influence of Netherlandish music and on the splendor which earned for it the unanimous admiration of the fine minds of its time.

CHARLES VAN DEN BORREN

Acknowledgments

I am grateful to my friend Herman Liebaers for having urged me to write this book and for having followed its writing step by step. Charles van den Borren, my teacher and master, has been so kind as to read the manuscript of this work and to give me his advice. H. Heckmann, A.-M. Pols and R. E. Wolf, the musicologists responsible for the translation into German, Flemish and English respectively, have not failed, in the course of their work, to make certain suggestions which have not been ignored. Madame Geneviève Thibault, Comtesse de Chambure, graciously permitted me to consult her iconographic documentation on fifteenth-century music. Certain problems connected with Florentine manuscripts were elucidated for me by Dottoressa Bianca Beccherini. My consultation of works in the library of the Brussels Conservatory was generously aided by Albert van der Linden. Pierre Baudson helped in the collection and description of the illustrations. Bernard Huys kindly agreed to prepare a basic list of phonograph records.

In the course of my work, I received much help from directors of museums, librarians and friends. I know they will forgive my not listing their names here. They can all be quite certain of my gratitude.

ROBERT WANGERMÉE

Prologue

Sabbato in aduentu do
mini ad uesperas super
psalmos. antiphona Se
nedictus. psalmus. Jpm.
Cum ceteris antiphonis
et psalmis. Jnfin. Caplm.

ce
dies
ueni
unt
diat
dns
et sustatabo dauid germe

2. Tree of Jesse.
Miniature.

A Question and Some Proposals

Even the bravest scholar hesitates when, in relation to the fifteenth and sixteenth centuries, he must speak of the "Flemish" music of the time, for the term "Flemish" is scarcely adequate to describe a complex historical reality. True, within the framework of present-day Belgium, it applies to people united by a common language, but historically it can either be limited to the inhabitants of the former county of Flanders or, in a larger context, extended to include all natives of the Low Countries. And yet, equivocal as it is, the term has for long been employed in the history of the arts and culture and enjoys therefore a certain prestige. This very indecisiveness makes it indispensable to specify just how it was used within the context of the Renaissance and to come to some decision as to whether or not one can apply a term, generally accepted by art historians, to the history of music.

At the start of the fifteenth century, in that region which, very much later, was destined to become Belgium, there were independent principalities which Philip the Good, Duke of Burgundy, succeeded in bringing under a common rule thanks to the fortunes of succession but thanks also to his political astuteness. The counties of Flanders and Artois, the duchies of Brabant-Limburg and Luxemburg, the counties of Hainaut, Holland and Zeeland, and the Domain of Friesland, all of these together constituted for the dukes of Burgundy the lands *de par-deçà* – the "distant" lands. Those territories retained a considerable degree of regional autonomy, despite which they had to submit gradually to a certain number of centralizing institutions. After Charles the Bold, these principalities passed to Mary of Burgundy, then, after a guardianship exercised by Maximilian of Austria, to Philip the Handsome. With the marriage of the latter to the daughter of the Catholic King, the fate of these regions was welded to that of Spain for two centuries.

Despite the fact that these principalities had common aspirations and a common civilization and displayed a certain solidarity among themselves, they still did not enjoy a perfect cohesion. Their territorial limits differed at various times and never at any time corresponded to those of present-day Belgium. Valenciennes, Bavai, Avesnes belonged to Hainaut, Lille to Flanders, while the bishopric of Tournai was not wrested from France until 1521. Charles V succeeded in extending his holdings considerably to the east and north by acquiring the duchy of Gelder and the neighboring regions, while Picardy and Artois endured many changes, being sometimes part of the Low Countries, sometimes of France. On the other hand, Liège, a prince-bishopric, contrived to retain its autonomy until the French Revolution. Cambrai also generally protected the autonomy of its small territory squeezed in between Hainaut, Flanders, Artois and France, but this may be explained by the fact that it was

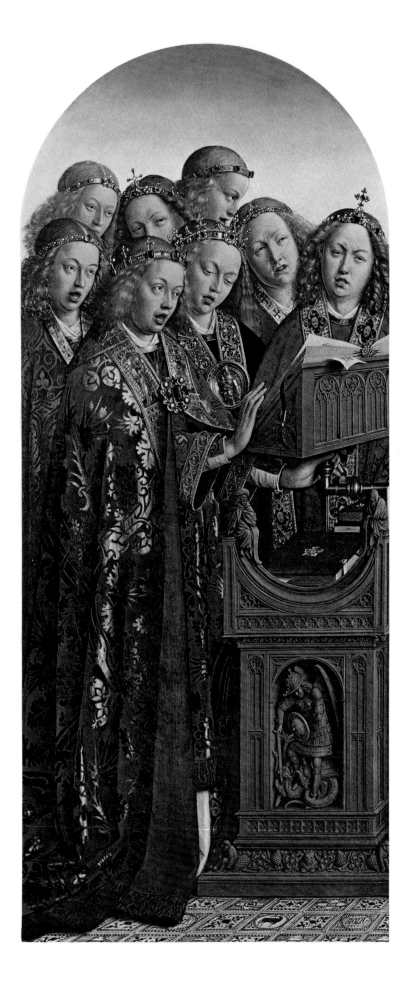

3. Singing Angels.
Jan van Eyck.

the seat of a vast bishopric whose ecclesiastical jurisdiction extended at one time or another to cities like Antwerp, Brussels, Tournai, Arras and Saint-Omer.

The territories assembled by the dukes of Burgundy and by Charles V were at first designated rather vaguely as *les pays d'embas* or *les pays de par-deçà,* the distant lands, or as the Low Countries (*Nederlanden* in Flemish), having in mind, no doubt, those vast flat stretches lying along the sea. Around 1570 they were called the Seventeen Provinces, but, as early as 1579, the seven principalities to the north, which were Calvinist, seceded to form the United Provinces (*Verenigde Provinciën*). In the seventeenth and eighteenth centuries, it was the southern principalities, finally determined to remain Catholic after their revolts and subject to the authority first of Spanish and then of Austrian governors, which were called the *Pays-Bas,* the Low Countries or Netherlands. This designation was given its widest extension in the short-lived kingdom of the Netherlands, which lasted only from 1815 to 1830, after which the name was applied only to the former United Provinces – now generally called Holland – whereas the country to the south was thereafter called Belgium.

Despite all this, historians and writers on music have often continued to speak of the "Netherlandish" music of the fifteenth and sixteenth centuries. In itself this need not be judged harshly as long as such writers are careful to specify that the terms used are merely conventional and also as long as they do not forget that the principality of Liège, which played such an important role in the music of the

4. Angel Musicians.
Jan van Eyck.

time, had never at any time been "Netherlandish."
The fact is that neither in French, Flemish nor
English is there an adjective which describes accurately a geographical-cultural entity which is at one
and the same time so united and so diverse.

And yet one simply cannot describe musicians of
the fifteenth and sixteenth centuries as "Belgian," for
this would be a flagrant anachronism, however frequently Renaissance Humanists may have called the
inhabitants of the territories assembled by the dukes
of Burgundy *Belgæ,* a literary but not a political or
ethnic designation and strictly confined to erudite
writings.

But since, to deal at all with this matter, we must
have recourse to some sort of conventional label,
why not simply speak of "Flemish" music? True
as it may be that in the sixteenth century Flanders
was no more one "land" among others in the Low
Countries, and that the Flemish were never confused with the natives of Brabant or Hainaut, it is
also true that in foreign parts, especially in the
South, all the people who came from any of the
Seventeen Provinces were often known as Flemish,
as *fiamminghi* in Italy, *flamencos* in Spain and *flamands* in France, thereby applying to the whole of
the territory the name of one of its most typical
regions. Indeed, it is so much the more legitimate
for us to use this name since, from the Renaissance
on, people have spoken of Flemish tapestries and
Flemish painters even more than of Flemish musicians. It is therefore in the largest context, that familiar from art history, that we shall speak here of
"Flemish" music.

This conventional terminology will prove acceptable if we can succeed in showing that in music as in painting it applies to a stylistic concept. We must therefore determine if, in the centuries which concern us, the music created by "Flemish" composers had sufficient homogeneity of idiom to justify calling it a single style. Such unity has generally been conceded by authorities on the subject, beginning with Kiesewetter and Fétis at the start of the last century down through Ambros, van den Borren, Besseler and others. Since, in any event, musical language went through considerable transformations in the course of the two centuries, some musicologists hold out for a succession of style periods, beginning with a Burgundian School followed by a First and then by a Second Netherlandish School. Others however, more cautious, think it better to characterize the successive periods by no more than the names of the most outstanding masters of each of them.

But throughout these several stylistic changes a certain type of counterpoint succeeded in imposing itself and was accepted as the normal language by most European musicians during more than a century. We must therefore determine to what extent Flemish composers contributed to its formation and to its widespread acceptance.

And yet, the true subject of this book is something else : it is concerned with seeing Flemish music within the context of the society of its time. If it is true that this music enjoyed long-lasting and, indeed, international success, if it was really adopted throughout Europe as a model to be imitated, it can only be because it succeeded in fulfilling certain artistic and spiritual desires of its epoch. In that event, it should be possible to arrive at a better understanding of what the science and pleasure of music signified to the men of the Renaissance. Because too often the history of an art is reduced to the history of its forms and language, we fail to understand its vitality, we strip it to bare bones. In this book, in which the pictorial image plays an important part, the attempt has been made to integrate the music of the past into the life of its time. We have tried to show how the music of the fifteenth and sixteenth centuries was linked to certain spiritual traditions, by what means it strove to satisfy the dual demands of moral edification and casual entertainment, with what appropriate techniques it endeavored to achieve both formal rigor and artistic dignity.

In this way we wish to help restore music to its rightful place in the history of culture. Although the visual arts together with literature and philosophy have for long been called on to shed light on past civilizations, music for its part has generally been ignored. It is virtually absent from such definitive syntheses as Burckhardt's *The Civilization of the Renaissance in Italy* and Huizinga's *The Waning of the Middle Ages*. By showing the important role played by music, both sacred and profane, in the daily life of men of the fifteenth and sixteenth centuries, we wish to prove that it is not possible to comprehend entirely any period if the music to which it gave rise is neglected.

It remains true that the actual sound of this music of past times is, for many, a scarcely explored world, even though many recordings are now available to provide an indispensable illustration and reference. Everything in this book leads back to the music itself : if we wish to make it better known, it is because we desire that others too will come to love it. We want to demonstrate that an art created in the service of the Church or for the festivities of princes or merchants of the past is able, today still, to touch us profoundly. Finally, we hope that it will be conceded that this music, conceived originally only to fulfill some function in church or court or dwelling, and not as pure art, is nevertheless worthy of surviving through the centuries and that a Guillaume Dufay or a Roland de Lassus occupies, in the museum of sound, a place as important as that of van Eyck or Bruegel in any museum of painting.

Chapter 1

Talking About Music

For the men of the Middle Ages and the Renaissance, what was meant by "music"? Throughout the centuries, theorists had prefaced their treatises with the question *Quis est musica*? True enough, this was often no more than a rhetorical question imposed by tradition, and yet, through their answers, frozen though they were in the mold of convention, we may nevertheless glimpse something of what music was for those times. Certainly it was not yet "the art of combining sounds in a manner pleasing to the ear" as the favorite definition of Jean-Jacques Rousseau put it, or at least it was not *only* an "art of combining sounds," pleasing or not. It was also something more general and certainly more profound.

ANCIENT GREECE :

THE PHILOSOPHERS SPECULATE

We must go far back beyond the Fathers of the Church, to ancient Greece, to find the origin of conceptions which in the Middle Ages no longer always had the vitality of ideas created out of experience and fortified by being lived with, ideas which, slowly only and even painfully, men came to suspect had become outworn.

One of the most meaningful myths of Greek Antiquity is that of Orpheus : poet and above all musician who, through the power of his song, succeeded in charming wild beasts and softening the hearts of infernal divinities. Orpheus the musician was also a magician whose incantations were the means of his magic-making. But Orpheus was more than a literary fable. There were Orphic mysteries with ceremonies of purification in the course of which collective dances mingled with song to wash away the impurities besoiling both body and soul.

Primitive Pythagorism also practiced purification rites which used music, and these go back to the very dawn of Greek thought. Onto the magical nature of music it grafted something more rational by establishing a relationship between two powers equally mysterious, music and mathematics : *What is most wise of all? Number. What is most beautiful? Harmony*. In bringing into concordance these two principles, it also laid the bases of an ethics and an aesthetics with some scientific pretensions, which were to endure for centuries. To the Pythagoreans goes the credit for having studied the mathematical relationships among the various tones of the scale. The seemingly natural laws which they discovered in music they attempted to apply to other domains. Thus, the harmony which reigns in the movements of the celestial spheres was, for them, not only a happy disposition of the whole and the parts : it was also a veritable musical concert. Indeed, the music made here on earth was itself no more than an imitation, an echo of the harmony which regulates the motions of the seven celestial bodies. By partaking

13

of music on earth, men could participate to a certain measure in the supreme harmony and thereby offer to the soul the possibility of liberating itself from human passions and stains, of winning back to the happy state of its original bond with divinity by recalling the experiences of its previous existences (the Pythagoreans were, in fact, firm believers in metempsychosis).

The network of concordances thus established among numbers, stars and the magical power of musical incantations was to undergo a moral and poetic transposition in the writings of Plato. Broadly speaking, Plato did not accord much importance to art, since art for him was no more than an imitation of this world we know through our senses, which itself is but an imitation of the eternal Idea : art is thus a mere copy of a copy. But among the arts music has a privileged position since what it imitates are states of the soul. The human soul can translate into songs and dances all the feelings it experiences, and, on the other hand, music can give rise, within the soul, to emotions identical with those it expresses. Music justifies its existence only in the measure to which it instills harmony into the soul and aids it to comprehend the harmony of the universe.

If good music is capable of producing this harmony in man, it is because it imitates divine harmony, because in its own way it is a counterpart of the Idea, and therefore can help man to understand both Truth and Beauty. For these reasons, it is urgent to distinguish clearly those melodies and rhythms susceptible of playing such a beneficent role and to reject all others without pity. But as early as Plato's times, the ethical significance of a certain kind of music was already merely a philosophical notion rather than a reality that men could experience in their daily lives. Plato himself complained that he could not find in the music of his days the moral values he prized so highly. The notion of an ethical music was already no more than a kind of moral speculation based on a body of traditional beliefs of religious origin.

For his part, Aristotle recognized that there was a place in society for music intended for diversion only. He even admitted that a type of music generally considered harmful might, in fact, have beneficial results. Transporting the soul into a state of exaltation, it could, like a purge, liberate it of everything noxious and, by expelling any excess of passion, restore to the soul its harmony. By thus according to music this power of catharsis, Aristotle preserved the concept of music as a moral ideal. This ethical conception prevailed throughout Antiquity. Along with it, as a kind of counterpoint, there were diatribes against the decadence of "modern" music and nostalgic laments for that golden age when, thanks to Orpheus and Olympus, music still possessed magical potency.

Only a few independent thinkers dared to oppose this traditional current and tried to measure what separated the moral ideal from the daily reality. At the same time as they carried on their assaults against a morality which pretended to be a science, a few Sophists of the fourth century attacked the alliance, which to others seemed so natural, between the Beautiful and the Good. Later, certain Epicureans and Skeptics attempted to show that the value of music does not lie in its own nature but, rather, in the opinion that men hold of it. They dared to challenge the belief that the destiny of the world was ruled by harmony and asserted that it was mere illusion to imagine that one must practice "good" music if one wished to live in conformity with the universal harmony and to achieve happiness. Music, they said, was merely something for relaxation, for diversion. Perhaps the mass of men held the same opinion of music, but the ethical conception continued to represent the principal current among moralists, philosophers and teachers.

Music may have played a really important role in education in archaic times. For the military state that Sparta was from the eighth to the sixth century B.C., education was based on athletics and music. Music in Sparta was an essential part of a primitive culture where, through dance, it was linked with gymnastics and, through song, became the adjunct of poetry. While solo vocal and instrumental music, choruses and poetry were finding their first masters, the entire citizenry united in active musical participation in the great religious festivals which, throughout the year, called for solemn processions, for athletic or musical contests, for choral singing and group dances.

According to Plato, education in archaic Athens had the same duality. Such a double training, gymnastics for the body, music for the soul, was intended to constitute a primary step in education, in the course of which the child was to learn to sing and to play on the lyre. But in *mousikè*, along with song and melodies, Plato made place for letters, for the study of the classic authors, whether poets or writers of prose, and even for mathematics, which was intended to form the child's judgment. Music was truly the "domain of the Muses." Secondary education, said Plato, should review all these elements and go deeper into them : literary, musical, gymnastic and mathematical studies were no more than a slow apprenticeship leading the best minds to higher studies, to philosophy.

The privileged place assigned to music (in the strictly limited sense of the term) in Plato's pedagogic program was even then out of step with the real state of things. Quite early the study of the *aulos* – a kind of oboe – had been abandoned, and in the classical period most children were not urged to study the lyre. Plato's fine saying "We consider as uncivilized anyone who cannot hold his own in a choir" no longer had any basis in reality. In religious ceremonies connected with the official cult of the city, citizen-singers had to be replaced by professionals. Like gymnastics, music appeared to be an archaic holdover in education, and in the course of the centuries both of them continued to lose ground to the profit of literary studies.

This does not mean that music ceased to be practiced, but it had become so complicated that performance on the kithara or aulos, solo singing or choral singing all required professional skill. Very much the same thing had happened in gymnastics : foot races, long jumps, throwing the discus or javelin had all gone out of common practice and become spectator sports. In education, while a major place was still granted to the cult of the Muses, this was no longer in relationship to music in the strict sense of the word but rather to literature, and it was only as a scientific discipline that music retained some place in the curriculum.

No small credit goes to the Greeks for having discovered how to measure the relationships between the length of strings or pipes and the pitch emitted. Certainly they do not seem to have progressed to the point of understanding the phenomenon of vibrations which, today, we know to be at the base of the science of acoustics. But those mechanical relationships they were able to find between sounds and the materials that can produce them permitted them to determine the numerical ratios controlling and ordering the various intervals. They observed that from the octave to the fundamental tone there exists the ratio of 2:1; for the fifth, 3:2; for the fourth, 4:3; for the major third, 5:4; for the minor third, 6:5; for the whole tone, 9:8, and so forth. Having discovered the possibility of representing a musical interval by an arithmetical ratio, and of symbolizing it thereby, the Greeks believed they had discovered the essential principle of music.

Understanding of music therefore seemed to them to lead to other clear and evident scientific truths :

16

the order which reigns in the domain of music appeared to be fundamentally a transposition of that which controls the universe. From Aristoxenus of Tarentum through Plutarch and Claudius Ptolemaeus to the Byzantines, most Greek theoretical writings were devoted to mathematical speculation; essentially, their analyses of musical modes and scales were nothing more than that. To this were added studies of rhythm, and these likewise ended up as problems in arithmetic, since the Greeks took as their basis the smallest rhythmic unit which could be considered indivisible and which could be applied to a single musical tone or to a sung syllable or to the most rapid dance movement, and this basic unit was combined into complex series of short and long values which, in turn, gave rise to other arithmetical ratios.

If then music could be reduced to a science of numbers applicable both to pitch and duration, it was normal that its study should be ranked among the scientific disciplines alongside geometry, arithmetic and astronomy. But, as a mathematical science, it no longer had anything in common with the practical art of the kithara player or of the singers in choruses. As a science, it was the object of noble speculations and its place was on the higher level of education, whereas the actual practice of music as an art was relegated to professionals, virtuosos who were not held in much esteem.

The same dichotomy was transmitted to Rome. There, music became fashionable as a Hellenistic refinement, but that elegant adornment to elegant living was purveyed by paid histrions who were despised and by courtesans and young girls trained

17

8. Theorica musica.
Franchino Gaffurio.

to play the flute. The music which had a place in education remained, in Rome as in Greece, a subject of mathematical speculation.

The Fathers of the Church inherited those conceptions. On the one hand, they hurled their anathema against music, that profane art so pernicious to the soul. But on the other hand they themselves pursued the study of musical theory which they considered, along with the other sciences, to be indispensable to the man in search of that knowledge which leads to the ultimate truth.

The literary and mathematical disciplines considered to be basic preparatory studies for philosophy were given the name of "Liberal Arts" in the second century by the Roman writer Varro, a name and function they were to keep throughout the Middle Ages and the Renaissance. In the fourth century, Martianus Capella depicted them in a kind of allegorical novel as young women, and their number was fixed at seven : Grammar, Dialectic, Rhetoric, Geometry, Arithmetic, Astronomy and Music.

The philosopher who was to influence most profoundly medieval thought, by transmitting to it a synthesis of the theories of Antiquity, was Boethius (ca. 480-524). It was as a preparation for philosophy, the supreme wisdom, that he urged the study of the four mathematical sciences forming the *Quadrivium*, the quadruple road to wisdom. Later, the three other disciplines, which are literary and aim at perfecting the modes of expression, came to be classed as the *Trivium*. Of Boethius' scientific studies, his treatises on arithmetic *(De institutione arithmetica)* and on music *(De institutione musica)* have come down to us. Basing himself on the work of Nicomachus of Gerasius, Albinus and Iamblichus, Boethius reworked all the Pythagorean and Platonic theories on music and number.

It is certain that for Boethius the word "music" was not limited to mere sound but designated, rather, all harmony. Moreover, he proposed a classification of music in which this harmony is manifested according to a universal hierarchy. *Musica mundana* is the music of the universe, cosmic music, that harmony which expresses itself in numerical ratios and which orders the movement of the stars, the mixture of the four elements of nature, and the regular alternation of the seasons. Such harmony of the spheres is not silent. It gives rise to a true, audible music, and if we earth-bound creatures cannot hear it, it is because we are so entirely immersed in it that our ears can no longer perceive it. Below this, in Boethius' hierarchy, comes *musica humana*, the harmony which rules over the microcosm of man. It is to be found in the soul and body when they are attuned to each other. It is an equilibrium between the faculties of the soul and particularly between the senses and reason, a harmony between the different organs of the body. *Musica instrumentalis*, finally, is that music made by man himself with the means available to him : his voice and the instruments he can manufacture. Such audible music, produced by art, is, as it were, an extension of the music of nature and, in imitating it, submits to the same laws. Its beauty is born from certain proportions, more specifically from a harmony of mathematical and sensory proportions. Indeed, Boethius does not deny the pleasure of the ear that can be derived from audible music. But this pleasure, he says, is related to the satisfaction of the intellect, and there is a concordance between the two types of judgment. The uneducated man can perceive no more than the exterior beauty that the sounds transmit to him, and the satisfaction he gains thereby, for all that it is real, is inevitably vulgar. The wise man, however, who knows the rational explanation for the pleasure he enjoys, draws from it a higher and therefore more complete satisfaction.

On the basis of this very intellectual aesthetics, Boethius tried to explain what a musician is and what hierarchy should be established among those who claim the title of *musicus*. The Latin word *ars*

19

does not mean what *art* means to us. It stands, in the first place, for knowledge of the rules which operate in creation, and then for a technique which puts to work the rules discovered by the intellect. Mind is superior to body : he who conceives something through reasoning is superior to him who realizes it through action; the general who thinks out the strategy is more important than the soldier who fights according to the orders received; the architect who draws up the plans is of greater worth than the mason who lays the bricks. In the same way then, the musician who comprehends the mathematical significance of the relationships between sounds is superior to the one whose only concern is with mere melody. Therefore, at the bottom of the scale are the instrumentalist, the player of the lyre or aulos, the singer ignorant of the science of numbers, all those who play or sing without knowing what they do, and these are all to be scorned. Then comes the poet, who is something more than a simple interpreter because he invents melodies and verses, but he unfortunately lets himself be carried away by inspiration without controlling it by sufficient reflection. The only true musicians are those who submit to the dictates of reason. The scholar, the sage, for example, is a musician, even though he may not concern himself with actual music in any concrete way, even if he deals only with the harmony of completely abstract proportions. The critic also is a musician if he uses his reason in judging the works he hears and if his judgment is based on scientific premises. Finally, also worthy of the high name of musician is the composer who invents melodies – on condition that he does not give way to flights of inspiration but is instead guided always by science in the largest sense of the word.

With Cassiodorus (480-575), classical education was subjected to a much clearer Christian orientation. Already with Saint Augustine the liberal arts had been considered as an introduction no longer to philosophy as such but rather to theology : they were the seven pillars of the wisdom which would, in the end, be attained thanks to theology. When Cassiodorus explains the pleasure listening to music gives, he justifies it by the secret power of the numbers and proportions it contains, and he adds that this harmony goes back to God, source of all beauty. The joy given by the sound of music prefigures the bliss of Heaven.

EARLY MIDDLE AGES :
THE MONASTERY SCHOOLS TEACH

While schools of the classical type were disappearing under the barbarian invasions, monastic and episcopal schools were coming into existence. In Italy, in Spain, in Ireland, and then in England and Scotland, then on the Continent at Saint-Gall and Reichenau, the monastery schools continued to teach the liberal arts as a preparation for theology. Often they did no more than recopy the fragments of ancient authors to be found in Boethius and Cassiodorus, as did Isidore of Seville in his *Etymologiæ*, which are summaries of his reading in which he borrows from everyone, jumbling together all sorts of notions without ever succeeding in synthesizing them into a whole. The science of music still formed part of the Quadrivium but merely repeated in mechanical fashion the old speculations about numbers. However, the monastery schools also had to concern themselves with music in the strict sense, with audible music. Their very nature and function obliged them to do so, for sacred music played a great role in the ritual of the Church.

Contrary to the tradition which considers all liturgical music as "Gregorian," there seems to be no proof that Gregory the Great, pope from 590 to 604, really created a *schola cantorum*. In his time, each church had only one reader who intoned the chant and one singer who taught the congregation a music which was as yet quite simple and which he intoned in alternation with them. Only in the eighth century did the church service begin to be lengthened and plain-chant enriched and complicated to such an extent as to require professional specialists, that is, cantors. After 750, after the agreements between Pepin the Short and Pope Stephen II, the Roman rite spread throughout Europe. Everywhere, except in Spain, which was occupied by the Arabs, it succeeded in displacing local rituals, and it was only then that the Roman style of chant also triumphed.

In order to impose a complex repertory which was, in part, entirely new, it became necessary to train cantors in each region. This involved a lengthy apprenticeship, since everything had to be memorized : the first books notated in neumes, which were still far from precise, do not date from before 820. As first step, apprentice cantors were taught certain stereotyped melodic formulas to be applied to the beginning, end and middle of phrases. The musical discourse was organized around these formulas, which were read over, repeated and extended according to certain rules. All this was simple enough when the chant remained close to recitation. But often there was more complex, positively florid ornamentation, and to master such difficulties cantors were led to do a further apprenticeship in Rome before returning to their abbeys – Saint-Gall, Metz, Rouen – to impart to others the Roman tradition. The chant was based on collections of liturgical texts, using more or less complex melodic formulas which were memorized and then organized during the execution itself, so that the interpreter had to remain firmly within a tradition while at the same time ever and again re-creating it anew.

Such a use of stereotyped formulas and their combination in an improvisatory style fixed by tradition is characteristic of Oriental thought and survives today still in the Orient in both religious and secular music. In the course of the Carolingian Renaissance, the attempt was made to subject this practice to the theoretical notions inherited from Greek science and perpetuated by Boethius and Cassiodorus. Numerous chapters in the theoretical writings of Antiquity had been devoted to the analysis of the modes and, in a somewhat artificial manner, the Carolingians tried to integrate the melodic formulas of Christian chant into a system modeled on the ancient modes. This they accomplished, but at the price of certain errors and of quite profound modifications which were made inevitable by the widely differing characters of these two types of music.

The entire liturgical repertory was forced into this system. This involved classifying the melodic formulas according to their range and final note, an effort far from useless as a means of putting order into a body of chants which was growing enormous and beyond the capacity of any one man to hold in memory. A similar task had been undertaken in Byzantium for the same reasons, and the example of Byzantium must have been known to the West. From the ninth century on, the various melodic formulas were set down in *Tonaria,* volumes in which chants were classified according to tones or modes. For each mode there were thenceforth available a certain number of melodic formulas, some very simple, others increasingly complex. With the exception of a few apparently very much older pieces which resisted being cramped into a specific mode, the bulk of the repertory was taken into the system, either without difficulty or at the cost of a few corrections.

The art of the cantor was thus developed in the course of an apprenticeship in which Antique theory also played a part. On the basis of the formulas now classified, the cantor practiced what Solange Corbin in her fine book *L'Eglise à la conquête de la musique* describes aptly as "regulated improvisation." He was, in fact, obliged to re-create the formulas, to give them new life by combining them and by inventing transitions between them, but in this perpetual improvisation he was expected to conform to both the rules and the tradition.

Thenceforth, even theory itself consented to go beyond mere speculation. Instead, it guided practice and, in so doing, itself became transformed. However, it still clung to the ancient classification of musicians according to their degrees of knowledge.

21

In the ninth century, Guido d'Arezzo was content to repeat that there is a great difference between a musician *(musicus)* and a cantor : *The cantor performs music, the musician understands it, and he who performs without understanding is nothing more than a foolish beast.*

The training of the musician took place in various stages. The first was a mere apprenticeship and purely practical, although it took much time : the student learned to sing the chant, to use the psalmodic formulas and melodies, and also to read Latin and pronounce it correctly. To this was eventually added the technique of reading music. On the basis of the neumes, which were no more than accents sketching out the general direction of a melody, there had been developed, little by little, an original method of musical notation which indicated precisely the pitch of the notes. The apprentice had to learn to sing the psalms according to the rules and formulas, as well as the anthems sung in the various services and during the mass. Finally he had to master the great solo chants which were highly melismatic with an elaborately ornamented melodic line requiring genuine virtuosity. The second stage of his training involved serious study of the intervals and modes. This training, which gave to the cantor the dignity of *musicus*, borrowed its terminology and methods of analysis from Antiquity. The highest stage comprised speculation on numbers and proportions, based at times on experiments with the monochord, an instrument whose single string could be divided into an unlimited number of proportional segments, thereby making possible acoustical measurements.

Such many-faceted training was provided in the great monasteries such as Saint-Gall in the ninth century and, a century later, in Reichenau. They were the great centers of diffusion of music both as *ars*, that is, as technique, and as *scientia*, as speculative philosophy. Tours, Auxerre, Saint-Amand and Fulda also acquired at the same period a great reputation in the practice of liturgical music and in the study of the liberal arts. Schools also came into being in the cathedrals of the first cities, at Canterbury, York, Reims and Chartres among others.

The masters of these monastery and cathedral schools wrote many treatises which have survived to our days. These might take the form of an "Exhortation to Study Music," often incorporated into a larger philosophical work, in which, faithful to the example of Boethius and aiming at the student of philosophy, the writer set forth the advantages of music, its classifications, and its relationships to the other arts. For the student already specializing in music, the teachers provided "Introductions" which, in a number of stereotyped chapters, developed rhetorical variations on the definition, etymology and origin of music, plus a description of its real or supposed effects and a discussion of the proportions. Many of these texts are nothing but copies of their predecessors, and the not very original contribution of most of the authors consisted of no more than commentaries added to notes borrowed from previous writers easy enough to trace to their sources.

Besides these "Exhortations" and "Introductions" concerned only with theoretical music conceived of as one of the sciences in the Quadrivium, a few treatises intended for the training of cantors dealt squarely with practical music. Typical of them is the *Micrologus* of Guido d'Arezzo written in 1025. It contributed to fixing a readable notation, and served for a long time as the pedagogic model for this kind of material. But even in this domain certain writers aspired to the greater dignity of speculation on intervals and proportions, so they began their textbooks with the standard chapters about the etymology and the origins and effects of music as if the repetition of commonplaces inherited from Antiquity might succeed in ennobling their books.

Beginning in the ninth century, polyphonic music began to appear along with plain-chant. At first there were only passing references to it in the treatises on liturgical music, a few words describing a usage which was becoming more frequent in the churches and gaining in importance. Soon special treatises had to be written about it because it posed specific problems. At the outset, there were problems of notation, since it was necessary to fix with precision the rhythm of the various voices. Only gradually, in close association with creative activity itself, was there developed a technique of notation adequate to express clearly the intentions of composers. Later, problems of melodic and harmonic relationships – the very essence of polyphony – had to be considered. These questions were so fundamental and so complex that musicians composing polyphonically were soon obliged to undergo special training. Much more obviously than had been the case in the monastic schools, it was becoming necessary to separate the practical training of polyphonic composers from the traditional teaching of music as a science in the Quadrivium.

FROM HUCBALD TO JOHANNES OF AFFLIGHEM
Northern France and the region that was to become Belgium seem to have been major contributors to the development of musical theory in this period of the Middle Ages, as seen, for example, in the work of Hucbald (d. 930), who was abbot of Saint-Amand in the diocese of Tournai near Valenciennes. Today only the *De institutione harmonica* is attributed to him with any certainty. But that treatise is enough to assure his fame, since not only does it propose a workable system of musical notation based on the alphabet but also, and especially, because it contains the first known reference to polyphony : "Consonance results from the calculated and concordant union of two tones; it is produced when two tones of different pitch are combined in a musical unity, as occurs when a man and a young boy sing together or in what we are accustomed to call an *organizatio*." The latter term refers, no doubt, to the *organum*, that primitive form of polyphony which is further and more clearly explained in two contemporary treatises formerly attributed to Hucbald, the *Musica enchiriadis* and the *Scholia enchiriadis*.

Hucbald himself was certainly not the inventor of polyphony but he was one of its earliest exponents. His text proves that polyphony was known at that time in the future Low Countries and even that it was used by the folk rather than confined to erudite circles. Another virtue of his manual is that it is essentially practical. Its aim is to teach beginners the rudiments of plain-chant, and at a time when other masters could only recommend committing everything to memory, Hucbald proposes a system of notation enabling singers to learn and perform even melodies they have never heard. Although he takes as his point of departure the theoretical concepts of antique music, he has the merit of not limiting himself to mere uncomprehending repetition of time-honored truisms. He tests them out on the music of his own time, cites numerous examples of plain-chant, exposes the contradictions between this music and traditional theory, and is not afraid to modify that theory to fit the living reality at the risk of being accused by posterity of having betrayed Boethius. In all this matter, Hucbald manifests primordial qualities which place him far above any other liturgical music theorist of the Carolingian Renaissance.

Smits van Waesberghe has written several extended studies in an attempt to prove that there existed in the Middle Ages a veritable "School of Liège" of musical theorists. His very ingenious hypotheses attribute, for the greater glory of the city of Liège, a certain number of authors and anonymous texts to that city. Unfortunately, not all are equally convincing. But in any event, it remains true that, between 1050 and 1125, various other treatises which have much in common were either written or copied out and studied in one or another of the abbeys of Liège and its diocese. Further there appears to be some truth in the claim that the author of a *De Musica* written around 1100 was not an English monk named John Cotton, as has been long believed, but instead a certain Johannes, perhaps of Afflighem, whose treatise shows unmistakable evidence of

23

acquaintance with the peculiarities of plain-chant as practiced in the abbeys of Liège. His *De Musica* belongs to the same line as the works of Guido d'Arezzo, an excellent introduction to the art of the cantor, and his theoretical speculations are always related to the teaching of Gregorian chant. While he may respect tradition sufficiently to continue to speak of *musica mundana* and *musica humana,* his real interest lies in *musica instrumentalis,* in the actual practice of music.

Within this so-called *instrumental* music, he distinguishes two types : *natural music* and *artificial music.* Natural music is that made by a man with nothing but his own voice, whereas artificial music involves the use of instruments specifically designed to make music. In dealing with this audible music, Johannes of Afflighem remains faithful to the ethical conceptions inherited from Antiquity. He attributes more or less arbitrarily precise expressive and moral significance to each of the liturgical modes : the first mode is sad and noble, the second rude and serious, the third energetic, the fourth full of sweetness, and so on. Though these expressive correspondences may strike us as dubious, they bear witness to a noteworthy sensitivity to the actual sound of music which is borne out by other opinions of the author.

Moreover, Johannes of Afflighem defends the right of his contemporaries to compose new songs, both sacred and profane, either monophonic or polyphonic. This is far from being as unimportant as it may seem. In the medieval conception, religious music, the only music worthy of consideration, constituted a single vast repertory which was sacred, inviolable and eternal. During the eighth and ninth centuries, liturgical chant had come to form a coherent ensemble sanctified by the authority of Rome and presumed to be the original, authentic repertory assembled several centuries earlier by Gregory the Great : many manuscripts of the period depict the dove, symbol of the Holy Ghost, perched on the shoulder of Saint Gregory and dictating to him the divine chants. Gregorian chant, being of divine

inspiration, could not therefore tolerate any alterations or additions. For the Ordinary and for the Proper of the liturgical festivals, there was a cycle of recitations and chants adapted to the needs of the different services of each day. No musician could have the ambition or the audacity to modify in any way these sacrosanct chants. His role, both modest and glorious, as a servant of the Church, was to learn, preserve and transmit the tradition. As we know, this tradition had for long been purely oral, based on stereotyped formulas which were combined and improvised upon; if later additions occurred, they were made, as it were, unconsciously. When at last the chants were written down in notation, the liturgical books were considered the repository of the divine word. By such rigorous control of music and ritual the Church manifested an insistence on unification which tended to impose Roman authority on local practices and on the spiritual powers of the various regions.

Only the introduction of new saints and new festivals into the calendar could justify the creation of new services. Thus, in Liège, in the tenth century, the bishop Stephen composed a new service in honor of his holy patron, but this service was never recognized by Rome and was only used in Liège and a few neighboring dioceses until the end of the eighteenth century. On the other hand, the mass of the Holy Trinity, composed by the same Stephen, was admitted by Rome and incorporated into the chants recognized by the Church when, in the fourteenth century, the feast of the Trinity was accepted into the Roman calendar. In the twelfth century, Rodulphe, abbot of Saint-Trond near Liège, composed various pieces in honor of his abbey's saint. Similar examples are known in the principality of Liège and elsewhere throughout Europe, but such

24

new chants, made legitimate only through the authorization of new feasts, were only exceptionally added to a repertory that was coherent and theoretically unchangeable.

Nevertheless, in the course of time, the repertory was further enriched by the addition of *tropes*. Tropes were finally banned by the Council of Trent in 1562, but from the ninth to the twelfth century it was through them that creative vitality was maintained within the plain-chant in a manner typical of the artistic conceptions of the Middle Ages. Because the sacred repertory was inviolable, it could only be by amplification and interpolation that new contributions were made to it, a procedure known to us only from the time written documents came into being but which must have been practiced earlier. A trope may consist of the invention of a new text to be sung to a pre-existing melody, particularly if that melody included a melismatic vocalise onto which could be grafted the new words, whether verse or prose, each syllable being set to a note of the melody. Most often the new text was an edifying or poetic commentary on the original text into which it was inserted. But a trope might also consist of the insertion of a new musical phrase, in the form of a vocalise, into almost any place in a chant. Or a new melody with a new text might be interpolated as a more or less extended lyrical and poetic amplification of the original. Finally, it might be a somewhat lengthier passage added as a prelude or postlude to a liturgical piece.

Scribes, theorists and philosophers of the Middle Ages often had recourse in their works to the analogous procedure of glosses and commentaries interpolated into an older text, so that the original text was used as something like a canvas on which to spin one's own reflections. That artistic creation was able to accept the same constraints, and that for so long it exercised the greatest prudence in insinuating itself into the frozen repertory of Gregorian chant, reveals something significant about the spiritual attitudes of the age. Most tropes and sequences (the latter are merely the application of the same procedure to the final vocalise of an Alleluia) were never integrated into the liturgy but enjoyed, nevertheless, great favor. Tropes on the Benedicamus Domino, the Kyrie and the Sanctus were frequent. In this way, a new poetic and musical style managed to introduce itself into Gregorian chant. Tropes in the form of dialogues eventually gave rise to liturgical drama. As for the introduction of polyphonic passages into the midst of a plain-chant, it may well have been at first no more than an original and unexpected application of the procedure of troping.

What, in fact, is an organum but a singular trope in which two melodies are closely combined? A newly invented melody is sung above a plain-chant melody in such a way as to concord with it, using the same text and rhythm, either note against note or in florid vocalises. The *motet*, a further step from the organum, is a still more complex trope : the second, newly invented vocal part is here provided with a new text, a syllable to each note, the text itself being in some way a comment on the text of the original Gregorian melody. For a long time, despite formal developments and refinements, the motet retained this character : over an entire Gregorian melody, or a fragment of one, presented in very long, slow rhythmic values, there were superimposed, according to rules which gradually became more precise, a second voice and then a third, each with a different text. In the early phase, such pieces were by and large merely an amplification of the original Gregorian melody which served as a basis for the entire composition. Later, concern for purely aesthetic values came to dominate more and more the initial para-liturgical intention, so that the Gregorian melody was most often reduced to fragments repeated and combined in complex rhythmic structures. As for the new voice parts invented over this armature, they did not hesitate to superimpose a love song in the vernacular onto a religious poem in Latin. In this way, polyphony came to liberate itself

26

from the limits imposed by plain-chant. It took on independent existence with its own exigencies and its own rules.

In the thirteenth century, the same principle of composition was applied in pieces no longer based on plain-chant but rather on some secular tune; soon, also, compositions were invented without using any pre-existing material whatsoever. This is the way by which, finally, polyphony came to make musical creation a truly autonomous activity.

For these reasons polyphony was to impose on the musician a specific and even more arduous apprenticeship. Henceforth, the demands of practical training were such that it was necessary to give over to the philosophers, to the erudite professors of the universities, remote as they were from any real contact with music, all the traditional speculations on music and number, those sterile commentaries which won for the scholar special prestige among his cultivated colleagues but which had nothing whatsoever to offer to the practical musician in the way of concrete bases for his art. More clearly than in previous centuries there developed a dichotomy between music as a theme for speculation and music as a creative art.

LATE MIDDLE AGES :

THE UNIVERSITIES DISCUSS

When universities finally appeared on the scene, music was integrated into the curriculum along with the other liberal arts. However, it would be wrong to imagine that music, as we think of it today, occupied any privileged position in university education. What was taught was almost always the abstract music of the theorists. The liberal arts were studied in what today would be called the Arts and Letters faculty in which Trivium and Quadrivium provided the groundwork of general culture for students who later entered the specialized faculties of law, medicine or theology. In the Quadrivium, music remained essentially a mathematical discipline, faithful to the tradition of Boethius, a *musica spec-*

ulativa. Indeed, the teaching of music was not always confided to specialists but rather, most often, to professors responsible for lecturing in all the general disciplines. Most of the treatises intended for use in education included only brief chapters on *musica practica.*

It must, however, have been in Parisian university circles that, at the beginning of the fourteenth century, there appeared the *Speculum musicæ*, the Mirror of Music, which aimed at being a compendium of everything known about the subject. It is true that general considerations and mathematical discussions still predominate in the *Speculum*, but actual practice is also treated and, in fact, two entire books are devoted to it.

The *Speculum musicæ* is one of those enormous encyclopedias so common in the last centuries of the Middle Ages and in all branches of knowledge, modeled after the great compendia of theology. For music there exists nothing comparable to this *Summa* with its seven books divided into 521 chapters in which the author – who modestly styles himself merely a compiler – gathered together the opinions of all those, since Boethius, who had treated the subject. Through Boethius he knows the philosophers, mathematicians and musicians of Antiquity : Plato, Aristotle, Aristoxenus, Ptolemy; he also knows Christian philosophers such as Saint Augustine and Hugh of Saint-Victor and the Arabs Al-Farabi and Averroës; he knows, finally, Guido d'Arezzo, Hermannus Contractus and the theorists of Liège with Johannes of Afflighem and their successors. Moreover, he does not merely pile up quotations but attempts, by comparing the various texts, to arrive at the truth, and he quotes fragments of the musical compositions he knows, judging and expressing his appreciations of them, though, it must be admitted, in a reactionary spirit, since he deplores and condemns the audacities of the *moderni.*

The identity of the compiler of the *Speculum musicæ* remains mysterious. He reveals no more than his Christian name, Iacobus. It is generally conceded

27

now that this Iacobus must have been a native of the region of Liège, and musicologists have given him a name that certainly was not his but that can be attributed to him with some degree of probability : Jacques de Liège. We know that he was a student at the Sorbonne in the last quarter of the thirteenth century and that he composed his vast encyclopedia after 1330, partly in Paris, where he had the great resources of a university library at hand, and partly in Liège, where he was able to delve into the works of the theorists and study the musical practice of the local churches. Like his predecessors, Jacques de Liège kept faith with the notion of the superiority of theory over practice. In line with the ancient convention, he grants the dignity of *musicus* only to the theorist, while the man who practices the art without understanding is worthy only of the name of *cantor* or, more modestly, is merely designated by the instrument he plays : organist, kitharist, fiddler.

Such certainty as to the superiority of the theorist was to prevail for a long time still in the minds of those who frequented the universities. It was, however, less and less justified. Once polyphonic music had appeared, composers served their apprenticeship in the churches themselves. In the thirteenth century, Leoninus and Perotinus attended Notre-Dame in Paris, not the Sorbonne. In the fourteenth century, Philippe de Vitry and Guillaume de Machaut, great poets as well as great musicians, never studied at a university. In the fifteenth and sixteenth centuries, only a few composers of importance had any connection with academic circles. A veritable divorce took place between speculation about music and musical life itself. This divorce had begun to take place in the abbeys after the Carolingian period, and the separation was henceforth to bring about the development of separate institutions. The higher education and general culture dispensed by the universities was countered by the technical apprenticeship offered in the choir schools of the great churches.

In *Music in the Medieval and Renaissance Universities,* Nan Cooke Carpenter maintains that a good many texts on music in those periods, including even introductory books in the practice of music, can be attributed to university circles. Certainly the best theorists did not fail to include in their treatises speculations on the music with which they were familiar. This was done by Jacques de Liège and also by his contemporary and adversary Johannes de Muris, mathematician, astronomer and professor at the Sorbonne, who, in his *Ars novæ musicæ,* had recourse to mathematical arguments to prove the merits of the innovations taking place in fourteenth-century music. Others after them did likewise, and it would be much too schematic to pretend that all teaching was concerned only with dead matter, without contact with reality. Many university professors leavened their speculative science with more or less developed ideas about real music, which, for them, meant essentially church music, *musica plana* (plain-chant) and *musica mensurata* (polyphonic music). In plain-chant, the modes lent themselves to interminable discussions, in polyphonic music the rhythmic structures and the proportions applied to the measurement of rhythms could be related to mathematics. When university scholars balanced their works on *musica theoretica* by writings on *musica practica,* they were still dealing with speculation, but at least there was some contact with living music.

It is quite certain, in any case, that practical music was simply not taught in the universities, with the rare exceptions of Salamanca, Oxford and Cambridge, which did, in fact, offer the doctorate in music. Music was made in the universities only to the extent that it was required in the chapels and churches attached to them, where it was employed to enhance both the liturgy and the academic ceremonies, though some music was made in the colleges themselves for the entertainment of the students. But none of this can be described as having any character specifically associated with a university,

10. An Aubade.
Colored woodcut

¶ Cõment paris et edouard faiſoient les aubades deuāt la chãbre de
Bienne.

Ors paris et edouard
ſaccorderēt enſemble
de faire aubades a Bi
ēne/ et mainteſ foiſ ilz
aloient enſemble de
nupct le pl⁹ ſecretemēt qlz pouoyēt
Bers celle part ou ilz ſauoyēt que la
chãbre de Biēne eſtoit. Et illecques
chãtoient moult doulcemēt/ et ſon
noient de diuers inſtrumēs/z eſtoit
tant plaiſant et tant doulce la melo
die des ſons z des chãs q̃ ilz ſaiſoiēt
q̃l paſſoit toutes aultres doulceurs
Et quãt le daulplphin et ſa femme
et Bienne leur fille ouyrent ſi douly

et ſi melodieuy ſons et chãs/ilz eu
rent grãt ioye/et p̃ p̃noient treſgrãt
plaiſir / et auoiēt gũt deſir de ſauoir
qlz eſtoient ceuly q̃ ſi grãt plaiſir et
ioye leur ſaiſoiēt. et pour les cuider
deceuoir/ le daulphin ſit faire Bng
grant cõuis/et ēuoya qrir to⁹ les ſo
neurs dinſtrumēs de toute ſa terre
et leur ſit cõmāder ſur grãt paine/ q̃
ilz fuſſent en leurs propres perſon
nes a celle feſte. Et quãt to⁹ les me
neſtriers du pais furēt Ben⁹/ on les
ſit ſoner!z lõ ne trouua pas ceuly q̃
ilz demãdoiēt. car ilz les euſſent Biē
cogneus/dõt il fut moult deſplaiſãt
et ſi eut pl⁹ grant deſir de ſauoir qlz
eſtoiēt q̃ deuãt. Et quãt Biēne ouyt
les meneſtriers q̃ ſonnoiēt en celle

a 3

neither in the works executed nor in the types of performers involved.

Traditions die reluctantly. Even in texts clearly intended for practical teaching and in no way associated with university education, it remained obligatory to include rhetorical excursuses on the origin, etymology, classification and effects of music, though these might be compressed into a few introductory chapters. Thus, even though he was writing for practicing musicians, one of the important theorists of the end of the fifteenth century, Johannes Tinctoris, did not feel free to neglect the speculative aspects, and he devoted two of his twelves treatises to them.

Born in Brabant around 1435, Tinctoris came to hold the title of canon in the church at Nivelles, probably his native city, but his real career took place in Italy up to his death in 1511. For many years he was in the service of King Ferdinand of Naples, and it must have been at that court that sometimes between 1470 and 1485, he wrote the twelve treatises that have come down to us.

One of the treatises, the *Proportionale musices*, deals with the application of mathematical proportions to musical notation. The most simple of these proportions were used to measure rhythmic variations within a single voice or between different voices in a polyphonic piece, but Tinctoris goes so far as to envisage hypothetical cases which would certainly create complex and subtle rhythmic overlappings not to be found in the practice of the period. Indeed, he allows himself to be carried away by the enthusiasm for speculative and hyper-rationalistic systems typical of the Middle Ages and constructs elaborate theoretical edifices of rhythmic possibilities that, however plausible they might be, were certainly not used in his time.

In the *Complexus effectuum musices*, Tinctoris recounts the effects of music. Less concerned with furnishing proofs out of his personal experience than with gathering together the assertions of venerable authorities of the past, he jumbles together indiscriminately Bible texts, the opinions of the Church Fathers and the poetic myths of Antiquity. These commonplace dicta of the past in praise of music are completed by a few more personal and more authentic remarks of his own. Such combination, in unequal doses, of conventional notions and genuine observation is characteristic of a period in which inherited notions were treated as eternal verities without, however, any real conviction as to their ultimate truth.

If Tinctoris begins by asserting that *music is pleasing to God* or that *music increases the joy of the blessed,* it is because for him sacred music is at the apex of the hierarchy of genres. There is little more than banality in his remarks on the effects of sacred music on men – *music prepares the soul to receive divine benediction, music leads hearts to piety, music elevates the earthly spirit* – but they at least help us to understand that for his time a motet or mass was intended to help men enter into contact with God. Music, then, was not mere audible decoration for the liturgy but rather a true adjunct to the prayers of the faithful. When Tinctoris, with a certain timidity, dares to enter the aesthetic realm in saying that *music renders praise to God more beautiful,* it does not seem to occur to him to choose examples from the music of his time but only from references to the art gleaned from Virgil, the Apocalypse, Ecclesiastes, and the Psalms. He readily repeats moralizing precepts – *music drives off evil tendencies, music softens the hardest hearts* – or magical ones – *music heals the sick, music provokes ecstasy, music expels the demons.* While he may have had in mind military music when he wrote that *music excites the soul to combat* or the polyphonic chansons of his time when he said *music encourages love,* his authorities for these were Ovid and Orpheus. Finally, however, to prove that *music increases the gaiety of banquets,* he does speak from

30

personal experience : *The custom has continued to our days of making music at banquets. During the splendid and ceremonious repasts of the great nobles, all sorts of musicians are heard – singers, flautists, dulcimer-players, organists, lutanists, oboists and trumpeters.*

It is evident that along with religious music, Tinctoris deemed other types of music – music of diversion, military music, love songs – also worthy of consideration. In admitting that music might have no other aim than entertainment, he openly acknowledged a function that had always been accepted by everyone but which the erudite authors had not wished to recognize. Yet, in connection with the proposition *music gives pleasure to men,* he tempers his audacity by saying that such pleasure may be more or less intense according to the degree of perfection attained and, further, that there are two ways of apprehending music : from within, by applying one's intelligence to grasping the inner structure of the composition, or from without, by merely basking in the delightful sound of it; finally he insists that, in any event, to understand a piece of music one must first have a certain degree of knowledge and to enjoy it to the full one must understand it completely.

It is when he declares that *music confers glory on those who are experts in that art* that Tinctoris formulates his most original proposition. Here he shows a new understanding of an art no longer held down by the collective anonymity of composers or by the dead hand of erudite authority, as had been the case in the Middle Ages, but instead oriented now toward the creative individualism of the Renaissance. Naturally, he still praises the Greek musicians and the philosophers of Antiquity, but directly afterward he extols the greatest musicians of his own time, and these are no longer mathematicians or encyclopedists but true composers : Dunstable, Dufay, Binchois, Ockeghem, Busnois, Regis, Caron, Carlier, Morton, Obrecht. And he exclaims: *Who would not accord the highest praise to those who compose works which are known all over the universe and which resound with supreme sweetness in the temples of God, the palaces of kings and the most humble of dwellings!* Polyphony, then, had become the true music, and the true musician was now the composer. For Tinctoris, musical composition, whether religious or profane, is not a humble kind of work : it can bring honors and glory to those who are worthy. In short, the notions of entertainment on the one hand and, on the other, of glory conquered by musical composition are new ideas which seem to emerge at last from the desert of platitudes about the ethical and magical significance of music. No small credit goes to Tinctoris for having been able to slip a few common-sense truths past the barrier of entrenched prejudices. Indeed, this is a measure of how much the fifteenth century remained obstinately faithful to broad generalizations lacking any connection with things as they really were.

THE SIXTEENTH CENTURY :
MUSICIANS MAKE MUSIC

Certain enlightened individuals in the sixteenth century strove to infuse new vitality into the old moralizing traditions by, for the first time, direct contact with the thought of Antiquity. It is not well enough known that alongside the humanism of literary men, sculptors, painters and architects there existed also a musical humanism which wished to return to what was considered the true source: Greek music. Music too felt the need to assert that, after a long decline, its art had also been born anew, and it too claimed the dignity of a return to the Antique. However, unlike the situation in the other arts, a direct linkage could not be proved, since there was nothing left of Greek music except for a few small, unimpressive fragments which were only beginning to be deciphered and that only with the greatest difficulty. Any return to the source in music could mean no more than a more careful study of ancient philosophy and theory. The piecemeal scraps of ancient texts gleaned from Boethius or Cassiodorus no longer sufficed. They were not only fragmentary but also warped and often distorted through the special pleading of the Medievals. As far as possible, then, the ancient texts were studied afresh, and their real meaning was liberated from all the encumbering glosses by which medieval erudition had done its best to make it appear that music was no more than a handmaid in the great task of glorification of God. Not only philologists but musicians also returned to Plato and Cicero as authorities for the prodigious effects of ancient music. Above all, for Renaissance musicians, this provided an arsenal of arguments in their polemic against certain tendencies in the music of their time.

If, indeed, the men of the sixteenth century believed in some special power in music, it was no longer in music as magic but rather as an art. This transformation is revealed quite clearly in a passage of the *Solitaire second* (1555) of Pontus de Tyard in which he evokes the impact of the lutenist Francesco da Milano on his auditors. The scene takes place after a banquet : *The tables cleared, he took up a lute and, as if merely essaying chords, he began, seated near the foot of the table, to strum a fantasy. He had plucked no more than the first three notes of the tune when all the conversations ceased among the festive throng and all were constrained to look there where he was, as he continued with such enchanting skill that little by little, through the divine art in playing that was his alone, he made the very strings to swoon beneath his fingers and transported all who listened into such gentle melancholy that one present buried his head in his hands, another let his entire body slump into an ungainly posture with members all awry, while another, his mouth sagged open and his eyes more than half shut, seemed, one would judge, as if transfixed upon the strings, and yet another, with chin sunk upon his chest, hiding the most sadly taciturn visage ever seen, remained abstracted in all his senses save his hearing, as if his soul had fled from all the seats of sensibility to take*

refuge in his ears where more easefully it could rejoice in such enchanting symphony. The ecstasy described here is no longer Pythagorean, based on a judicious mingling of numbers and proportions, nor is it Orphic and magical : it is nothing more nor less than true artistic pleasure.

Few texts of the period evoke the aesthetic experience in such glowing terms, but it remains true that the sixteenth century marked the beginning of the recognition that the primary aim of music is to produce a certain kind of pleasure. Traditions are tenacious and the theorists did not yet go so far as to reject the medieval classifications but they adapted them and set them into a new hierarchy. In his *Istitutioni harmoniche* of 1558, the Venetian Gioseffo Zarlino, disciple of the Fleming Willaert, continues to speak of *musica mundana* and *musica humana*, but he brings them together to form *musica animastica*, which is no more than the universal harmony ordering all things, and he opposes them to *musica organica*, which is music thought of only as combinations of sounds. He quickly disposes of *musica animastica* and its number-symbolism, relegating it to the domain of philosophy or theology. What interests Zarlino is, in fact, audible music only, and he studies it as both science and art : a science conceived more in terms of acoustics than of mathematics and which must be based on experience, an art in which one seeks to determine just what are the criteria of pleasure and of beauty. Zarlino proceeds to make analytical classifications for that music which can really be heard. He divides *musica organica* into *naturalis* and *artificialis* : natural music is that made directly by man with his lips, tongue, throat – in short, vocal music, which includes poetry

together with song, whereas artificial music has recourse to instruments, stringed, wind or percussion. Moreover, Zarlino insists that the principal role of music is to please and to entertain, and he specifies that this entertainment must aim at a certain high quality. Whether one listens to it or practices it, music helps *passare il tempo,* but in a manner ennobling to man. In his famous *Libro del Cortegiano* written at about the same time, Castiglione says much the same thing, that music should be made as a pastime in a small but select company.

The ideal of beauty by which sixteenth-century musicians judged specific works went beyond the Platonic notion of the alliance between the Beautiful, the Good and the True as well as the medieval conception of imitation of an ideal *pulchritudo.* For these new musicians, musical beauty was in the first place linked to a certain satisfaction, to the pleasure provided to the ear. The worth of vocal music resides in beautiful singing : *cantare bene.* Zarlino explains how this ideal can be attained : the musician must trace an elegant melodic line in light, flowing movements which yet retain a certain gravity, and he must avoid all harshness which might offend the ear, instead bringing out the *soavità* of his music with many happy inventions of details, harmonizing the whole into a well-balanced composition. Melodic lines must be so ordered as to form a polyphonic work which respects the rigorous rules of counterpoint.

In this way there came into being a veritable code of perfection elaborated by the greatest creators in their compositions and transmitted from masters to pupils. The art of counterpoint was recognized as the single fundamental technique of composition. On the basis of the practical teaching done by the composers themselves and of the works of those composers considered to be perfect models – Josquin, Willaert, Palestrina – the theorists strove to codify the principles governing the art of counterpoint. Only a profound acquaintance with those laws, they said, could form a true musician.

It was still true in the sixteenth century, as in the Middle Ages, that the perfect musician was certainly not the mere histrion, virtuoso or vocalist : the perfect musician was still *he who knows.* But what he was expected to know was no longer the mathematical science of proportions or the secrets of cosmology; it was, rather, the science of the rules of music. The musicians who were admired and even revered were no longer the theorists. In fact, theorists tended to present themselves humbly as disciples of some composer; having profited from the great man's teaching, they desired only to extol his art and science. It was agreed that the true musicians was the man who composed by applying that musical science which is the art of counterpoint.

Certain composers still seemed content to believe that it was enough to know the rules. But the more enlightened recognized that while this was an indispensable foundation there was needed also a lengthy practice and above all high skill in invention. The great composer, they realized, is not content merely to follow the rules. By applying his intelligence and his reason to the study of what has been accomplished before him, he learns how to use the lessons of the past in a new way and in order to create new masterpieces. It is in this precisely that invention in music resides, they said.

Sometimes clearly set forth by the theorists but most often merely implicitly accepted by everyone, these rules gave the sixteenth century a code of what could be considered both correct and beautiful. This system enjoyed an inner coherence which its contemporaries did not fail to appreciate : they called it, upon occasion, an *ars perfecta,* and it was Flemish music in the sixteenth century which provided the standards for this perfect art.

The chapters to follow attempt to make clear what was considered the ideal music in a given epoch. They are intended to describe the genesis of this *ars perfecta,* to measure the specific contribution of the Flemish to its elaboration, to tell of its glory and of its death.

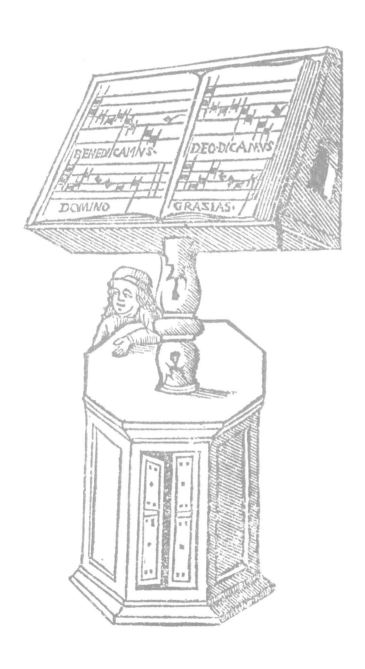

ous acomplissement ❧ · nous sommes enseignes que nous ne s

12. Music and Measure.
Jehan de Nizières.

Musica Practica

If in the first centuries of its history, polyphony had developed in the abbeys, later it was in the churches of the great cities that it flourished.

The new type of music required performers with special training. Priests skilled in plain-chant were not likely to be up to reading the new rhythmic notation and to singing the contrapuntal parts. For that, professionals were needed who had undergone a long apprenticeship. As early as the twelfth or thirteenth century, many churches had organized a plan of general education rounded off with special instruction in music, for which were recruited young boys chosen for the excellence of their voices and the aptitudes they revealed. These choirboys took part in all religious ceremonies, singing either plain-chant or polyphony. They were taught singing, certain instruments, and sometimes composition. Until their voices changed, they were maintained by the church and lodged in a house under the surveillance of a professor of grammar or music. Afterward, some might go on to a university, others perhaps became professional musicians, still attached to a church or in the service of some prince, while the humblest among them settled down to become minstrels employed by the town.

In all collegiate churches and cathedrals, one of the canons, the cantor, was responsible for the organization of the services. As long as the offices sung required only plain-chant, it was he who di-rected the ceremony, but the advent of polyphonic music created a need for a specialist who was a skilled musician. This new official often bore the title of *succentor* or vice-cantor, for he remained under the authority of the cantor, whose special task was to make certain that the liturgy was respected. He was also called *phonascus, magister cantus* or *musicæ rector* in Latin; in French, *maître de chant, maître de chœur* or *maître de musique*; in Flemish, *sangh-meester*. This choirmaster prepared and directed the performances of musical works and himself often composed some of the motets and masses needed for the service. In addition, he instructed the choirboys in the elements of music.

At the outset, one of the canons sufficed as school-master in the church schools. But he soon had to resign his tasks to a grammar master for general education and to the choirmaster for training in polyphony. The music master often took precedence since the Church needed good singers and was not over-scrupulous about skimping on general education in favor of practical training in music.

Inevitably, because of this, conflicts arose between the churches and the city authorities. There is a late echo of this in mid-eighteenth century in the disputes between Johann Sebastian Bach and the rectors of the school attached to the church of Saint Thomas in Leipzig. These were in no way caused by the lack of understanding on the part of

37

ordinary citizens for the genius of a great composer but rather represented a conflict of principles in which Bach stood for the medieval tradition. Originally the churches had been the only centers of education in the cities and, naturally, tended to emphasize training in music when polyphonic music began to increase the demands on the young singers. For their part, the city fathers preferred a general education to equip the young for the tasks of citizenry and were quite willing to do without so much attention to a musical training which they judged rather excessive. Such disputes over the importance of music in the curriculum often induced the city magistrates to deprive the churches of ultimate authority over education. No one in those times even imagined that there could be schools without the collaboration of the Church, but the communal powers come to exert more and more influence on the general orientation of studies, especially during the fifteenth century in Brussels, Louvain, Malines and most of the cities of Flanders and Brabant.

Thenceforth, choir schools were deliberately limited to the teaching of music, and general education in them diminished in importance. Until the end of the *ancien régime* all musical apprenticeship began in the choir schools.

A PEDAGOGY OF MUSIC

Some notion of musical pedagogy in the fifteenth and sixteenth centuries helps in understanding the music of that time, its language, and its subtleties. For this, the treatises of Johannes Tinctoris may prove a useful guide. Although they were not specifically intended for choir schools, in them are to be found all the factors involved in the training of musicians either as interpreters or as composers.

The writings of Tinctoris reflect the musical practice of the generation of Ockeghem as do his musical works also, since he was a composer also. The first of his treatises is a *Diffinitorium*. Although it did not have many predecessors, this glossary is not the earliest dictionary of music, and the definitions it proposes (301 of them) are not always perfectly clear. It pays particular attention to the technical terms useful in the various steps of apprenticeship but does not neglect those general notions which may serve as a basis for our investigation of the musical world of that time.

Tinctoris' definition of *cantus* – song or melody – as an assemblage of independent sounds is far from original, but he distinguishes several varieties of it. *Cantus simplex* consists of an isolated melody unrelated to other voices, that is, a monophonic melody which may be either *planus* or *figuratus*. In *cantus planus* (plain-chant) the notes do not have precise rhythmic values, unlike those in *cantus figuratus*, which is measured music. *Cantus compositus* (composed song) results from the relations established between the notes of one voice and those of another; this is, of course, polyphony, which when it is written out is commonly called *res facta* (the thing done) and when improvised, *cantus super librum* (song using the musical text as a point of departure). *Contrapunctus* (counterpoint) is a melody superimposed *point against point* on another melody. It may be *simple,* if each note corresponds to a note of the same duration in another voice, or *diminished,* if there are several notes in one voice to one in another. From a strictly musical standpoint, a *mass* is a vocal work of vast proportions, a *magnus cantus* comprising the five sections of the Ordinary composed polyphonically. The *motet* is a polyphonic piece of more modest proportions, a *cantus mediocris* on any kind of text, though most often sacred, and the *cantilena* is a short piece, a *cantus parvus* usually on a love poem.

The study of music was a long and difficult undertaking. It began with learning the notes and solfeggio plus plain-chant with its conventions and modes as well as the rhythmic signs of measured notation and the reading of figural music. It then went on to learning how to sing one's part correctly in a polyphonic composition and how to blend with the other voices. After this, there were the rules of counterpoint to be learned, and the way to improvise a new part above a Gregorian melody. Finally, the student was taught how to write polyphonic pieces for several vocal parts over a tenor and, as the last step, how to compose in the more complex forms, that is, the cantilena, motet and mass.

According to the medieval notions still prevalent in the Renaissance, a singer who had no more than a fine voice and only knew how to decipher notes was considered with a certain disdain for not being also a creative musician. After having assimilated all the rules, a musician was expected to be able to compose. Granted that everyone could not accede to this exalted level, the ideal of musical pedagogy was nevertheless the formation of composers of talent, as well as interpreters.

SOLMIZATION

To begin with, the student had to learn the names of the notes and their place in the scale. In the first treatise of Tinctoris, *Expositio manus,* are found the elements of a solfeggio system according to a technique generally ascribed to Guido d'Arezzo but which probably goes back even farther. Men had always used their fingers for counting and even as a calendar, so it is not surprising that the palm and fingers of the left hand came, finally, to be used for memorizing the names of the notes and thence for a procedure called *solmisation.* Most medieval treatises having to do with practical music began with a description of this "hand," generally called the *hand of Guido,* and the *manus* may be considered a symbol of this ancient type of pedagogy.

The use of the syllables *ut, re, mi, fa, sol, la* to designate the six tones of the scale was initiated by Guido d'Arezzo, who took them from the first syllables of the six hemistichs of the three first lines of the Latin hymn of Saint John the Baptist :

> Ut *queant laxis resonare fibris,*
> Mira *gestorum famuli tuorum,*
> Solve *polluti,* la*bii reatum,*
> San*cte Ioannes.*

Our modern system in the Western world is based on a scale of seven tones to which chromatic accidentals – sharps and flats – may be added at will. But the medieval system combined the six syllables indicated above into a series of hexachords, a system full of difficulties for modern minds accustomed to using the same seven syllables in every octave. In the Middle Ages and Renaissance, *si* – that is, B – could be either natural or flat, but there was no special name for the two forms. Formed from the initials of *Sancte Ioannes,* the syllable *si* was not used until the end of the sixteenth century. In our modern octave system there are two semitones in every octave, between *mi* and *fa* or, as we put it in C-major, E and F, and *si* and *do,* that is, B and C. In the hexachordal system there was only one semitone, and that was blithely called *mi-fa* wherever it chanced to fall, whether between *mi* and *fa* in the natural hexachord or between what we would call *si* and *do,* or *la* and *si*-flat.

To help the student in what even to its contemporaries must have been a difficult system, the so-called Guidonian hand was used as a mnemonic device. Specific places on the fingers of the left hand were associated with each solmization syllable of the three hexachords which covered most of the vocal range as used then. The instructor or choirmaster needed only to point with his right hand to one of those places on the left hand for the singer to know exactly what note was desired.

This was not very complicated as long as a melody remained within the range of a single hexachord. Trouble arose at the point of junction when it moved from one hexachord to the other, and here Tinctoris' *Expositio manus* offers invaluable directions for accomplishing such "mutations."

To teach correct intonation, the monochord was used. This instrument, whose use was virtually restricted to pedagogy, goes back perhaps to Antiquity. It consisted of no more than a long wooden sound-box over which was stretched a single string shortened at will by a movable fret which could be set in positions indicated by a graduated scale of mathematical proportions to produce the desired pitch. The monochord provided experimental proof of the concordances between sounds and the proportions arrived at in theory. Thus, when the movable fret was placed so as to divide the string into two equal parts, the instrument sounded at the octave of the fundamental tone. Divided into thirds, it gave the fifth, fourth and octave; into fourths, the higher octave, and so on. It is obvious that the monochord was a great help in teaching the correct intonation required in the difficult process of learning solmization.

Exercises in solfeggio involved, of course, learning to read notes from the musical staff, and this was further complicated by the use of numerous clefs (at least two F-clefs and four C-clefs) which not only varied from one voice to the other but also, often, within the same voice part in order to avoid using supplementary staff lines.

While Gregorian chant seldom used any accidental other than B-flat, polyphonic music often called for flats and sharps on many notes. As a rule, sharps did not affect solmization, except when applied to the leading-tone of the mode, in which case they were always sung as *mi,* whatever the normal name of the tone might be. In the same way, any note that was flatted was sung as *fa* and immediately called for a mutation into the hexachord in which that note normally was *fa.* As long as the modal system remained relatively stable, the associated hexachordal system could be maintained without too much difficulty. But the new style of the seventeenth century, in which numerous modulations occurred in the course of a single piece, made the system of mutations too ambiguous, and it had to be abandoned in favor of our modern regular heptachordal system.

PLAIN-CHANT AND THE MODES

Once the young musician had learned solmization, he set about studying plain-chant in order to be able to read and sing from the graduals and antiphonaries. The third treatise of Tinctoris, the *Liber de natura et proprietate tonorum,* dating from 1476, takes up the analysis of the modes, the essential material of the theory of Gregorian chant.

It is well known that the Gregorian modes undoubtedly sprang from the mnemonic formulas used in psalm recitation and that these, through a process of somewhat exaggerated codification, became confused with actual scales. Theoretically, the scales – that is, modes – are based on one of four final tones: D, E, F or G, and each mode is made up of an ascending fifth (for instance, D to A) to which is added a fourth (A to D, in this case) either above or below. Thus each final tone applies to two modes, one *authentic,* in which all the notes of the scale lie above the *finalis,* the other *plagal,* in which they lie on either side of the fundamental tone. All of the modes are purely diatonic : the intervals of the fifth and fourth on which they are based have a specific character determined by the sequence of whole tones and semitones. Tinctoris analyzes in detail the various fifths and fourths and the ways of arranging them to build up eight modes in all.

However, it must be recalled that from the tenth century on the modal theory had been imposed onto a vast repertory of chants not easily forced into the rigid discipline of these rules. In addition, the evolution of music itself raised still other problems. At the end of the Middle Ages, a certain number of new melodies – the sequences, among others – were added to the Gregorian repertory, and these were not usually confined to the narrow range in which the older melodies generally moved but quite simply burst through the rigid theoretical limits. This required the theoretical explanation of "mixed modes," which combined the authentic and plagal modes sharing the same *finalis* as well as modes with even more complex combinations. Polyphonic music was soon to introduce more serious modifications which led to even more radical, that is to say fundamental, readjustments.

As a matter of principle, Gregorian chant used no alteration other than B-flat, and this was employed to permit transposing the entire mode a fifth lower. But toward the end of the Middle Ages the flat appeared frequently in certain modes, for example in the mode on F, the Lydian, where the interpolated B-flat was a means of getting around the tritone F to B-natural, considered both too harsh to the ear and too difficult for correct intonation by singers. However, if a flat is introduced systematically into a melody, the result may be far from "accidental" : it may completely transform the mode, for in fact the modes are something more than scales, they are living melodies in which tones and semitones create subtle rapports of tension and relaxation in relation to the final tone.

Another important modification came to affect the tone immediately preceding the final. This penultimate tone has no special function in the Gregorian system and may be a full or half-tone distant from the final, according to the particular mode. Ends of phrases or entire melodies – the technical term is *cadence* – simply consist of a progression to the final tone from the nearest note above or below.

In counterpoint, in which at least two melodic lines converge to the final tone, the penultimate note acquired a special importance. To heighten the tension at the cadence, it was often raised a half-tone, thus bringing it as close as possible to the final tone and taking on the character of what today, in the diatonic system, is called, for obvious reasons, the "leading-tone." But this simple modification was enough to transform the very essence of the traditional modes, and the process was hastened in polyphonic music of the fourteenth and fifteenth centuries by raising also the fourth degree of the scale, so that at the cadence it slid by a half-tone into the fifth degree.

With such mobile tones, raised or lowered for melodic or contrapuntal reasons, the modes in which polyphony was composed became confused and difficult to define.

On the other hand, beginning with the fourteenth century, perhaps under the influence of popular or folk music, certain modes were preferred to others. Either in their normal form or transposed a fifth lower, the modes based on C and F occurred more and more frequently even though theory failed to bestow any sort of official recognition on them. It was not until 1547 that the Swiss humanist Glareanus in his *Dodecachordon* proposed a system of twelve modes with a ninth and tenth mode based on A and an eleventh and twelfth on C. Since, in practice, the authentic and plagal modes were not really distinguished and were, in fact, used simultaneously in polyphonic writing, such emphasis on certain more favored modes could only end in the eventual triumph of the mode on C, which, from the seventeenth century on, was to establish the scale as we understand it today : it was to become an absolute mode finally called *major* which tolerated no other mode except the *minor* (based on A), a mode which, by nature, is complementary to, and subordinate to, the major.

Modifications occurred also within the inner structure of the modes. In the Gregorian system, the *dominant,* which grew out of the "tenor" – the most important tone next to the final – could appear on various steps of the scale. In the new approach, it was confined to the fifth step and acquired a new function : to create in a melody a tension-point opposed to the sensation of repose associated with the final tone.

Finally, beginning in the fourteenth century, one further element deeply disturbed the nature of the Gregorian modes : the so-called *musica ficta,* meaning literally "feigned" or "imagined" music, also sometimes called *musica falsa,* "false" music. If nothing else, this practice demonstrates the formal respect paid to tradition by the men of the Middle Ages, a respect – something more than lip-service – which prevented them from simply abandoning certain rules considered "natural" in the deepest sense of the word, because they were believed to be

41

imposed by nature – which was equivalent to saying by God. Since doubt could not be cast on their validity, at least there were ways of making just a little spiritual "adjustment" which would permit one to employ them currently in daily religious practice.

Theoretically, the only notes which existed were those which could be pointed out on the Guidonian hand and which, with the exception of B-flat, formed a diatonic scale. In practice, composers simply went ahead and used tones below or above this scale as well as, and especially, complementary chromatic tones created by applying sharps or flats to raise or lower by a semitone any tone whatsoever. The existence of sounds which were *extra manus* – not on the hand – was not recognized *de jure*. It was extremely rare that such accidentals were written down on the music itself. They were quite simply treated as *musica ficta* and added by the singer in actual performance in accord with rules of solmization and counterpoint.

Modes were studied in the choir schools as part of a theoretical whole because it was deemed important that the musician should know the rules fixed by tradition and valid in plain-chant. The fact was, however, that all teaching actually centered around polyphonic music.

MEASURED MUSIC

Plain-chant notation does not indicate the precise duration of the notes. Even today its rhythmic interpretation is debated by scholars. As far as we can tell, each epoch had its own particular rhythmic system which varied according to the geographical center and to the types of chant in the repertory. Tinctoris tells us that in the fifteenth century Gregorian chant *was sometimes sung in measured fashion, sometimes not, sometimes in a ternary rhythm, sometimes in a binary, according to the liturgy of particular churches or the whims of the cantors.* In any case, rhythmic practice was transmitted orally and not written down.

It was polyphonic music and the obligation it imposed of co-ordinating the various superimposed voice parts which led to the working out of a notation system for time-values. The study of this rhythmic notation demanded of the apprentice musician a maximum of patience and industry. Tinctoris devoted to it five small treatises which form a single complete, coherent whole. Such music with precise rhythmic notation was called either *measured* (from *mensurabilis*) or *figured* (from *figurata*).

Except for their lozenge-shape, most notes of the fifteenth and sixteenth centuries do not seem much different from those used today, which, in any case, are derived from them although their meanings may be quite different. In descending order of duration, there were the *maxima*, the *longa*, the *brevis*, the *semibrevis* (our semibreve or whole-note), the *minima* (our minim or half-note). If Tinctoris admits *de facto* the *semiminima* (which resembles in appearance our crochet or quarter-note), he refuses to consider it a legitimate value, claiming that, by both nature and etymology, the smallest possible value can only be the minima. However, practice soon led to the acceptance even of the *fusa* (our quaver or eighth-note) and the *semifusa* (our semi-quaver or sixteenth-note).

Along with single notes, mensural notation employed ligatures which bound together two or more notes. These complex signs derive from the old system of neumes, which indicated no more than the general direction of the melodic movement and are preserved still in plain-chant, where they do not indicate any precise time-value. In mensural notation, seemingly identical ligatures have different values according to the direction of the notes, whether ascending or descending.

Problems arose as soon as it became desirable to measure the relative duration of notes. In the system which was to be established in the course of the seventeenth century and which we use today, everything is regulated on a binary principle : semibreve,

13. Musical Symbols.
The Brothers Mola.

minim, crotchet, every value in the series is half of the preceding value and double the following. However, in mensural music, a ternary system prevailed at the outset, followed by a period in which binary and ternary systems existed side by side but with the binary in a position of relative inferiority. Anything ternary was considered perfect, a symbol of the perfection of the Trinity, whereas what was binary was, by definition, imperfect.

Although bars were never used in the fifteenth century to indicate measures, the principle that governs our measures was not unknown. Conventional signs were placed at the beginning of each piece to indicate the method of measuring the time-values. The *modus* governed the values of the longa : if perfect, it meant that each longa contained three breves; if imperfect, two only. *Tempus,* perfect or imperfect, fixed the relationship between the brevis and semibrevis, and *prolatio,* that between semibrevis and minima. Other values were generally taken to be binary always. Highly complex mixtures of ternary and binary values could be set up by combining mode, tempo and prolation in various ways.

There is a further complication in the system. In modern notation, every figure has a fixed value; in mensural notation, each figure has no more than a theoretical value which can be diminished or increased by the notes that precede or follow it. In the perfect mode, for instance, the longa normally equals three breves, but the mere fact of being preceded or followed by a breve can make it imperfect. On the other hand, two breves placed between two longas suffice to create "perfection," the second breve (*brevis altera*) taking on the value of twice its normal duration.

Tinctoris devotes a small treatise to the rules of imperfection and alteration and another to the "dot" since in mensural notation the dot has a more varied function than in ours. By augmenting the note by half of its value, it becomes an agent of "perfection" which makes a ternary note of one that had been binary. But it can also be used merely to

separate groups of notes, to help make more clear the articulation of the modes, tempo and prolations, in which case it is considered a *point of division.*

Also, beginning in the fourteenth century, colored notes were used, generally red, later hollowed out to become white. Coloration made a note lose a third of its value, so that in a perfect mensuration it created imperfection and in an imperfect mensuration it created the equivalent of our present-day triplet.

In fifteenth- and sixteenth-century polyphony, the various voice parts were not written out one above the other as in modern scores. In the great choir books each voice appears separately, written on either the left-hand or right-hand page and at the top or bottom of the page. At times, separate small part-books were prepared for each voice. It is obvious that the rhythmic co-ordination of all these separate parts presented a special problem in performance. Time was beat, but in an infinitely less varied manner than today. *By measure,* says a theorist of the sixteenth century, *we understand a certain gesture or "tactus" which is made by an even lowering and raising of the hand or foot moved regularly and in proportion while singing.* Numerous pictures show us the singers beating time, most often with a slight movement of the wrist. The theorists confirm this : the *tactus* – as it was called in texts in Latin – was the only means of beating

15. A Chapel Choir.
Woodcut.

Practica muficae vtriufcǫ cātus excellētis Frā-
chini gaffoꝛi laudēfis. Quattuoꝛ libꝛis modula
tiffima: Sūmacǫ diligétia nouiffime ipꝛeffa.
✠

time throughout the Middle Ages and up to the seventeenth century. Already Hucbald advised the singing master *to indicate the duration by movements of his foot or hand in order to teach the children, from their earliest age, the discipline of rhythm.*

Modern measure is more complex : it is made up of the variable sum of several units of time in a more or less rapid movement. The beat in the Middle Ages and Renaissance was an invariable measure made up of two movements, one downward and one upward in a tempo which never varied. As a matter of fact, it was not until the seventeenth century that there appeared agogic indications such as *adagio, andante, allegro* and the like. Tactus, the beat, imposed a uniform movement on everything sung, so that greater or lesser speed in performance did not depend on the rapidity of these gestures, as it does today, but only on the number of notes contained within a single tactus. Many authors consider the speed of the tactus to be that of the normal pulse, which can be taken as a constant. What varied in different periods was the time-value taken to correspond with the beat : at first it was the longa, then the brevis, and finally in the fifteenth and sixteenth centuries the semibrevis.

But this is not the whole story. By using *proportions*, further complications could be introduced, adding richness and subtlety. The Flemish were masters at this in the second half of the fifteenth and the beginning of the sixteenth century, and to such an extent that their music has often been characterized by this practice and the notation of the epoch called *proportional*. Tinctoris devoted an entire treatise to this question, the *Proportionale musices*, which often indulges in mathematical speculation that has nothing to do with daily practice but which shows, nevertheless, that creative invention could occasionally take advantage of these a priori reasonings.

The only proportions used normally were *dupla, tripla* and *sesquialtera*. In double proportion a single beat included two semibreves (or an imperfect breve) instead of the usual single semibreve; in triple proportion, three semibreves or a perfect breve. Alternate use of these proportions led to subtle transitions from ternarity to binarity which are characteristic also of sesquialtera, in which three notes take the place of the normal two.

In theoretical writings, which continued to be based on the arithmetical notions of Boethius, there are distinguished the *genus multiplex*, proportions marked by fractions whose numerator is a multiple of the denominator, thus 2/1, 3/1, 4/2, 6/3; the *genus superparticulare*, in which the numerator is larger by one unit than the denominator, that is, 3/2, 4/3, 5/4, etc.; the *genus superpartiens*, with numerators at least two units more than its denominators, as 5/3, 8/5, etc.; the *genus multiplex superparticulare*, a combination of the first two types, in which the numerator is a multiple of the denominator but augmented by one unit, thus, 9/2, 10/3, etc; and finally the *genus multiplex superpartiens*, which combines the first and third types to give such proportions as 11/4, etc. All proportions represent diminutions : they mean that x number of notes indicated by the denominator and included within a single beat now correspond to y notes of the same value indicated by the numerator and included within the same duration of beats. These diminutions are, of course, balanced by inverse proportions, which are augmentations.

It is necessary to insist somewhat on these particularities of technique because they demonstrate the specificity of mensural notation. The presence of even the simplest proportions is enough to make exceedingly difficult the reading of certain pages of Flemish music of the end of the fifteenth century, especially because in polyphonic music each voice may be totally independent in rhythm, so that the only common indispensable regulating factor is the beat.

Although the Italian theorist Prosdocimus de Beldemandis provided a clear analysis of the proportions as early as 1408, both the technique and the style seem to have attained the maximum of virtuosity and subtlety at the end of the fifteenth century in the works of Flemish musicians and their imitators.

A SECRET ART ?

The complications in figural music are sometimes such as to raise the question as to whether perhaps they were not introduced deliberately and with some sort of secret intent. According to the musicologist Guillaume De Van, the teaching of mensural music involved a veritable initiation into an esoteric practice : music was conceived of as a discipline whose secrets could be communicated only to those worthy of receiving them. In this sense, there would have been no rupture between practice and science. Musical practice would have been the prolongation and incarnation of those mathematical speculations which, ever since Antiquity, had constituted the essence of music in the opinion of philosophers, and mensural notation would have been far more than a means employed by composers to set down their musical inventions : it would have been, rather, a symbolic illustration of truths that, in their essence, were mathematical.

However, there is no real evidence that measured notation was willfully hermetic or that it was intended to protect music against the curiosity of the uninitiate. There are, admittedly, works in which the composer may have taken perverse delight in piling complexity upon complexity, particularly at the end of the fourteenth century, but it really does not seem that they were conceived as some sort of dreadful test to be imposed. In fact, such a deliberate cult of the esoteric would not have failed eventually to make notation in some way independent of musical sense, but the fact is that from its origins to the end of the sixteenth century there was an ever closer relationship between notation and musical content. Progress in polyphony did not cease to go hand in hand with progress in notation. Polyphony

freed itself from the constraints of the rhythmic modes only when a means was found to distinguish clearly the longa from the brevis. Music became progressively enriched when, in the fourteenth century, the means were finally found to note unequivocally the semibreve and the minim and to integrate them into a general system. The *ars nova* of that century was truly a new art whose audacities were linked to progress in notation.

The complexity of measured notation thus grew out of the slow elaboration of a system of writing which would fulfill the needs of composition. It is difficult to be sure whether, in the Middle Ages, it was the theorists who, by inventing techniques of writing, made it possible to create works of an entirely new kind or whether it was the composers who finally evolved a new aesthetic out of a new system of notation.

In any case, notation affected intimately the very essence of the music of the Middle Ages and the Renaissance, and it is scarcely necessary to imagine that it had the further aim of creating some sort of esoteric mystery.

Furthermore, at various times and in various forms, measured notation gave rise to some works that are crystal clear and at others to works of extreme complexity. At the end of the fourteenth century, French music, represented by the successors of Machaut, became so addicted to rhythmic problems as to develop a special kind of notation we call *mannered*. On the other hand, the beginning of the following century, with Dufay and Binchois, brought in a somewhat less extravagant state of mind and, at the same time, a simpler way of writing. In the second half of the fifteenth century, Flemish music elaborated a characteristic style which was to dominate all of Europe, and there took place a return to complex techniques and highly erudite procedures on the part of musicians like Ockeghem, Obrecht and Josquin Desprez. After 1520, notation once more became simplified, giving up ligatures and most of the proportions in favor of simple rhythms with no attempt to combine complex and divergent rhythmic forms. Musical invention was channeled into other directions.

But, simplified as it might be, measured notation retained its basic principles throughout the sixteenth century. Some have held that complexities in rhythmic notation represent an archaic, reactionary attitude, but others consider them to be a trait of the austere art of the Flemish, no different in kind from other contrapuntal subtleties.

IMPROVISATION

Religious works in the fifteenth century were written for three, four or five voices; the sixteenth century chose sometimes even more imposing means. The upper parts, soprano and alto, were taken by choirboys, the lower by adult professional cantors.

For the young singer, the problem was to acquit himself honorably in the polyphonic ensemble. He began by learning how to sing along with only one other voice. Many teaching manuals have been preserved which contain fragments of masses and motets and original works which were used as solmization exercises along with little teaching pieces provided with edifying moral texts. Among these collections, often given the Latin name of *bicinia* (vocal pieces for two voices), are numerous compositions by Flemish musicians.

Together with such an introduction to notation and to polyphonic singing, the student learned the rules of counterpoint, the art of combining according to certain relationships several melodic lines which are heard simultaneously. Contrary to the general notion today, counterpoint was not sung from written texts alone. Initially polyphony was improvised, and the art of contrapuntal improvisation lasted until the eighteenth century, although it declined steadily. In the fifteenth century and even in the sixteenth, improvised counterpoint was still a lively art, generally called "singing from the book" (*cantus super librum*) or when it was done note against note, *discantus*. In Germany it was called *sortisatio*,

an allusion to the part played by chance (*sors*), which is inevitable in any kind of improvisation, while in Italy in the sixteenth century, the current expression was *contrappunto alla mente*.

The term "singing from the book" best suggests the actual method. Gathered around a choir book set up on a lectern, some of the singers intoned either a Gregorian melody in slow, equal time-values or else a measured melody with a definite rhythm, while other singers improvised over this pre-existing melody, called *teneur, tenor* or *cantus firmus*. Improvisation was subject to a number of rules also applicable to counterpoint which called for a subtle interplay of consonances and dissonances. Each singer was concerned only with the relations between the part he was improvising and the *cantus firmus*, with the result that when more than two voices were involved chance created some curious clashes.

Outside of certain efforts on the part of the avant-garde today, collective improvisation is no longer practiced except in popular and minor forms such as jazz. Since the Romantic era, the musical work has demanded of its interpreters complete subordination to the written text. However, in most non-European music everything depends on the interpreters, whose independence is, nevertheless, limited by respect for traditional formulas. Initially plain-chant had the same character. For singing from the book, with collective improvisation over a pre-existing melody, tradition had established rules and formulas which allowed skilled and well-trained singers to limit the disorder and cacophony that chance might introduce.

Even in written polyphony the Renaissance singer was not entirely limited by the text before him. Adrianus Petit Coclico, a Flemish theorist settled in Germany who claimed to be a disciple of Josquin Desprez, speaks in his *Compendium musices* of 1552 about ornamentation of the melody in polyphonic works. We know that such ornamentation was added by opera singers and instrumental virtuosos in concert music as late as the end of the eighteenth century, but we tend to condemn it in the name of good taste when it is applied to music by Handel or Corelli. Even less are we willing to admit that these fiorituras, colorations and diminutions may have been grafted onto the pure lines of Flemish counterpoint. Yet, various theorists confirm what Coclico says, and there are even some written-out examples of ornamentation of polyphony which survive. Unfortunately, today we can only reconstruct these ornaments in the most approximate way : we can apply the letter, but the spirit which gave rise to them escapes us. But the margin of independence allowed to singers – in an art, moreover, which demanded rigorous control – serves only to show us how ineffective are the texts we have when we wish to restore to life the music of the past.

For diminution as well as for "singing from the book," we have many more theoretical guides and examples from the sixteenth than from the fifteenth century, but it appears that the more precise the commentary, the more it simply indicates a hardened academic practice. Indeed, the very fact that these improvised elements were written out reveals that there was already at that time a growing distrust of freedom of interpretation. The specific indications provided by Vicentino in 1555 in his *L'antica musica ridotta alla moderna prattica,* and by numerous theorists after him, show how concerned the contemporaries were with eliminating from *contrappunto alla mente* all the barbarisms which might result from accidental clashes between improvising voices. Vicentino is concerned with furnishing formulas to prevent clashes and dissonances between the various voices. He is not satisfied, as was Tinctoris, with merely guaranteeing harmonious and correct relationships between each voice and the *cantus firmus.* Wishing to control everything, he limits the inventiveness of the singer, surrounds him with such restrictions that the entire practice of improvisation is drained of all its creative substance. Indeed, he goes so far as to assert,

without apparently even suspecting how paradoxical this might be, that the best improvised counterpoint is that which has first been written down and then memorized !

In any event, whether in a living or sclerosed form, improvisation continued to be practiced regularly in church music, using Gregorian melodies as its natural basis, in particular those of hymns, anthems, graduals, introits, and the chants of the requiem.

THE ART OF COUNTERPOINT

In his *Liber de arte contrapuncti* of 1477, Tinctoris distinguished written counterpoint from improvisation, calling it *res facta,* a thing made, or *cantus compositus.* In Germany, improvisation was called *sortisatio* as opposed to *compositio;* in Italy, *contrappunto alla mente* or *all'improviso* as against *contrappunto scritto* (written), *in cartella* (on paper) or *a penna* (with a pen).

A good *singer* was one who could read at sight measured notation, a good *contrapuntalist* one who was able to improvise on a given melody, a good *musician* one who knew how to compose for three, four or more voices.

Only gifted students, at the end of their apprenticeship, got as far as the study of written counterpoint. In the choir schools, no one made much ado about defining consonances and dissonances according to numerical relationships between simultaneous tones; what counted was the pleasant impression of fullness and repose that a consonance made on the ear. In earlier times, only the unison, octave, fifth and fourth had been considered consonant. By the fifteenth century, these were labeled perfect consonances (although Tinctoris stated that in two-part music the fourth gave an effect of dissonance), whereas thirds and sixths were imperfect consonances and seconds, sevenths and the augmented fourth (the tritone), dissonances. Counterpoint was worked out according to the relationships between consonances and dissonances.

50

How was counterpoint written down ? The problem was to invent a new melody over a given one by following certain fundamental rules : beginnings and ends of phrases must have a perfect consonance; two identical perfect consonances may not follow each other; dissonances may be used in passing from one consonance to another and must come about as the result of melodic movement, that is, in the terminology which later became current, must be prepared and also resolved by a consonance, preferably by conjunct movement.

Dissonances could not be used in *simple counterpoint,* in which several notes of the new melody was sung simultaneously with a single note of the *cantus firmus.* They were limited to *florid counterpoint,* in which several notes of the new melody corresponded to a single note in the given one. Theoretically, dissonance was an alien element to be passed over quickly and never emphasized. But in actual practice it was precisely in the treatment of dissonances that lay both the contrapuntal interest and the expressive beauty of the piece. In point of fact, a contrapuntal work is made up of a succession of tensions and relaxations, of disturbances brought to tranquillity, which perpetually arouse new interest. Progress in contrapuntal art in the sixteenth century was essentially a matter of the treatment of dissonance, of how to introduce it subtly or to intensify its forcefulness. In that century, it was seen clearly that dissonance was not an accident but rather an expressive means which could be used to bring out all the significance of a poetic text.

In the fifteenth and sixteenth centuries, all types of music were conceived contrapuntally, but an identical technical basis did not prevent a considerable diversity of style in successive periods. For the fifteenth century, a work in three or four voices was no more than a two-part work upon which a third or fourth voice was grafted. This was not merely a matter of custom but a positive principle of composition. As basis for a piece, as *tenor,* a com-

PRACTICA

MVSICA HERMANNI FINCKII, EXEMPLA VARIORVM SIGNORVM, PROPORTIONVM ET CANONVM, IVDI‑ CIVM DE TONIS, AC QVÆDAM DE ARTE SVAVITER ET ARTIFICI‑ OSE' CANTANDI CON‑ TINENS.

VITEBERGÆ EXCVSA TYPIS HÆREDVM GEORGII RHAVV, ANNO M. D. LVI.

16. A Chapel Choir.
Woodcut.

poser took some existing melody, often a fragment of plain-chant reworked according to mensural rhythms, or a bit of some popular tune. Each voice part invented to go above or below this tenor had to conform to the rules of counterpoint, first of all in relation to the tenor and then to the other voices. A fine piece of contrapuntal writing must perforce be made up of fine melodic lines. For this reason it is often said that fifteenth-century counterpoint was a style of horizontal writing. True as this is, it is equally true that such horizontal writing was regulated by a system of vertical relationships which were rigidly precise for the relations of each voice with the tenor and a little less so, but still definite, for the relations between each of those voices among themselves. While the tenor was often a pre-existing melody (*cantus firmus, cantus prius factus*), it could also be invented by the composer. In any event, the tenor was always well encased within the polyphonic web, a fundamental armature for the entire composition on which everything else was constructed.

By the end of the fifteenth century, the notion of reciprocal responsibility between voices had become more important. No longer was composition merely a matter of superimposing melodic lines, but, instead, it was conceived as an integral process in which everything was interrelated. This transformation was achieved in the generation of Josquin Desprez and Isaac, between 1480 and 1520. In order to invent a counterpoint in which everything hung together, some means had to be found to notate one voice above the other so that the composer could have the entire complex before his eyes while working, *tactus* by *tactus*. Thus were created the first scores, in the modern sense of the word. But tradition was still so powerful that such scores continued to serve only for the practical sketching out of a composition and not as a permanent record. In 1537, a German teacher named Lampadius referred to such a score as a *tabula compositoris*, pointing out that it could be written on a slate, a wooden

panel, or a sheet of paper. When the work was finished, it was copied out in the traditional manner either in separate part-books for each voice or else in a choir book in which the voice parts were laid out separately on the facing pages. This done, the sketch was rubbed out so the *tabula* could be used again.

As a result of this new way of composing, the tenor became less important. It began to be no more than one element among others and even to be omitted as a structural armature, thereby gaining greater cohesion and parity between all the voices. Having lost its former power to determine the structure, the tenor was now no more than one voice among others – a lower voice like the bass in contrast to the higher voices, soprano and alto – and the name itself denoted nothing more than a vocal tessitura, a voice range in the meaning we generally give the term today. One of the tendencies which grew out of this was to lead, during the sixteenth century, to the gradual abandonment of counterpoint and the triumph of harmony : greater cohesion among the voices tended to limit their melodic and rhythmic independence so that it was an easy step to a homophonic music in which vertical concepts predominated, with a single melodic line sustained by blocks of harmony.

But among Flemish musicians the principal tendency was to bring about such cohesion while still

respecting the independence of all the voice parts. This was done by *imitation,* a procedure in which a melodic motif announced by one voice was repeated more or less faithfully though at different pitches by the other voices in succession. As early as the thirteenth and fourteenth centuries polyphony had had recourse to imitation, but never consistently. The first example of strict imitation is the famous English canon *Sumer is icumen in,* which has been dated around 1300. *Canon* itself involves exact repetition of one melody by another which follows it after a few beats. This is often no more than a mechanical procedure, not unknown in primitive and folk music (as in *Row, Row, Row Your Boat* or *Frère Jacques,* for example) but it may also be a type of very learned and complex contrapuntal construction. In the latter case, the imitation may be at any interval – octave or unison, fifth, fourth, and so on – or the canonic voice may take up the melody in *augmentation* (the value of each note being lengthened in accord with the rules of proportions), or in *diminution,* or in *contrary movement* (each ascending interval of the initial voice echoed by the following voice but in inverse, descending direction); further, the canon may be *retrograde, crab* or *cancrizans* if the answering voice begins with the last note of the initial voice and repeats the melody in reverse direction. Canons may be written for two, three or more voices.

The canon was known already to the *ars nova* of the fourteenth century, but it was especially in the second half of the fifteenth century, in the generation of Ockeghem and then in that of Josquin, that it gained great favor. It was very often employed in masses and motets as a constructive means which displayed the composer's mastery of science and technique. Flemish music was particularly rich in such procedures, though often they degenerated to little more than school exercises or mere virtuoso

exhibition, as in the case of the *enigmatic canon* in which the key to the solution of the canon was given in a rebus or puzzle which had first to be deciphered. (As late as J. S. Bach, canons of this sort were still being written, for instance in his *Musical Offering.*)

Usually, at the beginning of the sixteenth century, imitation was not absolutely rigorous. The initial phrase was not repeated exactly. Instead quite brief melodic motifs were echoed back and forth in systematic fashion. Entire polyphonic works came to be made up of a series of imitative passages, each based on a different motif, one following the other without interruption, as in the motet. Such imitation is more free than the canon and leaves a larger margin to the composer's inventive powers. Nevertheless, as a structural device, it still often had to have recourse to procedures which had been developed through the canon.

Thus, in the sixteenth century, counterpoint became something more than the art of superimposing several melodies according to certain relationships between consonances and dissonances. It became also an art in which developments were worked out on the basis of imitation.

The great theorists of counterpoint in the sixteenth century were the Italians Vicentino and Zarlino, who had been pupils of the Fleming Willaert in Venice and boasted of it. Indeed, the art of counterpoint in that century seems associated with musicians from the Low Countries. They were the heirs of a tradition elaborated by masters such as Dufay, Ockeghem and Josquin Desprez. Even when this art was practiced by composers of other nations, it was always on the basis of the work done by the Flemish and in accord with their principles.

Next, therefore, we must try to see if it is correct to attribute to the Flemish the credit for the development of this art and for the creation of its most typical manifestations.

Chapter 3

18. Philip the Good Attends a Mass in Music Sung
by the Burgundian Chapel Choir.
Pupil of Jean le Tavernier (?).

A Perfect Art

In the fourteenth century, polyphony was, by and large, a French art. Its main achievements were confined to very few centers: the papal court at Avignon, great cathedrals such as those of Paris, Chartres or Rouen, the entourage of the King or of a few princes – Orleans, Savoy, Bourbon, Anjou, Burgundy. Outside France, it was practiced in such isolated courts as Cyprus or Aragon, where French models were imitated. A few Italian cities knew it also, as did some churches in England. Certainly the music of Italy and England had truly original traits, but it was French polyphony that dominated the entire period. And yet, the music which was composed and performed throughout Europe later, in the fifteenth and sixteenth centuries, undoubtedly had French antecedents, but by then it had taken on a profoundly different character.

How then, in the short span of a century, did a Flemish – or, in a sense, Franco-Flemish – art succeed in implanting itself everywhere and in becoming the model for all of Europe?

POLYPHONY IN THE NORTHERN
PRINCIPALITIES

Polyphonic music was not particularly favored in the fourteenth century in the northern principalities, if we may apply that term to the principality of Liège and those still independent regions of northern France later to be brought together by Philip the Good. The manuscript collection of motets, now in Turin, which was copied out in 1325 at the abbey of Saint-Jacques in Liège, did not originate in the latter city. The peculiarly Walloon spellings are deceiving, since they are no more than careless transcriptions of the original texts, and the music must have been composed in mid-thirteenth century in the circles associated with Notre-Dame of Paris.

Further, the *Mass of Tournai,* one of the earliest polyphonic settings of the Ordinary, bears that name only because the manuscript belongs (but since how long?) to the cathedral of that city. It is not a homogeneous work but rather a collection of anonymous fragments so varied in style that they must have been composed throughout half a century; moreover, the Credo and the Ite, missa est can be found in various other manuscripts in Las Huelgas, Apt, Madrid and Ivrea. Like the other settings of the Ordinary prior to Machaut's, this mass must have been composed at the papal court of Avignon. Though it may have been sung at Tournai as early as the fourteenth century, it was certainly not composed there.

Since these two important sources have been proved irrelevant, there remains very little in the way of polyphonic compositions that can be indisputably ascribed to the northern principalities at that period.

Perhaps, though, in the absence of other documents, we can learn something about the character of contrapuntal practice in this region through looking at the specialized teaching given in churches by the masters of music.

The earliest evidence of polyphonic practice in the North can be found in Liège and Cambrai. In Liège, the chapter of the cathedral of Saint-Lambert decided in 1291 to take care of poor children who would be charged with *reading and singing the services, both day and night, throughout the entire year.* The first *succentores* – masters of music – began to be listed by name in 1355, though the collegiate churches of Saint-Paul and Saint-Denis had begun to maintain choristers earlier, in 1331 and 1348 respectively.

In recent studies, Suzanne Clercx has proved that the composer Johannes Ciconia did not, as had been thought, pass most of his life in Italy. If it is true that he spent some thirty years at the end of the fourteenth century in his native city of Liège, then it was there that he composed some of his most important works. The outstanding figure of the latter fourteenth century and the early fifteenth, Ciconia was also the first of the great polyphonists of the northern principalities.

For Cambrai likewise, an independent city and seat of an important bishopric, the earliest evidence dates back to this period. In 1386 there were six boys in the cathedral choir, later eight and eventually ten, to participate, along with a dozen vicars, in the celebration of services in music. The first choirmasters whose names have come down to us were Etienne in 1373, Jehan in 1391, Nicolas Malin from 1392 to 1412, Richard de Loqueville until 1418, then Nicolas Grenon, who had previously been the grammar master. The bishopric of Cambrai has enjoyed special prestige, not only because of Loqueville and Grenon, who left works of considerable merit, but, above all, because Guillaume Dufay received his first training in that city and spent a good part of his life there. However, it is of note that Cambrai did not become a center of influence in polyphonic music until the fifteenth century, and the two choir books of the cathedral, the first collections of polyphonic music to be assembled in the North, were not written out before 1430.

Similarly, if in Flanders and Brabant there were signs as early as the second half of the fourteenth century of a musical life in which polyphony had a place, there was no original creative activity before the following century. In Bruges, a certain Guillaume Barbier was named *succentor* in 1365 by the chapter of the church of Saint-Donatien, and a text indicates that in 1421 four children trained in counterpoint sang Mass and Vespers. In Malines, a choir school existed as early as 1390 at the church of Notre-Dame-beyond-the-Dyle, and we can presume that there was a choir at the same period in the collegiate church of Saint-Rombaut even though the earliest documents referring to it date back only to 1433. The first *phonascus* cited in Courtrai appears in texts of 1410. At Sainte-Gudule in Brussels a foundation of *boninfanten* (deserving children) was set up in 1358 with the aim of maintaining and teaching twelve poor boys. It is possible that these children were used as singers from the outset, but it is not until the fifteenth century that there are specific references to choristers and *sanckmeesters*. A capitulary decision of 1446 ordered vicars under the age of fifty to learn *discantus*, which proves that polyphony was practiced at Sainte-Gudule at that time, although it also indicates that it was not as yet flourishing since special measures had to be taken to encourage it.

When polyphonic music began to be adopted generally, many churches must have run into difficulties. Documents in the archives of Notre-Dame in Antwerp show that at the beginning of the fifteenth century very few chaplains and canons knew enough of music to be able to sing in counterpoint, nor had they good enough voices to be able to sing polyphonic works at the services. At the request of the chapter and with the approval of the Duke of

Brabant, Pope John XXIII – during the Great Schism there was a pope of that name in Avignon – decided to divert the major part of the revenues of the twelve richest chaplaincies – revenues generally reserved for chaplain-priests – to the payment of professional musicians needed to perform the polyphonic music used in various services. This was in 1410, and at the head of the professional singers was placed a *magister cantus* who, at the same time, took on the duties of choirmaster since, in addition, it was felt necessary to organize a school for the training of children's voices. The former chaplain-priests protested energetically against these professional musicians who were depriving them of a large share of their income but were finally obliged to give in. Throughout the fifteenth century, the funds withdrawn from the chaplaincies and turned over to professional musicians continued to grow, which probably explains why Antwerp succeeded in attracting so many excellent musicians.

The practice of polyphony became widespread in the fifteenth century. Every church of any importance maintained a certain number of professional musicians : four, six, a dozen, sometimes more but not many more. The pontifical chapel in Rome had ten in 1442, twenty-four in 1483, and never more than thirty in the sixteenth century. These figures suggest a certain caution in whatever romantic illusions we may still have. No choir of the past ever attained the size of the immense choral groups of our days. Certain writers have claimed that Antwerp enjoyed an exceptional situation, citing the figures of fifty-one singers in 1443, sixty-three in 1480, and sixty-nine in 1549. The fact is, these figures include both the professional musicians and the chaplain-priests mentioned above, since the latter joined the choir on great feast days. There were never more than a dozen singers of polyphony in Antwerp in the fifteenth, and even the sixteenth, century. Besides the professional singers, there were an organist, occasionally a few instrumentalists, and the boy choristers, whose number varied from six

to twelve. Thus a good-sized musical group normally consisted of about twenty musicians in all.

The evidence is clear : if it was only in the course of the fourteenth century that polyphonic music began to be performed in the great churches of the northern principalities, it seems not to have been until the beginning of the fifteenth century that musical activity was organized in such a way as to encourage the use of contrapuntal music in religious functions. It may seem surprising that cities which were among the wealthiest of the time should have been so late, relatively, in developing such musical institutions. This delay, however, was not exceptional. In the fourteenth century it was in only a few centers that polyphonic music had established itself, and its use became widespread only much later.

Outside of the compositions left by Ciconia, the fourteenth century in the northern principalities was as poor in profane polyphony as in religious music. The few pieces with Flemish texts to be found in the manuscripts of Prague (Library, XI E 9) and Strasbourg (Library, 222 C 22, destroyed) seem to have been no more than adaptations of French or Italian originals. Nor need one count the few pieces in the Chantilly manuscript (Musée Condé 1047) by musicians of the dioceses of Cambrai and Thérouanne, since the fact is that all these composers worked at the courts of Foix and Aragon. In fact, for a long time the small courts of the northern principalities do not seem to have welcomed anyone but trouvères and minstrels with their traditionally monophonic songs. Almost a unique exception is Adam de la Halle, who composed in the polyphonic style in Arras as early as the thirteenth century.

But if little was done in the way of composition, already in the fourteenth century a method of training was initiated in a few churches which began to form musicians soon to be acclaimed throughout Europe. As early as 1389, the pontifical chapel included many cantors from Liège who were later joined by singers trained in Cambrai. The ecclesiastical constitution of Liège and Cambrai may account for their privileged position in relation to the pontifical chapel, and these two cities may have been the active intermediaries in establishing the new polyphonic art in the North.

THE BURGUNDIAN CHAPEL

The dukes of Burgundy were French princes : was not the first of them, Philip the Bold, a son of the King of France ? After him, John the Fearless and Philip the Good always considered themselves great vassals of the crown, rivals of the King, with ambitions to outshine him, if only by the splendor of their courts. Philip the Bold gathered together minstrels for his court entertainments and singers for the religious services in his chapel. A chronicler reports : *The holy offices were celebrated with great diligence, both day and night, and in royal fashion. There was even an excellent group of musicians especially maintained for this purpose, more numerous and more carefully selected than those of the kings, his ancestors.* His successors kept up the tradition, employing trumpeters for military functions, instrumentalists for entertainments, and for their chapels a half-dozen boy choristers plus cantors who were often priests but who, on occasion, also took part in performances of profane music.

In 1419, when Philip the Good succeeded his father, assassinated at Montereau, the personnel of the chapel was still exclusively French. The first chaplain, Jacques de Templeuve, came from Chartres, Pierre Fontaine and Guillaume Ruby from Rouen, others from Besançon or Toul; most of them had been recruited in Paris, at Notre-Dame or the Sainte-Chapelle. Later, Philip the Good was to continue to recruit his boy-choristers and musicians from the best choir schools of France, but he turned also to his northern possessions, to Cambrai in particular, which enjoyed great fame, and to Flanders and Hainaut. Fortegaire came from Bruges, Mathieu de Brakele and Jehan de Brouwer were Flemings, Constans was a native of Utrecht, Gilles Joye of the

19. Johannes Ockeghem and His Cantors.
Miniature.

diocese of Tournai. The most illustrious of them all, Gilles Binchois, was born in Mons, but his music belongs to a style no longer that of fourteenth-century France : from it we can see that, even if in numbers the French still dominated the chapel of Philip the Good, a new spirit was in the air.

From this time on, the French musicians of the chapel of Burgundy were to become in many ways more closely associated with the wealthy cities in the North. Often the chaplains held prebends in collegiate churches, and sometimes they left the ducal chapel to direct the music of some church in Flanders or Brabant. In this way, there took place a slow integration of French musicians into the Burgundian states.

Under Philip the Good, the chapel musicians accompanied the Duke whenever he moved his household from one dependency to another. From 1460 on, he settled in Brussels, and later the court was established more or less permanently at Malines under Mary of Burgundy, Philip the Handsome, Margaret of Austria, although still later, in 1531, under Mary of Hungary, it moved back to Brussels. All of this helped to broaden local recruiting, and there can be no doubt that the increasingly regular sojourns of the dukes in their northern territories stimulated the development of musical activity in those regions.

Beginning with Charles the Bold, the number of French musicians in the Burgundian chapel steadily decreased. The leading composers of the court were

the Fleming Hayne van Ghizeghem, Antoine Busnois, who seems to have come from around Béthune, and the Englishman Robert Morton. Pierre de la Rue, a native of Tournai, was the outstanding composer under Philip the Fair and, later, under Margaret of Austria. As for Alexander Agricola, the great composer who spent five or six years at the court of Philip the Handsome, nothing is known of his origins but he was certainly not French. Among the chapel musicians who were known as composers at the beginning of the sixteenth century, the organist Herry Bredemers came from Namur, Nicolas Champion from Liège, Jérôme de Clibano from 's Hertogenbosch, Godefroid Nepotis from Antwerp, Antoine Divitis from Louvain; there were almost no Frenchmen left in the Burgundian chapel.

When Charles V ascended the throne of Spain, he brought most of his musicians with him from the Low Countries. At home, a more modest chapel was promptly organized by the regent Margaret of Austria, for it was unthinkable that a Christian prince should do without a musical chapel. In any event, the former Burgundian chapel, which was continued in the Low Countries under the Spanish governors, and later under the Austrians, employed local musicians almost exclusively.

Although the dukes and their successors had a few great musicians in their chapels – Binchois, Hayne, Pierre de la Rue – despite all their munificence they were unable to attract as permanent members the best composers of the time. Dufay, Ockeghem, Josquin Desprez had only passing contacts with the court of Burgundy. For this reason, we cannot speak of a "Burgundian music" in the sense of an art inspired and protected by the dukes.

As soon as their worth began to be recognized, the musicians of the Low Countries made themselves known abroad. If the best of them succeeded in creating an individual style, it was through the synthesis of French style with what they learned from the Italians and the English. What resulted was in fact a truly European style in so far as it borrowed from diverse traditions which it blended into a unique language.

MUSIC IN THE FOURTEENTH CENTURY

The new style was in sharp contrast with the last phases of the *ars nova*, a term generally used by music historians to designate the music of the fourteenth century although it has much to be said against it, considering how often in history have appeared these *artes novæ, nuove musiche, modern musics* and the like.

Ars nova was the title of a treatise written by Philippe de Vitry around 1320 in which he dealt with musical notation, proposing new kinds of notes and a more precise, more rational method of measuring the relationships between them. The word *ars* in the Middle Ages did not refer to an aesthetic but only to a technique. Nevertheless, this new notation was used in music of a wholly new character against which Pope John XXII fulminated in 1324 but which was to triumph a few years later. Its foremost representative was Guillaume de Machaut, and typical of his work and of the new style was a predominance of profane over religious music. The polyphonic mass, which appeared at that time and which involved settings of the various sections of the Ordinary, was the only truly religious genre developed in the period. Most often the motet had no connection with the liturgy and instead used texts of moralizing, political or satirical content. It was constructed on the isorhythmic principle in which a rhythmic scheme was imposed a priori on the *cantus firmus* and sometimes also on the other contrapuntal voices.

In other types of pieces, literary forms determined a structure to which music was forced to conform. These are mostly rondeaux, virelais and ballades, forms which go back to the trouvères and troubadours.

Rather than by its genres and forms, the fourteenth century is characterized by its particular style. A subtle use of rhythm makes it seem that

20. The Emperor Maximilian Confides the Regency of the Netherlands to Margaret of Austria.
Miniature.

21. Belle, bonne ...

Baude Cordier.

each work is built up by juxtaposing perpetually varied small cells. One of the most severe strictures of Pope John XXII in a bull of 1324-25, heartily endorsed by the adversaries of the *ars nova,* was directed against the *hocket,* a procedure in which a melody is hacked up into tiny fragments — at times of two notes or even a single one — and distributed between the various voices. In addition, the fourteenth century encouraged a daring manipulation of counterpoint in which the structural points of repose were over and over again displaced to provide brief but constant tensions, with dissonances reconstituted as quickly as they are resolved.

Thus, from its earliest efforts, the *ars nova* showed itself to be an art both refined and learned. It was intended for the small cultivated circles of a few princely courts and was beyond the scope of any performers other than professionals skilled in rhythmic subtleties.

All of these traits became more pronounced in the last third of the century. In manuscript 1047 of the Musée Condé of Chantilly, the notation arrives at an extreme degree of complexity. It has been thought by some that such gratuitous difficulties were piled up willfully and without justification, but against this is the fact that mannered notation was a logical development from the rules in force ever since Philippe de Vitry. In the works in this manuscript the rhythmic displacements typical of the *ars nova* provoke chains of syncopations which seem over and over again to put off any feeling of repose. By skillful use of suspensions and anticipations, these syncopations often give the extraordinary impression of a *rubato* noted down in exact time-values. The voice parts seem exaggeratedly independent of each other. The rhythms of one voice part have nothing in common with those of the others or, if they do, the units of co-ordination are so large as to be scarcely apprehensible by the ear. Superimposed rhythmic sequences open the way to greater freedom in melodic counterpoint, to an accentuation of dissonances and tensions.

The parallelism between such subtleties of notation and the extreme refinement of the expressive content of these works can be seen in a rondeau of Baude Cordier in which the musical staffs are drawn in the shape of a heart. Even without hearing it, this music communicates to us as a calligram such as would have been enjoyed by Apollinaire or Mallarmé in modern France or by the seventeenth-century metaphysical poets in England.

In the Chantilly manuscript and a few others similar to it, the *ars nova* in its final stage reaches a kind of paroxysm of all its fundamental tendencies, achieving therefore at the end of the fourteenth century an ultimate mannerism in both technique and expression.

Nowhere outside of France did the movement go to such extremes. French notation was adopted by the English, but the surviving repertory, mainly religious, reveals no such extravagance. In Italy, polyphony seems to have been practiced by a kind of minstrel, heirs to the troubadour tradition, rather than by musicians formed in the discipline of chapel schools. Based on principles similar to the notation system of Philippe de Vitry, Italian notation nevertheless preserved its own character throughout the fourteenth century. Using poems of some literary quality, the musicians wrote *madrigali, caccie* and *ballate* for two or three voices. Syncopations and hockets were not lacking in their music, but the melodic line kept great suppleness and the counterpoint had a sweetness and charm not to be found in France. If at the end of the century a few musicians — Antonello and Filippo da Caserta, for example — indulged in French mannerisms, it was because they worked for French courts and had become in the long run, all things considered, French musicians.

However, in England and Italy the new style kept something of a local and even, one might say, provincial character. Only French music enjoyed international prestige and, to all intents and purposes, set the pace.

A NEW SPIRIT

A reaction in the direction of greater simplicity must have seemed desirable. When it came, it was due to Johannes Ciconia of Liège (ca. 1335-1411). What is outstanding about Ciconia is a certain international flavor in his style. He must have learned the French art in Liège, and he spent some time at the papal court in Avignon before moving on to Italy. His *madrigali* and *ballate* are wholly Italian in form and clarity of texture, and when he sets a *virelai* on a French text, he employs rhythmic superpositions of the three voices which recall the French *ars nova*. But his melodies are molded into sinuous vocalises with graceful curving lines which owe their inspiration to Italy. In the sections of the Ordinary of the mass he set, one can find traces of what he learned at Avignon, and in his motets there are occasional vestiges of isorhythm and, here and there, different texts for each voice, and these too are French traits. But he never uses a *cantus firmus,* and most often he assigns the same text to all the voices and bases the form of his motets on the Italian madrigals and ballades whose melodic turns he adopts. Also he employed systematically a procedure destined to know great success in the fifteenth and sixteenth centuries, *imitation,* often considered an essential trait of Flemish counterpoint.

This was not strict imitation as in the French and Italian *ars nova* with their *chaces* and *caccie* in which voices pursue each other like a hunter after his quarry. Outside of a few enigma canons, Ciconia preferred more flexible contrapuntal procedures offering greater possibilities for development. Transposition of a melodic line to other pitches often calls for minor readjustments which leave the melody clearly recognizable while, at the same time, reawakening interest through these minor variations. Not that Ciconia was the first to use imitation — examples can be found in his immediate predecessors in Italy and as far back as the thirteenth century in France — but he deserves credit for making it a normal factor in compositional techniques. Even in works calling for larger forces, he limits imitation to the two upper voices and often to the repetition of sequences alternating between the two voices and interrupted by pauses. At this still elementary stage even, imitation is already a dialectical process which pushes the composition forward step by step, a method of development not without a certain rhetorical quality but also of remarkable effectiveness.

To Ciconia is also attributed the honor of having replaced in his motets the *cantus firmus* (this was, after all, no more than a scaffolding for contrapuntal construction) with a freely invented tenor. This had already been done in the thirteenth-century *conductus,* but Ciconia's contribution was to convert it into a harmonic underpinning for the entire polyphonic web. He seems, moreover, to have been one of the first specifically to call for a chorus in religious music and to have conceived the idea of alternating a small group of soloists with the choral ensemble.

The essential virtue of Ciconia is undoubtedly his sense of construction. He reveals this in a striving for unity which leads him to utilize the same clearly recognizable melodic schemes in the course of a single work and also in apparently independent pieces. As a matter of fact, this is already essentially the notion of a *theme,* and so once again we find in Ciconia the origins of one of the most typical compositional procedures in Occidental music, thematic development becoming, much later, a basic principle of construction for music as we know it.

It is in this sense, and not from a strictly geographical point of view, that the German musicologist Besseler has justifiably acclaimed Ciconia as *der erste grosse Niederländer,* since all these procedures he developed were later taken up and exploited further by Flemish musicians.

At the beginning of the fifteenth century, there are glimpses of a new orientation in the works of other musicians. In Italy, Matteo da Perugia also shook off French mannerism by mingling French and Italian traditions in his work; in France, there were Carmen, Césaris and Tapissier. But, for the musicologist, these transitional figures are of interest only insofar as they announce the future. In the final analysis only the great artist *creates* his epoch: considered in historical perspective, his works seem to explain the works which precede them and to condition the evolution of those which precede him as well as of those which follow.

THE OPINION OF HISTORY

If, at the beginning of the fifteenth century, there was a single musician who can be said to have pointed toward the future, it was most certainly Guillaume Dufay. Even in his own time he was looked upon as an exceptional artist and an innovator.

Writing around 1480, a few years after the death of this illustrious composer, Tinctoris saw in him the dawn of a new era in music. It is true that Tinctoris seems to us to have had little real acquaintance with the history of the art. When, in the preface to his *Proportionale musices,* he summarizes the history of music, the names he cites are those of Jesus Christ, "the greatest musician of them all," Gregory the Great, Saint Ambrose, Saint Augustine and Boethius for Antiquity, and for the Middle Ages only the theorists Guido d'Arezzo and Johannes de Muris. Real music for him begins only with Dufay, Binchois and the Englishman John Dunstable, to whom he attributes the creation of an *ars nova,* followed

67

by Ockeghem, Busnois, Regis, Caron, his contemporaries whom he calls the *moderni* and who receive his full approval. Tinctoris ignores completely Machaut, and though living in Italy seems not to have heard of Landino or Ciconia. Yet, Tinctoris was one of the most learned musicians of his time, and his theoretical works are full of examples selected from the best contemporary music. Of the past he knew only the writings of the theorists but nothing at all of the compositions themselves.

Such ignorance of the past is of great significance to our study. It reveals to us one of the essential traits of medieval and Renaissance music. In those times, music was an art without a past or with, at most, a very restricted past. It lived in the present. We know that Tinctoris was one of the first to consider composers more important than theorists and to look on music as something other than a science. And yet, for all this, music certainly was not for him an art in the modern sense of the word.

For the man of today, something is characterized as a work of art to the extent that it invites aesthetic perception, that it can take a place in the universe of forms as well as in the evolution of history. The world of art is that museum without walls propounded by André Malraux in which works of every epoch and of all places dwell together, in a perpetual confrontation, within the aesthetic consciousness of modern man. Not only the visual arts but music also has created a museum in which Monteverdi holds his own with Mozart, Wagner and Stravinsky, to say nothing of a Javanese gamelan or some bit of folk song. In such a museum of sound all music is, as it were, up-to-date, of our time. Indeed, in the value judgments we form from this perpetual confrontation, it is the works of the past which are almost always preferred to those of the present. Ever since music became conscious of its own past, that past condemns both the present and the future. And yet, this is a recent attitude which goes back no farther than the Romantic nineteenth century.

For the Renaissance, music was much more a craft than an art in our sense. Even when it began to be recognized as an art, it was not as a pure art remote from its real social responsibilities but rather as something functional, an acoustical décor for daily living. It was precisely because music was so intimately linked with life, with tastes and sentiments, with fashions, that it was so rigorously tied to the present. Whether religious or secular, whether intended for edification or diversion, music was constantly transformed to conform to the spiritual and cultural evolution of the social group it aimed to satisfy.

When a work ceased to please because it was no longer in tune with the psychological needs of a society which had changed, it quite simply was no longer performed. It was relegated to dusty archives or outrightly torn up and thrown away, and its composer was soon forgotten. Even musicians themselves knew no more of the past than the works of the masters immediately preceding them whose language they adopted and then transformed without any revolutionary intent, acting within the most natural of dialectical processes.

Such unawareness of a remote past was responsible, perhaps, for the ready acceptance of the notion of a renaissance in music – which need not necessarily be identified with the specific epoch known as the Renaissance. This, in fact, worked to the profit of Flemish music because the latter seemed somehow to possess the very same qualities which, in the other arts, were associated with the movement of renovation and rebirth. For a long time, historians thought that the evolution of music always lagged somewhat behind that of literature and the visual arts. It seemed to many that the notion of a renaissance did not affect music until the end of the sixteenth century, when a Humanist current led to the invention of opera. Such an error could only be due to the mistaken notion that Renaissance meant no more than a revival of Antique classical ideals. The fact is that the idea of a rebirth of music appeared as early as the fifteenth century and according to a very simple schema : music had known its Golden Age in Antiquity either with the pagan philosophers or with the Fathers of the Church, after which it lapsed into decadence and lay fallow for many ignorant centuries until, in recent times, it had regained its original splendor. For the men of the fifteenth century and part of the sixteenth, this renewal had nothing to do with an imitation of Antiquity. According to Leo Schrade, it was the humanist Johannes Gallicus, a native of Namur transplanted into Italy, where he became a disciple of Vittorino da Feltre, who, shortly after the middle of the fifteenth century, was the first to formulate the idea of a musical *renovatio.*

Guillaume Dufay was the first musician to direct the art into truly new channels and to purge it of its errors. But since everything which has passed out of fashion was so quickly forgotten, throughout the sixteenth century the point of departure for the rebirth was constantly being corrected to a chronological distance within the memory of living men. Generally the title of founding father was attributed to some famous composer whose works were no longer performed but whose name was still recalled. Thus the glory was conceded to many, but in every case, even among the Italians, it was always given to a man from the North, a Fleming. In music, the Renaissance came from the North. For a long time also, one Fleming or another was acclaimed as having brought music to a point of ultimate perfection generally fixed at one or two generations after the beginning of the Renaissance.

For Glareanus, in the *Dodecachordon* (Basel, 1547), the *renovatio* was initiated by Ockeghem around 1475; in a second generation, around 1500, music continued to improve until it attained perfection with Josquin Desprez, who died in 1521, after which it was in danger of falling into decadence if the precepts of Josquin were neglected. In his *Compendium musices* (Nuremberg, 1552), Petit

Coclico considers Ockeghem, Obrecht and Agricola as almost mythological figures thrown in pell-mell alongside Orpheus and Amphion, but Josquin still represents perfection, the true Prince of Musicians; along with him Petit Coclico cites especially the Flemings Pierre de la Rue, Isaac, Willaert, Gombert, Crecquillon, Clemens non Papa, Pipelare and so on, and the Frenchmen Brumel and Lhéritier, the German Senfl, and the Spaniard Morales – but not a single Italian. According to Coclico, after Josquin there could only be a decline. For Hermann Finck (Wittenberg, 1556), the summit was achieved after Josquin, thanks to Gombert. For Zarlino (Venice, 1558), it was Adrian Willaert who had made of music a perfect art and it is in his works that one must seek for an exemplary model.

There is no equivalent in music for Vasari's biographies of Italian architects, painters and sculptors, or the *Schilder-Boeck* in which Carel van Mander studied and glorified Flemish artists. But the idea of a virtually biological development of music is implicit in sixteenth-century thought : after a rebirth there was a steady progress culminating in some especially favored composer, after which the art could only decline. Precise correspondences were rarely established between the evolution of music and that of the visual arts, but for Cosimo Bartoli, in 1567, Ockeghem rediscovered music just as Donatello had caused sculpture to be born again, and Josquin, the perfect and peerless master, was, in his domain, equivalent to Michelangelo.

It was only at the end of the sixteenth century that the artistic conceptions and merits of northern musicians began to be challenged. Before then, the perfect musicians had been considered to be, successively, Dufay for the period between 1430 and 1460, Ockeghem around 1480, Josquin Desprez around 1500 to 1520, Gombert and Willaert around 1550. If one adds to this list Roland de Lassus, who died in 1594, one sees the complete illustrious line of those Flemings who, in the eyes of their contemporaries, dominated music throughout two entire centuries. To them went – and goes still – the credit for the *renovatio* of music, and they made of it an *ars perfecta* which was based on the learned science of counterpoint.

With this in mind, we can now attempt to define the significance of this renewal and to see in what this perfection consisted.

GUILLAUME DUFAY
AND THE RENEWAL OF MUSIC

Present-day music historians agree with the opinion of Dufay's contemporaries that most of the secondary figures who preceded him, and in many ways anticipated him, can be neglected : it was, in fact, Dufay who renewed music in the years around 1430.

But who was this Dufay – whose name, incidentally, should be pronounced in three syllables ? It is not certain that he was born at Cambrai in 1400, but he appears in 1409 as a choir boy in the cathedral of that city and, in later years, as a chaplain there. His teachers must have been Richard de Loqueville and Nicolas Grenon. Quitting Cambrai for Italy at an early age, he embarked on one of those brilliant careers of which many subsequently would dream. From 1420 to 1426 he was at the court of the Malatestas at Rimini and Pesaro, where he composed his first works, then in Bologna, and later at the pontifical chapel in Rome, where he held only a modest position. In 1433 he entered the service of the Duke of Savoy, first as chaplain and then as master of the chapel. The court of Savoy at that time was most brilliant. A chronicler assures us that *at present the chapel of the Duke is held to be the finest in the world*. In June 1435, Dufay returned to the pontifical chapel in Florence and Bologna, where Pope Eugene IV had taken refuge because of political unrest. In 1437 he rejoined for seven years the ducal court of Savoy and, from 1445 on, using Cambrai as his base, he traveled throughout Europe and especially in Italy. As a reward for his merits, he was named canon of the cathedral of Cambrai and of the collegiate church of Sainte-

Waudru in Mons. In addition, he was awarded other lucrative posts not involving any definite tasks, among them that of *Chaplain and Most Illustrious Cantor for Monseigneur the Duke of Burgundy*. In his lifetime his works were known everywhere in Europe, as is proved by their presence in manuscripts of Italian, English, German, French and other provenance.

A long poem by Martin le Franc, the *Champion des Dames,* shows how highly his contemporaries valued his innovations :

> *Tapissier, Carmen, Césaris*
> *N'a pas longtemps si bien chanterrent*
> *Qu'ilz esbahirent tout Paris*
> *Et tous ceulx qui les fréquenterrent;*
> *Mais onques jour ne deschanterrent*
> *En melodie de tel chois*
> *Ce m'ont dit qui les hanterrent*
> *Que G. Du Fay et Binchois.*
> *Car ilz ont nouvelle pratique*
> *De faire frisque concordance*
> *En haulte et basse musique,*
> *En fainte, en pause, et en muance,*
> *Et ont pris de la contenance*
> *Angloise et ensuy Dunstable,*
> *Pour quoy merveilleuse plaisance*
> *Rend leur chant joyeux et notable.*

(Tapissier, Carmen, Césaris / In recent times so well did sing / They were the wonder of Paris entire / And of all those who gathered there. / But still their discant tunes were not so choice / Nor

70

Maistre Guille du Fay ~ Binchois.

Tapissier Carmen Cesaris
Na pas long tëps sy bien chätërët
Quilz esbahirent tout Paris

filled with charming melody / As – so I'm told by those who know them – / Those of G. Du Fay and Binchois. / For these have found a newer way / Of making fresh bright concordance / In public music and in private songs, / With *ficta*, rests and mutation. / Now they've learned the English way, / And Dunstable's their model / In making songs of wondrous charm, / Music joyous and far-famed.)

To Dufay, associated here with Binchois, is ascribed the merit of *a newer way of making fresh bright concordance*, and in this he is contrasted with Tapissier, Carmen and Césaris. The new manner is said to have been inspired by England and, in particular, by Dunstable. Tinctoris saw a link between Dufay, Binchois and Dunstable which brought in *such an astonishing progress as to deserve the name of an ars nova,* another indication, then, of a *new manner* quite different from the usual style of French musicians of the fourteenth century and which, apparently, influenced the entire period.

It has often been thought that this English way – *la contenance angloise* in the words of the poem – must refer to the adoption on the Continent of procedures employed in English discant, especially the extensive use of thirds and sixths in polyphony. As we know, originally these intervals were considered imperfect consonances and were, in fact, treated as dissonances to be reserved as passing harmonies between the structural perfect consonances. As early as the fourteenth century, however, English musicians had employed these intervals with growing frequency, not to render their counterpoint more harsh but, on the contrary, to increase its sweetness. This was done especially in *discant,* in note-against-note counterpoint, rather than in the melismatic style practiced, for example, in motets. In principle, discant excluded all dissonances, but alongside the traditional consonances – octaves, fifths and fourths – it introduced thirds and sixths to provide indispensable variety and a less disturbing tension than that produced by the harsher dissonances, the seconds and sevenths.

For a long time historians held the mistaken notion that discant consisted in the improvised addition of parallel lines in thirds and sixths above and beneath a Gregorian *cantus firmus* and that it was the source of the *fauxbourdon* style practiced around 1430 by Dufay and Binchois. In pieces in fauxbourdon, as in those in discant, two voices were written in counterpoint, most often note against note, the upper voice utilizing a plain-chant *cantus firmus*; a complementary voice, not written out, was patterned directly upon the *cantus firmus,* paralleling it mechanically a fourth below. To avoid any accidental dissonances with the unwritten improvised voice, the lowest voice maintained almost always the relationship of a sixth or an octave with the *cantus.* The result was a style of great simplicity in which dissonances were very rare. If these pieces are analyzed by the methods of classical manuals of harmony, in proceeding from the lowest voice to the highest, one finds a systematic use of thirds and sixths in parallel lines. Actually the procedure was used by Dufay and Binchois in only a limited part of their religious works, the hymns and Magnificats, which retain something of folk-song simplicity. But it impressed their contemporaries as a complete reaction against the mannerist excesses of the preceding period. By eliminating syncopations and dissonances, it introduced into polyphony a sound of great sweetness.

Dufay used this technique in some other works, these entirely written out, where, in brief sections which alternate with a more learned kind of counterpoint, there are passages where all the voices move together in the same rhythm with parallel melodic lines and superpositions of thirds and sixths in a kind of stylized fauxbourdon.

The German musicologist Heinrich Besseler is not mistaken in seeing in fauxbourdon the symbol of the new style imposed by Dufay and Binchois. On the other hand, it is not certain that English influence was responsible for the appearance of the new style. Extensive use of thirds and sixths is typically English but not systematic parallels in the voice lines. Rather it is to Italy, according to Suzanne Clercx, that one must look for the origins of the fauxbourdon, and she cites as proof a Credo of Ciconia in which all three voices – completely written out – move together in parallel imperfect consonances.

What, then, was this *contenance angloise* ? Manfred Bukofzer believed that it was a new way of approaching dissonances in counterpoint. When Tinctoris spoke of the music which had preceded the *ars nova* of 1430, he said it contained more dissonances than consonances. It would seem, then, that Dufay rejected certain harshnesses of the preceding epoch, and one can take literally Martin le Franc when he describes the art of Dufay as *a newer way of making fresh bright concordance.*

The fact is that the fourteenth century had treated dissonances with considerable freedom in the melismatic counterpoint which had developed out of the primitive organum. Theoretically, perfect consonances should have appeared at each regular structural point, and dissonances were *accidents* which could be distributed freely between consonances. In practice, however, rhythmic displacements could emphasize a dissonance and lessen the effect of consonances by delaying them or by introducing them before the structural point of repose. Indeed, dissonances might even be attacked directly, without preparation.

With Dunstable, Dufay and Binchois, a dissonance is always prepared : it is a passing event, strictly controlled, between two consonances. It could scarcely be used at a rhythmic point of emphasis, on what would later be called the strong beat of a measure, except as the temporary suspension of one voice over another in movement; any dissonance had to be resolved rapidly, dissolved into a new consonance, since syncopated sequences were no longer used. Moreover, whereas fourteenth-century counterpoint concerned itself only with the relationships of the various voices to one among them, usually the tenor, by establishing harmonious relationships between all the voices, Dunstable and Dufay avoid the accidental clashes which may thereby result.

But, once again, was there truly English influence on Dufay ? Such influence could have been transmitted to the Continent after the battle of Agincourt. It is known that the chapel of the regent, the Duke of Bedford, included between 1422 and 1435 both English and French musicians, and that Binchois was attached for a few years, beginning in 1424, to the chapel of the Duke of Suffolk. However, Italian influence must have been no less effective on Dufay, and certain innovations in his music can be linked with what he might have derived from Ciconia. This is true of the chansons in which a modern conception of tonality treats the tonic and the dominant as contrasting poles of tension and repose; often in such cases a counter-tenor acts as a bass part, moving by leaps of fifths, fourths or octaves and seeming to support all of the harmony.

Other profound changes affected rhythm and melody around 1430. The clearest evidence of this is the transformation of the notation system which resulted in a slowing down of the tempo. This was accompanied by a new melodic style which aimed at being more singable. In secular music, syllabic declamation – often integrated into a ternary rhythm with marked accents – and a new feeling of more popular inspiration put an end to the highly worked-out construction of excessively intellectual melodies typical of the fourteenth century. In religious music, there were wide-ranging, very free and very lyrical vocalises borne on a flowing and dynamic rhythmic base, these also very different from the complex juxtapositions of the preceding period.

All aspects of musical language were thus affected by the renewal : rhythm, melody, counterpoint, sense of tonality. The *ars nova* of the 1430's involved not merely a new technique but also a new aesthetic which may be considered the first sign of the Renaissance in music. Originating in French music,

73

the new art brought together, absorbed and amalgamated procedures borrowed from England and, particularly, from Italy. It was a truly international style, a reaction against the excessive refinement of the fourteenth century, against the Gothic.

Close examination of certain of the works thus produced reveals that there are still vestiges of the medieval approach, but this very ambiguity helps us to understand the complexity of such a civilization. The art of a Dufay was hailed as an ideal music at the papal court, the princely courts, and the court of Burgundy. When one measures all that separates it from what preceded it, as well as the renewal in depth which it introduced, this *ars nova* truly gave to its contemporaries the feeling of a renaissance.

The same transformation occurred in painting and to such an extent that the art historian Erwin Panofsky felt justified in borrowing his terminology from music. An *ars nova*, a "new practice," appears in painting around the same date of 1430 in the works of the Master of Flémalle and of Jan van Eyck as a reaction against the mannerism of the miniaturists of the beginning of the century, a mannerism to be found, for instance, in the manuscript copy of Boccaccio belonging to Philip the Bold and in the *Très Riches Heures du Duc de Berry*. In the new style there were revolutionary techniques – the use of oil paint – as well as a spiritual renewal : a striving for simplicity, for naturalness, for truth, with a new emphasis on religious themes. Just as we can attribute to van Eyck that *maniera fiamminga* which so deeply influenced all of European painting in the course of several generations, so also in music the international fame of Dufay can be said to have contributed to the association of musicians from the North with the prestige of the new art and with the feeling of a *renovatio* which it brought in.

At this time and in the same regions appeared other musicians who were to develop further the fundamental tendencies of the art by bringing into it those modifications which would evidently assure its further vitality.

A CLASSICAL ART OF COUNTERPOINT

Historians have often asserted that what they call Netherlandish music began with Ockeghem, while assigning Dufay to a Burgundian School. The fact is, however, that it is to Dufay that must go the credit for founding a new style based on counterpoint which was to dominate all of Europe throughout the fifteenth and sixteenth centuries, while Ockeghem, for his part, revitalized the art in certain of its most significant aspects.

Ockeghems have been found in Termonde and there is today still a commune called Okegem in East Flanders in the region of Alost. But all that is known of the musician himself is that, born around 1420, he was attached as chaplain and cantor to the cathedral of Antwerp in 1443 to 1444 and that the rest of his career took place in France, at the court of the Duke of Bourbon in Moulins and, mostly, at the court of the King. Appointed chaplain in 1453, then first chaplain and chapel master, he served under Charles VII, Louis XI, and Charles VIII. In addition, he was treasurer of the abbey of Saint-Martin in Tours, where he died in 1495. He was completely identified with French musical life and revealed his respect for the masters of the preceding generation by taking as his inspiration the later works of Dufay and by composing a lamentation on the death of Binchois.

Ockeghem has for long been considered the most typical exponent of Flemish music because of the complexity of his counterpoint. As proof of his extraordinary skill, his contemporaries were fond of pointing to his motet for thirty-six voices based entirely on an enigmatic canon. The *enigma canon* was a highly intellectual sort of puzzle which required the greatest skill in contrapuntal composition and in the reading of mensural music : all of the polyphonic parts had to be worked out from the single part actually written out and with nothing more to go on than a text in the form of a riddle. In the case of Ockeghem's thirty-six-voice motet, unfortunately lost, it appears that four voices were actually written out and from each of these a nine-voice canon was to be derived.

The truth is that such canons had been written long before Ockeghem, by Guillaume de Machaut, by the mannerists, by Ciconia and, occasionally still, by Dufay. Where Ockeghem's merit lies is in having made of this device something more than a scholastic exercise and in having been able to integrate it into serious works of art. His *Missa prolationum,* in which two voices in canon must be derived from two voices written out, is a prodigious demonstration of contrapuntal virtuosity. However, Ockeghem employed such procedures only rarely, and they are much more frequent at the end of the fifteenth century and the beginning of the sixteenth in the works of Josquin, Pierre de la Rue, Isaac and Mouton, although their use as part of the standard contrapuntal vocabulary was certainly fostered by Ockeghem.

Nor was Ockeghem the father of systematic imitative writing as has been claimed. The art of counterpoint, as practiced by Ockeghem with such supreme mastery, is roughly as described by his admirer Tinctoris in his *De arte contrapuncti* : it is not encumbered with any artifices of development, and imitation plays only a secondary role in it, since it is essentially linear. The fact is that Ockeghem generally wrote for four voices of equal importance laid out according to their ranges. Themes do not pass from one voice to another, and each melodic line is apparently independent and propelled only by its own dynamic energy. Autonomy is seen also in rhythm : phrases of variable length are superimposed in such a way as to avoid any coincidence of parts, so that the concluding cadences of each do not all come to rest at the same moment. This gives rise to a continuous movement renewed ever and again in one voice or another, and creating an inner life of its own.

The *Déplorations* – lamentations – written on the death of Ockeghem reveal how much he was still admired by the musicians of the succeeding generation. Guillaume Crétin, one of the so-called great rhetoricians, for instance, exclaims :

> *Chantres, plorez ce notable seigneur*
> *En visitant ses doulx chants angéliques...*
> *Agricola, Verbonnet, Prioris,*
> *Josquin Desprez, Gaspar, Brumel, Compère,*
> *Ne parlez plus de joyeulx chants ne ris,*
> *Mais composez ung "Ne recorderis"*
> *Pour lamenter nostre maistre et bon père.*

(Singers, mourn this worthy master / By repeating now his own angelic songs... / Agricola, Verbonnet, Prioris, / Josquin Desprez, Gaspar, Brumel, Compère, / Sing no more your merry ditties, / But each compose a "Ne recorderis" / To lament our master and kind father.)

In an epitaph set to music by Josquin Desprez, Molinet writes this :

> *Nymphes des bois, déesses des fontaines,*
> *Chantres expers de toutes nations,*
> *Changez vos voix fort claires et haultaines*
> *En cris trenchans et lamentacions;*
> *Car Atropos très terrible satrape,*
> *A vostre Obgam attrapé en sa trape,*
> *Vray trésorier de musique et chef d'œuvre;*
> *Grand dommage est que la terre le cœuvre.*
> > *Accoultrez vous d'habitz de dœul*
> > *Josquin, Perchon, Brumel, Compère,*
> > *Et pleurez grosses larmes d'œul;*
> > *Perdu avez vostre bon père.*

(Nymphs of the woods, goddesses of fountains, / Skillful singers of every nation, / Let your voices clear and proud / Now cry out laments alone : / For Atropos the frightful satrap / Has trapped your Ockeghem in his trap, / That true treasurer of masterworks and music; / Great pity it is that earth now covers him. / Don then your mourning habits, / Josquin, Perchon, Brumel, Compère, / And let great tears pour from your eyes : / Lost to us now is our kind father.)

24. Portrait of Adrian Willaert.
Woodcut.

In Venetia appreſſo di Antonio Gardano.   1 5 5 9.

Later, it was to be for his science rather than his sentiment that Ockeghem was lauded. He seemed to symbolize the basic principles of the contrapuntal art made famous after him by men like Antoine Busnois, Jacob Obrecht, Heinrich Isaac, Loyset Compère, Pierre de la Rue, and Josquin Desprez.

Josquin Desprez (ca. 1440-1521) seems to have come from around Saint-Quentin, but most of his career took place in Italy, in Milan and Rome. He was never actually a pupil of Ockeghem, but his art was a logical consequence of that of the older master. In any case, he had more frequent recourse to complex procedures, and he abandoned once and for all the conception of counterpoint as a superimposition of independent lines. He treated a work as an ensemble of voices linked indissolubly with each other. Voice parts were not invented one after the other as in the past but instead conceived simultaneously in their vertical totality. Much more than Ockeghem, Josquin employed the principle of imitation to guarantee that inner unity which henceforth was to hold together all the voices. Nevertheless, imitation was not often used throughout a work but rather alternated with passages in free style, and heaviness of texture was avoided through not using all of the voices all of the time.

This style was used with greatest thoroughness in his masses, but Josquin introduced it into all the genres, into secular chansons as well as sacred motets, and he imposed it on all of Europe as a model of unity possessed of universal validity.

DIFFUSION OF THE ARS PERFECTA
The examples offered by Josquin were followed, codified, often vulgarized by innumerable mere artisans in music. But they were also imitated and in part revitalized by a few artists of genius.

After Josquin, many musicians set about practicing the technique of imitation with greater rigor. Nicolas Gombert (1500?-1557), the chapel master of Charles V, is probably the best representative of the style which Charles van den Borren so happily named *imitatif syntaxique* (imitative-syntactic) and which Hugo Riemann called the *durchimitierende a cappella-Vokalstil* (through-imitated *a cappella* vocal style). In motets in this style, a particular theme is assigned to each section of the text and is freely imitated between the various voices; these sections flow into each other in a succession of developments uninterrupted by any conclusive cadence between them. Five, six, seven or eight voices are used, and rarely is the rather thick texture diversified by thinner passages employing a lesser number of voices. The result is an austere counterpoint in which all the marvelous possibilities of the science are exploited, sometimes even to the point of boredom.

After Gombert, the most authoritative exponents of this tendency in which the "perfect art" was gliding toward academism were Crecquillon and Clemens non Papa in the Low Countries, Vaet at the court of Vienna, Manchicourt in the service of Philip II.

Adrian Willaert (1480/90-1562), a Fleming settled in Venice, also practiced such a rigorous counterpoint larded with canons and strict imitation, but he was wise enough to prevent its hardening into a system. He alternated such passages with others in a quite different vein. In those, the voices proceed in the same rhythm and relieve the ear by vertical harmony from the continual horizontalism of counterpoint. The first examples of this style go back perhaps to the fauxbourdon so favored by Dufay, but it is from Italian secular music that this isometric tendency, which is, admittedly, an alien element within a contrapuntal texture, derives. It was adopted by the polyphonists for aesthetic reasons, to introduce an element of variety into rigorous contrapuntal writing and thus to reawaken interest. With Willaert, such isorhythm is accompanied by a more careful declamation of the text, by bringing out with musical means the expressive import of certain words, and by a greater use of chromaticism.

77

Intellectual as it might be, sixteenth-century music never forgot that it was meant for voices, that it was based on a text to which it must give the most sensitive expression. The composers of Italian madrigals – many of whom were Flemish – were so concerned about the relationship between text and music that their procedures have come to be called *madrigalisms* although, in fact, such devices can be found long before the madrigal as well as in many other genres, including the motet and even the mass. But through them, little by little, a new dramatic feeling insinuated itself into the art of counterpoint, so that, by the end of the century, the most violent attacks against the contrapuntalists were made in the name of dramatic expression.

Nonetheless, counterpoint itself made every effort to resist these antagonistic tendencies by assimilating them. Isometry, chromaticism, dramatic expression were, for a few great musicians, the means of instilling new life into a style which, in other respects, remained faithful to the principles of *ars perfecta*. In the second half of the century, Roland de Lassus was to become the most powerful exponent of a renewed aesthetic expressed in a language which remained true to the great tradition.

Ars perfecta, then, was a kind of music dominated by counterpoint, a style which despite notable variations preserved certain essential principles as great master succeeded great master : Dufay, Ockeghem, Josquin, Willaert, Lassus. This perfect art was born out of French music, but with Dufay it appeared as something entirely new, at least to the extent that he was able to graft English and especially Italian influences onto his French base. Thus, from its beginnings, this was an international art. In the fifteenth century, many of its outstanding representatives came from the Burgundian states, but there were also men from Liège – the Lantins – and Frenchmen – Compère and Brumel – and it never ceased to be fertilized by contact with Italy. In that country, where musical life was particularly active thanks to the pontifical chapel and to the numerous princely courts and wealthy cities, the *ars perfecta* was considered an art of the North. The designations *fiamminghi* and *francesi* were used without always making any clear distinction between them, and most often the northern musicians were simply called *Oltramontani* – men from beyond the mountains. Maximilian, Margaret of Austria, then Charles V and Philip II, all four great lovers of music and princely splendor, contributed greatly to spreading throughout Europe the fame of musicians from the Low Countries.

We shall see later how widespread after 1480 was the dispersion of musicians from the Burgundian states and then from the Low Countries. We shall see also how, in the sixteenth century, their style was more and more assimilated by composers from all over Europe, how it then became the basis of a truly international language which permitted great composers to express their individual genius within a common vocabulary.

Chapter 4

25. The Triumph of the Church over the Synagogue (detail).
Pupil or follower of Jan van Eyck.

Music in the Church

Music of the fifteenth and sixteenth centuries was never meant to be heard in a concert hall : it aimed at something quite different from aesthetic pleasure. An integral part of human activity, one of its principal functions was bound to be connected with religion. *Music,* said Tinctoris, *renders more agreeable our praises to the Lord.* Its role was to help the faithful to unite in prayer, to celebrate more intensely the joys and sorrows, the hopes and certitudes of their spiritual community.

It was also intended to make more splendid the rites of the Church. Huizinga, in his remarkable book *The Waning of the Middle Ages,* showed how much splendor and magnificence meant in fifteenth-century life. By such display, nobles and princes exhibited their own pride and their own glory, but the common man took pleasure in the spectacle thus offered him. If all important events of life — birth, marriage, death — provided the excuse for solemn ceremonies and were thereby rendered more exalting, if court entertainments — banquets and tourneys — always took a theatrical turn, if the most passing contacts between man and man took place according to an etiquette which was virtually a ritual, it was only natural that religious ceremonies should likewise take on an aesthetic aspect.

FUNCTIONALISM AND AESTHETICS

In primitive societies, religious music is essentially magical : it drives away evil spirits, it unites the participants, it throws the worshippers into trances and provokes an ecstasy which makes contact with the god easier. In the Catholic religion, such objectives have been progressively purified and stylized.

According to the Church Fathers, to drive out demons there is nothing more effective, along with prayer, than the singing of psalms and hymns. To bring about spiritual union, the faithful were encouraged to sing in alternation with specialized musicians. However, most often the Church has been content to make of the congregation no more than passive listeners to the divine service.

And yet, very early, the Church Fathers became aware of certain inherent dangers : they found that music tended to distract the attention of the faithful and so must be limited to the function of a *means,* never allowed to become an *end.* Saint Augustine, for one, admitted that he took pleasure in hearing melodies sung by lovely voices in church and this, he recognized, was a dangerous sort of pleasure : *When it so happens that I become more moved by the chant than by the words it accompanies, I confess that I become guilty of a grave sin.* And Saint Jerome counseled : *We should sing, in-*

81

*tone psalms and praise the Lord more with our souls
than with our voices.*

From the outset, therefore, there was conflict between the function of music in the Church, intended to bring about the communion of souls, and the artistic means used to enhance religious ceremonies but which tended to distract the soul from its proper concern.

In the Middle Ages, the chants of the Church were fixed in a ritual based on the Latin language, although Latin was no longer used except by the monks in their abbeys, secular priests in the cities, and a minority of intellectuals. Most of the faithful no longer understood the words and could not, therefore, be moved by the text as Augustine wished. For this reason, music became essential : added to the ritual of gestures and movements, it reached beyond the words of a strange, incomprehensible language to bring out the inner meaning of the mystery being celebrated. Every church ceremony was a joyous or sad solemnity which permitted the faithful to enter into a special relationship with God. If the music used were too ascetic, too frozen in an unchanging rite, its specifically religious function would be in danger of being lost : if it too were no longer understood, it could not serve as a means of intercession and communion.

Setting aside any romantic illusions we may have, we may well ask if, at the end of the Middle Ages, Gregorian chant had not become for most of the faithful a language as dead as Latin, and if polyphony was not introduced of necessity in the hope of restimulating the participation of the congregation by a more vital expression of their inner feelings.

Even in the abbeys where it was born, polyphony had been a means of inserting into a rigidly fixed liturgy something new more related to new spiritual needs. Still, in the early organum and motet, it was no more than an amplification and decoration of the liturgy. It was in the churches in the cities and in princely chapels that polyphony underwent the most original developments, because there it was required to respond to deeper needs. The nobility and the middle classes of the cities did not have the advantage of the same cultural traditions as the monks in their abbeys. To touch them more effectively, the Church might have had finally to agree to certain compromises such as the abandonment of Latin in favor of the local language in order to make the meaning of the ceremonies more comprehensible, and perhaps even to a simplification of the ritual. These were measures which the Reformed Churches were to take, in more or less radical manner, in the sixteenth century. Wishing to perpetuate both its liturgy and ritual, the Catholic Church was obliged to grant a certain creative freedom to music, and this permitted it to maintain bonds with the faithful which were so much the more solid for having thus become more emotionally affecting.

One of the justifications for religious polyphony and one of the causes of its great success may well have resided in the psychological transformations it introduced into the church service. Already, plain-chant was no longer sung in the fifteenth century in the same manner as in the time of Charlemagne. This deterioration, deplored by the purists, came about through a desire for a more intimate spiritual contact with the faithful.

But even this was not enough. The Church had finally to authorize the use of polyphonic pieces to replace certain Gregorian melodies. By the fifteenth century polyphonic music had become much more than a mere amplification of plain-chant. It was a new kind of music, much closer to the sentiments of the men of the time and made expressly for them, adapted to their spiritual needs. Such adjuncts to the liturgy could be dropped out without hesitation or regret as soon as they ceased to satisfy the psychological needs of the congregation. If, around 1500, the music of Josquin was preferred to that of Dufay, it was not because it was necessarily in itself superior but only because it expressed better the feelings of the men of 1500 than Dufay's music, conceived for the men of half a century earlier. It was *psychologically* more adequate to its task.

For these reasons, one can say that all this music was functional. Into a liturgy which by its very nature was frozen for all time, it introduced a spirit of renewal necessary to give force and life to religious feeling. In a church, illuminated by stained-glass windows and adorned with statues and paintings, it made the communion of souls more profound.

Also, it provided a sumptuous décor. The fifteenth and sixteenth centuries were addicted to festivities of all kinds, not the least of which, in number and splendor, were the religious celebrations which occurred throughout the liturgical year and, in addition, on the occasions of baptisms, marriages and funerals. At these solemn feasts, princes and nobles joined the middle classes and the folk in the cathedrals. But Gregorian chant was too modest a music to go with the resplendent tapestries hanging from the pillars of the nave, the richness of the priestly habits, the pomp and ceremonial. It was polyphony with its concert of voices and often of instruments also which contributed to such celebrations the splendor everyone wished for to brighten the dreary routine of existence.

Religious feasts had an advantage over profane festivities. Their ritual imposed a form and style which polyphonic music made more expressive, more touching and more brilliant. The decorative function of polyphony was not necessarily in contradiction with its religious function, for although religion was accepted by almost everyone without discussion or doubts, many knew no more about it than this official prayer in the collective manifestation of a festival. Such holiday joy brought men closer to God than solitary meditation.

Functional as religious music might be, this in no way meant it was without aesthetic value : it also aimed to give an impression of beauty which, moreover, was related to the very notion of the festivity itself. Obviously, some balance was necessary between aesthetic concerns and religious de-

26. Musicians in the Square Before a Church.
Miniature.
Reproduced by courtesy of the Trustees,
British Museum, London.

mands, for the ideal defined by the Church Fathers remained valid. The aesthetic factor must be discreet enough not to disturb the regular measure of the liturgy, it must be an implicit contribution strengthening religious sentiment without in any way conflicting with it.

This explains why music such as that of the fifteenth and sixteenth centuries is so profoundly different from ours. Today music has come to be considered a pure art, gratuitous, all function lost : we tend to think that any function brings with it, inevitably, servitude and impurity. It is true that in our society a functional art is an art for the masses and tends to become commercialized, uniform, and based on stereotypes of expression. But in the Renaissance religious music along with other art forms provided a particularly significant example of an art willing to take on a function, to exist within a system of commissions from Church and princes, to accept constraints of many kinds while, nevertheless, preserving intact its aesthetic imperatives.

THE ORDINARY OF THE MASS

In the Catholic liturgical calendar there are numerous feasts commemorating events in the life of Christ, His death and His resurrection which are grouped in four periods around Christmas, Easter, Pentecost and Trinity Sunday. To these are added the various celebrations of the saints. Each day of the liturgical year includes a mass and eight services for the canonical hours : Matins, Lauds, Prime, Terce, Sext, None, Vespers and Compline. However, in city churches and court chapels, all of these services did not retain the importance they may have had in the abbeys. Other than the mass, only Vespers and Compline were sung each day: the others were sung only on special feast days. To these, in the Middle Ages and the Renaissance, were added various offices in many localities. For feast days and Sundays something special was expected from the service, and it was for these occasions that polyphonic music was generally adopted. In the offices of the hours, as in

the mass, certain chants kept the same texts throughout the year and used only a limited number of melodies. Such fixed chants are called the *Ordinary,* whereas those specific to certain feasts, which vary according to the occasion, make up the *Proper.* For the canonical hours, psalms, canticles, anthems, responsories and hymns are sung.

As the principal action in the daily liturgy, it was natural that the mass should have attracted the particular attention of musicians. Each mass is a sacrifice of propitiation, centered on the words pronounced by Christ at the Last Supper, on the transubstantiation of the body and blood of Christ into bread and wine, and on the renewal of the sacrifice accepted by Christ for the good of mankind. Each mass includes texts spoken in a low voice (the Canon) or recited (the Epistle and Gospel) and ten chants. Five of these chants belong to the Proper : the Introit, which follows the entry of the priest into the sanctuary, the Gradual and Alleluia or, according to the period, the Tract (these are chants placed between the Epistle and the Gospel), the Offertory (which accompanies the offering of bread and wine) and the Communion. Five chants are included in the Ordinary : the Kyrie, Gloria, Credo, Sanctus and Agnus Dei, to which may be added, but not as part of the mass itself, the antiphon *Asperges me,* sung during the sprinkling of holy water preceding the mass on Sunday, and the *Ite, missa est,* which is a final benediction.

What musicians and musicologists mean specifically by a mass is a polyphonic setting of the five sections of the Ordinary. It seems to have been in Avignon in the fourteenth century that the idea first caught on of grouping these five sections (sometimes with a sixth, the *Ite, missa est*) into a polyphonic cycle. The first examples known – the so-called masses of Tournai, Toulouse, Barcelona and Besançon – are no more than artificial compilations of pieces by different composers which differ from one another in style. The first mass entirely conceived by a single composer is that of Guillaume de

Machaut. As a matter of fact, complete mass cycles remained exceptional throughout the century. Most often there were only separate settings of the various chants, sometimes in couples such as Gloria-Credo or Sanctus-Agnus. Settings of the Kyrie were still rare, and soon attempts to set the *Ite, missa est* were abandoned. There seems to have been very much less interest in the fourteenth century in composing music for the sections of the mass than for motets and secular music. In any event, for the form and technique of such settings of mass sections composers took as models other polyphonic genres such as the motet (from which they took the use of a *cantus firmus* and of isorhythm), the *conductus* (for the use of three voices in identical rhythm but without a *cantus firmus*) or the *cantilena* (for the arbitrary division of the liturgical text as if it were written in verses or strophes, with music inspired by secular polyphony).

In the medieval collections of plain-chant, the various sections of the Ordinary were arranged separately according to category : all the Kyries together, all the Credos, and so on. Today, liturgical books provide for certain feasts groups of four chants of the Ordinary – Kyrie, Gloria, Sanctus, Agnus Dei – but the Credos are always classed separately. This arrangement is recent, and instances of it were rare from the eleventh century on. In any event, in plain-chant as in polyphony, the earliest cycles have no internal unity but seem to be made according to a principle of selection we no longer understand and which offers no distinctive traits that might explain it.

THE ORIGINS OF THE CYCLICAL MASS

It was only at the beginning of the fifteenth century, and among polyphonic composers, that there sprang up the notion that the five parts of the Ordinary could be conceived as a unit. This aesthetic position may have provided some satisfaction to the composers, but it probably was not particularly evident to the listener. It must not be for-gotten that the polyphonic mass was not thought of as concert music. Outside of the Kyrie and Gloria, the five parts of the Ordinary were not intended to be heard one after the other; in the course of the service, they were separated by other chants and by recited texts. Be that as it may, composers exercised considerable ingenuity in working out subtle means to make of their settings a homogeneous whole.

For this, two procedures were used. In the first, at the beginning of each movement of the mass a characteristic melodic motif appears in one or two voices. At each new entry, despite slight variants, it is always recognizable to the ear. Strictly speaking, such a motif cannot be called a theme. A theme is a melodic pattern out of which an entire work is developed by means of repetition, imitation, extension and the like, whereas a motif becomes a theme only in so far as it may give rise to such developments. In the masses of the fifteenth century, the *head-motif* is no more than a somewhat artificial unifying device. It retains its original simple form, and in the course of any one piece is not subjected to imitation or even repeated after the beginning. Its only purpose is to attract the attention of the listener, and it does this by virtue of its position at the start of the piece. The second unifying procedure used was more closely linked to musical construction but was even less obvious to the ear. It consisted in employing, in each section of the mass, the same *cantus firmus* as a basis for contrapuntal elaboration.

At the outset, the head-motif was applied only to the paired movements, the Gloria-Credo or the Sanctus-Agnus. Later, two such pairs with different head-motifs were combined into a single cycle, and finally cycles were composed using only one head-motif for all the movements. The first examples of polyphonic Ordinaries thus unified seem to have been composed by men from Liège who had settled in Italy : Arnold de Lantins and Johannes de Lymburgia, worthy successors of Ciconia in the first third of the fifteenth century.

As for the second unifying procedure, it was from the motet that was borrowed the notion of using a *cantus prius factus* – a pre-existing melody – as basis for the composition. As far back as the fourteenth century, such melodies had already been employed in the separate movements of the mass, but what was new was the use throughout the five parts of the same melody as tenor, though repeated at times in variant forms. Here too, the technique was first applied to the usual paired movements, and the nature of the texts encouraged such coupling of the movements : the texts of the Gloria and Credo are made up of a succession of phrases of psalmodic character, whereas those of the Sanctus and Agnus Dei are shorter and their alternating structure tends to suggest a three-part form for the music (this is true also of the Kyrie, which later was often associated with the Sanctus and Agnus). The first examples of entire masses based on a *cantus firmus* are found in England, composed by Leonel Power and John Dunstable. In these, the tenor, based on a plain-chant melody, is provided in certain sections with a definite rhythm treated according to the isorhythmic principle. These two techniques were devised separately in Italy and in England between 1420 and 1430. Guillaume Dufay took full advantage of them both, utilizing them skillfully in combination.

Throughout his career Dufay continued to write independent mass movements and occasional paired movements, but we also have nine complete Ordinaries he composed, six of them based on a *cantus firmus*. It is to him that is due the honor of making the cyclical mass the most important genre in polyphonic composition.

There is probably some significance in the fact that in his first mass with a tenor Dufay used a *cantus firmus* borrowed from an English liturgical source. Through long, painstaking research, Manfred Bukofzer succeeded in identifying the mysterious tenor of this mass, which bears only the cryptic indication *Caput*. It proved to be the long melisma

on that word at the end of an antiphon, *Venit ad Petrum,* found only in the ritual of Salisbury and of very limited liturgical importance, having been used only in a small geographical area and there only during the characteristic vesper service of Maundy Thursday in the course of the ritual washing of the feet.

The reasons which induced Dufay to choose this antiphon as the basis for his work have nothing to do with the liturgy. The ritual of Salisbury had no influence whatsoever on that of Cambrai, and Dufay's mass was not written for England. His choice was exclusively artistic. There is much evidence that Dufay was interested in the English repertory and that he found therein the model for his masses based on a *cantus firmus* : it was not in a liturgical book that he found his tenor but rather in a polyphonic mass.

In line with the English practice and with what had been done in the motet ever since the thirteenth century and especially in the fourteenth, the Gregorian melody was shaped by Dufay into a rhythmic mold and repeated in each movement of the mass, first in triple rhythm, then in duple, but without any important melodic change. For the listener, the *cantus firmus* is not in any way obvious. Set into the center of the polyphonic web, the tenor has a second tenor below it and two other voices above. The entire contrapuntal construction was built upon the tenor in Dufay's usual style. Only the upper voices are made conspicuous, since these alone are meant to be sung, while the two tenors, in long note-values, are to be played by instruments. It is quite mistaken to think that a powerful instrument such as a trombone was intended to intone the *cantus firmus*. The tenor's importance is entirely contained in the act of composition itself : through its use as an armature, the mass acquires its profound architectonic unity and can spread out into a vast composition. Once the work is written, to the ear the tenor's function is merely that of one element within a polyphonic ensemble.

In the systematic use of a *cantus firmus* without any ulterior liturgical justification, there is implied, as Bukofzer pointed out, a deliberate aesthetic attitude characteristic of the Renaissance.

The same *cantus firmus* on the melisma *Caput* used by Dufay served later for masses by Ockeghem and Obrecht, and yet none of these musicians could have been acquainted with the Salisbury rite. The two later composers simply took the tenor from Dufay's mass and even preserved the rhythm he had imposed on it; they did no more than modify the sections and introduce between them pauses of variable duration. To all intents and purposes, a *cantus firmus* was considered no more than raw material to be used in any way one wished. The artist's work involved shaping such a basic, pre-existent melody into a precise form and then, and above all, inventing around it the other contrapuntal voices. The fact that they used the same tenor as Dufay did not in any way hinder Ockeghem, around 1470, and Obrecht, around 1480, from creating original works entirely different in style from the mass which Dufay began some twenty years before completing it in 1463.

Before and after the *Missa Caput*, Dufay wrote several masses for three voices which, despite innovations in idiom, grew out of the older style of the cantilena so common in the fourteenth century. Beautiful as these may be, his other masses based on a *cantus firmus* and dating from his mature period are much more important in several respects. One of them combines two vesper antiphons, the *Ecce ancilla Domini* sung at the feast of the Annunciation and the *Beata es Maria* sung at the feast of the Visitation. The fact that these melodies, deriving from the same service but from different feast days, could be integrated into a single mass shows to what extent the *cantus firmus* was no longer considered to have any liturgical significance. Even more convincing proof that religious music was increasingly being conceived according to aesthetic principles can be found in the several masses Dufay composed on tenors taken from popular songs. The fourteenth-century motet had already used such material, but those motets were not designed for the liturgy. What is novel here is the integration, for artistic purposes, of an alien element into a liturgical work.

In the *Missa Se la face ay pale*, Dufay took as his *cantus firmus* one of the voices of a ballade he had himself composed :

Se la face ay pale,
La cause est amer,
C'est la principale,
Et tant m'est amer
Amer, qu'en la mer
Me voldroye voir.

(If my face is pale, / The cause of it is love, / The chief and only cause / And so bitter is this loving / That drowned in the sea / I'd rather be.)

For his *Missa L'Homme armé* he adopted a monodic popular tune whose text reads :

L'homme, l'homme, l'homme armé,
L'homme armé doibt on doubter.
On a fait partout crier,
Que chascun se veigne armer
D'un haubergeon de fer.
L'homme, l'homme, l'homme armé,
L'homme armé doibt on doubter.

(The man, the man, the man-at-arms, / The man-at-arms he frightens all. / From everywhere there comes the call / That every man should take up arms, / A strong and sturdy coat of mail. / The man, the man, the man-at-arms, / The man-at-arms he frightens all.)

Dufay may have been the first to introduce secular tunes into a mass, but composers right up to the end of the sixteenth century followed his example. More than twenty composers, from Dufay to Palestrina, wrote masses on this same military ditty.

Was religious sentiment offended by this ? It does not seem so. Whether of profane or liturgical origin, the tenor was worked over and skillfully integrated into the polyphonic whole. Thus, the melody of

Se la face ay pale, which is quite long in the original, is divided into three fragments which are not all employed in any one movement. The original rhythm is transformed according to the rules of proportion, presented sometimes in values twice those of the original, sometimes in values three times as long, and while it is normally in triple rhythm, occasionally it is compressed into a duple rhythm; further, it is at times simply dropped out and at others repeated in different rhythms.

Since its role was limited to that of a unifying factor, of mere scaffolding, such a tenor was hardly likely to distract the listener or to shock him. Use of a popular melody in a mass was therefore in no way sacrilegious nor did it at all imply any weakening of religious sentiment. There can be no doubt that composers must have been concerned with something other than the liturgical function of their music and must have conceived their masses as works of art, though not, for all that, of what we would call "pure" art. A mass by Dufay sought to satisfy at one and the same time religious feeling and artistic values. Most often the musicians of the Renaissance succeeded in maintaining this delicate equilibrium, but it is surely paradoxical that precisely those works which today seem among the most perfect expressions of religious feeling should have been conceived according to aesthetic principles which were to triumph in the art of the time.

This attitude was to bring about a divorce between two contradictory types of music. Today, when music is conceived of as pure art, even a mass is intended not for the church but instead for the concert hall. From Beethoven to Stravinsky, great musicians have composed beautiful masses, but these are not acceptable within the church liturgy and rightly so, no doubt, for they would divert the faithful from their prayers. On the other hand, there is today a functional music which meets all the requirements for church use. It is much employed and perhaps really does encourage the congregation to pray, but it is of dubious value even

27. Mass on Christmas Day.
Jean Colombe (?).

for that. Its equivalent is the gimcrackery of gaudily painted religious images. As music, it lacks any style whatsoever. Its language is made up of bits and pieces of other styles. It has no artistic value. What a contrast with religious music of the Renaissance, which fulfilled a double function without sacrificing anything to one or the other!

For a long time the use of a *cantus firmus* was the most effective means of making a mass into a coherent work of art. Naturally, as styles changed, other ways were found to integrate the tenor into the polyphonic complex. Initially, with Dufay, there was always a voice below the tenor which tended to assume harmonic functions, and, above the tenor, there were two other voices which were much more mobile. Even in his most complex works, Dufay's melodies are clearly articulated with clear-cut cadences.

Of the fifteen masses by Ockeghem which have come down to us, nine are built on a *cantus firmus* derived from plain-chant melodies like *Caput* or *Ecce ancilla Domini* or from a popular source, in which case the tenor is sometimes borrowed from one of the voices of a polyphonic chanson such as Binchois's *De plus en plus*, Barbingant's *Au travail suis*, or Ockeghem's own *Ma maîtresse* or *Fors seulement*. Ockeghem's treatment of the tenor is much more varied than that of Dufay. He does not always subject it to strict repetition and sometimes it is ornamented in order to give it an importance equal to that of the other polyphonic voices.

Moreover, Ockeghem seeks to impose structural unity through new means. In the *Missa prolationum* the entire work is based on a series of double canons at intervals varying from the unison to the octave and utilizing the usual proportions of mensural notation. In such a work, the composer aimed at a grandiose ideal of formal equilibrium in which the logical, rational factor is never a mere scholastic exercise but is instead a stimulant to the composer's creative imagination. Such works were quite frequent in the sixteenth century after Ockeghem,

and even certain compositions of J. S. Bach, such as the *Goldberg Variations* and the *Musical Offering*, have much in common with them.

In his mass *Sub tuum presidium*, Jacob Obrecht attempts a total organization of another type. The *cantus firmus* used is an anthem in honor of the Virgin taken from the litanies of Loreto. As was customary, the composer reworked this plain-chant melody into a rhythmic form and divided it into three sections of sixty-six, forty-eight and seventy beats respectively. With only slight exceptions, these three sections reappear unchanged in each of the five movements of the mass, which thereby achieves an equilibrium despite the disproportion in length of the texts set. Further, Obrecht's counterpoint becomes increasingly more complex: the Kyrie uses three voices, the Gloria four, the Credo five, the Sanctus six, the Agnus Dei seven. Nevertheless, only two voices in the Kyrie and three in the other movements were entirely invented by the composer. Superimposed upon the *cantus firmus*, from the Credo on, are the melodies of six different Marian antiphons. Marcus van Crevel, the latest editor of this mass, has tried to prove that it has a secret structure in which the symbolism of numbers plays a determining role. According to this notion, Obrecht tried to realize a veritable cosmos of a mathematical nature, to give musical expression to the famous Golden Section of Leonardo da Vinci, and even to conceal within it certain Cabalistic and Gnostic symbols undecipherable except by a few initiates. Such theories are difficult to prove, but it is possible that such a work might embody in actual sounds – in *musica instrumentalis* – certain of those speculations about numbers so familiar in the thought of the Middle Ages and the Renaissance and which university scholars gleaned from their study of Boethius. In the principle of isorhythmic architecture which persisted in use until the sixteenth century, there may well have been an occasional but meaningful link between the science of music and *musica practica*. It is, however, from a more strictly musical point of view that one must understand the architectonic plan of this mass of Obrecht and those of others of the period.

The concern with aesthetic values that we can make out in the mass is also seen in the choice of a single mode for all of the movements even though such a respect for the modes is not to be found in the plain-chant literature itself.

The artistic unity of masses is well demonstrated by certain choir books in the form of most luxurious manuscripts which are written out most elegantly and provided with beautiful miniatures. In these, the Ordinaries are grouped together so that there can be no doubt that they were intended as unified works. One outstanding such example is the manuscript Chigi C VIII 234 of the Vatican Library, whose thirty-nine compositions in different forms include eleven by Ockeghem.

THE CYCLICAL MASS IN THE SIXTEENTH CENTURY

The *cantus firmus* remained for long the favored unifying device for the mass. It had been treated in various ways – left unchanged, divided into sections with definite rhythms but in slow-note values, as a crab canon or mirror canon, and in all the proportions of mensural notation. But in the sixteenth century it was more and more often paraphrased and varied in order to fit in with the other voices and to balance them. Such an approach made of it something more than simple scaffolding, and its melodic material was used as the point of departure for imitations in the other voices. Thus, the mass *Pange lingua* by Josquin takes the form of a vast contrapuntal fantasy on a hymn which is sung at the procession of the Holy Sacrament. Rendered more supple and paraphrased, the *cantus firmus* also absorbs the function of the head-motif and thereby makes the unity of the whole even more intelligible to the ear.

Another principle of construction also tended to dominate at this time, imitation, and it was capable of providing highly satisfactory coherence to an

entire work. But this unifying technique made a *cantus prius factus* superfluous. The composer could get along very well without a pre-existing melody as armature, replacing it by motifs of his own invention closely molded on the words and designed to stress what is important in them. The point of departure for this practice is development through imitation of the head-motif. In the sixteenth century, masses were often written without a *cantus firmus*, and these were called *missæ sine nomine*, although many of the masses so designated actually do contain a *cantus firmus* whose name the copyist or editor simply did not know.

It was in the motet that this procedure of imitation was to prove most useful, for in the motet it is important that text and music be closely related. The larger dimensions of the mass demanded a more ample basis for its construction, and this no doubt explains why the *cantus firmus* continued in use until the end of the sixteenth century though it had for long been an outmoded, archaic device; however, in this later period, most often the *cantus firmus* was subjected to paraphrasing which permitted a better integration into the polyphonic whole.

Occasionally a *cantus firmus* consisted of no more than a few solmization notes arbitrarily chosen. Thus, in his *Missa la, sol, fa, re, mi*, Josquin utilized

five notes and their transpositions, and in his *Missa Hercules dux Ferrariæ* he took from this title, which is a dedication to his prince, the vowels which gave him as his *cantus firmus* the notes *re, ut, re, ut, re, fa, mi, re*. As far as we can judge, the construction of a work as extensive as a mass must have been such a complex undertaking that composers hesitated to attempt it without some sort of underpinning which would determine the structure and permit them to solve more easily all the other problems.

In the sixteenth century, another type of mass was composed, the *missa parodia*, the so-called parody mass. Here the point of departure is not a melody but, instead, all or part of some piece already composed in polyphony which could be paraphrased. A remote ancestor of this device is found in the so-called *Mass of Besançon* of the fourteenth century as well as in certain pieces by Ciconia. Already Ockeghem, in his unfinished *Missa Fors seulement*, and Obrecht, in his masses *Malheur me bat*, *Je ne demande* and *Fortuna desperata*, had taken three-voiced pieces as a basis, borrowing one voice here, another there from which to construct an artificial, composite *cantus firmus* in no way different, in the final analysis, from a tenor derived from a monodic piece. In the same period, Barbingant, in his *Missa Terriblement suis fortunée*, superimposed several voices taken from a chanson, and Pierre de la Rue, in the mass *Ave Sanctissima Maria*, transposed canonic procedures borrowed from one of his own motets. What is novel in the parody technique is the fact that not only melodies but also harmonies are borrowed from another work and, in addition, the contrapuntal relations between these melodies with their interplay of consonances and dissonances and their characteristic cadences.

Josquin himself did not go that far. The parody mass did not become truly important until the second half of the century, and then among masters such as Roland de Lassus, Philippe de Monte and Palestrina, when it became the most frequently used form, revivifying the *cantus firmus* technique and adapting it to newer developments in musical language. By that period there had been achieved a global conception of polyphony, no longer viewed merely as superimposed lines but also in terms of the vertical relations, which, finally, were understood to play an important role in voice-leading. This then was the attitude which led beyond the *cantus prius factus* to the use of an *opus prius factus*, part or all of a chanson, madrigal or motet used as raw material for another and generally larger work.

In his mass for five voices on *Cara la vita mia*, Philippe de Monte takes as his point of departure a madrigal by Giaches de Wert. He does not hesitate to transcribe brief fragments of it which he places, for example, at the beginning of various sections as a means of imposing on the total polyphonic scheme a feeling of unity previously supplied by the head-motif. He also quotes certain characteristic cadences of the madrigal and even certain quite external effects such as rhythmic acceleration and echoes, although on the other hand there are places in which the borrowed themes are treated according to the old *cantus firmus* technique with new counterpoints embroidered above them. In these ways, then, the pre-existing work came to impregnate profoundly the entire mass with both its melodic and its harmonic material and even with its expressive character.

But, because of this, what was really no more than an artistic, technical procedure led to a situation the Church had reason to consider with suspicion. As early as 1549, certain finicky minds had caviled at the assigning to masses of titles such as *A l'ombre d'un buyssonet* (Brumel), *L'Ami Baudichon* (Josquin), *Baisez-moi* (Forestier), *La belle se sied* (Ghiselin), *Faulte d'argent* (Mouton), *Ma bouche rit* (Martini), all of these associated with more or less erotic and even bawdy songs known to everyone. And yet, as we have seen, the mere use of a tenor derived from a secular source in no way affected the religious character of the music. The situation was somewhat different with the parody mass.

VIDENDVM, VT NEC VOLVPTATI DEDITI PRODIGI ET LVXVRIOSI
APPAREAMVS, NEC AVARA TENACITATI SORDIDI AVT OBSCVRI EXISTAMVS

29. Temperance. Philippe Galle after Pieter Bruegel.

ENCOMIVM MVSICES

Quod ex sacris litteris concinnabat Philip. Gallæus Iconibus exprimebat pictor celeberrimus Io. Stradanus. Versibus illustrabat doctissimus Io. Bochius, urbi Antverp. a Secretis

Laudate eum in sono tubæ, laudate eum in psalterio & cithara. Laudate eum in tympano & choro, laudate eum in chordis & organo. Laudate eum in cymbalis bene sonantibus, laudate eum in cymbalis iubilationis: omnis spiritus laudet Dominum. Psal. 150.

AMPLISSIMIS ORNATISSIMISQVE D.D. EDVARDO VANDER DILFT ET CAROLO
MALINEO CIVITATIS ANTVERPIAE CONSVLIBVS PHILPPVS GALLAEVS D.D.

30. Harmony, Music and Measure. Philippe Galle after Johannes Stradanus.

In its decisions of 1562 and 1563 relative to the mass, the Council of Trent denounced what it considered to be abuses : vocal ornaments, excessively florid improvisations, too great prominence given to instruments when combined with voices, solo pieces for organ, contrapuntal over-complexity which made it almost impossible to understand the texts, and the introduction of profane elements into liturgical music.

Outside of Italy, the development of the parody mass does not seem to have been affected by these strictures, and even Palestrina himself, the most faithful exponent of the spirit of the Council, wrote masses based on chansons and madrigals. Nevertheless, music had reached a point where aesthetic concerns threatened to prevail over religious fervor and tended more and more to distract the listener's attention from the religious meditations the music should have inspired, and this the Church could not tolerate. The listener in question was a believer, and he listened to this music in a church, for despite everything the masses of the sixteenth century, like those of the fifteenth, kept their place in the liturgy and were never thought of as concert music. In those times, it would have been inconceivable to compose such a prodigiously lengthy masterwork as Beethoven's *Missa solemnis,* which, in length and aims, goes beyond any possible church function and can only be understood as a pure work of art. Whatever may have been the increasing concern with purely aesthetic problems, the contrapuntal mass of the Renaissance remained a functional work.

THE PROPER OF THE MASS AND THE REQUIEM
Initially it was the chants of the Proper which were more often composed in polyphony than those of the Ordinary. The *Winchester Troper,* which dates back to the eleventh century, contains some 150 organa on Graduals, Tracts and Alleluias. The same predilection for the chants of the Proper is seen in the repertory of Leoninus and Perotinus of the School of Notre-Dame in Paris. Polyphony was able to make a place for itself in a liturgical practice which called for alternation between soloist and choir in responsorial chants. Only those sections normally intended for a soloist were provided with a polyphonic setting for two or three voices, while those sections usually sung by the choir continued to be sung in plain-chant.

In the fifteenth century, composers tended to think of the various chants of the Proper as a unified body on which some sort of artistic order needed to be imposed, although they never went as far in imposing an artistic treatement on them as they did with the chants of the Ordinary. In any event, it was quite rare that chants for the same feasts were unified for any other than functional reasons, and they seldom reveal any obvious signs of an attempt at unification. An outstanding exception is the *Missa Sancti Jacobi* composed by Dufay in his youth, before 1430, in which he set a complete Ordinary and four sections of the Proper (Introit, Alleluia, Offertory, Post-Communion). This type of overall setting is called a *plenarium,* but the only evidence of any unifying factor is the final note of each of the movements, a D; there are variations in the number of voices employed (from two to four), in style (cantilena or motet) and in the manner of treating the *cantus firmus.* Another *plenarium* of the same period, the *Missa de Beata Virgine* by Reginaldus Liebert, has as the only unifying element in its eleven pieces a persistent use of three voices and of the cantilena style.

In seven great manuscript volumes of polyphonic music preserved at Trent which were copied between 1430 and 1460 in northern Italy, there are 250 Propers, often arranged systematically according to the order of the feasts. This repertory is not very well known, but it appears that most of the pieces are based on the Gregorian melody normally attached to a particular feast, but the melody is ornamented and often much modified. Four manuscripts from the beginning of the sixteenth century kept in Jena and Weimar are even less well

95

known, but they include almost 400 Propers and even some *plenaria* by German composers writing in the polyphonic manner of Ockeghem.

The most ambitious undertaking in the domain of polyphonic settings of the Proper, and the most perfect, remains the *Choralis Constantinus* of Heinrich Isaac, a major Flemish composer whose career took place in Italy and Germany. Begun in Vienna in 1508, continued in Constance and perhaps in Florence, it was left unfinished at the death of the composer in 1517 and had to be completed by one of his pupils, Ludwig Senfl. It was not published until some time between 1550 and 1555 in Nuremberg by Hieronymus Formschneider. It includes Propers for all the Sundays and feasts of the liturgical calendar as well as for a good many saints' days. The forces employed vary from two to six voices. The Gregorian melody appropriate to the feast is always present but more often ornamented than presented in its original simple form in slow note-values, and this helps it to become integrated with greater suppleness into the contrapuntal ensemble. In the first two books, the plain-chant melody is generally in the upper voice; in the third book it is in the bass. Despite changes, it remains always sufficiently recognizable, for Isaac does not stray far from the original melody, especially at the beginnings and ends of phrases, where the most characteristic motifs are brought out clearly.

Throughout his work, Isaac exhibits the greatest variety in writing as well as refinement in contrapuntal practice, and these stamp him as one of the great masters of his time. However excellent his music may be, it is the demands of the liturgy which remain foremost in his thinking. The different chants of a single feast are not unified by any formal device, and a certain number of them, the Introits for example, always conform to a rule of alternation between Gregorian chant and polyphony. Although Isaac may have striven for artistic perfection, these pieces are entirely appropriate to their liturgical function.

Among compositions including chants of both the Ordinary and the Proper, the *Missa pro defunctis* demands particular attention. It is sung on the second of November and at funeral services for the repose of souls, and is generally called a *Requiem* from the first word of its Introit. Dufay may have been the first to compose a polyphonic Requiem, but the work, mentioned in his testament, has been lost, and so the credit for the first work in this form must go to Ockeghem. The movements of Ockeghem's Requiem are not the same as those called for in the liturgy today, since until the Council of Trent the chants varied from place to place and at different times. Ockeghem's Requiem stops with the Offertory, has no *Dies irae*, and replaces the Gradual *Requiem aeternam* with *Si ambulem* and the Tract *Absolve, Domine* with *Sicut cervus*. Essentially Ockeghem's work is a paraphrase of the Gregorian melodies, which, in the upper voice, are often set out quite simply but may also be highly ornamented; in the Offertory, the melodies pass from one voice to another. Imitation is not used, but as is customary with Ockeghem the plain-chant is treated contrapuntally with considerable flexibility and freedom. The architectonic structure of the work is determined by the contrasts between different episodes for two, three and four voices.

The Requiem was treated in like manner by other composers, notably Pierre de la Rue, who maintained the plain-chant melody but occasionally made it serve as a motif for thematic imitation. Certain composers attempted to instill a more thoroughgoing unity into the form by employing for all the movements a single *cantus firmus* not connected with the liturgy. Thus, for example, Jean Richafort in the sixteenth century based his Requiem on a renowned canon by Josquin, *Circumdederunt me*. Most often, however, it was considered sufficient to make a more or less elaborate paraphrase of the plain-chant required by the liturgy and to surround his object with polyphonic voices in imitative style.

31. Sir Edward Bonkil, Provost of Trinity College,
Kneeling Before an Angel Who Plays the Organ.
Hugo van der Goes.

CEREMONIAL MOTETS
AND MARIAN ANTIPHONS BY DUFAY

In Tinctoris' definition, the motet is a polyphonic
piece of moderate length on an unspecified subject
though usually sacred. Broad as this definition may
seem, it is quite serviceable, since in the fifteenth
and sixteenth centuries all sorts of works were called
motets which had nothing more in common than
the use of Latin texts and the simple fact that they
were not part of the Ordinary of the mass. Thus,
there were liturgical motets which were polyphonic
settings of a Gradual, Offertory, Communion, or sections of the *Proprium missæ*, or of an anthem or
hymn from one of the services. There were also
non-liturgical motets of religious character sung in
church or elsewhere on special occasions, and these
had texts specially written for them. Finally there
were ceremonial motets having no connection with
a church service but intended, as a rule, for solemn
events in public life.

Descendant of the organum, by the fourteenth
century the motet had reached the summit of the
hierarchy of the various genres. It was especially
used for great occasions, when it lent a special brilliance to the celebration. Although not liturgical,
its structure was always based on a *cantus firmus*,
Gregorian or otherwise, upon which the other voices
were constructed. Most often, the tenor was treated
according to the isorhythmic principle and was broken up into a number of sections with identical
rhythmic schemes. The other voices were written on

different texts and at times they too were treated iso-rhythmically. This type of motet survived into the fifteenth century and, no doubt because of the solemn character of the occasions for which it was intended, it continued to exploit the outmoded and, indeed, archaic isorhythmic principle.

Like Ciconia before him, Dufay often preserved in certain of his larger ceremonial motets the tradition of plural texts and isorhythm. Toward 1420 he composed *Vasilissa ergo,* a motet in honor of Cleofe Malatesta's marriage to Theodore Palaiologos, son of the Byzantine Emperor Manuel III; in 1431, the motet *Ecclesie militantis* for the election of Pope Eugene IV; in 1433, *Supremum est mortalibus* to celebrate the treaty of reconciliation between Eugene IV and King Sigismund of Hungary, who was later to have himself crowned Emperor; in 1436, *Nuper rosarum flores* for the consecration by the Pope of the new cathedral in Florence. In a description of the latter ceremony, an eyewitness stressed the important role played by music, although we cannot make out at what moment this particular motet was performed. When the procession, led by players on wind and string instruments, arrived within the church, *there were heard voices in great numbers and of all kinds, and such symphonies rose to heaven that one seemed to hear a concert of angels... When the singing stopped, the instruments sounded so agreeably and so sweetly that the ecstasy provoked an instant before by the exquisite symphony of voices now began again and more strongly even... At the moment of the Elevation, the entire basilica resounded with such an harmonious ensemble of voices mixed with instruments that it was as if the music of paradise had descended on earth.*

In Dufay's youthful works, the *cantus firmus* was assigned to the lowest voice in accord with the fourteenth-century tradition, but in later works a counter-tenor played a functional role in the harmony below the tenor, as was customary in settings of the mass. Above this logically established scaffolding, Dufay invented other vocal lines in a style

owing nothing to the past, with bold, dynamic melodies to capture the listener's interest.

In marked contrast to his elaborate ceremonial motets, Dufay wrote others in a much simpler style, in particular compositions in honor of the Virgin, notably settings of the Marian antiphons *Alma Redemptoris Mater, Ave Regina cælorum, Regina cæli lætare,* and *Salve Regina,* which, at the end of the Middle Ages, were generally sung at a special evening service called the *Salut* in France or the *Salve* in England and Germany. This service, most popular among the folk, included group singing of anthems, hymns and canticles either around a statue of the Virgin or in a procession through the church. Most of the Marian antiphons of Dufay were composed for three voices, of which the upper sometimes includes the entire original Gregorian melody but in a triple rhythm modeled after the style of profane chansons then in vogue, while the lower voices were probably played by instruments, this too being a trait of the polyphonic chanson. Most often, however, the composer retained no more of the plainchant melody than a brief characteristic motif or else he provided an entirely original musical setting for the liturgical text. It might seem that this could lead to a certain worldliness in style, but the contrary was true : these works represent a revitalization of religious music and expressed a particularly vigorous popular fervor in a most direct manner.

Certain motets other than Marian antiphons were composed by Dufay in a free song style. *Inclita stella maris* and *Flos florum* do not borrow their

texts from the liturgy, although they too pay homage to the Virgin and reveal the same inspiration as the other Marian works, elegant and popular at one and the same time. Sequences and hymns were composed by Dufay in the same spirit of simplicity coupled with refinement. In the upper voice, the plain-chant melody is given a definite rhythm, para-phrased, rendered more animated and more affecting. In these works, Dufay often had recourse to the technique of fauxbourdon, in which only the outer voices are written out, while the inner voice merely follows the principal melodic line at the interval of a fourth. From stanza to stanza there is an alterna-tion between plain-chant, fauxbourdon and, at times, a more elaborate three-voice counterpoint.

Other composers in this period, among them Bin-chois, J. de Lymburgia and A. de Lantins, wrote hymns in a similar style. Afterward, a current of popular polyphony, quite different from the Flemish polyphonic tradition, grew up in various countries alongside or outside the mainstream of great art. The composers of these works were often anony-mous and apparently without any particular ambi-tions or any special interest in aesthetic values,

remaining humbly concerned only with the function of their music. These Italian hymn cycles included much writing in parallel vocal lines in a style de-veloped out of fauxbourdon. Later, Festa, Animuc-cia and Palestrina helped increase the dignity of this type of music by applying to it more learned techniques, while at the same time preserving the characteristic simplicity called for by the Council of Trent. This popular current, in which polyphony was reduced to essentials, was to have great appeal in Lutheran Germany. Thanks to the collections published in 1542 and 1545 by G. Rhaw, these *hymni sacri* became one of the important sources of the Protestant chorale, since these moderniza-tions of plain-chant melodies and these simple, mov-ing religious songs, once they were fitted up with a German text, ideally fulfilled the function required of them by the Lutheran liturgy, to aid in direct contact with the congregation.

Adrian Willaert in 1542, Jacobus de Kerle in 1558 and Roland de Lassus in 1581 all wrote cycles of hymns, but these were works of high purpose and skilled technique in no way alien to the general character of Flemish art. That art had not exploited

33. Acanthus with Musicians and Dancers.
Israël van Meckenem.

all the possibilities implicit in Dufay's work but only those which involved a certain rigor, a severity of style, and a scientific attitude toward the art of music. Such an evolution had, in fact, been anticipated by Dufay himself in certain motets in which he rejected both the pre-established scaffolding of isorhythm and the folk-song-like simplicity of his own hymns. In an *Ave Regina* for four voices, the Gregorian melody, very much ornamented, is embedded within the polyphonic web and its material tends to pervade all the other voices. This was the motet which Dufay wished to have performed at his funeral in Cambrai by the choir boys, two cantors and the singing master; in it he did not hesitate to add as a trope to the original text of the anthem as a personal prayer to the Virgin :

Miserere supplicanti Dufay
Sitque in conspectu mors ejus speciosa.

(Have pity on Dufay who prays to you / And grant unto him that he may die a good death.)

In a sense, this work may be considered Dufay's artistic testament. Flemish musicians took it as a model for the intricate counterpoint they composed to every kind of text, even for those with little in common with such learned music.

Johannes Regis (ca. 1430 - ca. 1485), singing master at the church of Our Lady in Antwerp and canon at Soignies, after having been Dufay's secretary became his perfect disciple, composing large-scale motets with *cantus firmus* technique. Antoine Busnois (d. 1492), court musician of Charles the Bold and author of delightful chansons, also wrote such learned motets as *In hydraulis,* whose tenor is made out of the persistent repetition of three slow notes, and *Anthoni usque limina,* a motet in honor of his patron Saint Anthony Abbot in which the tenor is reduced to a single note sounded by a bell at regular intervals. Most of Ockeghem's motets are in honor of the Virgin, but compared with those of Dufay the most simple among them appear highly complex. When they employ a plain-chant melody, it is boldly transformed and intricately woven into the contrapuntal texture. Further, Ockeghem's motets are set for four voices and even for five, and the latter, which are the most ambitious – for example, *Intemerata Dei Mater* and *Gaude Maria* – are highly worked-out vast constructions. Pierre de la Rue (d. 1518) was probably a native of Tournai, and he became one of the most illustrious musicians in the Burgundian chapel at the end of the fifteenth and the beginning of the sixteenth century. Without himself leaving the Low Countries, his numerous and diverse works came to be appreciated throughout Europe. Along with his secular chansons and his masses, his motets reveal his liking for canonic developments in a particularly austere style of great plastic beauty.

LITURGY, EXPRESSIVE MUSIC
AND PURE MUSIC IN JOSQUIN DESPREZ

It is in the motets of Josquin Desprez that one sees best what the form had become by the beginning of the sixteenth century. If musicologists have doubted – more perhaps than is necessary – that motets were really used in the liturgy of the period, it is because they have not been able to track down the origin of many of the texts used. Their error is in considering only the liturgy of today, which is sharply defined and the same everywhere. But in the sixteenth century there were many special practices which have since been abolished and a good many local traditions, limited sometimes to a single diocese, which have not survived. As an example, there were services in honor of the Virgin which, by

101

virtue of their popular, folk character, differed markedly from place to place, and there were also many saints' days peculiar to a particular locality. For these, music was composed on texts specially written for the occasion in a cadenced prose, in metrical verses, or on passages selected from the Old or New Testaments which were put together in something like the collages of which certain painters of our time are so fond and then made to fit their special purpose by the interpolation of a name or a phrase.

Particular circumstances – the death of a prince, a plague to be conjured away – also stimulated the writing of motets. Indeed, everything provided an excuse for new music, and new works were incorporated without difficulty into the services of the canonical hours, whose liturgy was relatively flexible, and even at times into the mass itself, into which motets could be inserted at places such as the Elevation or after the Kyrie, Sanctus or Agnus in order to enhance the solemnity of the office. In certain regions, northern Italy among them, sometimes even the chants of the mass were replaced by motets which paraphrased them, and these were called *motetti missales*. In this way, many motets could find a place in a liturgy which was still far from inflexible.

Moreover, the learned style of the motet little by little invaded the realm of chants, psalmodies and recitations, which certainly would not seem to lend themselves to such treatment. In the fifteenth century, along with the grand motets for special occasions which normally employed special texts, it was especially the Marian antiphons, sequences and hymns which were set to music. With Josquin, of whose motets some ninety have come down to us, the sources are much more varied. Fifteen of his motets belong to the Proper of the mass and replace not only certain chants – the Tract and Sequence, for example – but often also such recitations as the Epistle or Gospel for Easter, Pentecost, the feast of Corpus Christi and various feasts in honor of the

Virgin. Among the motets intended for the offices, there are four lessons for Matins, thirteen Marian antiphons, twenty-five psalms plus hymns, prayers and settings of the *Ave Maria* and *Pater Noster*.

Whenever there is a Gregorian melody associated with a liturgical text (as in Anthems, Responses, Sequences, Tracts and Hymns), Josquin used this melody as *cantus firmus*, though he paraphrases and transforms it, assimilating it into his style without, however, destroying its recognizable identity. Most often he divides it into a certain number of sections which are then treated one after the other, and at times he turns it into a canon which continues throughout the work. But whether it appears in long note-values or in an elaborate ornamentation, in the upper voice or buried within the texture, the *cantus firmus* for Josquin is never an alien element whose only purpose is structural. Instead, it is integrated into the polyphonic web, and its most typical motifs serve as bases for more or less concentrated developments in imitative style.

The creative method of Josquin is most clearly seen in those works in which normally the same plain-chant melody would be repeated for each verse. In these, Josquin is not satisfied with literal repetition, but instead, at each entry, the plain-chant is surrounded with new counterpoints for a different number of voices each time, and the *cantus firmus* passes from one voice to the other. From this takes form a work in vast dimensions, worked out on the principle – an innovation for the period – of contrapuntal variations. It is in this manner that are treated sequences such as *Victimæ paschali laudes* and *Benedicta es cælorum Regina*.

By one means or another, each motet tends to acquire a structural unity which makes of it a complete and independent work of art. Such unity, easy to achieve in motets of small dimensions, is less easily come by in larger works although Josquin never ceased to strive for it. Many texts used by Josquin are not associated with any Gregorian melody. Thus, prayers, readings from the Gospels and psalms are simply recited according to certain psalmodic formulas intoned at the beginning of each phrase. In setting such texts, Josquin often uses one of these formulas at the outset but in an ornamented version, and in addition he sometimes introduces them in passing in the course of the work, without, however, employing them either as *cantus firmus* or as motif for development. Instead, he has recourse to a melody associated with a text which is in some way related to the text he is treating, even if that melody is not Gregorian. Thus, in a *Stabat Mater*, a text for which contemporary liturgical books provided no plainchant melody, Josquin exalts the sorrowing Virgin at the foot of the Cross by utilizing as *cantus firmus* a chanson by Agricola whose text says : Like a disconsolate woman / The most abandoned of all / Who no longer hopes / Someday to be consoled / I only wish for death at morn and eve.

At times, he uses an even simpler procedure, taking as *cantus prius factus* merely a few solmization syllables which are obstinately repeated. A good many motets, however, use no pre-existing elements whatsoever, for the decisive factor in Josquin's invention is no longer the *cantus firmus* but, instead, a close bond between music and words. This had not always been the case in the past. In the fourteenth century, Aegidius de Murino gave the following advice : *When the composition has been completed, take the text of the motet and divide it into four parts and do the same with the music also; then fit the first part of the text to the first section of the music as neatly as possible, and continue doing this to the end. Sometimes you may have to use many notes for a few words in order to end up together.* According to fourteenth-century notions, the motet had a musical structure independent of the text, which was simply to be inserted after the music had been written, but in the fifteenth century this indifference to the text survived only in a few ceremonial works. Josquin, however, took the text as his point of departure and let himself be inspired and guided by it.

From this there grew a virtual rhetoric of composition in which the figures used could be specified precisely and classified together with their musical formulas. The simplest example is found when such words as *ascendit in cælum* or *resurrexit* are accompanied by a rising melodic line or *descendit de cælis* by a descending line. Josquin was not himself the inventor of this principle, which can be traced back at least as far as Dufay, but he seems to have gone about using these rhetorical figures in a very systematic way. In certain instances the musical illustration appears to be quite literal, but in others there is an attempt to permeate the entire composition with an atmosphere related to the text. Taking words as its point of departure, this expressive musical language came to acquire a considerable degree of autonomy, to have an existence of its own, and to communicate the overall meaning even when the listener was unable to make out clearly the individual words. Moreover, even the place assigned to a musical work in the liturgy usually helped the listener to grasp its significance, and by its own qualities the music did the rest. It is noteworthy that in his concern with welcome expressiveness, the sixteenth-century composer was partial to texts of emotional, subjective character such as the Lamentations of Job, David weeping over the death of Absalom, or Christ on the Cross.

Since he employed only exceptionally the large isorhythmic form and, at the same time, disliked treating the *cantus firmus* as nothing more than a structural support, Josquin sought to base his music on a more intimate connection with the text. Nevertheless, the relationship between words and music was not for him an aesthetic ideal but merely a stimulus to creation, and his central concern remained the music. Far from representing a capitulation to the text, this procedure, with Josquin, is an important stage in the evolution of the musical language. It would finally make of Western music a pure art, completely autonomous and, what is more, essentially instrumental.

103

If we wish to evaluate the contribution of Josquin and the Flemish musicians and to understand at what point they had arrived, we must situate them in their historical perspective. At the outset, polyphony was no more than a handmaiden to plainchant, merely a trope upon a pre-existing melody. When counterpoint was able to become more than a mere embellishment of a liturgical melody and began to become more complex, the *cantus firmus* for a long time seemed quite indispensable as an armature for the polyphonic structure, an armature which, in fact, determined the entire nature of that structure : once a functional element in the liturgy, the *cantus firmus* took on a structural role in polyphonic music. When the composer wished to free himself of the tyranny of the *cantus firmus,* he was obliged to seek other bases, and these he found in the text itself. The text, with its lamentations or jubilations, determined the overall expression of the entire work, and by association of ideas its key words suggested certain musical patterns which in their turn served as a base for development. As long as the *cantus firmus* remained strictly structural, it could be any fragment of a song, any casually chosen solmization syllables. In itself the choice had no importance. With Josquin, often the *cantus firmus* has its own expressive character. When it is not thoroughly blended with the melodic material invented by the composer, it is useful only to the extent that its melody is already known to the listener and is charged with a certain significance permeating the entire polyphony. It was for these reasons that Josquin at times replaced a Gregorian melody with a profane tune whose text was not itself sung but whose meaning was known to everyone and was germane to the composer's expressive purposes. Reduced to functioning as an element of expression, the *cantus firmus* was then obliged to compete with the composer's own melodic inventions. The question inevitably arose as to whether, in order to translate into music the sorrows or joys expressed by the text, it might not be more con-

venient and more effective to invent altogether melodies which would be so much the more moving because they could be more intimately related to the psychological character of the text. It was inevitable, then, that composers should finally reject entirely the *cantus firmus* and depend only on the text to determine the musical form of their works.

The particular merit of Josquin and his followers lies in the fact that they were able to take the text as their point of departure without, for all that, permitting it to dominate. Using the words as initial stimulation, the music could be developed according to its own laws : indeed, even when played on instruments, such motets do not lose their interest. It was soon seen that it was possible to compose contrapuntal fantasies (called *ricercari* in Italy) along the same lines as the motet. From these was born a pure music without precise function but with its own intrinsic value, a music from which were to spring the principal forms of the following centuries, the fugue and the sonata. Thus, the motets of Josquin succeeded in establishing a harmony between text and music which was entirely to the profit of pure music, and even their liturgical function did not prevent their acquiring an autonomy which stamps them as authentic works of art.

THE PREDOMINANCE OF THE MOTET

In the sixteenth century, the increasingly artistic character of religious music is revealed by what one might call its "motetization" : all religious music,

35. Madonna and Angel Musicians. Jan Sadeler the Elder.

no matter how humble in function, was treated with the techniques natural to the motet and thereby given added dignity. Josquin went so far as to put into rigorous polyphony passages from the Gospels which normally were only recited, and one of his motets is no more than the genealogy of Christ, a kind of musical Tree of Jesse. He was particularly fond of setting psalms. The first polyphonic psalms date back to the fifteenth century, but they were entirely functional in their simplicity. For his *In exitu Israel de Aegypto,* Gilles Binchois limited himself to the most rudimentary fauxbourdon : the upper voice intones the psalmodic recitation in a completely dry manner, while the two other voices follow it in parallel lines at the lower fourth and lower sixth respectively, without any variation except at cadence points. It was this type of pseudopolyphony that was most often used in Italy, and important examples for Vespers and Lauds are found in the manuscripts *Estense lat. 454* and *455* in Modena : the verses were sung in alternation between two three-voiced choirs either in rigorous homophony or in fauxbourdon, and the psalmodic recitation was maintained without ornamentation in the topmost voice. Throughout the sixteenth century, numerous psalms were based on an alternation of plain-chant with a psalmody tripled or quadrupled by voices which remained almost always rigidly parallel. It is possible that Josquin was not the first to write psalms in motet-style, but his prestige undoubtedly contributed to spread the practice to Brumel, Isaac, Mouton and later to Willaert, de Rore, Palestrina and Lassus. The liturgical tradition of psalmodic recitation was an obstacle to the general adoption of the motet-style, but artistic concerns won out among many composers.

The Magnificat likewise would not seem to offer much to polyphonic setting. This text belongs to the vesper service and is based on the canticles of actions of grace sung by the Virgin in reply to Elizabeth at the Visitation. In plain-chant it is a rather ornamented psalmodic recitation and, including the Doxology, it comprises twelve verses in Latin prose, each using the same melodic formulas at the beginning, middle and end of each phrase. The text of the verses remains unchanged from day to day, so that the Magnificat may be considered as part of an Ordinary of Vespers so to speak, but the twelve verses are preceded and followed by an anthem which varies according to the feast day. Since this may be in any of the eight modes, there are also eight psalm-tones which may be adapted to the Magnificat by varying their melodic formulas and the fundamental note which serves as pivot for the recitation; there are also eight ceremonial tones, more complex and more ornate. For this reason, when it came to composing the Magnificat in polyphony, it was necessary to write separate versions in each of the eight modes. Most often, the polyphonic verses alternated with plain-chant, so it was sufficient to compose either all the odd or all the even verses.

Once again it was in the circles around Dunstable and Dufay, before the middle of the fifteenth century, that the first polyphonic Magnificats appeared, and examples by these two masters have survived as well as some by Binchois, de Lymburgia and others who have remained anonymous. The *Magnificat in the Eighth Tone* by Dufay shows how, right from the outset, artistic character was given to this form. Dufay divides the twelve verses into four groups; in each group the first verse has the plainchant rather simply paraphrased in the topmost voice while the two other voices go along in fauxbourdon; the second verse is set for two voices only and recalls no more of the plain-chant than its characteristic formulas; finally, the third verse has nothing in common with the plain-chant except at cadence points.

Later, Magnificats were composed in motet-style with highly varied structure and language. At first, the recitation was often quite simple, the upper voice maintaining the psalmodic formulas and the other voices following it in fauxbourdon. In the generation of Busnois, the plain-chant was orna-

107

mented in accord with the aesthetic of the time, long melismas replacing syllabic declamation. Beginning with Josquin, there was a great increase in complexity. Because of their constant contact with Italy, the Flemish wrote many more Magnificats than in the preceding generations, since in Italy, more than elsewhere, the cult of the Virgin was celebrated with much pomp. Although there was at the time a renewed respect for declamation, often the psalmodic formulas were paraphrased and stretched out in long note-values or else assimilated to the other contrapuntal voices. Sometimes a *cantus firmus* from another source was added. The architecture of the whole was based on contrasts in the number of voices used in successive verses. In the second half of the sixteenth century, following the model of the parody mass, there were Magnificats in the parody technique based on either motets or madrigals. Most of the great contrapuntalists of the fifteenth and sixteenth centuries composed cycles of Magnificats in all the modes, and Lassus alone wrote 101 of them.

The Passion also was given polyphonic setting. The solemn recitation of the Passion, that is, of certain chapters from the Gospels, is called for during Holy Week : on Palm Sunday the Passion according to Saint Matthew, on Tuesday according to Saint Mark, on Wednesday according to Saint Luke, and on Friday according to Saint John. Ever since the Middle Ages this recitation has been done on certain psalmodic formulas and by three singers in alternation. One of them narrates the events (he represents, to all intents and purposes, the Evangelist himself), another speaks the words of Christ, and the third recites the parts of all the other personages in turn, including the crowd.

Polyphony was introduced into the recitation of the Passion in various manners. In the simplest cases, only the words spoken by the crowd (*turba*) were set to music. Obviously, this responsorial type of Passion modified only slightly the liturgical tradition. Certain composers, however, extended po-

lyphony to all the personages, including the Christ, and even to the narration of the Evangelist, and this, of course, led to the Passion entirely composed in polyphony. However, since the Gospel texts are long and, consequently, somewhat resistant to a complete setting in motet-style, Passion-motets are rather rare. In the fifteenth century only the *turbæ* were so set, as was probably the case with the *Passions en nouvelle manière* (in the new manner) by Gilles Binchois, unfortunately lost. In the following century, responsorial Passions remained the most numerous and most important; Lassus alone was to compose four of them.

The first Passion in motet-style dates from shortly after 1500. Long attributed to Obrecht, it is now known to be by a certain Antoine Longaval. It is almost entirely in four-voiced fauxbourdon with here and there somewhat more complicated contrapuntal developments, and its text is made up of selected passages from all four Gospels. In the same period, Pierre de la Rue wrote the motet *Vexilla regis* on a fragment of text of the Passion. The Fleming Cipriano de Rore composed a Passion-motet in 1550, and in Prague around 1580 Jacques Regnard did likewise. It was in Germany especially, at the end of the century, that this form had its most notable development. There is no doubt that the greatest attention has been paid to the Lutheran Passions of the seventeenth and eigteenth centuries which are in oratorio style, but it is important to realize that, long before these, a rather learned style of motet composition was frequently introduced into the liturgical recitation of the Passion and that attempts were made to incorporate even long narrative passages into the motet.

In the course of Holy Week, the Lamentations of Jeremiah likewise are recited. Matins and Lauds of the three last days before Easter constitute together the office of Tenebræ. Each time there are three Nocturns, and it is during the first Nocturn that the three Lamentations are sung. Until the Council of Trent, the selection of biblical verses

Excolit harmonicis diuinum Ecclesiæ cultum
Artibus, et varijs mysteria cantibus ornat.

Cornua multiplici vocum modulamine sacris
Dulce sonat adytis, Tyrrheno concinit æri

Fistula, delectatq̃ animos discordia concors,
Musaq̃ terrenas attollit ad æthera mentes.

36. A Religious Service. Philippe Galle after Johannes Stradanus.

used for these nine Tenebræ lessons varied considerably, although they always retained the Hebrew letters placed as a numbering indication at the beginning of each stanza; these were vocalized before the recitation of the text, which itself was chanted to a small number of melodic formulas. Dufay used fragments of the Lamentations of Jeremiah as the tenor of his great political motet on the fall of Byzantium in 1453, *Lamentatio sancte matris ecclesie Constantinopolitane.* The Lamentations supposedly composed by Busnois and Ockeghem have been lost, so that, with the exception of a few Italian fragments which are merely functional music without much artistic interest, the first important polyphonic Lamentations date only from 1505, and these are in two collections published by the Venetian Petrucci in which works of Tinctoris, Agricola, Weerbecke and Ycaert appear alongside those of Italian musicians. Later in the century polyphonic Lamentations became far from rare : Crecquillon, Arcadelt, de la Hèle and Lassus composed them, as did also Festa, Carpentras, Palestrina, Morales, Tallis and Byrd. The Hebrew letters – *Aleph, Beth, Gimel,* and so on – always provide the excuse for contrapuntal developments in a decorative style. The text itself, because of its length, offers varied musical possibilities, ranging from simple fauxbourdon to the most complex style with the most intense expression.

These extreme cases indicate how very important the motet-style had become and also how determined composers were to apply their most erudite skills to all the texts of the liturgy, even to those which would seem least amenable to polyphonic treatment. Taking as point of departure melodies rather popular in style, such as those of hymns and sequences, but also even the dry recitation of psalmodic formulas, there was brought into being a music liberated from plain-chant and focused on its own artistic ends.

It was the motet-style as worked out by Josquin Desprez that was considered in the sixteenth century as the perfect art, the *ars perfecta.* Whatever historical transformations occurred, whatever local peculiarities there were, or individual turns given by musicians of genius, the style continued along the lines of a tradition already firmly established at the beginning of the sixteenth century.

The style was handled with great rigor by musicians like Gombert, Clemens non Papa, Crecquillon, Manchicourt, Vaet and a few others who, even more than in the mass, applied to the motet the principles of the so-called imitative-syntactic style. Among the Flemings settled in Italy, such as Willaert, Rore and Wert, the approach is less austere. More faithful to the spirit of Josquin, they lightened the contrapuntal texture by inserting episodes in homorhythm and also concerned themselves with the relationship between music and words. In Italy, the motet was influenced by the secular madrigal but also, and in a diametrically opposed direction, by the edicts of the Council of Trent. In the latter part of the century, musicians such as Palestrina in Italy and Monte and Lassus in Germany continued to respect the basic principles of Flemish counterpoint but, at the same time, brought about a profound renewal in its spirit.

SACRED MUSIC AS ART
AND THE RELIGIOUS SENTIMENT

It suffices for the moment that we have seen how very much concerned with aesthetic values composers of religious music had been ever since Dufay. While maintaining the inevitable bonds between their creations and the liturgical ceremonies for which they were intended, composers wished also to give them artistic value. The tradition thus created, and which remained dominant for almost two centuries, was able to preserve a satisfactory equilibrium between functional requirements and the demands of the artistic conscience and proved thereby that functional art need not be any the less noble. Indeed, function offers to the work a frame of reference which is both a support for the composer and an

37. Angelic Choir.
Simon Marmion (?).

aid to the listener. Functional requirements act as a guide to the musician, setting before him specific tasks, and they also provide him with a public he must satisfy. Moreover, they do not prevent him from respecting his own aesthetic imperatives and from moving freely within purely formal complementary limits, nor do they forbid him the pleasure of giving rein to his own fancy.

For most musicians, religious feeling must have been both natural, that is, in conformity with the spiritual climate of the age, as well as professional, a part of their daily work. But one may also ask if such music also succeeded in expressing something of that Flemish spirituality marked in the fourteenth and fifteenth centuries by the writings of the Blessed John Ruysbroeck and Thomas à Kempis. In the masses of Ockeghem or the motets of Dufay, is there to be found some echo of these mystic doctrines ?

Various music historians have attempted to establish some link between these composers and the movement of *Devotio moderna*. Around 1380, in the bishopric of Utrecht, Geert Groote had founded the Brotherhood of the Common Life. In the fifteenth century, communities of both men and women were created at Brussels, Louvain, Ghent and Liège on the model of the chapter at Windesheim. The New Devotion movement wished to realize in daily existence certain precepts of the mystics, and its ideal was a community life which would nevertheless remain in contact with the world. The Brethren of the Common Life continued to practice various professions without taking vows, subjecting themselves nevertheless to severe constraints of humility, practicing a rigorous asceticism, partaking of the sacraments with particular assiduity, and devoting themselves to prayer with intense fervor. They seem to have had most success in Holland and in the Rhine regions, whereas in Flanders, Brabant, Hainaut and the principality of Liège their importance was always much less and in France almost nonexistent. The ideal of austerity which inspired the Brethren, and which was revealed in the garments they wore as well as in the life they led and in their spiritual preoccupations, appears to have had as its primary aim to reaffirm and purify individual piety. But this aim left them indifferent to the magnificence characteristic of the Roman liturgy and all that that implied for music. The attitude toward art of the Brotherhood seems to have had something in common with Calvinist strictness, which tolerated in the sacred service no more than the singing of psalms in a form not at all conducive to artistic development.

In any event, there seem to have been no connections whatsoever between the Brethren of the Common Life and the court circles in which Dufay and Ockeghem lived and worked. It is only in the most arbitrary and artificial manner that one may discern in the linear counterpoint of Ockeghem or in the dynamic melodies of Dufay a realization in sound of the austere ideals of the Brotherhood. The most that can be admitted is that the renewal of religious enthusiasm which sprang up in the fifteenth century in certain cultivated circles of the Low Countries found particularly accomplished expression in the music of Dufay and Ockeghem, as it did also in the paintings of Van Eyck and Van der Weyden.

But we must admit that it is most difficult for us today to measure how much and what kind of religious feeling might be contained in a musical work of the past. In the museum of sound into which we place all works of the past in order to compare and judge them, the only thing that truly counts is their artistic quality. To determine this, we can only use aesthetic criteria, by means of which we form, more or less arbitrarily, some idea of the religious sentiments those works contain. We know that if we limit ourselves to passing aesthetic judgments only we shall not betray the wishes of the composers themselves, for we know also that whatever the function they may have designated for their works, they never ceased at the same time to pursue artistic ends.

Recent studies in the sociology of religion teach us, moreover, to be wary of preconceived ideas and romantic notions. They have shown that even in Flanders, generally considered an ideal terrain for faith, an authentic piety was no more frequent at the end of the Middle Ages than at any other period. We know that the practice of the sacraments was very lax and that ignorance of religion was deeper and more widespread there than has been imagined hitherto. For men of the fifteenth and sixteenth centuries, the finest occasions for instruction and participation in a spiritual life were offered by the church holidays, which, fortunately, were numerous. On the one hand, the sermon was addressed to their minds; on the other, the music appealed to their hearts. For many men these were the only ways of rising above the tedium of daily existence.

Music helped the faithful to participate in the divine service, and it was precisely because it was useful that the faithful were interested in it and strove to comprehend not only its content, which was religion, but also its form, which was art. Thus the faithful became also auditors of music. There was no divorce between form and content but only a profound and intimate union, and through this there could grow up a solidarity between the composer and the crowds who frequented the church on feast days. Far then from being rivals, religion and art offered each other reciprocal aid in rising to greater heights in their respective domains.

Chapter 5

Music of Court and City : The Chanson

In the Western world, music was at first written down only for use in church. Not until much later were profane works so perpetuated, at first as simple monodic songs and later in polyphonic settings.

In the fourteenth century, profane polyphony included two important genres : the *song-motet* and the *cantilena,* whose most significant examples were provided by Guillaume de Machaut. Whereas the song-motet, generally isorhythmic, was composed on the basis of a tenor and by superposition of melodic lines with different texts, the cantilena consisted of a melody which followed the form of the poem being set – *virelai, rondeau* or *ballade* – and was supported by one or two complementary melodies confided to instruments. Although the virelais of Machaut are relatively simple, his rondeaux are much more worked out and his ballades even more complex. After Machaut, composers were to favor the ballade above the other forms. Like the motet, from which it borrowed certain of its techniques, the ballade was often written for special occasions and dedicated to some nobleman in celebration of a marriage or even a military victory.

By the end of the century, the style became so complicated as to merit the name of "mannerist." This was essentially a music of the court which could only be performed by highly skilled professionals for the entertainment of what must have been, necessarily, a limited élite.

However, a tendency toward simplification had already appeared at the beginning of the century among musicians such as Johannes Césaris and Baude Cordier as well as, later, Richard de Loqueville, Nicolas Grenon, Pierre Fontaine and Jacques Vide.

The last four named were men of the North : Loqueville and Grenon held various positions at the cathedral of Cambrai, Grenon was in the service of John the Fearless, Vide was a valet at the court of Burgundy, and Fontaine served three dukes as chaplain. But all these musicians seem to have been caught up in contradictory tendencies. Although their melodic lines already seem less finical, less minutely worked over, and their rhythmic movement more regular, with some restraint placed on the excessive independence of the polyphonic parts, yet they do not really succeed in freeing themselves from the tendency toward ornamental over-refinement. The return to a less agitated style is most clearly seen in those musicians who were in contact with Italy : in Ciconia, or in Matteo da Perugia, who was master of the chapel of the cathedral of Milan at the beginning of the fifteenth century and had worked at the papal court in Avignon. Matteo's work more and more abandoned the mannerist artifices to become more controlled and more expressive. As for Grenon and Fontaine, they too had worked in Italy at the papal court, and their works were much appreciated there.

115

Since the most important sources for the French chanson in the first third of the fifteenth century are Italian manuscripts, it is evident that in the domain of secular music, as in that of religious music, the new orientations came about through foreign influences – Italian above all – on French art. A new style was coming into being which would be international in character. From 1430 on, it was to manifest itself in a decisive manner with Dufay and Binchois in both the chanson and the motet.

The question arises as to whether this evolution toward greater simplicity of language was perhaps especially due to the increased importance of secular polyphony, which was reaching the widest social strata of the time. The fact is, however, that in the first half of the fifteenth century, polyphonic music was still confined to aristocratic circles.

Like Dufay, whose career we already know, Gilles Binchois was a court musician who wrote both secular and sacred music. Son of a middle-class citizen of Mons who at the end of the fourteenth century was counselor at the court of the counts of Hainaut, Binchois served Philip the Good from 1430 to 1460. His position as chaplain required him to participate in liturgical ceremonies and to compose religious music; in addition, he was canon at Mons and Soignies. However, his secular works are much more numerous than his motets and settings of mass sections, and it need not surprise us that a man of the Church should have written so many love songs, since this was not at all exceptional. In the centuries which concern us here, composers wrote masses and motets but also rondeaux and chansons and employed in both types of music exactly the same techniques : the same mensural notation and the same contrapuntal practice, at least in its basic principles, served for both. After all, the art of music could only be studied properly in churches and princely chapels and nowhere else, so it was perfectly natural that musicians should apply to ditties and love songs the techniques learned in church.

The profound and almost natural unity which existed between secular and sacred polyphony was therefore the result of a common technique. Secular polyphony, like sacred, was made by professional musicians. But in the fifteenth century it tended, more than religious music, to discard the complexities of the preceding period and to become easier to read and less encumbered with artifices of notation. In the period of Machaut, secular polyphony could only be performed by professionals; in that of Dufay, while it continued to be composed by specialists, it admitted certain simplifications which allowed it to be read and performed by amateurs under the guidance of professionals. It is in this, perhaps, that resides the great difference between the music of the fourteenth century and that of the fifteenth. In any event, this secular polyphony was not concert music in the modern sense. It was not listened to passively and merely for its beauty, as today we listen to symphonies and concertos in halls specially designated for that purpose. This music was not pure but was, rather, a certain type of functional music whose principal role was social diversion; for the participants, aesthetic criteria were secondary.

MUSICAL AMATEURS :

PERFORMERS OR LISTENERS ?

It was principally on the basis of pictorial evidence that the musicologist Heinrich Besseler was able to prove that amateurs participated actively in the performance of this music.

Particularly suggestive for this is the painting in the museum at Versailles depicting a scene at the court of Philip the Good, a copy whose original must have been painted around 1430 or 1431. Here there is a brilliant assembly of noblemen and their ladies within a grove, almost a garden, near a lordly château, gathered together after the hunt. In the distance, a few hunters obstinately continue the chase while others hasten toward the castle. Some guests are gathered around a table set up in the middle of the grove. The Duke is there : he holds a falcon on his left fist, a dog nuzzles close to him. Lords and ladies promenade in couples or in groups of three or four. Musically, two groups are of particular interest. At the left, in the middle ground, three players of wind instruments form a sort of small orchestra playing in the open air, while on the right, close to the Duke, there are five singers. Facing us, a man in black holds a piece of music whose notation is barely

legible, although Besseler supposed that it may be a few measures of the tenor from the chanson *Filles à marier* by Binchois, and he thought also that this man, the only one actually holding any music, may be the composer himself. Surrounding the man in black there are two gentlemen and two ladies in rich court habits, and three of them are actually taking part in the music : the tall woman beside the man in black, the man seen in profile with open mouth who seems to be beating the measure (his right hand raised toward his chest may correspond to a movement of *tactus*, and his left hand resting on the shoulder of his neighbor may help in setting the rhythm), and finally the woman with her back to us (her neighbor's hand on her shoulder shows that she too is participating in the song). One may conclude from this that in this court entertainment noble amateurs are amusing themselves by singing to the Duke, aided no doubt by a professional mu-

117

sician. The other personages pay no heed to them, for here there is neither concert nor public. The only passive listeners here are the Duke himself with an attendant holding a sword and, perhaps, the nobleman with a black hat on his back who stands a little apart from the singers.

That musical pleasure was considered to reside in active participation rather than mere listening seems to be borne out by many other works of art. A tapestry of Tournai from around 1480 depicts a curious scene at the court of Maximilian of Austria and Mary of Burgundy. While the archdukes play at chess, lords and ladies gossip near a table set up for a banquet and, in the foreground, two groups make music : to the left, three ladies and a man sing, all reading from the same piece of music, while one of the women beats time; at the right, a woman plays the harp, another the lute, one man the recorder and a second man the fiddle.

A similar scene is found in a Brussels tapestry from around 1500, now in the Germanisches Museum of Nuremberg. In a garden before a castle five personages are seated : three women playing, respectively, the rebec, harp and dulcimer and a man playing the lute and another a shawm. Others approach them, apparently to join in the music-making : to the left a man carrying a lute, to the right two couples among whom one of the men also carries a lute. To judge by the richness of the robes and costumes, these must be lords and ladies and therefore musical amateurs, but it may be that two men in simpler dress – the shawm-player and the man at the far right carrying a lute – are of a different social class, in all likelihood professional musicians. Indeed, it is not surprising that certain wind instruments should have been considered vulgar and fit for playing by professionals only, perhaps even by professionals of modest rank. Other French tapestries of the end of the fifteenth century show us scenes of noble persons making music : the *Concert at the Fountain* (Musée des Gobelins, Paris), where two women play the organ and fiddle and a man

the lute, or the *Scene from Courtly Life* (Musée de Cluny, Paris), in which a woman in her bath is entertained by a woman who plays a lute while seated on the edge of the basin and by a man standing who plays the shawm and who must be a professional musician.

There are rather startlingly worldly miniatures at the bottom of the pages of a Flemish choir book devoted to Ockeghem and his contemporaries which must have been prepared for Philip the Handsome in the first years of the sixteenth century and is now preserved in the Chigi collection of the Vatican Library. Here, for example, are two couples who sing around a fountain, two of the women and one of the men holding music, or again two couples in a grove who play various instruments, lute and harp for the women, shawm and fiddle for the men.

Among the engravings in which, around 1490, Israël van Meckenem depicted scenes from daily life there is one in which a man plays a lute while a woman sings from a small music book, and another with a woman playing the harp and a man the lute. In the fifteenth century there are also many illustrations of so-called Gardens of Love where there are always groups of singers and instrumentalists, men and women, whose amorous activities seem to be aided and abetted by music.

Certainly one may ask just how realistic these depictions were meant to be, and the answer seems

41. Two Musicians : Lutenist and Singer.
Israël van Meckenem.

to vary from one work to another. The tapestries of the Loire, for instance, appear to be highly stylized, but they reveal such careful attention to details of movement, costume and musical instruments that they can surely be taken as trustworthy. The Gardens of Love are not very likely to represent scenes from life as it was lived, but they obviously have some basis in reality, even when they seem very much idealized. There is therefore no reason for skepticism about what the pictorial evidence of the time can teach us.

What may be the earliest example showing a lady of quality interpreting a musical work is found in a French tapestry from the beginning of the fifteenth century (Musée des Arts Décoratifs, Paris). Here a lady plays a harp while, at her knees, a gentleman unrolls a parchment on which can be read musical notes and the title *De ce que fol pense*. There is a ballade for three voices from the second half of the fourteenth century attributed to Pierre des Molins which begins with these same words, but the tapestry must date from a half-century later and probably alludes to another composition.

Fortunately, musical texts confirm the iconographic documents. Thus, whereas previously high voices were only rarely used in secular works and were intended for young boys, after the change in musical style around 1430 pieces with a soprano part became as frequent in the works of Binchois, Dufay and their contemporaries as those requiring only low voices, and were certainly meant to be sung by women.

Furthermore, the new simplicity of style encouraged performance of polyphonic music by non-professionals. Certainly long before then noblemen had sung and played on certain instruments – hunting horn, harp or fiddle – but the music they performed was monodic. What was new in the fifteenth century was that lords and ladies took part in polyphony, could read music, knew how to sing as well as to play instruments, and could hold their place in a vocal or instrumental ensemble.

In the famous book in which he set forth what the perfect courtier must be and must be able to do, Baldassare Castiglione, in 1528, showed to what an extent music had become an established part of court life. *My Lords*, says one of the characters, *you thinke I am not pleased with ye Courtier, if he be not also a Musition, and beside his cunning and understanding upon the booke, have skil in like manner on sundry instruments. For if wee weigh it well, ther is no ease of the labors, and medicines of feeble mindes to be found more honest and more praise worthie in time of leisure than it. And principally in Courtes, where (beside the refreshing of vexations that musicke bringeth unto eche man) many things are taken in hand to please women withall, whose tender and soft breastes are soone pierced with melodie, and filled with sweetnesse.* However, in the name of warlike virtues, some consider that the true and principal profession of the courtier should be that of arms and believe that *musick... together with many other vanities is meet for women, and peradventure for some also that have the likenesse of men, but not for them that be men in deede : who ought not with such delicacies to womanish their mindes, and bring them selves in that sort to dread death.* But, calling to his defense all the literary and philosophical commonplaces in praise of music, Castiglione concludes finally *that musicke is not only an ornament, but also necessarie for a Courtier.* What matters, says he, is knowing when and how it is proper to practice it.

In the sixteenth century, in France as in Italy, music was a part of the etiquette of court life. In the fifteenth century, secular polyphony had been essentially music made at court.

COURT MUSICIANS

Gilles Binchois, who passed most of his career at the court of Burgundy, left fifty-five chansons of whose authenticity we are certain, and of these forty-seven are rondeaux as against only seven ballades and one song in free form. Favorite genre of the time, the rondeau was a brief piece which, musically, was made up of two more or less symmetrical parts adapted in conventional manner to the poetic scheme by repetitions and alternations. More ambitious and more ample, the ballade comprised several stanzas which, for musical purposes, were divided into two groups of unequal length.

In the fourteenth century, Machaut had continued the tradition of the trouvères in setting to music, either monodic or polyphonic, verses he had written himself. This, however, does not seem to have been the practice in the fifteenth century, and it does not seem likely that Binchois contributed anything besides his music. Few of the poets whose texts he set can be identified, but we do know of at least three. This text, of somber grandeur, is from the pen of Christine de Pisan :

> *Deuil angoisseux, rage démesurée*
> *Grief désespoir plein de forcènement*
> *Langueur sans fin et vie malheurée*
> *Pleine de pleur, d'angoisse et de tourment.*
> *Cœur douloureux qui vit obscurément,*
> *Ténébreux corps sur le point de partir*
> *Ai, sans cesser continuellement*
> *Et si, ne puis ni guérir ni mourir.*

(Anguished grief, rage beyond measure, / Despairing sorrow beyond bearing, / Languishing ever and joyless life / With tears, with anguish and with torment. / Dolorous heart that lives in shadow ever, / Dark-humored flesh so close to death / Have I, and this unceasingly, / And cannot heal, nor can I die.)

To Alain Chartier is due this fragment of a rondeau :

> *Triste plaisir et douloureuse joie*
> *Apre douceur, réconfort ennuyeux*
> *Ris en pleurant, souvenir oublieux*
> *M'accompagnent, combien que seule sois.*

(Woeful pleasure and dolorous joy, / Bitter sweetness, painful consolation, / Smiles through weeping, forgetful memory, / All these attend me, yet solitary ever am I.)

121

And to Charles d'Orléans, this charming and amorous quatrain :

> *Mon cœur chante joyeusement*
> *Quand il lui souvient de la belle,*
> *Tout son plaisir se renouvelle,*
> *De bien en mieux certainement.*

(My heart sings joyfully / When it recalls that beauty, / All its pleasure is renewed, / And surely goes from good to better.)

Whether their texts are taken from famous poets or from others whose names we shall probably always ignore, the chansons of Binchois are all conventional variations on the same theme : love, with its hopes, leave-takings, memories and regrets, and always in the thrice-familiar vocabulary of courtly verse, with allegories derived from the *Roman de la Rose,* with all the rigmarole which that long novel in verse places in the mouths of allegorical personages named Evil Tongue, Bright Welcome, Danger, Envy or False Seeming. To this hodgepodge, seldom of any particular literary worth, the music brings a note of freshness. Almost always it is written for three voices, but only the topmost one was meant to be sung, the two others being instrumental. The melodies flow along in rhythms which correspond to our 6/8 or 3/4, and the latter gives rise to firmer and more varied rhythms typical of the modernism of the new school.

The chansons of Guillaume Dufay, written most often for three voices but sometimes for four, are generally cast in rondeau form, occasionally as a ballade and, exceptionally, as a virelai, while a few cannot be classed in any fixed form. Again the subject matter is courtly love in a general climate of melancholy, regrets and laments :

> *Adieu, m'amour, adieu, ma joie*
> *Adieu le soulas que j'avois*
> *Adieu ma léale maîtresse.*
> *Le dire adieu tant fort me blesse*
> *Qu'il me semble que mourir dois.*

(Adieu, my love, adieu my joy, / Adieu the comfort once I knew, / Adieu my mistress ever-faithful. / To say adieu doth wound me so, / Methinks that death must surely come.)

But there are also drinking songs in which the topers challenge each other :

> *Hé ! compagnons, réveillons-nous*
> *Et ne soyons plus en souci...*

(Hey ! comrades, be lively now / And cast away all hint of care...)

And songs which celebrate the coming of spring:

> *Ce mois de mai, soyons liés et joyeux,*
> *Et de nos cœurs, ôtons mélancolie...*

(In this month of May, be gay and joyful, / And from our hearts drive melancholy...)

And songs for the New Year :

> *Bon jour, bon mois, bon an et bonne étrenne*
> *Vous doint celuy qui tient tout en demaine,*
> *Richesse, honneur, santé, joye sans fin,*
> *Bonne fame, belle dame, bon vin,*
> *Pour maintenir la créature saine.*

(Good day, good month, good year and good gifts / May you receive from Him who ruleth all. / Riches, honor, health and endless joy, / Good repute, sweet dame, fine wine / To keep in health the human creature.)

Contrary to what had been thought for a long time, this secular music was intended for soloists and not for chorus. Nor was it purely vocal, for most often instruments were mingled with the voices and could even double or perhaps ornament the vocal lines. Presumably there was nothing to prevent an occasional performance of these chansons by instruments alone. All that we know for certain about the entire problem is that there is much uncertainty about it. Contemporary documents are vague and say nothing at all about the use of particular instruments, so that we can only conjecture what was meant to be sung and what to be played. In any case, there must have been a certain latitude allowed to the performers, who could thus take advantage of whatever instruments or voices were available and could dispose them in accord with traditional practices.

As a general rule, not much care was exercised in placing the words below the notes to which they were to be sung, and composers did not seek to establish a close rapport between the syllables of the poem and the notes of the melody, so that often there are long vocalises on short syllables as well as on long ones.

It was only exceptionally that Dufay and his contemporaries made any effort to adapt the musical declamation to the text, and this was the result not of lack of skill but rather of a precise aesthetic position. Besides, the poetic text did have a certain importance, since in rondeaux and ballades it determined the musical form even though the composer himself might be indifferent to questions of unity between verbal rhythms and musical rhythms. Music simply took hold of the text and used it for its own ends.

In chansons based on fixed forms such as rondeaux and ballades, all of the musical material was newly invented by the composer. There were, however, certain chansons based on a *cantus firmus*. In *La Belle se siet au pied de la tour*, Dufay utilized text and music of what may very well have been a folk song or, in any event, a song which remained popular throughout at least two centuries and which, under the name of *La Pernette*, lived on in the oral tradition of Romance-language folklore.

We simply do not know if already in Dufay's time this song was sung by peasants and city folk, and today no one has any romantic illusions about collective and spontaneous creation of folk songs. Whoever many have been the author, *La Belle se siet* already enjoyed at the time a popularity proven by the fact that a court registrar of Namur, Noël de Fleurus, wrote it out at the end of an account book of the bishopric of Namur. Perhaps it was not truly a folk song according to the rigorous definition of the ethnomusicologists, but it certainly was purely monodic and by an anonymous author and its success was definitely not limited to court circles. In its subject, it escapes from the rather precious high-flown matter of the usual rondeau to take up one of the favorite themes of traditional folklore :

La belle se siet au pied de la tour,
Qui pleure et soupire et mène grand doulour.
Son père lui demande : "Fille, qu'avez-vous ?
Voulez-vous mari, voulez-vous seigneur ?"
"Je ne veux mari, je ne veux seigneur,
Je veux le mien ami qui pourrit en la tour."
"Et par Dieu, belle fille, à celui faudrez-vous
Car il sera pendu, demain, au point du jour."
"Père, si on le pend, enfouissez-moi dessous !"
Ainsi, diront les gens, voici loyaux amours...

(The maiden sits at the foot of the tower, / And weeps and sighs and has great sorrow. / Her father asks, "Girl, what ails you ? / Do you sigh for a husband, do you long for a lord ?" / "I wish no husband, I wish no lord, / I want my true love who's locked in the tower." / "By God, my daughter, he's not for you, / For tomorrow at daybreak he'll go to be hanged." / "Father, if he's hanged, then bury me too !" / Then the folk will say, there's true love for you...)

Dufay placed the original melody in the tenor of his composition in long note-values like a *cantus firmus*. On it he superposed two contrapuntal melodies which divert attention from the original tune and which differ in no way from those of his other works except for a more rapid syllabic declamation.

From this we can see how limited was the influence of popular music on Dufay : it was no more than a theme to set off his inspiration, and its substance was absorbed and integrated into his own learned and highly refined art.

Nevertheless, compared with the mannerism of the end of the fourteenth century, the secular music of Dufay has an overall simplicity different also from the complex constructions of his masses and certain of his motets. Yet, in no way is this a popular art. It may be relatively easy to perform, but it has great subtlety of writing, which is seen in the richness of its melodic invention and in the elegance and mellifluousness of its counterpoint.

These same qualities are found in some degree or another among certain of Dufay's contemporaries, especially among the natives of Liège who lived in Italy and wrote on French texts, composers such as Hugo and Arnold de Lantins and Johannes Franchois of Gembloux. And yet, in the chansons written by Dufay toward the end of his life and in the works of the next generation, once again compositional techniques became more complex and overall style more learned.

One of the most important of those musicians, Antoine Busnois, lived at the court of Burgundy at the time of Philip the Good, Charles the Bold and Mary of Burgundy, and died in 1492. He was a priest and exercised various functions in churches at Mons, Lierre, Furnes and Bruges. His chansons

124

seem to have enjoyed much favor, since the sixty-three known to us are scattered widely throughout Europe in thirty-five manuscripts, and theorists and poets of his time were lavish with praise for him. Indeed, Busnois was himself a poet and wrote dialogues in verse with Jean Molinet as well as texts for some of his own chansons. He was most partial to the rondeau form but also contributed to the success of the *bergerette*, a short form which was nothing more than a virelai reduced to a single verse.

Among the composers of his generation were Hayne van Ghizeghem, the English chaplain of the Duke of Burgundy Robert Morton, Gilles Joye, Philippe Caron, Tinctoris and Ockeghem, though the latter wrote few chansons but all of remarkable quality and with a simplicity of expression which may seem surprising in a composer whose partiality for technical complications is too often stressed. In addition, many of the pieces in the *chansonniers* have remained anonymous.

It may seem surprising that these musicians did not avail themselves more of the texts of the great poets of the time. François Villon, for one, was called on for no more than a single rondeau, *Mort, j'appelle de ta rigueur*. They seem to have been equally cool toward the learned constructions of the masters of rhetoric with their intricate manipulation of rhymes and words. Instead, they were content to use poetry in the most traditional of forms whose content was no more than one more variation on the limited theme of courtly love.

For a notion of what was considered a pleasing text, we may look at a verse set to music by Hayne van Ghizeghem which enjoyed great popularity:

> *De tous biens pleine est ma maîtresse,*
> *Chacun lui doibt tribût d'honneur;*
> *Car asservie est en valeur*
> *Autant que jamais fut déesse.*
> *En la voyant, j'ai tel léesse*
> *Que c'est paradis en mon cœur.*
> *De tous biens pleine est ma maîtresse,*
> *Chacun lui doibt tribût d'honneur.*

(With all virtues is my mistress blessed, / All mankind pays her homage; / For she is as high in worth / As ever was a goddess. / At sight of her, I have such joy / That my heart is filled with paradise. / With all virtues is my mistress blessed, / All mankind pays her homage.)

There is no point in attempting to conceal the fact that the texts used for chansons were often poor indeed, their workmanship conventional, their vocabulary banal. As one would expect, these poems do not appear in collections with any literary pretensions. They were specifically conceived for music and generally have no independent value, nor do they hesitate to repeat over and over again the few key words that stimulated the musical imagination of the time. Many hundreds of such chanson texts are found in anthologies such as *Le Jardin de plaisance et fleur de Rhétorique* (The Garden of Pleasure and Flower of Rhetoric), prepared by an anonymous compiler for publication in 1501 by Antoine Vérard. Whatever the title may say, it includes no works by rhetoricians such as Molinet or Crétin, which must have been considered obscure and pretentious and scarcely apt for music. Instead, there are many rondeaux and ballades (some of them quite old), all that court poetry so attractive to musicians, but also there are more popular genres such as theater songs of all kinds : satirical, bawdy or moralistic.

In the same way as the chivalric ideal, which an evolving society had left behind, continued to haunt daily life like a dream only half-remembered, so

courtly love became a social pastime with poetic forms and a repertory of images and fancies artificially held over from the vanished world of the trouvères and troubadours. Personal feelings were expressed only by allusion to some literary tradition, and no one bothered to experience what he could not express in that fixed manner.

Cultivation of the polyphonic chanson seems to have been a prerogative of aristocratic circles in the fifteenth century. Even when it was taken up by the middle classes and changed somewhat in character, the chanson preserved its traditional character at the court of Margaret of Austria, governess of the Low Countries from 1507 to 1530. Several anthologies of poetry bear witness to this late survival, but the traditional themes of unrequited love, with laments and complaints, continued to be exploited without any very deep originality. One of these chansons begins thus :

Allez regrets, videz de ma présence;
Allez ailleurs quérir votre acointance,
Assez avez tourmenté mon las cœur.

(Away, regrets, quit my presence; / Go elsewhere seeking company, / Torment enough you've brought to my sad heart.)

And another goes :

Venez, regrets, venez, il en est heure,
Venez sur moi, faire votre demeure.

(Come, regrets, come, the time is ripe. / Come to me, take up your dwelling here.)

And still another :

Les grands regrets que, sans cesse, je porte
Et nuit et jour, tourmentent tout mon cœur.

(The great regrets I bear, unceasing, / Both day and night torment my heart.)

The first phrases of a few other songs reveal quite clearly the morose self-indulgence the times seem to have enjoyed : *Pleine de deuil et de mélancolie* (Full of grief and melancholy), *Deuil et ennui, souci, regret et peine* (Grief, care, worry, regret and pain), *Pour un jamais, un regret me demeure* (For one forever one grief remains for me). Fortunately,

two of the collections preserved in the Bibliothèque Royale of Brussels also include music for these chansons composed by Agricola, Compère, de la Rue and Isaac and various other composers, some of them anonymous. If this repertory has survived, it is due only to the quality of the music. Whatever novelty the chansons may have is contributed by the music alone. Notwithstanding certain conventions imposed by the texts, and despite the use of melodic or rhythmic formulas all cast in the same mold, there is constant musical invention to be found in their charming melodies and elegantly written counterpoint.

The music has the same somber quality as the texts. These courtly songs never aim to divert; theirs is a climate of melancholy and reserve, alien to any excess of passion but, nevertheless, moving and seductive. Composed by court musicians who most often were also in the service of the Church, these rondeaux, ballades and bergerettes make only slight use of technical artifices but still belong to a learned art which for long appealed only to the happy few.

THE POLYPHONIC CHANSON IN URBAN SOCIETY
The diffusion of the chanson to other social strata came about by a psychological process of imitation of the tastes and diversions of the aristocracy. It is impossible to state flatly when this took place, and the most that can be said is that the polyphonic chanson did finally spread beyond the court circles, that it came to be appreciated by the urban middle class, rich merchants, jurists and financiers who served princes, but that it never became a truly popular kind of entertainment.

Searching study of the manuscript collections including polyphonic songs would almost certainly provide the basis for a reply to questions as to the practice of this music in different strata of society. There are a good many such collections, and in a bibliographical study, Madame Geneviève Thibault was able to locate thirty for the period from 1400 to 1450, nineteen for 1450 to 1480, fifty-six from

1480 to 1520. While at first these secular pieces were bound together with religious works, later anthologies were confined to the chansons. The chansonniers which have been preserved are volumes written on parchment or paper, most often of oblong format and small size. Gathered around one of these tiny books, the performers could find all three or four voices of a chanson written out on two facing pages, sometimes on a single page when the piece was especially short. The vocal parts were not written one above the other as in modern scores. Instead, each voice was copied out completely, so that the *superius* would be on the left-hand page, the tenor and counter-tenor on the right-hand page. Certain chansonniers were beautifully written out and adorned with miniatures; these luxurious manuscripts were obviously intended for princely libraries, but many others were copied out in a simple, utilitarian manner and must have been meant for practical use.

The two chansonniers of the Bibliothèque Royale of Brussels which we have already mentioned (Mss. 228 and 11239) bear the arms of the House of Savoy; in one of the miniatures Margaret of Austria herself is seen at prayer in her oratory. It is likely that the chansonnier now held by the library of the city of Dijon (No. 517) once belonged to the dukes of Burgundy; one in the Bibliothèque Nationale of Paris (Ms. fr. 9346) belonged to Charles de Bourbon, and another (Ms. fr. 1597) was copied out in 1495 for the Duke of Orleans. The Medici Codex (Rome, Vatican Library, Cappella Giulia, XIII, 27) was prepared for Pope Leo X; the British Museum Harley manuscript 5242 was owned by Françoise de Foix, mistress of Francis I, and another in the Bibliothèque Nationale of Paris (Ms. fr. 1722) bears the inscription : *Verses and poems of Marguerite d'Orléans, Duchess of Alençon, sister of King Francis I, who ... became Queen of Navarre.*

Beginning in the second half of the fifteenth century, some ordinary citizens also came to own chansonniers. The oldest collections that we know for certain to have been in the hands of a commoner is the *Liederbuch* of a doctor in Nuremberg, Hartmann Schedel; this was begun around 1456-61 while Schedel was a student at the University of Leipzig. Manuscript 463 of the abbey of Saint-Gall is a *Liederbuch* which belonged to the Swiss humanist Egidius Tschudi.

As long as secular polyphony was transmitted in manuscript copies only, it could reach only the restricted circles of the nobility and the wealthy middle class. Printing, however, guaranteed for it a widespread diffusion. In the fifteenth century there had been printed only a few books of plain-chant and occasional fragments of polyphony inserted as examples in theoretical works. The first edition of polyphonic music appeared in Venice in 1501, the *Harmonice musices Odhecaton A,* published by Ottaviano de' Petrucci; its erudite-sounding title means no more than *One hundred chansons in polyphonic settings,* although, in fact, it includes only ninety-five. Two other volumes followed it : in 1502 the *Canti B Numero cinquanta,* with fifty-one chansons instead of the fifty announced by the title, and in 1504 the *Canti C Numero cento cinquanta,* with 139 rather than 150. These three volumes, which include also a few religious works, constitute a virtually complete anthology of the chanson from Busnois and Ockeghem up to the generation of Josquin. Although the pieces include only the first few words of the songs, the *incipits,* and not complete texts, nothing indicates that they were intended as instrumental music. The selection was made on the basis of a great number of manuscript chansonniers, most of them written in Italy. The great majority of the composers were Flemish — in the broad sense of the word — along with some Frenchmen writing in the same style : Agricola, Busnois, Compère, Ghizeghem, Isaac, Japart, de la Rue, Morton, Obrecht, Josquin, Stokhem, Tinctoris and others. There is still a preponderance of rondeaux and bergerettes, but there are also chansons made up of several verses plus a refrain which is often no more than a sort of catchword easy to remember, such as :

> Et qui la dira, dira
> La douleur que mon cœur a.

(And he who would tell it, would tell / The sorrow in my heart.)
or even nonsense phrases like *Viragon, vignette sur vignon* or *Latura tu et nennin dea.*

In texts, if not in structure, chansons of this type have a light, popular character which distinguishes them clearly from the usual repertory in court circles. They appear to have originated from well-known tunes which were purely monodic and likely to have been hummed by everyone after being heard in farces, *soties* (comedies) and morality plays.

In a recent study on music in the French secular theater, H. M. Brown proposed the name *chansons rustiques* – rustic ditties – for these theater songs. It is true that occasionally in the sixteenth century a distinction was made between *chansons rustiques* and the apparently more elaborate *chansons musicales*, just as, in a related sense, Molinet had already spoken of *chansons rurales*. However, such terminology is ambiguous, at least insofar as it suggests a peasant origin for these songs.

Whenever in the fifteenth century a theater song was used as the basis for an art-chanson, its original character was changed by integrating it into a more learned style which gave it new dignity. Thus, it might be employed as a *cantus firmus* and have contrapuntal parts added to it along with a new text which quite literally camouflaged its humble origins. In the *Odhecaton*, the chanson :

> Il est de bonne heure né
> Qui tient sa dame en ung pré
> sur l'herbe jolye.

(He is born to good fortune / Who embraces his lady / On a grassy sward.)
becomes the basis for a sophisticated and elegant rondeau : *Amour fait moult, tant que argent dure* (Love achieves much, as long as the money lasts). In the *Canti C,* Japart with exceptional skill super-imposed this same chanson on another famous tune, *L'Homme armé.*

However, at the end of the fifteenth century the original text was often kept in all the voice parts; confided to the tenor, the melody of the rustic chanson underwent various imitations, and it impregnated quite thoroughly the work based on it. Starting with a simple, unpretentious tune, the end result was a carefully worked-out music which no longer revealed any popular traits. Even more severe in style were those pieces in which a theater tune was systematically echoed in canon by a second voice while complementary counterpoints produced less systematic imitations, as can be seen in Josquin's *Allégez moy, douce et plaisante brunette* for six voices or his *Faulte d'argent* for five voices, as well as in Jean Mouton's *Je le lesray* for four voices and Adrian Willaert's *En douleur et tristesse* for six. Sometimes the tune of the theater song was ornamented and paraphrased. It remained exceptional for the tune to be given to the topmost voice and made further conspicuous by having the other voices follow its rhythms and its syllabic declamation. And yet, exceptional as such a practice was, it was the basis for an overall lightening in character which was to become typical of a good part of the chanson repertory in the sixteenth century.

In Josquin's generation, it was the severe style which continued to dominate any others. Whether it conformed to fixed forms or was cast in verses with refrains, whether it clung to the mannered declarations of courtly love or appropriated more varied subjects from the theater, the chanson remained always a learned art form. What was modern in it was the increasingly regular use of imitation. At first, imitation was applied only in passing to two voices above a freely composed counter-tenor, then to three voices as a rather more permanent trait, and finally in a systematic manner to all four voices, for henceforth it was the rule to write for four or five voices. Certain procedures typical of religious music began then to appear frequently in secular music : the canon, for example, and the *cantus firmus*, and although they were not rigorously subjected to as complex manipulations as in masses, they contributed to establishing a common language between all the types of music in current or daily use.

There is therefore nothing surprising in the fact that the great composers of chansons were also the luminaries of religious music : Josquin Desprez above all others, and Pierre de la Rue, Loyset Compère, Agricola and Isaac. Lest any be omitted, we can quote the prologue to the fourth book of Rabelais's *Pantagruel* : *And I remember (for I have a member, and a memory too, ay, and a fine memory, large enough to fill a butter-firkin) : I remember, I say, that one day of tubilustre [horn-fair] at the festivals of good-man Vulcan in May, I heard Josquin Des Prez, Olkegan, Hobreths, Agricola, Brumel, Camelin, Vigoris, de la Fage, Buyor, Prioris, Seguin, de la Rue, Midy, Moulu, Mouton, Gascoigne, Loyset Compère, Penet, Fevin, Roussée, Richard Fort, Rousseau, Consilion, Constantio Festi, Jacquet Bercan, melodiously singing.*

Most of these musicians achieved their fame at the end of the fifteenth and the beginning of the sixteenth century, and despite the rather curious spelling we can make out their names from the list. Rabelais distinguished them clearly from a second group of younger musicians still active in mid-century among whom were composers whose major activity was writing chansons : *Nine olympiads and an intercalary year after ... I heard Adrian Villard, Gombert, Janequin, Arcadet, Claudin, Certon, Manchicourt, Auxerre, Villiers, Sandrin, Sobier, Hesdin, Morales, Passereau, Maille, Maillart, Jacotin, Hurteur, Verdelot, Carpentras, Lhéritier, Cadeac, Doublet, Vermont, Bouteiller, Loupi, Pagnier, Millet, du Moulin, Alaire, Maraut, Morpin, Gendre and other merry lovers of music, in a private garden, under some fine shady trees, round about a bulwark of flaggons, gammons, pasties, with several coated quails, and laced mutton, waggishly singing.*

45. An Organist and His Wife.
Israël van Meckenem.

Rabelais had each of these groups sing songs so bawdy that we cannot possibly print them here. Yet they were not inventions of his imagination. In a repertory much more varied than in the past, the sixteenth century saw the success of many songs which never fussed about offending prudish ears.

Such changes in the spirit and the form of the chanson can be explained by a marked increase in favor on the part of a much wider public.

THE URBAN PUBLIC

The development of music printing played a part in these transformations. In the first half of the sixteenth century, the polyphonic chanson was published in three major centers: Paris, with Attaingnant, who, from 1528 to 1552, published in the neighborhood of fifteen hundred *chansons nouvelles* in some fifty collections; Lyons, with Jacques Moderne, who, from 1538 to 1543, published in the ten books of the *Parangon des chansons* and the two of the *Difficile des chansons* about three hundred *chansons nouvelles au singulier prouffit et délectation des musiciens* (new songs to the singular profit and delight of musicians); finally, Antwerp, where Tielman Susato, between 1543 and 1555, published more than four hundred chansons in four volumes. To these anthologies must be added numerous publications devoted to individual composers.

There can be no doubt that music printing stimulated composers and encouraged many more musicians to try their hand at composing: in the fifteenth century composers were few in number and the same names reappear from one manuscript to another, whereas in the following century hundreds of musicians turned out chansons and got them published. For this to occur, there must have been a market at hand. The fact that an edition appeared in a thousand or fifteen hundred copies shows that the polyphonic chanson was in demand by a large public, though it certainly should not be presumed that everyone, from the top to the bottom of the social scale, went about singing in counterpoint. Polyphony

was unknown in country places and among the humble artisans of the towns, and its practice required a certain culture which in the sixteenth century might reach as far as the urban middle class but certainly not to humbler folk.

Pictures may help us understand the situation. It is possible that the engravings of Israël van Meckenem dating from around 1490 and illustrating, presumably, everyday life may, in fact, depict members of the nobility, as is suggested by the palace setting and the costumes of the two couples of whom one man plays the lute and one of the women the harp while the other woman sings from a sheet of music. But there is certainly a middle-class family in another engraving in which a man plays a positive organ set up on the dining-room table while his wife works the bellows. The miniaturist of the *Hortulus animæ* (1510-1520) likewise shows a middle-class setting with a woman standing to play the spinet while the meal is being prepared and a man and a child warm themselves by the fire. Other illustrations are less certain: the serenade on the canals of Bruges which illustrates the month of May in the *Heures de Henessy* may well depict nobles – a man playing the flute, a woman the lute, and another singing – whose little boat is being rowed by valets. And the three charming young women in a painting in the Harrach Museum, Vienna, who make up a trio of flute, lute and voice are just as likely young ladies of the aristocracy as elegant middle-class girls. On the other hand, there can be no doubt about the middle-class van Berchem family painted by Frans Floris: the woman is at the spinet, the man at the lute, while around them are the grandmother peeling an apple, children at play, other relatives and a dog.

Spinet, harpsichord, organ, lute, flute could be employed variously in the performance of polyphonic chansons, and in themselves they indicate a certain social level. They are never found in the hands of a peasant or poor person, nor does one ever see a peasant reading music from a manuscript or a

132

printed book. As a matter of fact, the habitual or common music of the poor or the peasants was in reality something quite different, neither written down nor in polyphony.

In ceasing to be exclusively an art of the court and in assuming bourgeois attire, the chanson did not, for all that, stop being a functional kind of music, a convivial or family entertainment in which the pleasure of being a performer was undoubtedly greater than that of being a listener. For this reason, most publications allowed considerable liberty to the performers, limiting themselves to saying, for example, that the songs were adaptable to both voices and instruments or, as the title of one of Susato's publications put it, *Twenty-nine love songs in four parts fit for all musical instruments, with two pieces to be sung as grace before and after the meal.* There were also publications of chansons arranged for harpsichord or lute in which the polyphonic voice parts were reduced and combined so as to permit individual performance on an instrument. Ideally, an ensemble of homogeneous sound was preferred, either all voices or all instruments of the same family, as, for instance, viols or flutes in their various forms and registers from low to high. In writing for four, five or six parts, all voices were of equal importance and contributed equally to the polyphony. But in actual practice, if the ideal of homogeneous sound proved not to be feasible, there was nothing against using whatever forces might be available.

There are not many precise documents to explain the social uses of the chanson at the time, but quite picturesque descriptions may be found in Flemish handbooks of conversation intended both to improve social behavior and to teach a more refined use of the language to the middle class. Naïve as they are, these texts often provide us with first-hand evidence of what was considered "nice" comportment. One of these handbooks from around 1540 gives us a glimpse of life in a bourgeois family of Brussels. After dinner in the home of Master Jacob

46. Promenade on the Canals in the Month of May.
Simon Bening (?).

van den Dale, the company prepares to entertain itself :

— *Master Jacob* : And now, should we not sing us a little song ? Willeken [the page-boy], would you go get my books ?

— *Willeken* : What books d'you want, Sir ?

— *Master Jacob* : The books in four and three parts.

— *Willeken* : Where d'you keep 'em, Sir ?

— *Master Jacob* : You will find them on the side-board.

— *Willeken* : I'll go get 'em, Sir.

(The company drinks their wine.)

. . . .

— *Master Jacob* : Now where's that Willeken got to ?

— *Willeken* : I can't find 'em, Sir !

— *Master Jacob* : You go look for them, Antoni, and pick us out something pretty.

— *Antoni* : Right, Sir. Would you like to hear a song in four parts ?

— *Master Jacob* : It's all the same to me. Sing what you like.

. . . .

— *Antoni* : Dierick, here's the superius. It's not too high for you ? The children can help you out.

— *Rombout* : Give me the counter-bass part.

— *Antoni* : I'll do the tenor.

— *Dierick* : Who'll sing counter-tenor ?

— *Ysaias* : I, I'll sing it !

— *Dierick* : Who begins ? Is it you, Ysaias ?

— *Ysaias* : No, not I. I've a four-beat rest.

— *Antoni* : And I one of six.

— *Ysaias* : Well then, you come in after me ?

— *Antoni* : So it seems. It's up to you, then, Rombout !

— *Rombout* : Yes, I've only a crotchet-rest. But we'd better get the pitch.

— *Dierick* : What note do you begin on, Ysaias ?

— *Ysaias* : I start on E la-mi.

— *Dierick* : And I on C sol-fa-ut.

— *Antoni* : That makes a sixth. And you, Rombout ?

— *Rombout* : I begin on F fa-ut.

— *Master Jacob* : Thomas and Felix, you children sing along with Dierick !

— *Felix* : Yes, Father.

— *Master Jacob* : Have you studied this song ?

— *Felix* : Yes, Father.

— *Master Jacob* : And you, have you learned it ?

— *Thomas* : No, Father, but we'll be able to do it all right.

— *Rombout* : Steven's not singing with us ?

— *Dame Catelyne* : No, he's too young yet, but he'll soon begin to learn, and his sister also. Now, Steven and Cecily, you go eat.

(The company sings the song.)

. . . .

— *Master Jacob* : Now that's what I call a pretty song. Who made it up ?

— *Rombout* : I think it's Gombert.

— *Master Jacob* : Who's he ?

— *Rombout*: He's singing master for the Emperor.

— *Master Jacob* : Well, that's really a pretty song. And who made up the other one ?

— *Dierick* : Johannes Lupus, the singing master at Cambrai.

— *Master Jacob* : That's pretty too. And now, Ysaias, I drink to your health.

Such a document situates the chansons in a precise manner in the daily life of the time and helps us understand that music was first and foremost a form of social diversion. People learned to read notes, they tried to sing on pitch and in time under the direction of the most skilled among them, they played the lute or some other instrument. Mensural notation was always much simpler in chansons than in motets, and in the sixteenth century virtually all chansons were written in rhythms which were not difficult to sight-read. However, composition remained a matter for professionals. Even if it was easy to sing, the work might be complex in structure and studded with close imitation or chromaticism.

134

On the whole, the sixteenth-century polyphonic chanson must be considered what we call light music. Aesthetes would like to think that there is only one sort of music worthy of esteem, that music which, somewhat over-earnestly, they have labeled *serious,* the kind of music which today is confined to the concert hall, where it is listened to, as Jean Cocteau said, with head in hands. Its history is that of an art of high culture in which masterpieces of the past and present now exist side by side in an imaginary museum of the ear. Those masterpieces command the respectful admiration of a public initiated into their language and convinced, therefore, that it enjoys the dignity of a certain spiritual superiority. But alongside this art of high culture there exists another : *popular music, light music,* and these are the art of the masses.

Opposition between serious music and light music has not always existed. The schism did not begin to take place until the nineteenth century, when new notions and new democratic horizons became accessible to a wider population. Learned art, formerly the exclusive property of limited and homogeneous social groups, found that all of society was suddenly available to it as a field of expansion. Art seems then to have feared becoming degraded by too great popularity. To escape from this threatened taint, it felt obliged to seek constantly after novelty and to reject all social function. Thus it became *pure art,* art for art's sake, free of any social ties, and the artist became a lonely figure responsible only to his own conscience, an individualist who seemed to seek deliberately the opposition of society. The arts took refuge in language known only to initiates.

Parallel to that art was developed a utilitarian art intended for the masses, and this the artists themselves held in no esteem. Unlike the art of high culture, which is a pure art, this art of the masses is functional, seeking to satisfy a vast public whose rather vague artistic needs are always closely linked with their daily activities.

It is within this frame of reference that the opposition between serious music and light music takes place today, symbol of a struggle between art of high culture and art of the masses, between pure and utilitarian art, between an art of form and an art of content, between a refined art reserved for the pleasure of the élite and an art of facility intended as food for the many.

This was not always the case. In the sixteenth century the polyphonic chanson was light music but not prone to the flaws of popular music today. Because of its consummate dignity of style, we tend to think of it as high art, and because we have ripped it from its natural surroundings – something we do to all music of the past – it has become for us a pure art. It disturbs us to admit that formerly such music was thought of as a mere diversion without ulterior over-excited pretensions and that the extra-aesthetic pleasure it gave was much like that to be had today from any of the tunes our radio sets blare out.

Like light music today, the polyphonic song functioned both as entertainment and as an article of commerce. The success of these songs in the sixteenth century is shown by the many editions published. And yet the example of this music of the Renaissance proves that functionalism and commercialization need not necessarily involve artistic mediocrity. It seems strange to us to admit that music could have been *light* and still of high standards in language and style, and we think it odd that the same musician could turn out masses and popular songs. Yet this was the case of Lassus, composer of the *Penitential Psalms* as well as of the flippant ditty *Quand mon mari vient de dehors.*

The greatest composers of chansons were also among the greatest composers of religious music : Josquin, Willaert, Gombert, Lassus, to name only Flemings. This happy versatility was long-lived : Mozart wrote contredanses and minuets for the balls of Vienna at the same time as his *Symphony in G Minor.*

135

How can we explain this? First of all, in the sixteenth century, all music of any type whatsoever was functional. There was no conflict between pure music and utilitarian music: the motet functioned in the liturgy, the chanson in entertainment. Any functional art sets up close ties with the public it must satisfy, and this reduces the distance composers are sometimes inclined to prefer between themselves and their listeners. The composer must always preserve his contact with his audience, must always be understandable to them, or else be cast off, condemned to sing unheard. The great musician of the fifteenth and sixteenth centuries was never the Romantic creator, *dark-browed, widowed, unconsoled*, as the poet put it. He was not a solitary in revolt, an individualist wrapped in his own pride, contemptuous of others. Not that he may not have been conscious of the importance of what he was doing, of the value of his creations. But such legitimate pride did not lead him into a position of opposition, into a disdain for the admiration lavished on him. In those times, the composer often lived in relatively modest circumstances, serving a court or church, writing not for his own pleasure but on command. If he felt that he was understood by those he worked for, it was because there existed between them and himself a fundamental agreement on the essential values of existence, which meant religion, morality and politics as well as culture and aesthetics.

Society was organized according to a strict hierarchic plan in which the only people who counted were kings, princes, nobles and a certain upper middle class made up of merchants and functionaries. For a van Eyck or Bruegel, a Josquin Desprez or Roland de Lassus there could be no question of satisfying all of society. Himself part of a homogeneous environment, the artist addressed himself to a specific public and not, as today, to a faceless mass. With this public he shared a common respect for identical values. In creating for others, he created for himself; by serving others, he satisfied his own conscience. He felt no need for whatever special distinction might be gained by inventing an individualistic idiom. The complex art he mastered – counterpoint – could be placed at the service of others without compromising, because those others had the same aspirations he had and the same tastes.

If a style could be developed and maintained on an aesthetic level, it was because the best artists felt themselves in spiritual accord with a limited and homogeneous public. This accord involved certain bonds of subordination for the musician, a subordination he considered natural and satisfying. The acceptance of these bonds allowed him to assume without any psychological qualms his function as an entertainer just as, at other moments, he could assume his function as servant of God and the Church.

As a matter of fact, the chansons of the sixteenth century are highly diversified in both treatment and artistic ambitions. There are tiny pieces which are very simple, popular – or pseudo-popular – in spirit, and there are also highly worked-out compositions which have recourse to the most learned artifices. There are certain stereotyped procedures which, precisely because they were successful, were imitated more or less happily in numerous instances. Be that as it may, as always in any great mass of artistic work, truly inspired masterpieces are more rare than good or mediocre copies.

THE PARISIAN CHANSON AND FLEMISH ART

When it lost its exclusively aristocratic character, the chanson lost also its unity of inspiration and style. By becoming bourgeois, it gained in versatility.

Without doubt, the new trends were already apparent at the end of the fifteenth century in the repertory of *chansons rustiques*. After Josquin and Compère, they reappeared in the *Chanzoni franciose* of Adrian Willaert, in the *Chansons à troys* published in 1520 in Venice by Antico and Giunta, as well as in the *Couronne et fleur des chansons à troys* published by Antico in 1535. But in these works, the popular tune was not made prominent and was

136

always thoroughly integrated into a tightly worked-out counterpoint.

On the other hand, the most significant of the chansons published by Attaingnant beginning in 1528 seem to have something entirely new about them. Such novelty is not to be found in those chansons which maintain the traditional fixed forms, however simplified, nor in those which preserve the courtly character and continue to celebrate love in conventional flowery language and with outmoded images. The innovations occur rather in the descriptive chansons such as *La Bataille de Marignan* (The Battle of Marignan), *Le Chant des Oiseaux* (The Song of the Birds), *La Chasse* (The Hunt) or *Le Caquet des Femmes* (Women's Chatter) which used and abused highly evocative onomatopoeias; innovations occur also, and even more, in the chansons inspired by the theater : drinking songs, satirical songs, dialogues, narratives, bawdy ditties. The basic material was the same as in the old rustic songs, but what was new was the way it was used. In the new style, the music follows the text closely and almost always uses a syllabic declamation. Contrapuntal writing is restricted to brief imitative passages, and much is made of the contrast between two pairs of voices. Alternating with contrapuntal episodes are others in which all the parts go along in the same rhythm and seem to form chords to such an extent that the effect is vertical and harmonic. One voice clearly dominates the ensemble : the superius, the topmost voice, and it carries the principal melody and is the focus of attention; the other voices seem quite subordinate to it and limited to providing for it a harmonic coloration.

Let there be no mistake : this is still the same learned art, but its structures are simpler and it is easier to grasp by ear; the theater tune used is made to stand out more conspicuously in the upper voice at the same time as its material is made to impregnate all the other parts of the polyphonic web.

Quick to respond to the new vogue, poets took to turning out pastiches of theater songs, and these were

47. A Woman Standing at the Spinet.
Simon Bening (?).

snatched up for polyphonic setting by the composers. Because of Attaingnant's publications, musicologists have given the name of *chanson parisienne* to the new genre which gained favor from 1528 on and whose most typical composers were the Frenchmen Claudin de Sermisy, Clément Janequin and Pierre Certon along with many others more modest in fame. Attaingnant also published works by Flemings such as Willaert, Gombert, Crecquillon and Clemens non Papa.

At this time the Parisian chanson, which had been derived from the rustic chanson, began to differ from the chanson as conceived by the Flemish, whose character was more reserved and which remained faithful to the counterpoint and manner of Josquin. The Parisian chanson was to achieve its most characteristic expression in the second half of the century with pieces sometimes called *vaudevilles* or, after 1570, *airs* or *airs de cour*. Pierre Certon's *Premier livre de chansons* (1552) provides the best examples of this type. For the Parisians, the chanson was most often *strophic,* cast in verses, with literal repetitions of the music from stanza to stanza, whereas the Flemish preferred a chanson to be *through-composed,* with music which was constantly invented anew as the piece proceeded. For the Parisians, the text was set in *syllabic* manner, a syllable to a note, but the Flemish did not hesitate to unroll long *melismas* on a single syllable, with the result that the text lost its original rhythm while the music profited thereby. For the Parisians, the chanson was *homorhythmic,* with the principal melody in the top voice and all the voices going along together singing the same syllables at the same time; the Flemings continued to prefer a more supple counterpoint which maintained the independence of lines.

In Lyons, Jacques Moderne published works by Frenchmen and a few Italians along with Flemings, and this was the practice in Paris also. But in Antwerp Susato gave small place to the Parisians in his editions, publishing mostly works by Flemings currently living in the Low Countries or attached to the court of the Emperor – Payen, Crecquillon, Canis, Richafort, Clemens non Papa, Manchicourt, Gombert, Susato himself – or living in Germany – Guyot and Vaet – or in Italy – Willaert and de Rore. Susato allowed an important place to Josquin, the uncontested master of the beginning of the century, and this reflects a deliberate attitude : in choosing for his anthologies the most contrapuntal and complex chansons, Susato proclaimed his loyalty to the tradition of Josquin, which had remained vital in the Low Countries, however much it may seem to have been put in the shade by the great number of editions of Parisian music brought out by Attaingnant. With Crecquillon and Richafort, the chanson approached closely the style of the motet, from which it differed only by more emphatic rhythm and clearer cadences. In the chanson as in the motet, Gombert had recourse to the imitative-syntactic style, in which each phrase of text gives rise to a motif imitated by all the voices, and this is so not because Gombert did not know how to write more simply – certain of his chansons published in Lyons prove he could – but because he preferred closely woven counterpoint, which made whatever he wrote seem austere regardless of the text and its character.

In the middle of the century, lighter pieces were rare among the Flemish, although some were written by Clemens non Papa, who modeled both text and music on the Parisian chanson, as in this example :

> *Entre nous, filles de quinze ans,*
> *Ne venez plus à la fontaine,*
> *Car trop avez les yeux friands,*
> *Tétin poignant,*
> *Bouche riant,*
> *Connin mouflant,*
> *Le cœur gai plus qu'une mitaine.*
> *Entre nous, filles de quinze ans,*
> *Ne venez plus à la fontaine.*

(Take it from me, you teen-age moppets, / Better keep away from the fountain : / Your eyes are much too inviting, / Your breasts too pointed, / Your mouths too mocking, / Your headgear too showy, / And your hearts more gay than a cozy mitten. / Take it from me, you teen-age moppets, / Better keep away from the fountain.)

Whatever might have been the musical and poetic trends, there were a great many publications, and yet many chansons remained unprinted. In 1551, Adrien Le Roy and Robert Ballard opened a publishing house in Paris which remained prosperous until the eighteenth century. Between 1552 and 1585 they published no less than twenty-five *Livres de chansons nouvellement mises en musique à quatre parties par bons et sçavans musiciens* (Books of songs newly set to music for four parts by good and learned musicians), which enjoyed such success that they were often reprinted, the sixteenth book alone having gone through nine editions. Nicolas Du Chemin, who published music in Paris from 1549 to 1570, paid particular attention to chansons, as did Pierre Phalèse, publishing in Louvain from 1553 to 1560, whose productions went through numerous re-editions. In Germany French chansons were published by Kriesstein in Augsburg and Ott in Nuremberg, and in Italy by Gardane in Venice.

Avid for profit, publishers often printed the same songs as their competitors. Along with anthologies, there were often editions devoted to a single composer. Also, many chansons were published in versions for keyboard instruments or lute, and as early as 1531 Attaingnant had put out *Dix-neuf chansons musicales réduites en la tabulature des orgues, espinettes, manicordions et tels semblables instrumentz* (Nineteen songs in music transcribed into tablature for organ, spinet, manicordion and similar instruments) and lute arrangements in tablature were published by Adrien Le Roy in Paris and by Phalèse in the Low Countries. Such arrangements are positive evidence of the popularity of this music.

POETS AND MUSICIANS

More often than for the preceding century, it is possible to identify the poems that were set to music, among them texts by Mellin de Saint-Gelais, Marot,

Ronsard, Jean-Antoine de Baïf, and Philippe Desportes. Marot alone contributed 118 poems – songs, epigrams, rondeaux and the like – which served in the sixteenth century for 234 compositions by 65 musicians. The Flemish were as fond of him as the French and if they were a little tardy in discovering him, he nevertheless remained in favor among them at a time when the Frenchmen had already taken up Ronsard and Baïf. In a painting by the Master of the Half-Figures, there are three young women making music, specifically the chanson of Marot *Jouyssance vous donneray*. The same song appears in another painting of the same period in which there is a young woman accompanying herself on the lute. Marot's text was set to music as early as 1528 by Claudin de Sermisy and published by Attaingnant in that same year; it was later set by the composer-publisher Gardane in 1539, by Willaert in 1540, by Gerard van Turnhout in 1574 and, in part, by Lassus in 1577. *Mon cœur se recommande à vous* was set by F. De Lys in 1536, by Severin Cornet in 1574, and by René de Mel in 1597. There can be no doubt of Marot's popularity among musicians and the public. He continued to exploit the traditional themes of courtly love : *Secourez moy, ma Dame, par amours.* (Succour me, Lady, by your love.) but also treated others which were more earthy, indeed pseudo-popular and in the manner of theater songs, such as :

> *En entrant en un jardin,*
> *Je trouvay Guilloy Martin*
> *Avecques s'amye Héleine.*

(When I came into a garden, / I discovered Guillot Martin / With his little friend Helena.)

From 1552 on, Ronsard was the favorite poet of musicians. At that date appeared the first edition of his *Amours*, with, as a supplement, compositions for four voices by Certon, Goudimel, Janequin and Muret. By 1580, some two hundred poems by Ronsard had been set to music by about thirty composers, including Frenchmen like Costeley and de la Grotte and Flemings like Philippe de Monte, Jean de Castro,

Regnard and Lassus. However, what the musicians took from Ronsard were not his ambitious efforts stuffed with mythological allusions but rather songs, sonnets, odes and fragments of hymns, and above all those special favorites, *Mignonne, allons voir si la rose, Amour, amour, donne-moi paix ou tresve,* and *Si je trepasse entre tes bras, madame.*

Ronsard and the Pléiade poets typify the desire to establish a closer and deeper union between text and music. Though poems no longer necessarily determined the musical form, certain composers compensated for this independence by establishing a unity of atmosphere based on intimate correspondence between poetic rhythm and musical rhythm; Baïf, for one, asked musicians to pay close heed to the rhythms of his *vers mesurés à l'antique* (verse scanned according to Greek meters). Many composers, however, preferred to concentrate on bringing out the meaning of the words through the innner expressiveness of music.

In Italy, meantine, a new genre, the *madrigal,* had been developed, applying music of great refinement to poems of high literary quality. Without rejecting the subtleties of counterpoint, the madrigalists paid close attention to relationships between music and text. Foreigners such as Willaert, Arcadelt and Verdelot had been among the first great creators of this genre, which, itself, was a new product of the profound link between the Italian spirit and the Flemish technique. When around 1550 the madrigal style began to affect the French chanson, this was more than a sign of the current marked Italian influence on French literary inspiration, in which a new enthusiasm for the sonnet resulted from the resurrection of Petrarch; it was also the proof of renewed Flemish influence on musical style. Alongside *vaudevilles* and chansons which used the same music for every stanza, alongside court airs which continued the style of the rustic songs but in a refined, more intellectual manner, and alongside chansons *mesurées à l'antique,* many chansons followed the model of the madrigal and thereby ac-

quired a new dignity from the more attentive choice of poems and from more painstaking work in composition. The musician who best qualifies as an exponent of the chanson in the second half of the sixteenth century is Roland de Lassus, born in Mons in the Low Countries, educated in Italy, and finally attached to the court of Bavaria in Munich.

ROLAND DE LASSUS

Roland de Lassus was only twenty-three in 1555 when Susato in Antwerp published his first chansons. These were the first of a long series of chansons destined to make of him the most successful composer of his time right up to the end of the century, with numerous publications by Phalèse in Louvain and Le Roy in Paris.

Lassus was quite eclectic in his choice of texts, not even hesitating to disinter such forgotten poets as Alain Chartier (*Quand un cordier*) or François Villon (*Gallans, qui par terre et par mer*), and taking from Marot poems neglected by composers before him (*Bonjour et puis quelle nouvelle*) as well as selecting liberally from Ronsard, Baïf, Du Bellay, Belleau and anthologies like *La fleur de dame* besides a good number of anonymous poems written especially for music.

Infinitely versatile, Lassus moved freely from the subtle refinement of Ronsard :

O doux parler dont l'apast doucereux,
Nourrit encor la fin de ma mémoire,
O front, d'Amour le trophée et la gloire,
O doux souris, ô baisers savoureux !

(O sweet speech, whose honeyed lure / Still nourishes the dregs of remembrance, / O forehead, Cupid's trophy and glory, / O sweet smile, O luscious kisses !)
to the realistic accents of the folk-style complaints of unhappily married women :

Quand mon mari vient de dehors
Ma rente est d'estre battue.

(When my man comes home at night / I'm paid off with a drubbing.)

140

Sometimes he borrows a text from a folk song :

O vin en vigne, gentil, joly vin en vigne,
Vignon, vigna, vigne sur vigne...

(O wine still on the vine, sweet jolly wine on vine, / Vinon, vina, wine on vine...)

and he does not hesitate to choose bawdy texts and others which, because of their double meanings, might be judged blasphemous if one did not keep in mind that they are merely part of a solid tradition of satire :

Il estoit une religieuse
De l'ordre de l'Ave Maria
Qui d'un Pater estoit tant amoureuse,
Que son gent corps avec le sien lia.

(There was a nun / Of the order of Ave Maria, / So much in love with a Pater, / She surrendered her sweet body to him.)

To this diversity of texts corresponds a prodigious variety of music. When he borrows the Parisian style, Lassus uses it with complete ease and with a comic verve superior to that of his predecessors, writing in a harmonic manner with all the voices moving along together. However, what he prefers generally is an extremely flexible contrapuntal style in which imitation is not pursued beyond the entries of phrases. The fact is, it is the text which determines the nature of his music : it is the source of all inspiration and it dictates the style of the piece. Phrase by phrase, the literary ideas call forth new melodies and, as in the Italian madrigal, certain words are set in relief to enhance their expressiveness. In his chansons Lassus avoids complex artifices of composition, but his counterpoint is noteworthy for its subtle treatment of dissonances and for the discreet but effective introduction of chromaticism.

It is safe to say that with Lassus the polyphonic chanson attained a veritable perfection. Bawdy or dignified, popular or aristocratic, simple or learned, it aroused enthusiasm among the most varied publics throughout Europe and provided a form of entertainment adapted to every humor, to all circumstances, to all spiritual and cultural attitudes.

THE POLYPHONIC LIED IN FLEMISH

The success of the French chansons is revealed not only by the dispersion throughout Europe of an abundant repertory created by the French and Flemish, but also by the fact that it stimulated the composition of works of the same nature in many languages. In Italy, Spain, Germany and England, equivalent forms were developed, some of them of great originality, others no more than fashionable imitations.

It may seem surprising that polyphonic chansons with Flemish texts are relatively few. But first it must be remembered that the native language of many composers we call Flemish was, in fact, French. And then, musicians never wrote for personal satisfaction but only at the command of a public. It is only natural that most of the ballades and rondeaux of the fifteenth century were written in French since they were composed for princely courts and French was the international language of the aristocracy in England, in certain courts of Italy, in Cyprus, at the court of Aragon and, obviously, at the court of Burgundy.

Chansons on Flemish poems scarcely appear before the end of the century. There are twenty-five in a manuscript of the British Museum (Add. Ms. 35087), sixteen in the first editions of Petrucci (the *Odhecaton*, the *Canti B* and *C*) and about fifteen scattered here and there. From around 1511 there are seven chansons on Flemish texts along with fifteen in French and three Latin pieces in the little *Chansonnier de Tournai*, a volume decorated with charming miniatures which contains the separate tenor part of a polyphonic ensemble. If there was occasional interest in Flemish texts, it must have been to the extent that the chanson was beginning to move out of aristocratic circles to reach the urban middle classes. And yet the polyphonic lied was confined to certain localities; one should not be misled by Petrucci's publications since he printed only the music and not the texts. The art of the Flemish musicians of the fifteenth and sixteenth

141

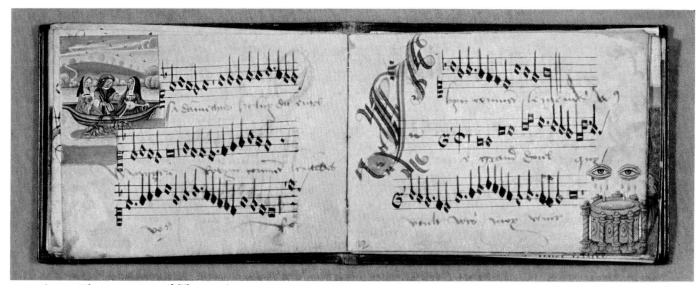

48 and 49. Chansonnier of Tournai.   Pages illustrated with miniatures.

centuries was international : Adrian Willaert, Cyprien de Rore and Philippe de Monte had their careers in Italy or Germany and composed on French, Italian or German texts, never, however, on Flemish.

At the turning point between the two centuries, a few great musicians had written a few such Flemish songs : Agricola and Obrecht two each, Busnois, Pierre de la Rue, Brumel and Isaac one each. The Germans were the first to publish chansons in Flemish : Formschneider in Nuremberg in 1538, Kriesstein in Augsburg in 1540, Georg Rhaw in Wittenberg in 1542, but in each case this meant a few pieces only.

The first collections entirely devoted to Flemish polyphonic chansons do not date from earlier than 1551 and are due to the publisher Tielman Susato of Antwerp : *Het ierste musyck boexken met vier partyen daer inne begrepen zijn XXVI nieuwe amoreuse liedekens in onser nederduytscher talen, gecomponeert by diversche componisten, zeer lustich om singen ende spelen op alle musicale instrumenten* (The first music books in four parts, including twenty-six new love songs in our Low German tongue, composed by divers composers, most pleasant to sing and play on all musical instruments).

The enterprise was so exceptional that Susato thought it necessary to justify it in a preface : *Musica is een sunderlinghe hemelsche gave van God geordineert, ende den menschen gegeven, niet tot onheerlijcke of lichtverdigen misbruycke, maar om hem voer al dankelijck, te lovene, ledicheit te schouwene, tyt te winnene, melancholie te verjagene, omlust te verdrivene, sware geesten te verlichtene, beroerde herten te verhuegene. En waerome en soude men dat voortane niet also wel met gelijcker konst ende soetigheid in onser moedersp raken connen gedoen, als men tot nu toe in latijnse, walsche ende italiannsche sprake gedaan heeft ? Ist de konst ende soeticheheid even gelijck, waerom sal men die meer om dene dan om dander wille verachten ?* (Music is a remarkable gift, instituted by order of God and offered to man to be used not for dishonest or thoughtless ends but, above all, to render thanks and praise to the Lord, to shun idleness and make good use of his time, to drive out melancholy and dark thoughts, and in order to restore joy to hearts sorely tried. And wherefore then should this not be done henceforth in our own mother tongue with the same skill and the same harmony as, until now, have been lavished on Latin, French and Italian ? Our art and our harmony being the equal of those of others, for what reason should one language be scorned to the profit of another ?)

In the same year Susato published two other *Musyck boexkens,* one containing twenty-seven chansons in Flemish and the other instrumental dance pieces. Most of the chansons are anonymous, and

142

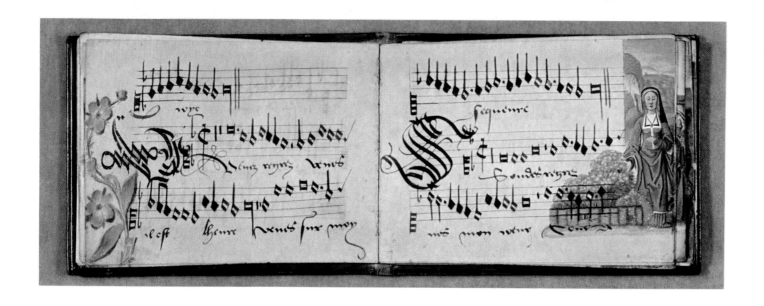

only a single composer of great reputation, Clemens non Papa, is included, the others being musicians of second grade, unimportant local masters belonging to several generations : Verbonnet and Nicolas Liégeois, Antoine Barbé, Josquin Baston, Benedictus Appenzeller, Lupus Hellinck, Jerome Vinders and Tielman Susato himself. Most often they are love songs of no great originality, but there are also narrative texts of more popular inspiration as well as drinking songs. Musically there are the same discreet imitations, rhythmic vitality and syllabic text-setting characteristic of the French chanson of around the middle of the century.

A very few collections appeared in the following years. In 1554 Jacob Bathen published at Maastricht *Dat ierste boeck van den nieuwe duytsche liedekens*, including chansons by Clemens non Papa, Petit Joan de Lattre and Ludovicus Episcopius; in 1568 six *liedekens* by Noël Faignient were included among French chansons, madrigals and motets in a volume published in Antwerp by the widow of Jan Laet; in 1571, seven Flemish songs for two voices – four anonymous and three by Jan Verdonck – were printed in a *Liber Musicus* published by Phalèse in Louvain and by Bellère in Antwerp; in 1572 there came from the same editors *Een Duytsch musyck boek* in which one finds again Clemens non Papa, Hellinck, Episcopius, Faignient along with new names, Jan Belle, Jean and Gerard van Turnhout.

There are in this anthology songs of May, drinking songs, moralizing songs and quite pleasant love songs like this one set to music by Jan Belle :

> *O amoureusisch mondeken root,*
> *naer u staet mijn verlanghen;*
> *toont mij uws herte grondeken bloot,*
> *en u roozierighe wanghen.*
> *Ghij hebt mij toch ghevanghen*
> *door dwezen gracieus;*
> *ghij brenght mij heel in pranghen,*
> *met sinnen rigoreus.*

(Those love-ripe lips / Shall not wait long to still my ardor; / Reveal then the secret of your heart, / And offer me the roses of your cheeks. / Long have I been the prisoner / Of your abounding grace; / Long have I sought deliverance / With never-failing desire.)

As we have seen, the repertory of Flemish polyphonic chansons is not large, and while it is generally of good artistic quality, it must be admitted that it was produced for local use only and did not arouse the interest of the greatest composers.

SOUTERLIEDEKENS AND SPIRITUAL SONGS

The most important collections for the history of song in Flemish are the translations of the Psalms of the Bible, the *Souterliedekens* by Clemens non Papa, published by Susato in 1556 and 1557 as volumes IV to VII of the series of *Musyck boexkens* (*Souter*

is the equivalent of the modern Flemish – and English – word *psalter*).

In 1540 Symon Cock had published in Antwerp a volume of *Souterliedekens* containing rhymed verse translations of all the Psalms done, it is believed, by a nobleman of Utrecht, Willem van Zuylen van Nyevelt. The melodies applied to the Psalm texts were not original but were borrowed from well-known French or Flemish songs and from fragments out of serious compositions. Thus a well-known song such as, for instance, *Ghequetst ben ick van binnen* was used as a basis, replacing the amorous verses with an exact translation of Psalm 101 (*Domine exaudi orationem meam*) :

> *Hoort mijn ghebet, o Heere,*
> *Mijn roepen wilt ontfaen.*

(Hear my prayer, O Lord, / And let my cry come unto Thee.)

The German translation of the Psalms by Luther had been published in Antwerp in 1526 and must have influenced the Flemish version found in the *Souterliedekens*. As is known, Calvin had undertaken in Geneva the French translation of the Huguenot psalter in collaboration with Clément Marot and Théodore de Bèze and with musical settings, adaptations of existing melodies either profane or sacred, provided by Louis Bourgeois.

The *Souterliedekens* were not explicitly intended for adherents of the Reformed religion, but it is likely that they were conceived and published in a climate of sympathy for Protestantism such as existed then in various circles in the Low Countries. Obviously their originators counted on a certain ambiguity, since to justify a publication which enjoyed official sanction they presented these *Souterliedekens* as hymns in the vernacular fit to be sung by all good Christians and not intended to be used in any specific cult.

Whatever may have been the pretext, the fact is that the *Souterliedekens* became particularly popular among the Protestants. In a sense, from the time the Reformed religion became illegal in the southern provinces, the *Souterliedekens* may have been considered something like the songs of a resistance movement, although the Catholics themselves seem to have accepted them as simple hymns. In any case, this enthusiasm from both sides explains the numerous editions which appeared in the sixteenth century.

The polyphonic versions of the Psalms made by Louis Bourgeois in 1547 at Geneva probably served as models for Clemens non Papa's three-voiced settings of texts and melodies taken from the *Souterliedekens* published by Cock in 1540. Officially Clemens was a loyal Catholic and the composer of many Latin motets. His polyphonic versions of the Psalms were never used in the Protestant service but were conceived to be sung in the intimacy of middle-class family circles, not by choirs but by amateur soloists. It is characteristic moreover that Clemens should set them for various combinations of voices of different ranges. The original melody is used as a *cantus firmus* placed most often in the center of the polyphony, but there is much emphasis on the invention of complementary contrapuntal lines to adorn the original melody, which, itself, is always presented simply and without notable modifications, remaining clearly recognizable in the midst of the contrapuntal convolutions. In 1561 Susato published a new version of the *Souterliedekens*, this one polyphonic for four voices, composed by Gerard Mes, said to be a disciple of Clemens non Papa, but this volume unfortunately has not survived.

145

Under Protestant influence, there appeared in the second half of the century chansons with moralizing or religious texts. Thus Hubert Waelrant and Jan Laet published in 1556 at Antwerp *Le Jardin musical contenant plusieurs belles fleurs de chansons spirituelles* (The Musical Garden, containing several beautiful flowers of spiritual songs), two volumes with chansons on edifying texts composed by Crecquillon, Jean Caulery, Clemens non Papa, Waelrant himself and a few others. Seemingly Waelrant was a sympathizer of the Reformed religion, since in 1555 he also published fifty psalms in the French version of Marot, and eight of the pieces he composed for the *Jardin musical* utilize psalms by Marot. Nevertheless, it is certain that such spiritual chansons, intended for the familly circle or friends, enjoyed the favor of Catholics also.

The success of one of these songs proves how great was the interest of the public in this edifying genre. A Huguenot poet, Guillaume Guéroult, wrote the text as a paraphrase of the story of Susanna and the Elders :

> *Suzanne un jour, d'amour sollicitée*
> *Par deux vieillards convoitans sa beauté...*

(Susanna one day, her love solicited / By two old men lusting after her beauty...)

A composer in Lyons, Didier Lupi, had set the poem to very simple polyphony in 1548. The text, sometimes adapted into Flemish, English or German, and very often Lupi's melody also – used more or less faithfully as a *cantus firmus* – gave rise to a great number of polyphonic settings. Before the end of the century thirty-five of them were published in Louvain, Antwerp, Lyons and Paris. Roland de Lassus set the text twice, once in 1560 in French and again in 1576 in German, and among the Flemings there are versions by Faignient, Castro, G. van Turnhout, Rore, Episcopius, Cornet, De Paepe and Pevernage.

Among these composers there are more Catholics than Protestants, and it appears likely that the success of the spiritual song may have been due as much to the Counter Reformation as to the Reformation, the Catholics seeking to outdo their adversaries in austerity. Since all styles were used for these songs, from homorhythm to the most complex counterpoint, one can conclude that, musically at least, these spiritual songs differed in no way from profane chansons. It is not surprising that well-intentioned editors were often content merely to publish highly popular profane chansons fitted out with new texts, as was the case, for one, in the volume published in Geneva in 1555 *in which are contained many songs chosen from among the best, ancient as well as modern, composed by divers excellent musicians, of which we have changed the licentious poems into spiritual and Christian words.*

Thus, one of the most famous songs of the Renaissance, *Faulte d'argent, c'est douleur non pareille* (Lack of money brings grief beyond compare) was transformed into *Faulte de foy, c'est erreur non pareille* (Lack of faith brings error beyond compare). A charming poem by Marot :

> *Tant que vivray en aage florissant*
> *Je serviray d'amour le Dieu puissant.*

(As long as I live in healthful age / I'll serve the powerful God of Love.)
was paraphrased into :

> *Tant que vivray en aage florissant*
> *Je serviray le Seigneur tout puissant.*

(As long as I live in healthful age / I'll serve the powerful Lord of all.)

The spiritual chansons do not really count as an important genre, but they round out our picture of the subjects used for polyphonic chansons in the middle-class society of the sixteenth century. Mindful of the warnings of Calvin, certain Protestants went so far as to banish all "lascivious and shameless songs" which might trouble the soul, but the Catholics were more flexible. For them, good sentiments and pious feelings served as a salutary diversion in the midst of the pleasures of a society which, moreover, never wearied of singing of love, sometimes bawdily, sometimes with precious affectation.

Chapter 6

51. Carole in the Orchard.
Master of the Juvénal des Ursins (?).

Music and Life

Polyphonic music enjoyed a privileged place in the church, in the princely courts, in middle-class homes. Pictorial evidence proves that in all strata of society songs, dances, fanfares and all the other kinds of music provided an indispensable concomitant of most events in life. But it was not always the same music : the choice varied, and greatly, according to time and place, to special circumstances and social level. Books, however, unlike pictures, are less revealing about the many kinds of music made, and that is because much of it was never written down but only improvised. Compared with other civilizations, our Western culture is unique in the importance it assigns to the notation of a certain kind of art music; nevertheless, it is likely that the amount of music actually written down in the fifteenth and sixteenth centuries was no more than a tiny part of all the music sung and played.

There is no hope of rediscovering any significant traces of all this music. When a learned musician noted down the melody of a popular song or dance, he transplanted it into a quite different world where it became something quite different. Folklore of today is not of much help in disinterring the popular music of the past, for with time traditions degenerate or become modified. The most we can hope to do is to try to decipher, from all sorts of secondary sources, the nature and importance of the unwritten music which played a part in the great and small happenings of existence in every walk of life.

THE BURGUNDIAN FESTIVITIES

In modern society, public festivities have lost the intensity of participation, the seduction and splendor they once had. They have dwindled in significance as modern man demands and enjoys more leisure, which he spreads throughout the year in weekends and holidays. In the Middle Ages and the Renaissance, work was interrupted only by Sundays and the holidays of the religious calendar, by the festivities marking the return of the seasons, and by public ceremonies called for by the prince or the city.

It is only recently that these festivals and ceremonies of the past have begun to be studied systematically. In an attempt to rediscover them in all their diversified aspects, historians are now collaborating with specialists in the history of literature, theater, painting, architecture, music and dance.

Political circumstances were often more than the excuse for such public festivities. They also determined their content, their themes, and their forms. Here we must limit ourselves to pointing out the part played by music in them.

The splendor of the court of Burgundy was legendary throughout Europe. Of all the celebrations in the reigns of Philip the Good and Charles the Bold, none created more stir than the Banquet of the Oath of the Pheasant, which took place on June 17, 1454 in Lille. We are familiar with the political reasons which lay behind this lavish show and the nostalgia for a waning feudal world it re-

149

vealed. In those years, the idea of a new Crusade was arousing the enthusiasm of the great lords. After the fall of Constantinople, in response to a plea from the Pope, Philip the Good wished to take a solemn vow to come to the aid of the captive Church. He therefore invited a brilliant company to the ceremony so that it might bear witness before all men and posterity to Philip's noble determination.

The festivities at Lille were described in detail and at length by the chroniclers of the time, notably by Olivier de La Marche and Mathieu d'Escouchy, though both seem to have made use of the same official account. Every detail of the grand occasion was painstakingly worked out as part of a theatrical staging intended to direct the onlookers' thoughts to a single focus : the aim pursued by the Duke. In re-reading these accounts, one sees how much the very notion of "spectacle" has become restricted today.

The banquet hall at Lille was hung with great tapestries depicting the Labors of Hercules. Three tables with silk damask cloths were set up under canopies of precious materials, and the guests took their places on benches with cushions embroidered in coats-of-arms. There were so many guests, the chroniclers tell us, that even knights and ladies of great houses had to content themselves with places on platforms set up nearby. The tables were decorated with enormous constructions – the *entremets* – which were either automatons or handsome settings from which emerged personages and animals, and some of these fabulous displays were made of nothing less than pastry !

On the central table reserved for the Duke himself there was *a church with vault and windows made most beautifully, wherein a bell sounded and four singers sang and played on organs when their turn came.* On the second and longest table, at which sat the Count of Charolais, the future Charles the Bold, there was *a pastry within which twenty-eight live persons played various instruments, each one when his turn came.* The third and smallest table,

reserved for the squires and their ladies, held a marvelous forest with strange beasts *which moved by themselves, almost as if they were alive.* Elsewhere in the hall there were pieces of lesser importance, all of them concealing allegorical enigmas.

The banquet was interrupted by *lively, animated and diverting interludes* consisting of brief dramatic or lyrical scenes. When everyone was seated, *in the church, which was the first interlude, a bell sounded very loudly and when it had ceased three little choir-boys and a tenor began a very lovely chanson, though what it was I cannot say,* declares Mathieu d'Escouchy, *but for my part I found it a pleasant Benedicite for the beginning of the supper. After those in the church had done their turn, a shepherd played a bagpipe in a fashion never heard before. Then sixteen knights in livery led in a richly caparisoned horse walking backward, and on the horse two trumpeters seated back to back and without saddle ... played a very long fanfare.*

When the interlude of the horse walking backward had passed ... the organ in the church began to play most sweetly, and when this had finished in

the church, within the pastry was played a German cornett most strangely. After a buffoon had made the round of the hall, those in the church sang and in the pastry was played a cromorne with another instrument, and after that there sounded most loudly four bugles [clairons] in a most joyous fanfare. The buglers were behind a green curtain stretched across a great platform set up at one end of the hall. The curtain was drawn and Jason appeared, the hero-patron of the knights of the Order of the Golden Fleece, and he fought against bullocks that were both great and horrible to look on. In the course of the banquet, three tableaux in pantomime recounted the adventures of Jason in Colchis.

After this mystery, the organ in the church was played again and within the pastry was sung ... by three sweet voices an entire chanson entitled "La Sauvegarde de ma vie." Then appeared a white stag with gold horns mounted by a lad of twelve, and upon entering the hall the said boy began to sing the top voice of a song loud and clear and the stag itself sang the tenor without any other person being visible save the boy and the device of the stag : and the song they sang was called "Je ne vis oncques la pareille." So, singing as I tell you, they made the round of all the tables and then departed.

There exists a rondeau for three voices, Je ne vis oncques la pareille (I never saw the like), which according to the sources is attributed either to Binchois or to Dufay and which is no better and no worse than the other songs then fashionable. Since on this occasion it was sung by only two voices, it must have been the counter-tenor which was omitted, which proves once again how much liberty was allowed in performance of a polyphonic piece constructed by the superimposition of relatively independent voices.

After which, in the church they sang a motet and in the pastry a chanson for two voices accompanied by a lute : in this way the church and the pastry always performed something between the courses. The second episode of the history of Jason was announced by a fanfare on four bugles. Then a musical interlude : the organ in the church was played and in the pastry four minstrels played flutes. After a dragon passed through the hall, another

151

motet was sung in the church, and in the pastry blind minstrels played fiddles accompanied by a lute *and there sang with them a young girl from the service of the said duchess named Pacquette ... and it was a fine and sweet melody to hear* – one more proof of the participation of amateurs in polyphonic singing. Then a heron was let loose in the hall and a falcon which killed it *and then once again there was singing in the church, and in the pastry three drummers played together a very gay song* (it is likely that the players of tabors played at the same time a little fife or *flajol,* just as in the folk music of Provence today where the *galoubet* and *tambourin* are played for rounds and dances). The four buglers on the platform introduced a final scene from the exploits of Jason. This was followed by an interlude on the organ in the church, and in the pastry there took place a hunting scene with ingenious automatons during which one heard the greyhounds bark and the hunters call and sound their horns.

After these *entremetz mondains* there arrived the solemn moment which was the reason for the entire celebration. A Saracen giant led into the middle of the hall an elephant on whose back was set up a fortified tower within which was a lady *dressed in a robe of white satin very simply made in order to show her high birth and the noble place from whence she had come.* This lady attired as a nun symbolized the Holy Church held in thrall by the Saracens, but she leaned on the rampart of a tower and this represented the faith which lives in the hearts of men. *As soon as her elephant had stopped, she began her complaint and lamentation in a piteous womanly voice,* and addressing the Burgundian nobles and in particular the Duke, she begged them to take up her defense.

Dufay wrote four *Lamentacions de Constantinople* but only one has come down to us, the *Lamentatio sanctæ matris Ecclesiæ constantinopolitanæ,* which is a four-voiced motet whose *cantus firmus* is borrowed from the Lamentations of Jeremiah recited during Holy Week. The *Complainte*

de la dame as reported by the chroniclers does not seem to agree at all with the motet, but it is possible that it was one of the lost *Lamentacions* by Dufay.

Surrounded by numerous officers, the master-at-arms of the Order of the Golden Fleece then presented to the assembly a live pheasant decorated with pearls and precious gems *in view of the fact that it is and was the custom to bring a peacock or some other noble bird into our great festivities, in the presence of the grandees, the princes, lords and nobles, in order that they may make useful and worthy vows.* It was to God, to the Virgin, to the ladies and to the pheasant that Philip the Good addressed his vow to embark on the Crusade, and a similar vow was promptly taken by the Count of Charolais, the Duke of Cleves and the principal lords, as well as some hundred others who swore their vows the next day.

After the noble lady personifying the Church had expressed her gratitude, the final scene was a sort of ballet. The tables were taken out and *into the hall entered by the great portal a horde of torchbearers followed by many players on divers instruments such as tabors, lutes and harps.* They preceded a lady symbolizing the Grace of God who was followed by twelve masked knights, each bearing a torch and leading in a lady. These twelve ladies symbolized the twelve virtues necessary to the Duke to succeed in his undertaking, and *they then began to dance a kind of mummery and to make much jollity so that the festivity might thereby end more joyously.*

We have lingered over this scenario because, despite the wealth of details, one can decipher in it the profound underlying significance of a festivity whose magnificence was encumbered with a hodgepodge of literature, in which refinement mingled with vulgarity, where chivalric ideals and religious sentiment were both expressed in a theatrical manner, but in which the theater was linked with a meaningful action in life and thereby ennobled it.

It is clear what a considerable place music had in such pageantry. It was of three types : religious

53. A Tourney.
Jean Dreux.

music in the church with four cantors, organ and a bell; profane music in the pastry with minstrels playing bagpipes, German cornetts, flutes, fiddles, lutes, tabors; fanfares in the hall with trumpets and bugles sounding flourishes. To this must be added the lament in the form of a motet sung by Mother Church and also the final dance of the Twelve Virtues.

Many other festivities of comparable extravagance took place in the fifteenth and sixteenth centuries. Among those of which we have descriptions may be mentioned the wedding of Charles the Bold with Margaret of York in Bruges in 1468. From the minutely detailed account by Olivier de La Marche a few remarks about the music will suffice. The marriage was celebrated at Damme, and in the procession which welcomed the new Duchess into Bruges, music had its part : *after the nobles, there marched all sorts of instruments ordered according to their divers nations, and after them came buglers, minstrels, trumpeters and both English and Burgundian, who made themselves heard with force.* In this procession were also the white palfreys and litters of the great ladies of England, the Burgundian gentlemen, the magistrates of Bruges, the knights of the Order of the Golden Fleece, the clergy, ambassadors, foreign merchants and others.

This celebration in Bruges continued for ten days. Each day there were dinners, balls, dramatic scenes in mime, and various interludes of which we need single out only those of the third day. In the middle of the hall was set up a high tower painted gold, azure and silver from whose summit a watchman *sounded most loudly upon a cornett,* whereupon, at the four windows at the top of the tower, appeared four boars bearing the banners of Burgundy *and they sounded a long fanfare.* Later appeared three female goats and one male, and *the latter played on a sackbut* [trombone] *while the three nanny-goats played shawms* [oboes], *all of them combining to play a motet, after which they returned as they had come. Then, suddenly the windows flew open,* and *in them appeared four wolves with flutes in their paws and the said wolves struck up a chanson, and then went away as the others had, after which came four large asses very well counterfeited, who recited a chanson in four parts specially written for them on the words "Art being an ass, my mistress?"; and finally for the last interlude monkeys danced a moresque playing pipes and tabors.*

Another day there was a great ballet with sirens and knights emerging from the belly of a whale, and a lion and another animal sang a chanson for tenor and treble specially composed for the new Duchess :

Bien viegne la belle bergère
De qui la beaulté et manière
Nous rend soulas et espérance.

(Welcome to the new shepherdess / Whose beauty and grace / Restore to us hope and solace.)

Throughout the ten days of the fête, trumpets punctuated the most memorable moments with their heroic fanfares. Trumpets and bugles were always employed in the Burgundian festivities and above all in those favorite entertainments of the nobility, jousts and tourneys. Olivier de La Marche reports that the jousters were accompanied by *heralds, drummers and trumpeters,* and the chroniclers never fail to mention in their accounts of tourneys *the trumpets, clarions and minstrels who made such a fine melody it was a joy to hear them.* Many miniatures show musicians marking the different phases of the tourneys with their fanfares, in this way rendering such spectacles more solemn, imposing upon them a formal order by which a combat became a kind of ballet, and conferring upon the entire event the solemn dignity of a work of art.

The great lords always maintained military trumpeters as part of their establishments. The Duke of Burgundy had twelve of them who preceded him upon his entry into a city and who accompanied him to festivities and tourneys and, in the event of war, to his camps.

154

There are no illustrations surviving for the most spectacular celebrations of the Burgundian court, but they do exist for festivities elsewhere and provide a welcome complement to the copious chronicles of the time.

There is, for example, in the church of Notre-Dame de Nantilly at Saumur a great tapestry from the Tournai workshops of the second half of the fifteenth century which depicts a *Ball of the Wild Men*. As was typical of tapestries of the period, it contains a great number of figures. Mingled with the lords and their dames in rich attire are "wild men" completely covered from head to toe in the fleece of some animal or other (such disguises often played a role at one and the same time picturesque and psychologically disturbing in the entertainments of the Middle Ages and the Renaissance). On a dais, five musicians play various instruments for the dance in which most of the figures join except for a few bystanders who seem to be conversing.

In banquet scenes one often finds musicians. In a fifteenth-century manuscript of the *Histoire du Grand Alexandre* (Paris, Petit Palais), two Flemish miniatures depict sumptuous banquets : in the middle of the hall, before the guests at table, instrumentalists make music : on one side, three players of harp, fiddle and portative organ; elsewhere, four players of recorder, sackbut and lute; in the courtyard of the palace one can glimpse two jousters.

A miniature of the *Chronique de Hainaut* by Jacques de Guise (Brussels, Bibliothèque Royale) shows a banquet hall with guests and attendants while, on a balcony, three musicians play shawms.

On the engravings and drawings depicting Herod's banquet in which Salome after her dance carries in the head of the prophet, there is traditionally a group of musicians, as for example in the engravings by Israël van Meckenem and Martin Zasinger.

Another banquet scene with dancers and masquers is found in *Der Weißkunig,* the somewhat fanciful autobiography Maximilian of Austria wrote, or had written for him, between 1505 and 1516. In it he designates himself as the White King, alluding to the armor he wore in tourneys and military actions, and speaks at length of his sojourn in the Burgundian states and of his marriage with Mary of Burgundy, daughter of Charles the Bold. Among the engraved illustrations, one shows a group of women seated at a table presided over by Mary of Burgundy enthroned under a canopy. In the middle of the hall, a group of masquers approaches Maximilian. They are led by a torchbearer and wear plumed turbans and are armed with swords and clubs; their masks are in the shapes of birds of prey. There can be no doubt that this was some sort of dance, since there are also three musicians playing flute and drums.

THE FESTIVITIES AT BINCHE

Festivities with masquerades, mummeries and interludes were not the exclusive speciality of the court of Burgundy with its love of medieval pomp. They were practiced widely and for a long time everywhere and ended up finally in the *ballet de cour* in France and the *masque* in England. Further, this same sort of entertainment larded with interludes in antique manner, pastorals, allegories and triumphs finally spawned a new form, opera, at the court of the Medici in Florence.

The style of these festivities often differed somewhat in the sixteenth century. An attempt was made to give greater dramatic unity to the various interludes, as in the *Ballet comique de la Reine* conceived by Balthazar de Beaujoyeulx and presented in Paris in 1581 at the wedding of the Duke de Joyeuse and Mademoiselle de Vaudemont. Nevertheless, traditions which some have thought of wrongly as medieval survived very late and more often than is generally thought.

This is true of the celebrations organized at Binche in Hainaut in 1549 by the Governess of the Low Countries, Mary of Hungary, in honor of Charles V and his son Philip on the occasion of their visit to their northern territories : *I can truly say,* declared the French annalist Brantôme, *that never*

155

was anything done or seen more splendid, not even the Roman magnificences in their games of yore, if we leave aside the gladiators' and wild beasts' combats; those excepted, the festivities in Binche were more sumptuous and pleased more, were more diversified and more consistent.

Throughout nine days a magical world of chivalric romance was brought into being. After a tourney and masquerades, there unfolded a long dramatic action in which reality mingled with fantasy. A petition was presented to the Emperor by the knights-errant of Belgian Gaul requesting his protection against a sorcerer who lived in a castle perpetually swathed in a cloud so thick that no one could ever hope to pierce it. A mysterious knight, aided by the Enchanted Queen, thereupon set forth on a quest for a magic sword. This found, they were enabled to break the evil enchantments and to destroy the Dark Castle after a goodly number of heroic exploits. The incidents in this complicated action did not take place on a stage but, rather, in the many halls of the castle, in the gardens and forests round about. The participants experienced a kind of intoxication in reliving these scenes from a legendary past, and this too served the political scheme which lay behind the allegory : the determination of Charles V to oblige the Low Countries to accept the legitimate right of his son Philip to the throne. Thus, at the end, there was general delight in recognizing Prince Philip in the mysterious Knight of the Magic Sword. Tourneys, banquets, balls and festivities of every kind were mingled with this fiction and formed an integral part of it.

The chief organizer of these festivities seems to have been the organist Roger Pathié, favorite musician of Mary of Hungary. Nothing is known of the music used, but it must certainly have intervened at several moments in the celebrations. On the seventh evening there was a veritable ballet. First, four ladies of the court, masked, entered on the arms of four knights in Venetian costume, *all dancing an allemande with so much rhythm and*

156

54. Philip the Good Preceded by His Trumpeters Is Welcomed at His Entry into Dijon by a Procession of Burghers.
Miniature.

such precision that it was a marvel to behold. The dance was interrupted by four other knights with armorial bearings in white, preceded by drummers, who pretended to provoke the first four to combat. This new group danced with the ladies, and the combat also seems to have been danced according to stylized figures and with swordplay such as are described by Thoinot Arbeau in his *Orchésographie.* Then suddenly there burst in eight new personages in green capes – wild men – against whom the knights united in combat. Their entry and the simulated fight were the excuse for new dances during which the wild men and their squires succeeded in making off with the women by force. The next day it was necessary to deliver the kidnapped ladies, after a veritable siege, from the fortress where they were held prisoner.

A drawing of the period makes it plain that what was involved was a ballet : in the great hall of the palace of Binche, in the presence of Charles V, Prince Philip, Mary of Hungary, Eleonore of Austria and the principal nobles, a highly stylized combat takes place of eight knights against eight wild men, during which squires lead off the ladies, all still dancing.

According to a convention which was to survive for a long time in court ballets, most of the dancers

were not professionals but courtiers who took pleasure in participating in such ludicrous masquerades with scenes in mime or dance, in short, in showing themselves off.

THE MORESQUE

One of the dances most often mentioned in medieval and Renaissance texts is the *moresque*, which Thoinot Arbeau in his *Orchésographie* characterized thus : *In my youth, I saw that in good company, after supper, there entered into the hall a lad with skin all smudged and blackened, his brow bound round with white or yellow taffeta, and wearing little bells on his leggings, and he danced the dance of the Moors, marching from one end of the hall to the other, making a sort of passage. Then, returning on his steps to the place where he had started, he began another new passage, and in this way continued making divers passages most agreeable to the onlookers.*

The moresque appears then to have been a sort of ballet danced by a person in disguise, his face blackened, in motley costume, little bells on his legs — in short, the traditional figure of a Moor. It is thought that the dance may have originated in the court spectacles which depicted combats between Crusaders and Saracens, and as a matter of fact the moresque was often a sword dance and seems to have been an artistic reworking of a folkloric theme. The irruption of a Black Man in rather wild and at times even obscene dances may have some connection with very primitive social myths which have survived through the centuries although in less ominous and milder form.

It is significant, indeed, that the Moor should often have been a wild man, a madman, death. The dance is found in many countries besides France and the Low Countries — in England it is known as the *Morris dance*, in Germany as the *Morischentanz*, in Spain as the *Morisca* and in Italy as the *Moresca*. It was always an exceptionally eccentric dance which might be presented on the stage of a theater,

or at the conclusion of a banquet or as an interlude in the course of a ball. In a miniature of the *Roman de Paris*, the Master of Wavrin has depicted wild men and a madman in the throes of an unbridled dance, and an engraving by Israël van Meckenem displays all the *bizarrerie* and boisterousness of the moresque.

Without doubt, the *Gille* of Binche — certainly the most extraordinary and picturesque personage of all the carnivals in present-day Belgium — is a descendant of the medieval wild men and Moors. An insistent local tradition asserts that it was at the festivities of Mary of Hungary in Binche that these *Gilles*, first appeared and that they were originally Indians brought specially from America for this entertainment. Whatever truth may be in the tradition, there seems to be something in it to which the popular fancy clings. In any event, the dances of the wild men in the festivities at Binche were certainly not imported from America, since they were no more than a dramatization of an age-old theme from folklore. Incorporated into a court entertainment, the dance of the wild man continued to symbolize the intrusion of nature into society, of violence and unreason as opposed to order and conventions. It perpetuated in much changed circumstances the fertility rites of primitive societies. But at the same time it accepted a stylization which

158

disciplined such outlandish and barbaric folly by imposing on it the rules of art.

What is remarkable about Binche is that, after having borrowed from folklore one of its essential subjects, a court festivity was able to return it to the people enhanced with a certain aura, a new prestige, and this has played a part in keeping the tradition alive through the centuries. Changes may have taken place in the costumes and dances, but, in essence, with his motley raiment, his forehead swathed in a white band, the tall plumes in his headgear, the little bells which jingle at his arms, legs and waist, the *Gille* of the carnival of Binche is a living image today still of the Moor and the wild man of the festivities of the Middle Ages and the Renaissance. Even, despite inevitable alterations, the traditional music hammered out and blared out for his dances may be some sort of echo of the once celebrated moresque.

DANCES AND BASSES DANCES

The moresque was an exceptional dance, something more like a pantomime, a spectacle or even a ballet. In many other dances, the relative importance of the spectacle tended to be less than the social pleasure to be derived from participating in an entertainment in which, after being spectator and listener, one became also actor.

The dance which enjoyed the greatest favor in the Middle Ages was perhaps the *carole*, apparently a dance done in the open with music sung by the dancers, who held hands to form a chain. For accompaniment, almost any instrument could be played by the jongleurs or minstrels, who either themselves led the chain or stood on the sidelines to make their music. A soloist sang the verses in alternation with the refrain, which was sung by all the dancers. During the verses the dance was interrupted, everyone remaining in place and beating out the rhythm, then its snake-like windings began again with the refrain. Originally this type of dance must have been connected with folk diversions. It probably

56. The Tidings Brought to the Shepherds.
Follower of Simon Bening (?).

160

used music of great simplicity with a monotonous refrain of marked rhythm and with verses which permitted the soloist to improvise on a well-known tune, to draw out at length the story and to interject witticisms to the delight of the company. Later, with the rise of forms such as the rondeau, virelai and ballade, the carole too was subjected to poetic stylization. The music intended for dancing must have been monodic with at times some sort of improvised polyphony, and was only rarely written down. As a matter of fact, even the few pieces we have in notation are of dubious authenticity, since most often they were no more than dances invented by skilled poets and musicians in what they pretended, or imagined, was a folk style.

Medieval texts often make a distinction between the carole, which was a round dance, and the *dance* proper, which was performed in couples or small groups and which was often quite formal and more complicated, with steps, movements and changes of partners. These dances might have been performed among the people, but it was in the courts that the many varieties were invented, developed and grew fashionable. Among the most frequently cited dances of the Middle Ages was the *estampie,* but by the fifteenth century it had gone out of style. The manuals written then by dancing masters – the *De Practica seu arte tripudii* by Guglielmo Ebreo, the *Libro dell'arte del danzare* by Antonio Cornazano, the *De arte saltandi et choreas ducendi* by Domenico Piacentino and the *Art et instruction de bien dancer* by Michel Toulouze – all are evidence that the court dance was becoming an art no longer dependent on mere tradition but was, instead, acquiring more elevated status through artistic stylization and through being subjected to inflexible rules.

The *basse dance* seems to have been the most important court dance in the fifteenth century, as we know from the manuals which tell us all about the choreography but little or nothing about the music. What we know of the music is mostly due to an admirable manuscript, now in the Bibliothèque Royale of Brussels, which belonged to Margaret of Austria but, in fact, dates back to the fifteenth century. In this small oblong volume, written in gold and silver on black parchment, are the melodies of fifty-nine basses dances without precise indication of rhythm but with conventional letters representing the various steps. Most of these pieces are also found in the manual by Michel Toulouze published in 1495.

It was long believed by scholars that basses dances were simply played as monodies, and no one saw very clearly in what way the rhythm was to be marked. Did the interpreter have the freedom of choosing whatever rhythm pleased him, or did he apply to the tunes certain conventionally fixed rhythmic schemes which perhaps he had to ornament by more complex figurations? Only recently – thanks, in particular, to Gombosi and Bukofzer – has it become evident that the basses dances were a form of polyphony, but of a polyphony that was improvised, using melodies such as those in the Brussels manuscript as *cantus firmus* in the familiar contrapuntal technique. The tune, already known to the dancers, was played slowly, perhaps by a sackbut, in equal time-values, with each note corresponding to a step in the choreography, while above it two oboes added improvised counterpoints which respected certain rhythmic structural points.

Several melodies in the volume of Margaret of Austria have been identified by Charles van den Borren. *Sans faire de vous départie* is the tenor of a chanson by Pierre Fontaine, *Triste plaisir* and *Le doux espoir* are borrowed from chansons by Binchois, *Une fois avant que mourir* and *Languir en mille détresses* are the tenors of anonymous polyphonic chansons, while others, such as *Roti boully joyeulx* and *Marchon la dureau,* may well come from theater songs which had never been arranged polyphonically; finally there are certain themes which must have been written directly as dances : *La Margarite, La Franchoise, La Danse de Clèves, La Danse de Ravestain.*

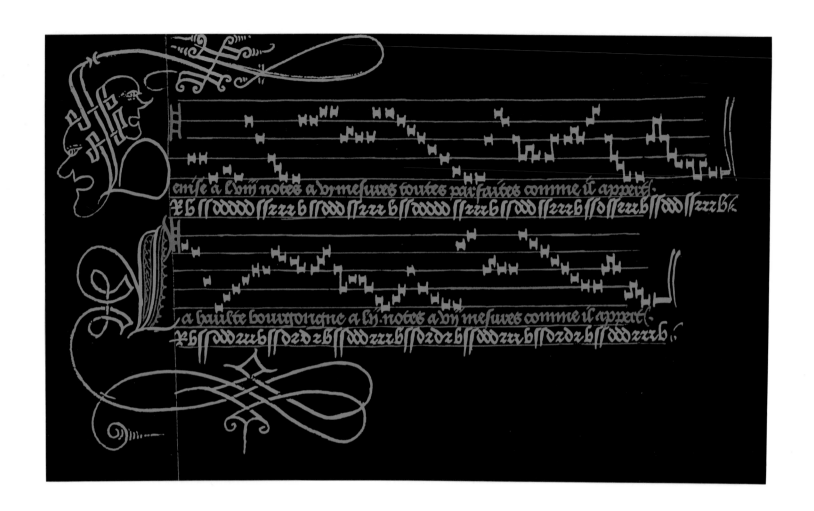

57 and 58. Basses Dances.
Musical manuscript.

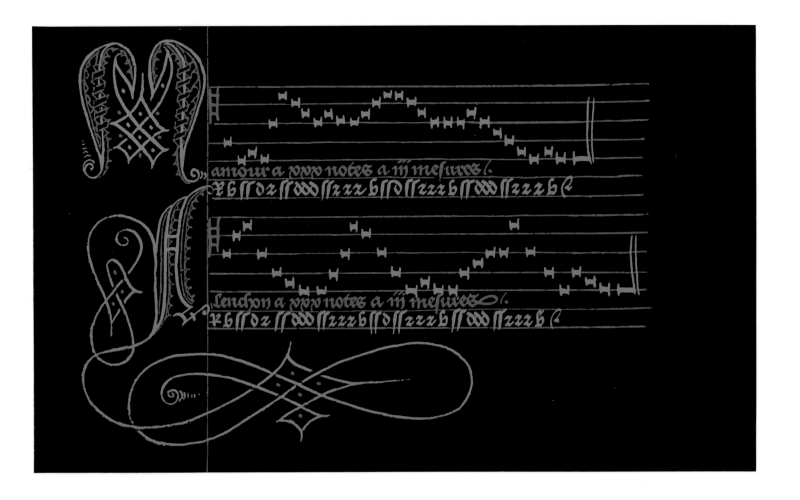

In the fifth book of *Pantagruel*, Rabelais, addicted as always to bizarre enumerations, gives a long list of 180 basses dances, taking the titles from an anonymous collection which specifies the choreography but makes no mention of the music. A few of these titles can be cited for their picturesque character and to prove that often well-known chansons provided the basic melody : *Dessus les marches d'Arras, Par trop je suis brunette, La mousque de Biscaye, En l'umbre d'ung buyssonet, Bon pied, bon œil, Hé ! Dieu, quelle femme j'auoys.*

What seems to be a basse dance is depicted in a miniature by Loyset Liédet in a manuscript of the history of Renaud de Montauban in the Bibliothèque de l'Arsenal in Paris. This shows a ball at the court of King Yon of Gascony on the occasion of the marriage of his daughter Clarisse with the oldest of the four sons of Aymon. Accompanied by three musicians (two shawms and a sackbut) seated on a platform, the couples make a solemn entry into the ballroom with gliding steps of the sort which probably explain the term *basse* – low – in the basse dance.

There is also a *bassadanza* depicted on a marriage chest of the Adimari family in Florence. These marriage chests, known as *cassoni*, were large coffers presented to brides in which they could store their clothes, gifts and dowry. On this famous panel, which must have been painted around 1450 (it is in the Accademia in Florence), one sees the wedding of Boccaccio Adimari with Lisa Ricasoli : under a canopy and facing the loggia of a palace, five couples dance, holding each other by the hand, to the music of four musicians – three oboes and a sackbut – seated on a great chest; in the background is seen the baptistery of Florence.

The basse dance seems to have been most often a ceremonious and grave dance performed in gala attire, the women swathed in long skirts with trains, the men sometimes still wearing their swords. However, according to the manuals of the fifteenth-century Italian dancing masters, the *bassadanza* was a general term which covered four dances of different rhythm and tempo : the *piva*, the *pas de Brabant* or *saltarello*, the *quaternaria* or *saltarello tedesco* and the *bassadanza* proper. The same tune was used for each of the four, intended often to be danced one after the other as a suite, and this explains why such tunes were noted down in equal time-values or in breves and semibreves only, since they were no more than a scaffolding whose articulation varied with the dance chosen, each note corresponding to a step in the choreography.

DANCES OF THE SIXTEENTH CENTURY

In the following century it became more common to note down dances in their polyphonic versions. This innovation coincides with the beginning of emancipation of instrumental music, which, until then, had not been considered apart from vocal music or had been too humble in function to merit being written out. In the sixteenth century, along with certain pieces which had always served as dances, other instrumental pieces retained nothing of dance character except the formal schemes and rhythms, neglecting any functional use and becoming truly a kind of pure music. An important body of material grew out of these, including such forms as the *pavane*, which was composed with high art and was full of harmonic experiment. Dances were also organized into unitary cycles : contrasted in tempo – either fast or slow – and in rhythm – triple or duple – they were grouped into a *suite* which remained in the same key and often constituted a series of variations on a single theme.

The Flemish did not play as important a part in the history of music for the dance as in other types of music in this period. Their style dominated the mass, motet, chanson – those genres that were basically vocal – but in dance music they merely followed the fashions of France and Italy. Nevertheless, the collections published in the Low Countries by Susato and by Phalèse and Bellère are in no way inferior in quality and quantity to those published in France by Attaingnant and Moderne.

164

59. Ball at the Court of King Yon of Gascony Before the Betrothal of His Daughter Clarissa with Renaud de Montauban, Eldest of the Four Sons of Aymon.

Loyset Liédet or workshop (?).

The most important collection produced in the Low Countries was *Het derde musyck boexcken*, published in Antwerp by Tielman Susato in 1551 and containing *alerhande danserye* (all sorts of dance tunes) : thirteen *basse dansen*, nine *ronden*, six *branlen*, eight *allemaingien*, seven *pavanen* and fifteen *nieuwe gaillarden*. The names suffice to show to what extent these were mere copies of the French dances in vogue. As music, they are merely utilitarian with no great ambitions to be more. The principal melody is carried by the upper voice, and the other parts keep pace with it in chordal manner which helps stress the rhythm. Nevertheless, Susato preserves some rudimentary polyphonic style, which perhaps makes his arrangements more attractive than his French models. No indication is given as to what instruments are to play the four parts, the title itself asserting that they are *bequaem om spelen op alle musicale instrumenten*, just as Phalèse in his publications was to say that his dances were adaptable for voices as well as for all musical instruments.

Although *Het derde musyck boexcken* states that the dance pieces were *gheecomponeerd ende naer d'instrumenten ghestelt duer Tielman Susato*, there is no reason to suppose that Susato was the composer in the modern sense of the word, for most often he merely adapted into polyphonic style and arranged for dancing these pieces, which he had borrowed from all sorts of sources. The pavane *Mille regrets* takes its tune from a chanson by Josquin, the basses dances *Le cueur est bon* and *C'est une dure départie* come from Claudin de Sermisy, and certain dances are based on monodic theater songs. For a galliard, Susato appropriated the melody of a well-known Flemish song, *Ghequetst ben ick van binnen*, which had also served for a *Souterliedeken*. Finally there are pieces which may derive from peasant dances, for instance the *Hoboecken dans*, whose title refers to a village near Antwerp and which seems very popular in character.

Many of the melodies used by Susato had been used before him by Attaingnant; others were to be

taken up by Phalèse and Bellère, who published two other dance collections, one in 1571 whose title announced it to be a *First book of dance pieces, containing several pavanes, passamezzos, allemandes, gaillardes, branles, etc., the whole fitting for all musical instruments, newly put together from several books*, and another in 1583 which proclaimed itself a *Collection of dance tunes, containing almost all sorts of dances such as pavanes, passamezzos, allemandes, gaillardes, branles and many others, arranged for the voice as well as for all musical instruments, newly put together by certain learned musicians and other lovers of all sorts of harmony*. The titles make no fuss about admitting the borrowings which were customary for such merely functional music. Written in a style quite different from what must have been the improvised polyphony of the basse dance in the fifteenth century, and different also from the complex polyphony of motets and masses, these dance pieces, despite their simplicity, possess much charm.

Certain dances retained a highly aristocratic character, above all the pavane, about which the *Orchésographie* states : *It serves for kings, princes and dignified noblemen to display themselves on days of solemn feasts in their great cloaks and robes of state. At such times they are accompanied by their queens, princesses and ladies, the long trains of their gowns let loose and trailing, or sometimes*

borne by maidens. And the said pavanes are played by oboes and sackbuts, and lead off the great ball and make it last until the dancers have circled the hall two or three times. Such pavanes are also employed in masquerades for the entries of triumphal chariots with gods and goddesses, emperors or kings full of majesty. The music of the pavane preserved a certain melancholy and grave distinction inherited from its origins, and the galliard was generally associated with it, succeeding it in a more rapid rhythm, often merely a variation on the same tune.

The branle, however, drew its origins from the people. The branle, asserts the Orchésographie, is danced by valets and chamber maids, though sometimes by young gentlemen and ladies when they go masked as peasants and shepherds, or when they wish to amuse themselves privily. The numerous varieties of branles described by Arbeau testify to their peasant origins : branles of Burgundy, Champagne, Poitou, Avignon, Hainaut, Scotland, trioris of Brittany, as well as branles of the peas, of the clogs, of the horses, of mustard and the like, and besides there

167

are simple branles, double branles and finally "gay" branles. Branles were not danced in couples but, as so often in peasant dances, in a line or circle.

In the sixteenth century – and this was typical of the period – aristocratic dances like the pavane and popular dances like the branle were mingled in the princely courts as well as in middle-class frolics. Some attempt was made to resist the *danses modernes* such as the *volta* and the *courante,* which came from Italy and were often viewed with disapprobation. But the moralizers made no headway, and, like Brantôme, most contemporaries appreciated the volta, which *by causing the gown to fly up always reveals something so agreeable to the eye that I have beheld many men simply lose their heads and float off in ecstasy.*

In the ballroom, the dancers were also actors playing roles, for themselves as much as for others : the bourgeois played at being nobles when they danced the pavane, princes played at being peasants by dancing branles and rounds, and princesses and middle-class misses alike boldly delighted in playing the hussy in voltas and courantes.

Basses dances in the fifteenth century were strictly reserved to the courts and were not danced elsewhere. But in the following century both bourgeoisie and aristocracy performed the same dances, although the nobility continued to set the tone by imposing a certain formality on the choreography. But just as had been the case with the chanson, a wider public brought about a profound modification in the spirit and form of the dances.

MUSIC OF THE PEOPLE

The kinds of music practiced by peasants in the country and humble folk in the towns must have differed much from the songs and dances we know from surviving texts. But we are condemned to know little of it, scarcely more than the distorted echoes to be found in the art music of the time, for it was neither written down nor transmitted in any way save by oral and direct tradition. When scholars

began to take an interest in it, when it became a concern of the cultured, this sort of music was dubbed *folkloristic* but, at that very moment and through that same fact, its authenticity became threatened and compromised, because learned music, which was then tending to spread out to all of society, impregnated it and absorbed it. It was not until the nineteenth century that anyone began to note this music down carefully, and at that time it was already becoming frozen and unproductive; its decline and death were at hand. Such notation came too late and could trace no more than a distorted picture of the authentic music of the peasants and common folk of the past.

The rare attempts made in the past to write down such music are no more reliable. Rounds like the *Hoboecken dans* found in Susato's collection are not authentic transcriptions of popular pieces but only stylizations inspired more or less remotely by folk music. We must resign ourselves to the conclusion that to understand the popular diversions of the past, we must depend on literary allusions, miniatures, paintings, engravings in which we find peasants forming circles or snakelike chains in the tradition of the carole and sometimes also dancing in couples. But we shall never know how the music sounded in those peasant dances with fiddle and bagpipes that Bruegel delighted to paint.

The songs of the people are scarcely better known. Folklore experts consider as authentic only those pieces that have survived in the oral tradition, and they compare the different versions they find in regions sometimes widely separated in order to measure their areas of diffusion. By studying pieces which have come down in folklore, it is at times not impossible to discover historical allusions which permit us to date them to some extent, and by analyzing the internal structure of the music one can attempt to determine the period from which it sprang. But this is work of dubious value, because what characterizes the oral tradition is its mobility and its vagaries. In the course of centuries a song rarely

61. Peasant Dance.
Pieter Bruegel.

remains unchanged : a word grown incomprehensible is replaced by another, an archaic inflection is modernized. On the basis of all the variants of a song, the folklore experts succeed in singling out the strata laid down by traditions through the centuries, and they strive to reconstruct what may have been the original schema, the *Urmelodie*, the archetype. But they no longer believe today that it is possible to discover the primitive and pristine state of a song known only through oral tradition, for a folk song has no existence other than in its mobility and its multiplicity.

Another method that has been tried is the examination of the written-down material of the fifteenth and sixteenth centuries in an attempt to isolate the essence of the folk songs of the period. But how can one know what was truly a folk song in those times ? No one believes any more in the myth of collective authorship of a folk song. Its author was never the people : the author may have been some kind of minstrel practicing a traditional art but he may also, and just as likely, have been a learned musician. What makes a song into a popular song, into a folk song, is not its origin but rather its diffusion into social groups which do not practice a learned art. What counts is the function it might assume in a certain society and also the way it was transmitted without ever having been written down.

In short, then, it is as difficult to determine if some song surviving in the oral tradition today really dates back to the fifteenth or sixteenth century as it is to decide if some other song, noted down in some form in the Renaissance, was really a popular song in that time.

There is a tendency to think that certain tunes must have come from the people merely because they have come down to us as monodies. But the fact is that monodies also may very well have been written by learned musicians and been diffused only in such limited social circles as those which practiced polyphony. Among the monodies of the fifteenth century found, for example, in the Bayeux manuscript (Paris, Bibliothèque Nationale) there are ballades and virelais no different in form and spirit from polyphonic works of the same period. The songs included in the collections of the clerk of Namur mentioned earlier must have had the same function and the same public as the polyphonic music of the fifteenth century.

In the following century, a large repertory of monodic songs on political subjects sprang up in Flanders, the *beggars' songs,* which date from the time of the so-called Beggars' Revolts against the Spanish, among them the very fine *Slaet op den trommel* (Beat the drum) and *Wij Geuskens willen nu singhen* (We beggars would like to sing). Songs of this type became very popular, but their origins are to be found in learned music. Often they were simply adaptations of new words, inspired by political events, to the well-known melody of a love song, a drinking song, a *Souterliedeken* or a theater song.

Of peasant music in the Renaissance we seem to know nothing whatsoever, unless it be a few vestiges surviving in a confused oral tradition. And yet it is in that tradition that can be found the most authentic documents of an autonomous art independent of all learned creation. The pieces which appear to be most closely related to the folk character are, in fact, the theater songs, which were so success-

63. A Moresque.
Workshop of the Master of Wavrin.

ful as to reach all classes of society, including those who could not read music, and to have passed into the countryside after having originated in the towns.

MUSIC IN THE THEATER

Songs were introduced under the most diverse pretexts in moralities, farces and other entertainments. Indeed, sometimes no pretext at all was needed. It had simply become the custom to begin or end a play with a song :

> En prenant congé de ce lieu,
> Une chanson pour dire adieu.

(In taking leave of this place, / We'll sing a song to say farewell.)

Or then again, the action might be interrupted to provide a little musical diversion :

> Chantons un motet d'apparence
> Afin que la noble assistance
> En soit un petit consolée.

(Let's sing a stately motet / So that this noble company / Some pleasure yet may take.)

As we see from this verse, comedians needed to know how to sing and also to play :

> Vous verrez jouer farces
> Dessous les establis
> Badines et moralles
> Des enfans sans soucy.
> Ensemble la musique,
> Farces et rhétoriques,
> Chanter et triumpher.

(Farces you'll see played / Upon this wooden stage, / Gay ones and moral, / By our happy-go-lucky crew [the enfans sans soucy were a troupe of actors, probably most of them students]. / Along with music, / Farces and proud speeches, / We'll sing and win your praise.)

Theater songs were most often sung unaccompanied, as monodies. Brown found more than four hundred in French farces and moralities between 1400 and 1550, and tracked down the music for many of them, either as monodies in the chansonniers or as tunes incorporated in polyphonic works, or again in what England and Germany called a quodlibet, France a fricassée, Spain an ensalada – polyphonic potpourris jumbling together bits and tag ends of all sorts of songs in public favor.

Such a bibliographical study helps us see how, once introduced in the theater, a song could launch off on an independent career. Thus, Je voys, je viens, mon cœur s'envolle, which had been sung in the farce of the Pèlerinage de mariage, was transformed into a Christmas song, Chantez Noël, clergeons d'escolle, and into a Protestant spiritual song, En esprit jusqu'au ciel je volle. The drinking song Nous sommes de l'ordre de Saint Babouin, which began in the farce La Résurrection de Jenin à Paulme, became the Noël Nous sommes de l'ordre du corps Jésu Christ, and was also given a polyphonic setting in a four-voice piece by Loyset Compère found in the Odhecaton.

Despite these deliberate and conscious adaptations, the true process by which a song is taken up by the folk escapes us, and it is scarcely possible to follow the avatars in text and music a song went through in oral transmission and diffusion throughout society.

Music was also used in the theater for dances and various kinds of intermezzos. The book of instructions for the stage-manager for the performance at Mons in 1501 of the Mystère de la Passion by Arnoul Gréban provides a document of exceptional interest since it has preserved all the stage directions. Thus we know that music was required for every change of scene. While the actor was moving toward the next "mansion" called for by his role, there could be an interruption which the medieval stage-manager called a pose in French or a silete in Latin, the latter being an imperative which means literally "be quiet." The two terms express very well the notion implied, that at these moments, when the audience might become distracted, it was most necessary to keep them quiet, and this could best be done by music. It was thus that the words pose and silete became synonyms for musical interlude.

173

Also in the *Mystère de la Passion* the stage-manager specifies that when Noah steps out of the Ark after the Flood he is to kneel and address a prayer to God; *then, when he has said his prayer, a silete is sung in Paradise, or the minstrels play, or some instrument is heard, or there is a pose on the organ.* Often it is specified that music must be adapted to the necessities of the actors : *when they go off stage to make themselves ready, if they take too long there should be a pose on the organ in Nazareth.* After the Annunciation, the Angel cries :

> *Chantons à dextre et à senestre*
> *De tous poins nous resjoyra.*

(Sing to the right, sing to the left ! / On every hand let us rejoice !)

and the stage-manager adds : *In Paradise there is great joy and they should sing,* giving the text of the song. After the Nativity, he notes, *one should take pains to show the exultation in Paradise.* God the Father concludes a tirade of fifty verses with these words : *Now let there be heard a beautiful silete,* and the stage-manager adds : *Now there must be great rejoicing in Paradise, and there should be sung as a finished thing* [that is, in counterpoint, *res facta*] *what follows,* and he specifies a chanson for all the angels together. When the shepherds rejoice together at the birth of the Lord, the scene ends thus :

Gombault : *Bien en devons faire grand joye*
S'en yray chantant par la voye.

(Now must we proclaim our joy, / I'll sing the news on every hand.)

Rifflart : *Commence donc, je te ayderay*
Et avecques toy, chanteray.

(Begin then and I'll help, / I'll join my voice to yours.)

Allars : *Et moy aussi, de ma musette*
Car bien debvons joye mener.

(I too, and with my bagpipes, / For now must we rejoice.)

and the stage-manager notes : *And then they sing and dance.*

An angel is to make pronouncement in the name of the Lord. *Then he must sound the trumpet and afterwards he reads from a scroll what follows.* At the banquet of Herod, Florence – who corresponds to Salome – *dances a moresque to the sound of a small drum and then the drum is silent a while and the girl continues to dance.* When, on the morning of the Resurrection, the Son rejoins the Father, it is indicated : *Here, God speaks with three voices,* which is clearly a musical symbol of the Trinity; a manuscript states : *Note that the allocution of God the Father can be delivered understandably and attractively by three voices, that is, a treble, a countertenor and a bass in tune together.* There are directions also for the singers to change mansions according to the needs of the dramatic action : *Here those who sing motets in Paradise should be given a signal to climb down from Paradise to Limbo to sing a motet there at the right moment.*

The mysteries played in Flemish used music in the same manner. For the performance on the Grand-Place of Brussels in 1444 of *De eerste bliscap van Maria,* first of a series of seven mysteries representing the Seven Joys of the Virgin, the musical interludes were designated as *Silete, sanc of spel, Hier sal men singhen of spelen, Pause, sanc of spel.*

Music also had a part in the *montre,* the parade of the actors through the city to advertise their performance on the days preceding it. The day of the performance itself the procession formed at the place where the actors dressed. It paraded around the playing area *to the sound of trumpets, clarions, busines, organs, harps, drums and the like, playing all the time.*

Although little documentary material has survived, once again pictorial evidence provides us with interesting details. In a series of tapestries illustrating the morality play *La Condamnation de Banquet,* now in the Musée Lorrain, Nancy, there are several musicians, and in a large canvas painted around 1540, now in Reims, which depicts the mystery play *La Vengeance de Jésus Christ,* four musicians on a platform play for a round danced by around a dozen men and women.

In the life of the time, all public occasions tended to take theatrical form. Weddings, funerals, the Joyous Entries of princes and potentates provided all that was needed in the way of a simple and effective dramatic plot, and the entire city became a stage to be decorated lavishly. A total spectacle was created with the collaboration of architects, painters, actors, mimes, mountebanks, acrobats and musicians; even the citizens themselves had a role to play. The entire city was decorated with banners, tapestries and triumphal arches; in the processions there were chariots with symbolic groups, and dramatic spectacles were presented in public places or palaces.

The music involved in these festivities and ceremonies was so linked to its immediate function that generally nothing was done to write it down for posterity. To recover at least the spirit of it, we are obliged to depend on literary accounts, but unfortunately the reports of sixteenth-century eyewitnesses are much less prolix than those of their Burgundian predecessors and do little more than mention the trumpets and oboes *which sounded most melodiously* or the tumult in the streets when instruments brayed out along with the acclamations of the crowd in holiday mood.

Pictorial evidence is more profitable here. The *Triumphs of the Emperor Maximilian* are particularly remarkable documents for our study although they depict an ideal, imaginary celebration, not a historic one. Maximilian wished his memory to be glorified by the publication after his death of a considerable number of works whose themes he set and whose contents he sometimes himself dictated. There are epics such as the *Theuerdank*, the *Freidall* and the *Weißkunig*, and leading the series, where one might have expected a genealogy or a calendar of the events in the Emperor's life or at least a book

of the saints, there is instead an *Arch of Triumph* and a *Triumphal Procession*. All of these books were to be illustrated with engravings.

The *Triumphal Procession*, whose publication was completed in 1526, contains 135 woodcuts of which 67 were designed by Hans Burgkmair. The entire series of prints was so arranged that they could be pasted together to form a long scroll which, unwound, revealed a sumptuous procession. According to the program established in 1512 by Maximilian, the procession was to include, as Pierre du Colombier reports, *a herald mounted on a griffon, the title, drummers on foot and horseback, hunts, five dignitaries of the court, musicians on five chariots drawn by elk, buffaloes and camels, two chariots with buffoons, masqueraders, then twenty-five plates devoted to fencing, combats on foot and horse, tourneys, horsemanship, the procession of the Burgundian marriage with the countries of Austria and Burgundy, the small triumphal chariot or marriage chariot designed by Dürer, the wars of Maximilian, trophy-wagons, vessels, his famous artillery, treasures, the statues being cast at Innsbruck for the mausoleum of the Emperor, fifers and trombonists, heralds with trumpets, the triumphal chariot of the Queen, the cup-bearer with the banner of the Empire, the Marshal of the Empire with his sword, the great triumphal chariot, the princes, counts, lords, knights, the chariots used in a military manœuvre of which Maximilian was particularly proud, savages, baggage-trains, and finally the two men who had drawn up this entire notion : the historian Stabius and the painter Koelderer.*

The very idea of such a cortège was inspired by Humanism, but its imitation of the ancient imperial Roman triumphs did not go so far as to dress it up in antique garb. Although the engravings at times indulge in mythological allegory – the great chariot of the Emperor is drawn by horses representing the Virtues and they are guided by a female figure who stands for Reason – there is nevertheless a constant concern with realism, and actual personages of the entourage of the Emperor are portrayed. There is the organist Paul Hofhaimer in a chariot drawn by a camel, playing his instrument while an assistant works the bellows. In another chariot ride the cantors of the Imperial chapel choir, while still another carries three lutanists and two viol-players, and a fourth has performers on lutes, viols, tabors, flutes and oboes. While the players of drums, trumpets, trombones and oboes occupy the places one would expect in such a procession, lute players and singers are depicted mostly to bear witness to the magnificence of the Imperial household, although such musicians may in fact have participated occasionally in such public displays as this procession.

It was in Bruges in 1515 that Charles V opened the cycle of great fêtes of his reign. The Joyous Entry of the young prince into that city was described in detail by Remy Du Puys in *The Triumphal and Solemn Entry Made upon the Coming of the Most High and Most Powerful Prince Monsieur Charles, Prince of the Spains, Archduke of Austria, into His City of Bruges.* The theme chosen was the greatness and decline of Bruges and its hopes for a renascence to be brought in by the Prince. The communal authorities insisted on presenting, as part of the pageantry, tableaux vivants which, by analogy with biblical episodes, showed the time when Bruges had been a prosperous city under the dukes of Burgundy; for their part, the foreign merchants established in Bruges also desired to contribute to the glorification of the young Prince. All of this has been preserved in the miniatures in the manuscript of Du Puys, now in Vienna, and in the woodcuts of the publication drawn from them. Among these tableaux vivants there were, for example, Orpheus playing his harp in a pleasure garden, the garden representing the kingdom of the young Prince, who, like Orpheus, was invited, to *tune the instrument of his conduct, that is to say the institution of his reign, in perfect consonance and melodious harmony with all excellent virtues.* In the miniatures and engravings, we glimpse the streets

hung with tapestries, the banners, the instrumentalists in motley costumes who play from towers, battlements and windows, and finally the Prince seated on a throne surrounded by his aunt, sisters and a trio of musicians.

There are innumerable other examples of these solemn fêtes and Joyous Entries. We have descriptions of the entries of Charles V into Antwerp in 1515 and into Cambrai and Valenciennes in 1540, and the receptions of Prince Philip, the future Philip II, into Brussels, Louvain, Ghent, Bruges, Lille, Tournai, Arras and Antwerp in 1549. These provide material for the study of the change in taste from Gothic decoration to a classicizing style as well as for the role of the Chambers of Rhetoric in the execution of dramatic scenes and tableaux vivants. About music, however, they reveal little, for relevant documents are exceptionally rare.

Nevertheless, a booklet dating from 1515 recounting the spectacles organized for the entry into Antwerp of the young Archduke Charles and of Maximilian was accompanied by the publication of two motets by Benedictus de Opitiis, thus providing evidence that, at least occasionally, polyphonic music had a place in these fêtes. Further confirmation is given by the texts of numerous ceremonial motets of the fifteenth and sixteenth centuries.

When, in 1540, on his way from France and accompanied by the Dauphin and the Duke of Orleans, Charles V entered Cambrai, at that time an independent archdiocese, he was welcomed by the notables of the city and by twelve trumpeters dressed in black and red. After the official salutations, *the said twelve trumpeters began to play most melodiously, and without interruption, preceding His Majesty on the way to the episcopal palace.* The bells began to ring when the procession approached the

176

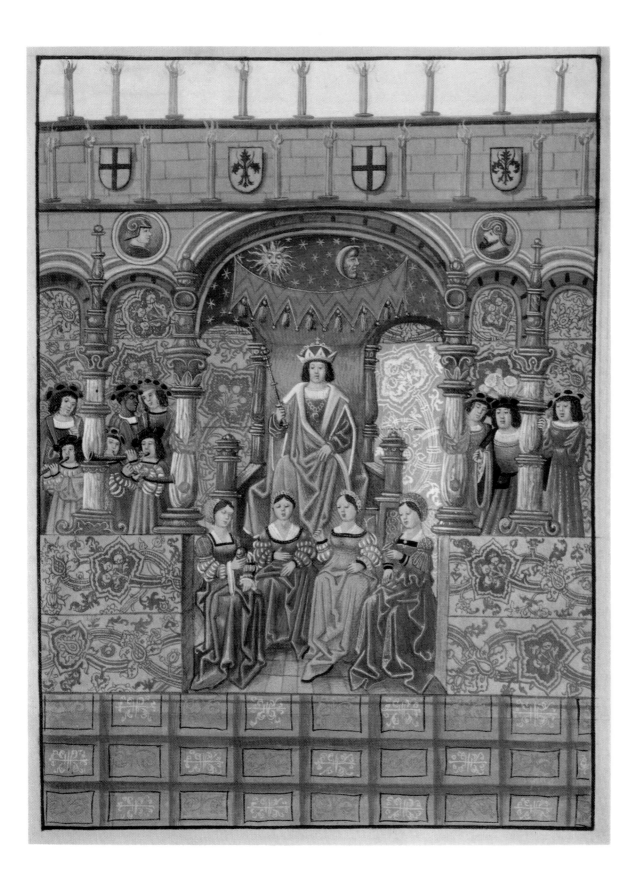

city, and the Emperor traversed streets illuminated by 7,500 torches (it was six in the evening) and adorned with triumphal arches and heraldic trappings. On many squares and in the streets farces and mystery plays were performed on platforms set up on trestles. Among the actors of the *Mystery of the Holy Trinity,* played in the Rue Saint-Georges, *there were handsome young boys and girls who, when the said Majesty passed under the said arch, began to sing in beautiful, sweet and harmonious counterpoint, "O vera unitas."* At the moment the Emperor stepped into the market place with his suite, *besides and along with the splendid resonance of the said trumpets, there were, at the top of the city hall ... a great number of instruments called clarions and oboes making great melody. And a great many little children all crying out loudly in the Italic fashion, "Imperio! Imperio!" which filled the said market place and all the town with delightful joy and harmony.*

At the episcopal palace, the Emperor was welcomed before the open door by the bishop, the chapter, and the choirboys dressed in cloth of gold, and from the summit of a triumphal arch the cantors of the bishop *sang melodiously songs and motets made and composed in honor of His Majesty and all the said princes, and notably a motet with excellent music composed by Master Jehan Courtois, Master of the Chapel of the said Most Reverend Monseigneur,* after which a Te Deum was sung within the church. The next day, in the course of mass in the cathedral, *the cantors of the chapel being in the choir loft above and very numerous, they sang with great melody the above mentioned motet by Courtois... Directly this was finished, the vicar-cantors of said church, who were XXXIII in number, being below in the said choir, sang in honor of the glorious Virgin Mary the motet "Præter rerum seriem."* During his exit from the city, as he traversed the market place, the Emperor was saluted by fanfares of trumpets and clarions played from the top of the city hall.

The motet *O vera unitas* must have been composed especially to celebrate the ephemeral friendship between the Emperor and the King of France. *Præter rerum seriem* is a well-known motet by Josquin Desprez, and *Venite, populi terræ* is a motet by Courtois which has been preserved and which sings of the virtues of peace.

Funerals also served as the pretext for lavish ceremonies intended to impress the citizen-spectators. The obsequies for Charles V at Brussels on December 29, 1558 were commemorated in a luxurious volume published by Plantin with drawings by Jean Duatecum engraved by his brother Lucas. At the head of the procession, which marched from the palace to the church of Sainte-Gudule, came the clergy and musicians with trumpets and kettle-drums, followed by the notables of the city, 200 mourners dressed in long robes and hoods as they appear on the tombs of the dukes of Burgundy, the officers of the Imperial household, standard-bearers, an allegorical ship recalling the victories of the reign, captains and dignitaries bearing the insignia of Imperial majesty, the Emperor's horse riderless and with black plumes, nobles representing the Imperial possessions, Philip II in long black robe and hood wearing the Order of the Golden Fleece around his neck, and finally the knights of the Order. Music was heard during the cortège and in the course of the funeral services, which went on for two days.

Along with these civic ceremonies – Joyous Entries, triumphs, funerals – whose primary aim was to strengthen the bonds between the prince and his people, there were other festivities of more strictly local character, such as those processions in which participated the religious orders, the various parishes of the town, the city magistrates, the high dignitaries and the entire citizenry, marching with banners, statues of the Virgin borne aloft, precious reliquaries and the Holy Sacrament. A painting by Van Alsloot, now in the Prado Museum, shows in painstaking detail one of such processions in Brussels, and in it we can make out a group of musicians playing oboes, bassoons and sackbuts.

The *ommegangs*, wich ever since the Middle Ages have enjoyed such popularity in the cities of the Low Countries, were at the outset no different from other processions, but various new elements progressively enriched them. To the customary parade of religious confraternities, artisan guilds and city authorities were added chariots honoring the saints of Brabant, and later there were also tableaux vivants organized around a theme which varied with the circumstances. Thus, at Antwerp in 1559 was celebrated the return of peace and abundance; in 1561 the vicissitudes of all things mortal in war and peace and richness and poverty; in 1562 the Ages of Man, Time and Eternity; in 1564 the good and the evil use of wealth. Music contributed to the procession with singers of hymns and instrumentalists playing marches or musicians playing from the chariots : Licentiousness played the flute in an languorous pose, Madness beat upon a tabor, the Muses warbled a polyphonic chanson.

TOWN MUSICIANS

The musicians who took part in these processions and festivities were mostly communal minstrels, drummers and players on wind instruments – oboes, flutes, trumpets, cornets and sackbuts.

Ever since the Middle Ages, in the Low Countries most towns of any importance had musicians in their employ. There was, for example, always a watchman on one of the city towers with his trumpet, shawm or cornet to sound the curfew or give the alarm. In Germany, France and the Low Countries, many songs present this personage who warns lovers of the coming of dawn : *die wachter blaest sinen horen* say those songs which, in French, are called *chansons d'aube* – aubades, songs of dawn – and in Flemish, more explicitly, are termed *wachter liede-ren* – songs of the watchman. The watchman's principal jobs were to announce official communications and to serve as messenger.

65. Town Minstrels.
Heinrich Aldegrever.   179

On an artistic and social level higher than that of
the mere watchman, the city musicians were called
minstrels, *menestreux, ministrelen, speellieden* or,
from the names of their instruments, *stadtspijpers,
schalmeypijpers* or *trommelslaeghers*. They wore
livery – a costume of colored cloth and often a
wide collar with a pendant – and their instruments
were decorated with streamers bearing the arms of
the city. A decree of 1505 regulating the functions
of the town musicians of Malines tells us that they
were to play on cornets and other instruments during solemn masses celebrated by order of the magistrates; they were to play at the town hall *met
schalmijen, trompetten ende andere instrumenten*
late mornings every Saturday, Sunday, holiday and
days preceding public festivities; in the course of
banquets organized by the town, they were to entertain on stringed instruments and flutes; they
could not refuse to participate in any service required by the town; in order to maintain a desirable
standard of performance, they were ordered to re-
hearse together at least twice weekly and to obey
a leader.

This official document helps us understand what
these musicians contributed to the life of a city.
They played for fêtes, processions, *ommegangs*;
they offered serenades before houses in which distinguished foreigners were stopping; they entertained at banquets and feasts; they gave open-air
concerts. In short, they served the town in the same
ways as court musicians served princes, and there
can be no doubt that the towns aped the princes in
their use of music.

Socially, town musicians were rated lower than
musicians of church or court, but if the *torenwach-
ter* and the *trommelslaegher* were also messengers
and public servants of humble rank, the players of
cornets, sackbuts and shawms could be musicians
of quality. They frequently played polyphonic chansons and dances, and the best of them were educated
in choir schools and could aspire to permanent positions at some court or in a church.

66. Oboists and Sackbut Players.
Hans Burgkmair.

MINSTRELS AND INSTRUMENTALISTS

Alongside these town musicians, there were also
players of instruments who quite independently
offered their services to individual citizens for private festivities, weddings and balls. Throughout the
Middle Ages there had been minstrels wandering
from castle to castle to sing ballads and play on the
fiddle or harp, and these were, in the words of Colin
Muset :

> *... gent qui vont contant*
> *De cort à autre et vont trouvant*
> *Chansonètes, mots et fabliaus*
> *Pour gaaigner les biaux morsiaux.*

(... folk content to go / From court to court and
make up / Songs and ditties, poems and fables / To
line their paunches with the choicest morsels.)

The fiddle player Lodewijc Van Valbeke, *de goe-
de vedelare* boasted of in the *Brabantsche Yeesten*
for his talent in inventing estampies, was famous
throughout Brabant at the end of the thirteenth
century :

> *Hij was d'eerste die vant*
> *Van stampien die manieren*
> *Die men noch hoert antieren.*

(He was the first of all / To invent the way of
playing estampies / In the way still done today.)

Vagabond musicians who lived on the gifts and
bounty of anyone willing to listen had not disappeared in the fifteenth century, but they often
sought to be taken into the regular service of some
prince. Philip the Good and the dukes of Burgundy
permanently maintained a dozen of them, and they
always welcomed heartily the minstrels other lords
sent to them as messengers. Moreover, whenever

they visited a town, they were always willing to listen to the local musicians.

As far back as the thirteenth century there were minstrels in the towns who played and sang for the common citizenry. All of these minstrels, no matter where they lived or whom they served, met together each year during Lent, when musical entertainments were banned. Their gatherings often took place in the cities of the northern principalities, and there are mentions of minstrels *going to school,* as the chroniclers put it, at Bruges in 1318, Ypres in 1313 and 1432, Brussels in 1370, Ghent in 1378, Beauvais in 1398 and 1435, Mons in 1406 and 1422, Cambrai in 1427 and 1440 as well as *en Allemaigne,* which could mean either Germany or the eastern regions of the Low Countries. It seems that these annual conclaves were the occasion to compare techniques and for every minstrel to broaden his repertoire with new songs and dances. However, the practice appears to have been abandoned in the second half of the fifteenth century.

At that period, the unattached players of instruments in the cities organized themselves into guilds modeled after those of the other trades. There had already been such groupings in the fourteenth century, but it was in the fifteenth and sixteenth centuries that they acquired some importance. At Mons there was a Confraternity of Saint Cecilia and at Brussels a Brotherhood of Saint Job, and their principal purpose, or at least the one most insisted on, was charitable and religious, grouping the town musicians together to lend help in case of need, to make their devotions in common to a patron saint, to do charity. However, other, less altruistic concerns were more discreetly put forward and created solid ties among the members. They were especially interested in barring from any remunerative musical activity those who were not citizens of the town or members of the confraternity, thereby guaranteeing that musicians merely passing through the place might not be allowed to work. These confraternities gathered together all those in any city who wished to

earn their living by playing some instrument. At Mons, in 1588, to be accepted by the assembly of masters, the candidate had to be able to play the oboe, cornet, flute and violin and must have served as an apprentice for at least two years. Elsewhere, the apprenticeship might be as long as six years. *In order to become a master,* said the regulations at Mons, *he must be able to play two pieces of music on each of said instruments, such songs as the masters see fit to choose;* the test imposed to become a master was not the composition of a piece of music but merely the performance of certain pieces from memory. For many, however, music was no more than a means of picking up a bit of extra cash on holidays.

These, then, were musicians who have left scarcely any concrete evidence of their activity, an activity which was, for all that, intense and, in relation to the mass of inhabitants of a city, perhaps played a part more important than that of musicians educated in the learned art of counterpoint.

Besides the theoretical and systematic instruction dispensed in the church schools, there was then another kind of apprenticeship which was strictly practical as well as traditional. Instrumentalists thus trained were held in contempt by the singers of polyphony as much as by the learned theorists : they knew nothing of the harmony of numbers and of the subtleties of mensural notation and were furthermore quite incapable of writing a bit of counterpoint. In the opinion of the educated classes the minstrels were at the very bottom of the hierarchy of musicians. Nevertheless, they were the ones who served up musical entertainment for a good part of society. Regrettably, it is difficult to know to what extent the music they made may have differed from that of learned musicians.

What matters here is that, to satisfy highly diverse needs, society in the fifteenth and sixteenth centuries could call on a great variety of musicians according to the functions they were to fulfill and according to the public they were to satisfy.

Chapter 7

67. The Prodigal Son Among the Courtesans.
Oil on wood.

The Sound of the Past

When we attempt to study any music of the past, to situate it within its historical period with all the social and cultural aspects thereby implied, to analyze it and to pin down its place within an organic evolution, we do it not out of mere intellectual curiosity but rather in response to deep-lying artistic necessities. Music of past times is an integral part of the aesthetic universe of the man of today, for that universe includes all music whether of the present or past – a past no longer confined to a few privileged great names like Bach, Mozart or Beethoven. Just as in painting we do not now dismiss as "primitives" van Eyck, van der Weyden and Memling but have come to understand and love them, so today we admit that the motets or chansons of Guillaume Dufay, Josquin Desprez and Roland de Lassus can stir the listener as deeply as any symphony of the eighteenth century or any Romantic concerto. In the museum of the ear – an imaginary museum embracing all music – music of all times is subjected to the same value judgments. But these judgments are neither spontaneous nor naïve. They are conditioned by a storehouse of culture which is, as it were, in a perpetual state of siege : some new work may appear at any moment to overthrow all the carefully established hierarchies. Historical consciousness is a part of our judgment, shaping it and underpinning it. Every work captures our interest at first contact and stirs us to the extent that it

is authentic, to the extent that it makes us perceive the unique character of its beauty, to the extent, finally, that in its language – less rational but more concrete than that of words – we discover in a very special way the world of values with which it was freighted by the epoch which conceived it.

A work of art of the past offers us more than itself : it uncovers the past for us or, rather, it offers us some still-warm morsel of the past within a present world. Because of this, the demands we make upon it are proportionate to the importance we accord to it. Van Meegeren and his fake Vermeers have taught us how much our value judgments may be affected by criteria of authenticity. In essence, then, the awareness of history we glean from a work of art of past times deeply influences the aesthetic judgments we pass on it.

THE NOTION OF MUSIC OF THE PAST
In many civilizations a work of art is only appreciated for the function it fulfills and is promptly discarded when it ceases to be effective. As long as music of their own times satisfied what they expected of it, men disdained music of earlier times or considered it with condescending indifference. But at the moment when a gap opened between the composer and his public there appeared the need to seek in the past those artistic satisfactions the present no longer afforded. The men of the early nineteenth

century who disinterred the music of earlier times did so precisely because the music of their own time spoke a language difficult to decipher, and they hailed what had gone before as something truly admirable. It is this rather odd angle of vision that explains why at first men insisted that this inadequately understood art of former times – with which, in fact, they were barely acquainted – must have been as different as possible from that of the present, something quite rare and exotic. They wanted old music to be completely unlike modern music, to be, in fact, in frank opposition to what was going on around them. A similarly warped attitude led Viollet-le-Duc, when he was disclosing to the world the beauties of medieval architecture, to add to the buildings he restored arches, battlements and capitals dreamed up in his own mind, to make of the Gothic something larger than life, something more gothic than the Gothic.

It was the *Concerts historiques* organized in Paris from 1832 to 1835 by the musicologist Fétis which provided almost the first contacts of modern men with old music. Music of the sixteenth century was played on old instruments and the oddness of the sound counted for a good deal in charming the public. In the same frame of mind as Viollet-le-Duc, Fétis made rather peculiar arrangements of these pieces and perhaps even fabricated some of them – those which, as it happened, enjoyed the greatest success !

Ever since the seventeenth century there had been a science of the history of music whose bases met certain criteria. But it was only when early music fulfilled a real and deep need for men of a certain culture that the science emerged from mere archaeological dilettantism and developed with great rapidity.

Today we tend to lessen the distance between us and the past, to enjoy all the present there is and all the pasts there ever were. As our museum of the ear makes new acquisitions, the musical universe continues unceasingly to push back the frontiers

which once limited it. Johann Sebastian Bach was the first musician to be rediscovered after long neglect and his was the first music of the past to be assimilated into the aesthetic present of the men of the nineteenth century. Since then we have continued to push our explorations farther and farther back : Monteverdi, Palestrina, Lassus, Josquin, Dufay, Machaut, Perotinus and, of course, Gregorian chant have each in turn been resurrected.

Our aesthetic awareness is also a historical awareness: we wish to perceive in works of art of all ages both their uniqueness and their continuity. One of the basic tasks of musicology is therefore to recover the works of earlier times in their most complete authenticity. Just as some people insist on liberating Romanesque churches from the Baroque stuccos which they imagine disfigure them, so also do we aspire to establish what the authentic sound of a mass by Dufay must have been in the period in which it was created.

What the Germans call *Aufführungspraxis* – performance practice, the science of interpretation – is now one of the principal studies of musicology. This must be so because music is an art of a peculiar sort. A painting as we see it at first glance enjoys its own complete and autonomous existence, but a work of music, when we decipher it from a sheet of parchment, has only a potential existence and is not truly born until the moment it is performed; only then does it become something concrete, a sonorous object. A painting offers itself passively to our judgment : music, however, unrolls in time, and in order to do so requires our active participation. To come into being music demands interpreters especially gifted in re-creating it. While any such interpretation is necessarily linked to that certain way of feeling which must be ours in our own time, it also takes as its point of departure the material elements we can glean from texts as well as from an intangible tradition.

For periods still relatively close to us – those of Beethoven and Wagner, for example – texts and traditions furnish bases that are more or less stable and so are only rarely debated. The genius of the interpreter is at one and the same time limited and sustained by objective criteria which must be respected at the risk of falsifying or denaturing the work. The Ninth Symphony of Beethoven has no existence as we find it printed in the Collected Works, it only comes to life in the interpretations of a Karajan or a Kleiber. Different as any two interpretations may be, they reveal to us complementary aspects of the genius of Beethoven, but both are of equal validity since both respect the objective bases furnished by Beethoven's text and by the conventions of performance native to all the symphonic literature of the nineteenth century.

TASKS AND OBSTACLES

Reconstruction of earlier music as it must once have sounded poses problems which are so much the more formidable because the work itself is so remote from us, its objective criteria fewer and less certain, its traditions indecisive and equivocal. Lest the interpreter simply give way to his own inspiration and indulge in poetic fantasy, all the elements available must be pinned down with the greatest rigor.

A few examples may help to show how difficult it is to arrive at an authentic interpretation of music of the fifteenth and sixteenth centuries. First of all, we must be able to decipher the original texts. Mensural notation poses problems normally beyond the scope of the average musician trained in a conservatory, so that specialists in musical paleography must be called on to transcribe the old notation into the only system known and used by musicians of our times. Such transcriptions must be faithful to the original but, at the same time, comprehensible to the uninitiated. That is far from easy. For a long time scholars transcribed the old note-values into modern forms which, in appearance at least, seemed most closely related to them : thus, for example, a semibreve of the fifteenth century was made equivalent to our modern semibreve. But our modern semibreve is, in principle, a note of long duration, whereas the old semibreve normally implied a moderate tempo and even, when subjected to proportional manipulation, a rapid tempo. By reason of a psychological quirk difficult to get rid of, this has led many people to think that all old music was slow and solemn and has simply reinforced their unjustified prejudices against it.

Another delicate problem : the bar, or measure, was virtually unknown in the sixteenth century and only became common in the seventeenth, and yet this device is an absolute necessity for performers today. Earlier music was sung according to the *tactus*, a regular beat more or less corresponding to the normal heart pulsation. The modern measure, on the other hand, involves a more or less complex combination of a variable number of beats at variable speeds. Now, in theory it should be logical to draw a bar-line after each tactus, but the jumble of lines which results from this makes it painful, to say the least, to read music so barred. And yet, if we squeeze music of the past into the straitjacket of our modern measures, we run into another psychological difficulty, since in music of our time the bar-line implies necessarily a stronger beat on the first note of each measure, the so-called down-beat. In Renaissance music, certain works have a periodic down-beat while others flow along in level rhythm with stronger accents which vary according to the phrasing. If we simply place bar-lines wherever there is a stronger accent, additional difficulties are created, since in many polyphonic works the accents do not come at the same time in all the voices. The only solution, therefore, which will make the work readable for modern musicians is the compromise of using bar-lines which are valid for all the voices but, at the same time, of adding complementary signs to specify the articulation and to underline the structure of the phrases.

The task of an editor of early music is not done when he has transcribed the old text into legible modern notation, since all notation is merely a

68 and 69. Angel Musicians.
Hans Memling.

framework and does not reveal the great number of conventions involved in a proper interpretation. Earlier music was often performed only in a small and culturally unified circle which had no need to have explained again what everyone knew about interpretation; after all, no one was likely to err since everyone practiced the same style. Greater precision in signs only becomes necessary when several styles compete. Today, when such multiplicity of styles has gone beyond any limit, the interpreter runs the risk of applying too widely the conventions familiar to him and of presuming that they are universally valid. Only utmost precision in notation can avoid the risks thus created.

We must therefore reduce as much as possible what seem to be the indeterminate factors in old music by rediscovering all the conventions which governed interpretation in the past. This means making explicit what formerly was simply taken for granted. Thus, for example, medieval and Renaissance notation did not always specify the accidentals, sharps or flats, which occurred in the course of a melody. They were left to the singer to interpolate, especially in the cadences at the ends of phrases, according to certain rules of solmization and counterpoint. If these chromatic accidentals, called in the past *musica ficta*, are not indicated, our modern transcriptions falsify old music and make it seem grotesquely archaic. On the other hand, musical texts were not always interpreted as simply, as severely as the notation seems to indicate. Singers and instrumentalists often ornamented them according to certain formulas in order to display their virtuosity, but these *colorations* could also constitute expressive commentaries on the original melody. For this reason, any re-creation of sixteenth-century polyphony must take into account this custom and seek to rediscover the secrets of improvisation.

Another fundamental problem is the determination of correct tempos. Obviously, Renaissance texts include no metronome indications, and yet the tempo was not left to the discretion of the performer's

feeling for the literary text or the expressive character of the piece. If it was not specified, it was because it also was governed by rigorous conventions. The problem is not resolved by saying that all music was performed according to the tactus, since we still must find, for each case, the basic unit of beat, and this varied from period to period and even between different works.

Finally, the musical documents of the Middle Ages and the Renaissance do not specify the nature or the number of the forces required for performance but simply consign the different voices to two facing pages of a large choir book or else to separate booklets, one for each voice. Therefore, one must first determine if the work was intended for voices, for instruments, or for both, and if it utilized a few soloists or a larger ensemble, and also, in the event that instruments seem to be called for, just what those instruments were. For what type of music was the flute used and for what other the trombone? And the fifteenth-century flute, just what did it sound like? And the fiddle, the *vièle*, exactly how was it played?

All these remarks, then, tend to prove that in the field of early music the task of the musicologist is only completed when he has furnished to the interpreters of today, with the greatest possible precision, all the elements necessary to aid them in performing the work in a version as close as possible to that ideal but unknown model it had once been. To do this, the musicologist must know how to fill in innumerable gaps in the old documents, and he can do this only by impregnating himself with ancient traditions, with knowledge of past styles, and by disinterring with utmost patience all of the conventions needed to make possible an adequate modern performance. He must dare to adventure beyond the texts themselves, to take risks. But they must be calculated risks, for the margin of uncertainty is great and can only be reduced little by little thanks to a more and more intimate knowledge not only of the texts and musical practices but also of the entire artistic, spiritual and social world from which the work sprang : a thoroughgoing performance practice touches on every aspect of the history of music.

GOALS AND LIMITS

The quest for authenticity in the re-creation of works of the past is imposed on us by our historical conscience. In many ways, that quest is vain.

The historian tries to explain, for instance, that works of earlier times were not appreciated for their pure beauty and that their primary aim was functional, any aesthetic significance being incidental. By this means he seeks to replace these works in their social environment and to help the listener acquire a greater intellectual comprehension of them. But when we ourselves today listen to such music it is no longer in a church or princely palace but in a concert hall or in the intimacy of our home, on records or the radio. It is no longer for us liturgical music or table music, an expression of religious feeling or an adjunct to some festivity. It has been drained of all the substance in which at the outset it was so rich. It is no longer anything more than music, pure music. However accurate and faithful may be its reconstruction, it is irremediably something other than it was once. Whenever we listen to a mass only as a work of beauty, everything in it is transformed and it is no longer heard in the same manner.

On the other hand, for a man of the Renaissance, the music of his time was an absolute : he knew no other. For the listener of today every work is no more than a point on a line of historical evolution, a link in a chain, and it interests him or moves him because of everything in the history of the art that it represents, of everything it explains or foretells.

And for this reason the illusions and ideals of the historian are inevitably tempered. However scientific our knowledge of performance practice may be, a work of the past will never again be heard as it was by those for whom it was intended. The past cannot be recovered as one recovers some objective reality. The past is a construction we ourselves make on the basis of certain data which we should like to control rigorously but which, in fact, we ourselves lay out after having chosen what is relevant to our purposes. It is, therefore, we ourselves, with our own aspirations and our own sensibility that we project into the past. And this is why such a past touches us so deeply, because it is never established once and for all, it is constantly corrected by taking into account both the objective elements available to us as well as our own present experiences. It is the present which modifies our understanding of the art of the past. Stravinsky, Schoenberg and Boulez have helped us listen to the music of the fifteenth century with different ears than the Romantics had; they have pushed us to rediscover it. Modality is no longer a curious exotic variant of tonality, because modern composers have taught us that the tonal principle is not the ultimate end of music. Isorhythm does not seem to us some sort of bizarre device, now that we know *Le Sacre du printemps* and the works of Messiaen. We know, because of the serial composers (if we failed to learn the lesson from Johann Sebastian Bach), that the artifices of counterpoint are not obstacles for composers of genius but, rather, means of achieving, through discipline, a certain formal perfection.

The work of the musicologist is therefore like that of the historian, at one and the same time science and art. Beginning with a rigorous scientific method, the musicologist must exercise truly creative audacity and yet remain free from illusions. He knows perfectly well that he will make mistakes: he can only approximate the reality of the past. And the reality which seems right today will not be right tomorrow, when certain new criteria will have modified the point of view and when men's sensibilities will have somehow changed, asking of works of the past something other than is asked today. No matter. Is not such a constantly threatened existence the condition of all works of art ?

191

70. The Trials of Job.
Jan Mandyn.

The transcription of ancient musical texts into a meaningful and usable form is difficult, but it is an even more delicate task to adventure into the forest of conventions not specified by notation. To begin with one must be able to decipher theoretical writings which over and over again make one regret that they dally over defining an ideal pedagogy instead of describing the practices of their times. To complement these, one must also explore literary sources for any references to music, however slipshod, erroneous or merely fantastic and capricious these may often be.

When one reads these verses of Jean Molinet, it is easy to see that they are no more than a poetic pleasantry not to be taken seriously :

J'ay veu, comme il me samble
Ung fort homme d'honneur
Luy seul chanter ensemble
Et dessus et teneur :
Okeguem, Alexandre,
Jossequin ne Busnois
Qui sçavent chant espandre
Ne font tel esbanois.

(I saw, meseems, / A sturdy gentleman / Who sang alone / Both discant and tenor : / Ockeghem, Alexander, / Josquin nor Busnois, / Who know the art of song full well, / Not even they could do this feat.)

But one is tempted to trust the same rhetorician when he evokes the magnificent display made by Charles the Bold at the siege of Neuss in 1474 : *Melodious sounds of wind instruments, trumpets, clarions, flutes, bagpipes and shawms floated through the air and made such delectable harmony that they drove away all melancholy, gave rise to new joy, and elevated the care-fraught hearts to the throne of perfect bliss.* Still, one begins to doubt the value of such evidence from Molinet when it becomes clear that in works of pure fiction his descriptions of music employ very similar details and an identical vocabulary.

The fact is, Molinet delighted in juggling with the musical vocabulary and his technical explanations are quite dubious. He was a poet who used music as a pretext for his verbal fancies. If he enumerated instruments it was only for the pleasure of arranging them in elegantly flowing phrases, as can be seen in this poem celebrating the defeat of the French at the battle of Guinegatte in 1479, in which he was obviously indulging his taste for assembling sonorities and rhythms :

Sonnez tambours, trompes, tubes, clarons,
Fluctes, bedons, simphonies, rebelles,
Cimballes, cors, doulx manicordions,
Décacordes, choros, psalterions,
Orgues, harpes, nacquaires, challemelles,
Cornemuses, timbres et cloches belles,
Pipes, flayos, luctz et marionnettes,
Venez jouer dedans nos maisonnettes.

(Sound out drums, trumpets, tubes, bugles, / Flutes, kettles, symphonies, lyres, / Cymbals, horns, sweet manichords, / Decachords, drones, psalteries, / Organs, harps, nakers, shawms, / Bagpipes, tambourines and pretty bells, / Pipes, fifes, lutes and marionettes, / Come play your pieces for us in our little houselets.)

For a good many other writers of the Middle Ages and the Renaissance – Rabelais, for one – enumerations of this sort were no more than rhetorical exercises without any realistic intentions. The names of instruments – preferably the most rare, bizarre and magniloquent names to be found – were brought in to give color to descriptions which, in any event, were themselves patterned on interchangeable formulas. Music and its particularized vocabulary were exploited as means to purely literary ends.

Not that one cannot make use of such evidence, but it must be subjected to the most severe critical examination. Sometimes it helps us to determine what were the social conditions of musical performance, or even to discover styles of interpretation, or to get some idea of the actual tone color of works for which we have no more than the dry notation.

PICTORIAL EVIDENCE

Similar caution is advisable in the use of iconographic documents. Emanuel Winternitz was quite right to point out certain very common errors that come about when musicological research puts too much trust in images as documentary evidence, for the fact is that painters are not always scrupulously realistic. They are not photographers but painters, and Picasso and Braque, with their cubist guitars, are not alone in distorting reality.

The artist employs a plastic language which sometimes deliberately leads him away from a literal representation and which may induce him to schematice or even destroy natural forms. He is subject to his material, to stone or wood or canvas, to his tools whether pencil, brush or chisel, and to a technique. Sculpture, for instance, does not permit great precision in details. It needs only to simplify and suggest, whereas painting reduces everything to two dimensions according to laws of figuration which have varied throughout time. The artist may utilize personages as elements of composition without concerning himself with realistic depiction. Winternitz has shown also that artists may wish to display their erudition by placing in the hands of an Orpheus or a David a lyre or harp which is no more than a dubious archaeological-literary fabrication.

There are subjects in which fantasy is the rule, such as the illuminations in the margins of choir books of the fifteenth and sixteenth centuries with their grotesque caricatures in which the shape and details of musical instruments are deliberately distorted. In the infernal scenes of Hieronymus Bosch, a harp or lute may become an instrument of torture or even an erotic object. Musicians and instruments may be deliberately made ugly in the interests of satire, caricature or some poetic invention of demoniac character. On the other hand, in other works, they may be considerably embellished, but this too is a sort of distortion for aesthetic ends and realism is once more sacrificed, this time for an ideal of formal beauty.

In certain subjects, symbolic or allegorical elements impose conventions which the artist strives to respect at the cost of authenticity, or which he translates into inappropriate contemporary terms. As is known, musicians frequently figure in depictions of biblical episodes. If the four-and-twenty elders of the Apocalypse who prostrate themselves before the Lamb to *sing a new song* are usually shown with instruments with plucked strings, it is because the biblical text describes them as *having*

194

every one of them harps, but they have also been shown with other instruments copied from contemporary reality.

In religious iconography, angels frequently figure as musicians. Pseudo-Dionysius the Areopagite in the sixth century was the first to describe the celestial hierarchy as divided into nine choirs whose essential task is to praise the Lord. In the earliest representations, the angels were singers only, and the only instrument they carried was the *tuba* mentioned in the Vulgate, an instrument of glory, summons or magic. Later, notably in scenes of the Last Judgment, this trumpet took on many forms suggested by contemporary instruments. It is not before the twelfth century that one finds angels playing various other instruments which are not sanctioned by the sacred texts.

Little by little, angels were introduced into other types of scenes. Beginning with the fourteenth-century Sienese and Florentines, they are shown as a triumphal cortège leading the Virgin into Heaven for the Assumption, a notion inspired by the *Golden Legend* of Jacobus de Voragine, which enjoyed immense success in the Middle Ages and supplied painters with a rich arsenal of devout images. Later, the saints underwent the same apotheosis : processions of angel musicians, singers and players bore the saint's soul to Paradise. The music of glory the angels make before God was extended to the Virgin in her Coronation. If the Virgin sings a Magnificat of gratitude after the Visitation, she is

surrounded by angels. At the Nativity there are worshipping angels and they, at least, have scriptural authority for their presence there. Finally, the Virgin and Child enthroned, surrounded by angel musicians, is a theme which appeared in the fourteenth century and which was to have a long life in devout imagery.

It was only in the fifteenth century that painters – and first of all Flemish painters – began to place angels in scenes borrowed from daily life and no longer in idealized processions. The celestial hierarchy was deliberately carried over into the ranks of men. Here artists were most often obliged to take as models what they saw about them, and such works are particularly useful as evidence of the musical practice of the time. The angel at the organ behind a donor in prayer painted by Hugo van der Goes is depicted within a church, reading from a book of music and with an assistant to work the bellows. The Berlin *Madonna and Child* of van Eyck is placed in a Gothic church where two angels, far back in the choir, are intent upon a large music book : surely they must be singing in counterpoint. On one of the panels of the *Mystic Lamb* of van Eyck, the angel musicians really do sing in polyphony, as is proved by their open mounths and the expressions on their faces. Probably they are singing a work with different melodies in each of the three voices, and in the foreground one angel leads the others, one hand beating the tactus.

Generally the depictions of musical instruments by fifteenth-century Flemish painters are quite accurate. They take deliberate pains to find visual equivalents for the performance of polyphony, which was, as we know, the music appropriate to solemn events and therefore fit to be the music of angels. The precision of the settings and the realism of certain details seem to indicate that these painters took as their models scenes from life around them. Nevertheless one must beware of trusting them too far, since elements taken from reality may be used in an arbitrary, non-realistic manner.

Furthermore, even an exhaustive study of a great number of Angelic Concerts does not give us the solution to the most important problem : the way voices and instruments were actually used in religious music of the fifteenth and sixteenth centuries. The frequency of instruments in the iconography of the period – despite the fact that they are so seldom mentioned in biblical texts – seems to show that, in life, they were often used together at that time, but the pictures do not tell us just how they were used. The groupings depicted by the painters do not necessarily correspond to those in real life. On the second panel of angel musicians of the *Mystic Lamb,* there is an angel playing a positive organ, another holding a harp and still another a fiddle, but they do not play on these. The instruments are painted with the utmost precision, but were the organ, harp and fiddle really often used together ? Are they not combined here simply to illustrate the Psalm text written later at the foot of the painting, *Laudent eum in chordis et organis ?*

Because Memling painted on the panels of an organ case angels playing the psaltery, tromba marina, lute, oboe, trumpet, portative organ, harp and fiddle, are we to believe that such perfectly realistic but highly varied instruments formed a harmonious ensemble that might actually have been heard at the time ? It seems more likely that Memling merely wished to place around the Lord, along with the singers, a certain number of instruments in a hierarchic order.

Similarly, one can glean little of value about the musical practice of the Renaissance from the innumerable depictions of the Madonna and Child seated on a throne and surrounded by angel musicians. In the simplest types, there is an angel at either side of the Virgin, often with one playing the lute, the other a harp, as in numerous miniatures and paintings, notably in a painting by Gerard David in the Louvre and one by the Master of Saint Lucy in the collection of Baron Van der Elst. In a famous painting by Memling in the Uffizi, the lute is replaced by a fiddle, but the angel does not play it and is merely offering an apple to the Child. A similar device is used in another work by Memling in the National Gallery, London, but there the lute is replaced by a portative organ and there are two female saints and the family of the donor. A painting in Brussels by the Master of the Morrison Triptych shows angels holding a lute and a fiddle; elsewhere one finds a portative organ and a harp or a flute and a lute.

The two angels have an obvious significance: they symbolize the praise of the glory of the Madonna and Child. But they have an ulterior aim, that of providing a harmonious balance to the composition, and therefore we must be wary of attributing any precise intention to the choice of harp and lute or harp and fiddle. The same caution is necessary when the painter elaborates on the theme, using three, four or more angels. In a work by the Master of the Embroidered Foliage in the Féral collection, Paris, there are at one side three singing angels bent over a polyphonic choir book (in which one can make out an *Ave Regina cœlorum* by Walter Frye), on the other side three instrumentalists with lute, fiddle and recorder. In a triptych by Gossaert in the Museo Nazionale, Palermo, there are three cherubs singing from a book and two little players of lute and recorder. In a *Madonna and Child* by Memling in Munich, one angel plays a portable organ, another a lute, a third a harp, and the fourth holds a fiddle on his lap and proffers a fruit to the Child, while the background shows an exterior view of a castle and countryside. A work by Gerard David in Darmstadt, in which one sees on one side a group of four singers and on the other an organist, seems clearly inspired by the panels of van Eyck.

In such images of angels, it is the harp, lute, fiddle, recorder and organ which appear most often. They may all have been used together in church, but one wonders if the trait they have in common – which may be their sweetness of tone – is not primarily intended to characterize the expressiveness of the charming scene of the Madonna and Child or if, on the other hand, the frequent grouping of lute, harp and organ is not merely an illustration of some Psalm text. Since angels were above all intended to celebrate the glory of God, it seems that these depictions may have been inspired more by Psalm 150 than by examples from contemporary life.

It must be admitted also that painters in the fifteenth and sixteenth centuries exploited the theme of the Virgin and Child in what we might call a rather commercial manner. They introduced variations in the pose of the figures and in the background – drapery, church, castle or landscape – and increased the number of secondary figures, the angels, and diversified their accessories, that is, their musical instruments. But concern with pictorial composition rather than realism seems often to have determined what musical forces were depicted.

Among the biblical texts which often gave rise to musical depictions is the Tree of Jesse, which derives from a passage in Isaiah. As we find it in many miniatures and paintings, the genealogical tree of Jesus and Mary grows out of the sleeping Jesse, David's father. On its branches appear the twelve kings of Judah, and each of the crowned figures plays an instrument in honor of Christ. But if we find a miniature in which they play the lute, harp, fiddle, portative organ, psaltery, shawm, bagpipes, drum and tromba marina, there are no grounds for concluding that such an ensemble could or would ever have played together in life.

A similar critical spirit must govern the study of other documents illustrating the sacred texts or themes popular in medieval traditions, such as David, Orpheus, Jubal, Tubal-cain, the Adoration of the Shepherds, the Banquet of Herod and Salome's Dance, Saint Cecilia, Job, the Liberal Arts, the Muses, and the Five Senses.

And yet it remains true that such pictorial evidence can be a precious auxiliary source of information for the history of music, a source not yet adequately explored. It can provide first-hand in-

197

formation on instruments, on the musical forces employed, on groupings of instruments and voices, on how ensembles were conducted, on the functions of music, on the social situation of musicians, and on the conditions in which music was listened to. But all such data must be treated with rigor.

HIGH INSTRUMENTS

The Middle Ages and the Renaissance lacked the conception of a balanced standard orchestra such as that adopted in the eighteenth century. However, instruments were not used casually but often had specialized functions and were associated with veritable social hierarchies.

Today, instruments are generally classified according to the large families which go to make up a symphony orchestra: stringed instruments, wind instruments, divided into woodwinds and brasses, and percussion. Specialists in the field of instruments long ago dropped such an imprecise classification and prefer to speak of chordophones, aerophones, membranophones and idiophones, with each class further divided according to the way the sound is produced, whether by pinching, rubbing or striking.

The medieval classification, used in erudite treatises but also in common speech, was infinitely more simple and repays attentive study since it casts light on certain aesthetic problems and reveals the role played by tone color and dynamics. Instruments were quite simply merely ranged in two categories according to their relative volumes. Frequently one finds allusions to minstrels or players of instruments *tant hauts que bas,* that is, both high and low. Olivier de La Marche speaks of the *six high minstrels* of the Duke of Burgundy but also of his *four players on low instruments.* High and low, this was the fundamental classification. In modern terms, this means simply loud and soft. "High" instruments are loud, "low" instruments are soft, and the terms have nothing to do with their pitch and range : a tiny high-pitched flute is a "low" instrument, the trombone a "high" instrument.

72. Young Girl Playing the Lute.
Master of the Half-Length Figures.

Among the high instruments there were first of all percussion instruments either using a membrane (a stretched skin on a drum, for instance) or made of metal. Those with membranes included *drums* and *nakers – naquaires* or *nacaires* in French – which were small kettledrums brought into Europe by the Crusaders and used on the battlefield, in tourneys, banquets and fêtes. In metal there were *cymbals* – two discs struck against each other – and *bells.* In the Occident, the oldest bells date back only to the end of the twelfth century, when they already possessed their characteristic tulip shape. Certain miniatures show small bells suspended from bars and struck by hammers, and these could be tuned to make complete scales. There were also great bells in the churches which struck the hours and sometimes were combined into carillons such as are still heard in Flanders.

When it arrived in Europe from Byzantium in the tenth century, the *horn* was made of ivory and called the *oliphant* and, as we know from the *Song of Roland,* was a part of the warrior's accoutrement to be used in hunting, expeditions and battles. Later it was often made of metal but retained the curved shape recalling the horns of an animal. It was used exclusively by the nobility and, limited in possibilities as it was, it served for no more than to blow the few notes of a signal or call for help.

Throughout the Middle Ages, brass instruments were associated with kings, princes and nobles. The *trumpet* or *buisine* was first intended for military uses. It was a long metal tube with a mouthpiece

and ending in a large bell. For fêtes and tourneys it was adorned with a long streamer bearing the arms of some nobleman. The tube was sometimes bent into an S-shape and later, for larger forms, twisted backward to form a U. In a princely court, the trumpeters were the most important among the so-called high minstrels and for a long time formed a special caste proud of its role and contemptuous of other musicians. They accompanied the prince on his voyages and sounded their horns at the entrance to a city; also they announced proclamations, summoned the court to table and marked the different phases of a tourney. The use of trumpets was a mark of distinction that the nobility for a long time tried to reserve to itself but which was seized upon by the cities to assert their independence and power. Backed up by kettledrums, the trumpet was the perfect instrument for occasions of pomp and brilliance, although the number of notes it could play was small, no more than the series of harmonic tones determined by the length of the tube, the same few notes found in the present-day bugle.

The *sackbut trumpet,* on the other hand, could play all the chromatic tones since it was made up of two tubes fitted together so as to slide in and out. It was around the middle of the fifteenth century that the bass trumpet underwent the technical improvement which is reflected in its name, since *sacquer* means to pull and *bouter* to push, and the sackbut is really nothing more nor less than a slide trombone.

The *shawm – chalumeau, chalemie* or *chalemelle* in French, *schalmey* in Flemish and German – was composed of a conical wooden pipe pierced with holes and with a double reed, the legitimate ancestor of the oboe. In the fifteenth century shawms and sackbuts formed an ensemble typical of the kind of music made in princely courts. Tinctoris, in his unfinished treatise *De inventione et usu musicæ,* calls it *alta,* that is, music of high, loud instruments, and according to Besseler the peculiar tone color of such ensembles can still be heard in the *cobla*

which plays for sardanas in Catalonia. The musicians in pictures of court dances are usually players of shawms and sackbuts (or trumpets); they are to be found in the hunting scene at the court of Philip the Good in the Versailles museum and on the wedding chest of the Adimari family in the Accademia in Florence. It will be recalled that in the basses dances it was the shawms which improvised counterpoints over a tune played in the bass register by the sackbut.

The same ensemble sometimes played a kind of fanfare such as we can easily imagine sounded by the players on horseback in the *Triumph of the Emperor Maximilian.* Exceptionally the sackbut could also take part in the performance of a polyphonic chanson as we know from the counter-tenor trumpet part called for in a three-voice chanson by Pierre Fontaine, *J'aime bien celuy qui s'en va.* Heinrich Besseler has shown much discernment in linking this innovation with the evolution in musical language fostered by Dufay and the appearance of a functional harmonic bass in polyphonic music.

Shawm and sackbut lost their aristocratic connections in the sixteenth century, when the shawm became the usual instrument for town musicians, who played it solo as a signal instrument or in groups for serenades, cortèges, processions and *ommegangs.* When they hired out to the bourgeoisie or peasantry to play at weddings, banquets or balls, minstrels usually played the shawm, and Arbeau in his *Orchésographie* (1588) was already aware of this decline in prestige, pointing out that there was henceforth not a single bourgeois who did not insist on oboe players at his wedding.

The *cornet* did not appear until the end of the fifteenth century. It was an instrument with a mouthpiece like a trumpet but its pipe, either straight or curved like a horn and with holes like a shawm or flute, allowed it to play all the tones of the chromatic scale. Often in the sixteenth century it was associated with shawms and sackbuts for mu-

73. Two Musicians near a Fountain.
Israël van Meckenem.

sic outdoors, and because of its clear and expressive sonority it was also used in churches together with the voices.

LOW INSTRUMENTS

Low instruments – those that play softly – were especially appreciated by the great personages as a sort of chamber music. Philippe de Mézières, in his advice to King Charles VI of France, told him : *Another thing fitting for you is to have minstrels to play on low instruments for your every recreation and to calm your royal person after the councils and labors of Your Royal Highness.*

Low instruments figure in the account Christine de Pisan gives of a royal reception : *After supper, the King retired into the parliament chamber, and with him the son of the Emperor and as many barons as could enter, and there, as was the custom, there played minstrels on low instruments as sweetly as they could, and there were seated the two kings in two high chairs on each of which was embroidered a fleur-de-lis.*

Among the low instruments especially prized for their sweet tone were the *flutes*, among which were distinguished, according to Guillaume de Machaut, *flautes traversaines* – transverse flutes – and *flaustes dont droit jouer quand tu flaustes*, flutes you must play straight on when you flute, and which are still known as *recorders*. Then came the *douçaine* or *dulcina*, a double-reed instrument of the shawm family but with less powerful sonority, and the *cromorne*, whose crooked tube explains its name (in German, *Krummhorn*).

All stringed instruments were low instruments. Known as far back as Assyrian and Egyptian Antiquity, the *harp* arrived on the Continent around the ninth century from England and Ireland. Often it was of a small, portable type. In the twelfth and thirteenth centuries, the jongleurs played it to accompany their recitations of poems. There were still harpers among the low minstrels of the Burgundian court, but the instrument was also used by amateurs, particularly by women of the aristocracy in the fifteenth century, as we know from the French tapestry in the Musée des Arts Décoratifs, Paris, in which *De ce que fol pense* is being sung, and also from the Brussels tapestry in Nuremberg depicting an outdoor concert as well as from several engravings by Israël van Meckenem.

The strings of the *psaltery*, of a variable number ranging from twenty to sixty, were no longer stretched across a wooden case but along the soundboard, and the little trapezoid instrument was played held against the chest, as we see with an angel in the triptych by Memling in Antwerp. The strings were plucked either with a plectrum or directly with the fingers, but however it was played, it must have had only the faintest sonority.

The *dulcimer* (*tympanon* in French, *Hackbrett* in German) is very much like the psaltery but was played with two little hammers and either held flat on the lap, as shown in the *Triumph of the Church* of the Prado, or placed in front of one, as in the *Tree of Jesse* in the Breviary of Philip the Good in the Bibliothèque Royale, Brussels. Like the psaltery, the dulcimer seems to have been principally a woman's instrument. Both instruments fell into neglect in the sixteenth century, when they were supplanted in favor by keyboard instruments.

The *marine trumpet* must have been used rarely, but it has exerted a peculiar fascination on painters thanks to its bizarre form and its name has intrigued poets right up to Guillaume Apollinaire. In English it is known also as *sea trumpet* or *nun's fiddle*, in Italian as *tromba marina*, in German as *Nonnengeige*, *Marientrompette* or *Trumscheit*. There is one on one of the panels (finger-board covering ?) of the *Angel Musicians* of Memling and in the *Triumph of the Church*. It was shaped like a very long tapering pyramid and usually had only one string which was played by a bow.

Introduced from the Orient by the Arabs and Spaniards, the *lute* became one of the most widely used instruments in the fifteenth and sixteenth centuries. Its swelling pear-shaped body, its flat belly and the strings stretched along its neck are depicted in precise detail on the panel by Memling mentioned above, on the *Reliquary of Saint Ursula* in Bruges, and in the engravings of Israël van Meckenem. Through time its strings have varied both in number and tunings, and the plectrum originally used was abandoned in favor of plucking with the fingers; in the fifteenth century, there were not always frets on the neck to locate the half-tones. According to Tinctoris, the lute was used for fêtes, dances and public and private entertainments. One of its principal advantages was that polyphonic music could be played on it, and this explains its popularity as a solo instrument. Exclusive property of the aristocracy in the fifteenth century, later it was much appreciated by the middle classes, and in all cases was the ideal instrument for intimate music-making. Most of its literature was intended for amateurs and consisted especially of adaptations of popular chansons and dances, of reductions which did not always carry over all the original polyphony and sometimes of arrangements in which the lute was used to accompany a singer. But among the tablatures (tablature is a specific type of notation by letters or ciphers used for the lute repertory) there were also original pieces, fantasies or variations of considerable difficulty since the lute also had its professionals and virtuosos.

The *vièle* – the medieval fiddle – was held flat against the chest, had four or five strings, and was played with a bow. Illustrations of it are found in one of Memling's panels in Antwerp, in the *Reliquary of Saint Ursula* in Bruges, in the *Triumph of the Church* of the Prado, and – in a larger format, the tenor *vièle* – on a panel of the *Adoration of the Mystic Lamb*. It was used by jongleurs to accompany poems, and according to Tinctoris was still in use at the end of the fifteenth century in the recitation of epic poems. It served also to accompany dances, and at banquets was played in concert with other instruments.

Whereas the so-called high, loud instruments were associated with war and tourneys and made a manly music, the more refined low, soft instruments were more pleasing to women and young gentlemen, as at the Burgundian court, where the players of fiddles, harps and lutes were in the service of the Duchess and of the young Count of Charolais. For his part, Tinctoris was particularly fond of the fiddle because it best aroused in him feelings of piety, and he wished that *it might be reserved for sacred music and the secret consolation of the soul rather than for profane occasions and public festivities*.

Tinctoris was also fond of the *rebec*, a small pear-shaped fiddle with three strings, a good illustration of which can be seen on the Brussels tapestry in Nuremberg.

In the course of the fifteenth century increasing favor was given to a hybrid instrument which was to enjoy great success during the succeeding three centuries, the *viol*. This was a kind of lute but with a flat back like that of the guitar and played with a bow instead of plucked. In Spain it was called *vihuela de arco* – the bowed viol – to distinguish it from the *vihuela de mano,* whose strings were plucked. Because it was held between the knees, it was often given the name of *viola da gamba,* leg-viol. In the sixteenth century there were viols of various sizes, ranging from soprano to bass, but in every case they had six strings tuned in fourths separated by a third and with frets on the neck. Lutenists were able to play it without difficulty, and like the lute it was used by both amateurs and professionals and gave rise to an original repertory, particularly in England and Italy, where Flemish composers such as Buus and Willaert were especially fond of it.

Around 1550 *violins* appeared, born from the same line as the fiddle, rebec and *lira da braccio*. Their four strings were tuned in fifths and the neck was not fretted. Since at first they were used only by professionals for dance music in court ballets or

74. A Woman Playing the Portative Organ.
Drawing.

middle-class and peasant entertainments, they were given much less consideration in the sixteenth century than the various kinds of viols. As we all know, they were later to enjoy a healthy revenge for such neglect.

KEYBOARD INSTRUMENTS

Ever since the Middle Ages, the *organ* has been associated with sacred music, but its popularity was not, in the past, restricted to the church. An immigrant from Byzantium into the Western world in the ninth century, it is a wind instrument into whose pipes air is pumped mechanically and controlled by a keyboard. There were organs of all sizes in the fifteenth century, all the way down to the *portative,* called in Italy *organetto,* a small instrument held in front of the player like the accordion today and played with only three fingers of the right hand while the left hand worked the bellows. A perfect example showing twenty-six pipes is found on the *Reliquary of Saint Ursula.* It was played during processions, but a miniature in the *Histoire du Grand Alexandre* (Petit Palais, Paris) proves that it was used also by minstrels since it appears there together with a fiddle and a harp as entertainment at a banquet. In a Flemish drawing in the Louvre it is played by a lady, apparently of the nobility. In the course of the sixteenth century, the portative organ passed out of favor and disappeared.

The *positive organ* was of larger dimensions, quite different from the small model, which could be carried. Played with both hands, it could make polyphonic music. In an engraving by Israël van Meckenem it is shown resting on a table, played by a bourgeois while his wife works the bellows, but one of the *Weißkunig* engravings shows a much larger model in the palace of Emperor Maximilian which sits on the ground, has a pedal board and some fifty pipes. As early as the fifteenth century, the positive had reached its full development, often having a second manual, a pedal manual, and enough

pipes to form homogeneous ranks of contrasting tone colors. Admirable examples can be found in the *Adoration of the Mystic Lamb* and on a panel by Hugo van der Goes in Edinburgh.

The organ was normally placed in the choir in a church. When installed in a tribune or loft suspended from one of the walls of a church, it could be even more elaborate, with thousands of pipes and, consequently, numerous stops imitating the sound of instruments in use at the time. From this arose the stops known as clarion, viola, virginal, chalumeau, cromorne, dulciana, sackbut and theorbo, names which are still used and which are largely responsible for the aura of poetic mystery the instrument continues to hold for the layman. This was the *great organ* used exclusively in churches, illustrated in one of the miniatures of the *Très Riches Heures du Duc de Berry.* In the sixteenth century, organs made in Brabant and Flanders were much appreciated in the countries along the Rhine and in Denmark, France and Spain. The organ literature, written down in tablature notation, included transcriptions of secular polyphonic pieces, variations on chansons and dances, but above all religious works to be performed during church services either in alternation with the voices or to fill in silences, and it could of course also play along with the singers.

The keyboard principle came to be applied to stringed instruments during the Middle Ages. The *monochord* was never more than an instrument used as a teaching device to demonstrate the physical relationship between pitch and the divisions of a string, and it was not from it but rather from the psaltery and dulcimer that, in the thirteenth century, there was developed the *manichord,* later to be called *clavichord,* in which the strings were struck by a tangential jack fixed on the end of each key. The clavichord was a small instrument which could be placed on a table, and its sonority was so delicate that it could only be used in the privacy of a dwelling for the personal pleasure of the player. A wood sculpture by Adriaen van Wesel offers one

205

75. Spinet-Harpsichord.
Ruckers.

76. Apollo and the Muses.

Martin De Vos.

of the earliest illustrations, an angel playing it beside Saint Joseph and two fiddlers. However, it is likely that it was only the artist's fancy thus to replace in a sacred concert the usual portative organ with a clavichord, since the latter could never make itself heard in a church, never being louder than what was later jocularly dubbed a concert of buzzing flies. It is as an instrument for private use that it appears in a painting by Van Hemessen (Worcester, Massachusetts) dating from around 1530 in which Mary Magdalene is portrayed as a richly dressed young noblewoman in whom some chaim to recognize Eleanore, sister of Charles V. A drawing by Vermeyen in Berlin likewise shows a young woman playing the clavichord for her own entertainment in a serious manner.

There had been another keyboard instrument in existence since the fifteenth century, but its strings were plucked by a kind of plectrum attached to a jack. Its body need be no more than a simple rectangular case that could be set on a table, as in the engraving showing Maximilian among his musicians. This was the *spinet* – in French, the *épinette* – which, except for a few minor details, did not differ from its English counterpart, the *virginal*. But it could also be a larger instrument standing on three or four legs, with strings set perpendicular to the keyboard, not parallel to it as in the spinet, and which, like the organ, could have a second manual and several registers with contrasting timbres. This was the *harpsichord,* known in French as the *clavecin,* in Italian as the *clavicembalo* or *gravicembalo.* Antwerp in the second half of the sixteenth century became the most important center of harpsichord manufacture, thanks to the Ruckers family, who invented many technical improvements and sold their instruments throughout Europe. Eventually harpsichords often became fine pieces of furniture ornamented with paintings and gildings.

Modest or splendid, clavichords, spinets and harpsichords were the instruments most appreciated by sixteenth-century amateurs, whether noble or mid-

dle class, to judge by the pictorial evidence which so frequently shows women especially playing them. An important independent literature grew up for the instrument, including, as for the lute, arrangements of chansons and dances but also original pieces composed by virtuosos for their own use.

MUSICAL INSTRUMENTS IN SOCIETY

As we have seen, some sort of social or ethical character was attributed to most instruments, either by association with their function or by tradition. The horn, instrument of hunt and battle, was sounded only by noblemen. The trumpet, used for war and celebration, commanding in character and virile, could be played only by specialized minstrels. Likewise reserved to professionals were the shawm, sackbut and other loud instruments, both at the time when they were still used only for court dances as well as later when cities employed them in public ceremonies and the middle classes for their private diversions. Though it was also played in palaces and bourgeois dwellings, the organ was above all devoted to religious music, and the organist was generally a church musician, a cantor specially skilled in reading mensural notation and in composing counterpoint.

Among the low instruments, the harp, fiddle and lute were at first played by minstrels but beginning with the fifteenth century were also taken up by amateurs. The nobles prized above all else skill in arms. For them, music was really no more than the food of love, a lively adjunct to their festivities

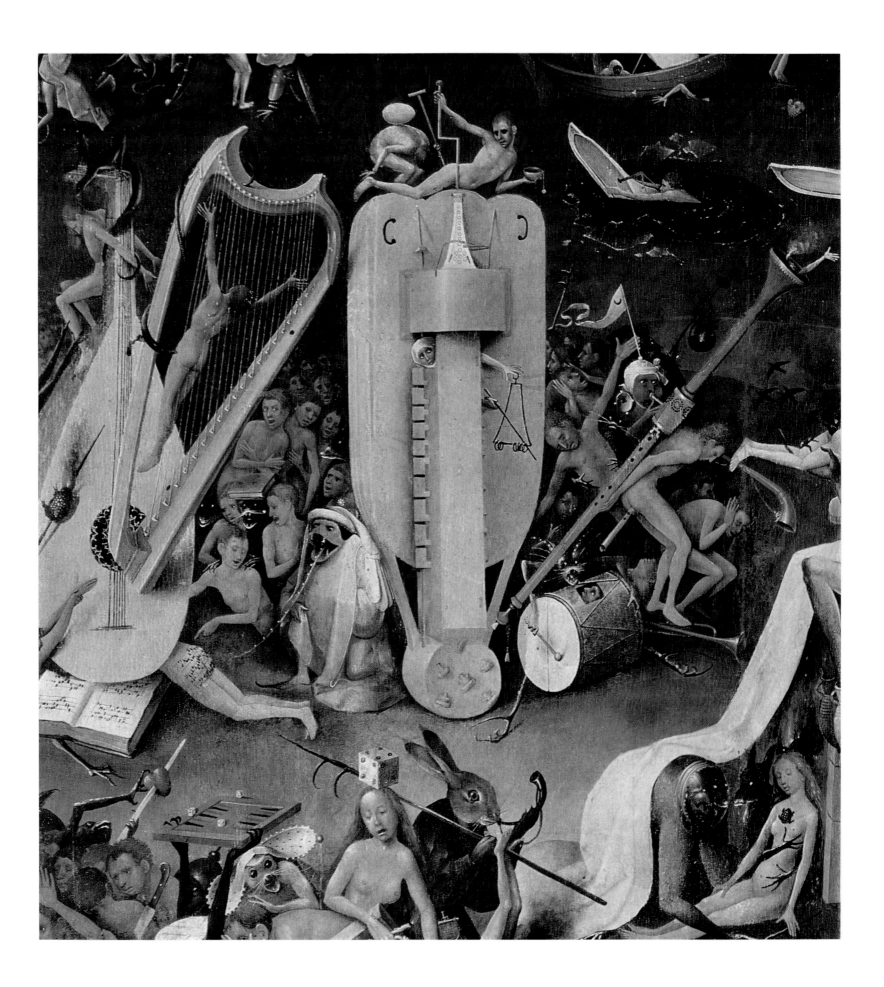

but perhaps not truly fitting to a manly man and better left to women and fledgling youths. Pictorial evidence indicates that music, unless executed by professionals, was mostly a matter for women, and it is women one sees most often playing the harp, psaltery, dulcimer or portative organ and later the lute, spinet, clavichord or flute. Even when music had won over the middle classes, women seem to have been involved in it more than men. This is not to say that in the sixteenth century many men, both nobles and commoners, did not play the lute, for by that time music had become for many something more than an elegant diversion : it had become a veritable passion to be allowed free rein in the playing of several instruments and in singing polyphonic chansons or madrigals.

Still, certain instruments never attained either aristocratic or bourgeois dignity, remaining tied to a more vulgar music. There was for example the *whistle flute* or *fipple flute – flageolet* or *flajol –* used only for dance music, a tiny fife played in the right hand while the left was busy beating out rhythms with a stick on a small drum or tabor.

The *hurdy-gurdy – vièle à roue –* was shaped like a lute or guitar and the strings were sounded both by playing on a very rudimentary keyboard and by turning a wheel with the right hand which made the strings vibrate in a steady drone. Possibly at the outset this wheel-viol, then called *organistrum* or *chifonie,* may have been used in the abbeys along with the portative organ, but from the fourteenth century on it was played only among the peasantry for dances and fairs and declined so much as to become the characteristic instrument of beggars. Bruegel made a special place for it in his *Hell.*

The *bagpipe – cornemuse* in French, *Dudelsack* in German, *piva* or *zampogna* in Italian – was always the instrument of the peasant, the poor, the beggar. With its reed pipes attached to a windbag, it could play a very elementary type of polyphony, no more than a tune with a drone accompaniment, and this no doubt was responsible for its success,

since a single bagpiper could provide dance music for a village. Every time Bruegel depicts peasant festivities there is a bagpiper sounding a dance or backing up the lively clatter of a rural wedding, and the shepherds at the Nativity often bring their bagpipes with them. Rabelais's Pantagruel made no bones about declaring his preference for *the rustic bagpipe* over *the murmurings of lutes, rebecs and antique violins,* but for Hieronymus Bosch and many others, the bagpipe was a symbol of vile sensual indulgence, and this because of a folk tradition which found something rather suggestive about the shape of the instrument.

Fife, hurdy-gurdy and bagpipe therefore made music for the many who knew nothing of learned music, as they still do in peasant communities, and it is they which we generally associate with folk music.

So musical instruments came to take their places on a social scale : the trumpet for noble warriors, the organ for churchmen, the bagpipes for peasants. But such specialization was never rigid and time brought many changes. Many of those changes came about in the course of the fifteenth and sixteenth centuries. The medieval distinction between high and low instruments faded out in the latter century. People then began to study instruments in more systematic manner and often to perform on them in the best society, to say nothing of the development of virtuosity among professionals. Indeed, to judge by the little treatise by Sebastian Virdung, *Musica getutscht,* which appeared in 1511, or the

highly detailed descriptions by Praetorius in his *Syntagma musicum* of 1619 there was an astonishing variety of instruments in the sixteenth century. A great many of them simply passed out of existence later when the Baroque awarded the palm to stringed instruments as against the Renaissance attitude that held flutes and cornets to be as important as viols. In addition, since instruments were generally turned out by local artisans, there was no tendency to standardization and the result was a great diversity in forms and timbres.

Beginning with the fifteenth century, many instruments began to be made in different sizes and consequently in different registers. Since sixteenth-century polyphony was generally written for four, five or more voices, families of instruments were devised in from four to eight different sizes with which this polyphonic music could be performed in a tone color as homogeneous as that of voices. This was what the English called a *whole consort,* the Germans an *Accort.* Instruments of different kinds – within certain limits – also could be combined into what was called a *broken consort,* and the mixture of instruments among themselves and together with voices presents some of the thorniest problems in our modern attempts to reconstruct the performance practice of the past.

THE SOUND OF EARLY MUSIC

In Dufay's time, ballades, rondeaux and chansons were most often composed for three voices, a principal voice which was sung plus, below it, tenor and counter-tenor parts intended to be played by instruments. This constituted a kind of chamber music in which flute, fiddle, dolcian, harp and lute could take part, perhaps also less usual instruments like the psaltery or dulcimer. Tinctoris tells how he heard at Bruges the Orbus brothers playing together with polyphonic vocal music on a soprano fiddle and a tenor fiddle, an example of homogeneity in the forces used. The outdoor fête depicted on the Nuremberg tapestry shows a more varied ensemble, with lords and ladies playing fiddle, harp, dulcimer and lute and a professional at the *bombard,* a bass shawm.

Compositions in which the parts seem stylistically homogeneous must have been performed by singers alone. Thus, in the hunting scene at the court of Philip the Good, there are no instruments in the group around the Duke but only singers. Likewise, the songs described by Olivier de La Marche in his account of the Banquet of the Oath of the Pheasant seem to have been performed unaccompanied by *three little choirboys and a tenor* or by *three sweet voices* or by a young boy and a tenor. Nevertheless, it could often happen that instruments entirely replaced singers and formed consorts which were either uniform or varied in tone color.

Usually soft instruments were used to play chansons, and the trombone part added to the rondeau by Pierre Fontaine in the Escorial chansonnier seems quite exceptional. However, at times, outdoors or in a great banquet hall, loud instruments performed chansons with excellent effect on shawms, bombards and sackbuts, the ensemble mentioned by Olivier de La Marche in his report of the wedding of Charles the Bold.

As for vocal music, we know already that besides men and young boys – professional musicians, chaplains, choristers and minstrels – women too began to sing as soon as secular polyphonic music was taken up by amateurs.

Thus it is clear that no one was very certain about the forces called for, the composer rarely specifying exactly what he wished, leaving it up to

213

his interpreters to distribute the parts in accord with traditional practice and unwritten conventions.

In any event, dances and chansons used a very limited number of performers. The fifteenth century could not even have imagined anything like our gigantic modern orchestras. In the most grandiose festivities only a small number of musicians was employed : players of flutes, shawms, sackbuts, fifes and drums formed small ensembles used separately, never together. The Duke of Burgundy maintained no more than six to eight minstrels for soft music, and according to the pictorial evidence, there were never more than a half-dozen performers at a time used in secular music. The music of the time was a music of soloists.

The forces required for religious music are more problematic. We already know that pictorial evidence is unreliable and that concerts of angels were not modeled after those of humans. Nor are the texts very explicit. In the first centuries of Christianity, the Church Fathers inveighed against musical instruments as tools of the devil. But such severity does not seem to have troubled the fifteenth century, although councils and synods throughout the Middle Ages had condemned instrumental musicians in terms that seem to be more the exploitation of a traditional literary topic than the expression of real feelings.

Other instruments than the organ, acknowledged to be the ideal sacred instrument, must have participated in performances of masses and motets. A certain number of religious works by Dufay and his contemporaries are written in a cantilena style like that of the ballades and rondeaux with one or two voices to be sung together with a tenor and counter-tenor. The latter were apparently instrumental, having no text, making much use of unvocal large melodic leaps, and being written in slow note-values in contrast to the liveliness of the upper voices. The praise lavished by Tinctoris on the fiddle and rebec shows what use these instruments may have had in religious music. In the

80. Maximilian with His Musicians.
Hans Burgkmair.

Trent manuscripts can be found a *Kyrie tubæ* (no. 891 in the thematic catalogue) and a *Missa tubæ* by Cousin (nos. 1123 to 1125); in addition, there is a *Gloria ad modum tubæ,* and all of these suggest the use of the sackbut in the mass.

However, one of the great specialists in fifteenth-century music, Heinrich Besseler, argues that voices could also have sung these apparently instrumental parts. Indeed, among the musicians of the Burgundian chapel only chaplains and choirboys are mentioned, with no reference whatsoever to any instrumentalist. The miniature in the manuscript *Traité sur l'oraison dominicale* (Bibliothèque Royale, Brussels) which shows Philip the Good in his oratory depicts singers only and no instrumentalists, and the same is true of the miniature with Ockeghem and his singers gathered around a lectern. As for evidence from the archives, it was only in the course of the sixteenth century that churches and princely chapels engaged specialized instrumentalists, before then usually relying entirely on the organist. An engraving by the Master of Petrarch from around 1518 depicts Emperor Maximilian at mass in Augsburg : to the right the cantors and choirboys are gathered around the lectern, to the left an organist plays a regal, a small organ with reed pipes only, but there is no other instrument.

It is certainly possible that in the Burgundian chapel some of the singers also played instruments, and minstrels who played shawms, sackbuts, fiddles or flutes may have joined the singers in masses and

motets. Yet, instruments must have been used only exceptionally in religious music and then only in certain works and perhaps only on the most solemn occasions. As for voices, we know that women did not sing in church and that treble parts were sung by the choirboys.

Today we know that, at its beginnings, medieval polyphony was reserved to soloists. In those pieces in which polyphonic sections were inserted into the middle of a plain-chant, the sections traditionally intended for soloists were composed in counterpoint, while those usually sung by the choir were done in plain-chant. It was not before the end of the fourteenth century – and for the first time in the works of Ciconia – that there occurred the first mentions of choral polyphony. In mass fragments, certain three-voice sections bear the indication *chorus* in contrast to two-voice sections normally meant for soloists. This did not necessarily mean a chorus in which all three parts were sung, since apparently at first the choir sang only the upper part, leaving the other two to instrumentalists; in some cases, the two upper voices were sung and the lower one played. Eventually the entire polyphonic ensemble came to be sung by the choir.

At the beginning of the fifteenth century, polyphony was still only occasionally confided to an entire chorus, but this became more frequent between 1430 and 1440. If between those dates precise indications become more frequent in the manuscripts, it is perhaps because it seemed advisable to give specific directions to the performers at a time when traditional practices were being dropped, since once choral polyphony had triumphed and set up its own traditions such directions no longer seem to have been thought necessary.

One positive proof of the change from polyphony sung by soloists to choral polyphony is the change in the dimensions of manuscripts. As long as the music was intended for soloists, one singer to a part, choir books remained small, no more than about ten by twelve inches. But when larger groups began to sing from them they became very much larger – indeed, some of them were more than three feet tall – and were set up on a lectern around which the entire choir gathered. Not that those choirs were large. The most important of them had no more than a dozen singers in the fifteenth century, twice that a century later.

We know too that in the second half of the fifteenth century a change of style came about, and counterpoint was normally no longer written for three voices but for four, and these four voices were all of equal importance. With this change, it was natural that an effort should be made to balance the sonorities by confiding all the voice parts to a chorus, a practice which was maintained when composers took to writing for five, six and even more voices.

This does not mean that instruments were not used in motets and masses. On the contrary, they seem to have been called for more frequently in the sixteenth century than earlier. However, they no longer replaced singers but merely doubled the voice parts, thereby amplifying and reinforcing them to enrich their sonority. In the *Triumph of Maximilian,* there are a player on a sackbut and one on a cornet among the singers of the imperial chapel. An engraving by Philippe Galle in the *Encomium musices* depicts a religious ceremony with singers and players of sackbut and cornet divided into several groups. On the first page of Herman Finck's *Practica musica* of 1556 we see seven choirboys, a dozen cantors, two cornetists and a sackbut player gathered around an open choir book on a lectern. Cornets and sackbuts seem to have been used most often, together with the organ, in choral polyphony, no doubt because they helped to keep the singers on pitch and blended harmoniously with the voices.

Sometimes other instruments were brought in. Various iconographic documents prove this, as do certain publications from the second half of the sixteenth century which mention explicitly the use of instruments in church music. But it was not before 1587 that a composer thought of specifying exactly what instruments were to be used and how : in some of his motets, Giovanni Gabrieli juxtaposes and contrasts a four-voice chorus with passages for a soloist accompanied by the organ, or with purely instrumental passages for three cornets, one violin and two trombones, or with others for two soloists and instruments, or, finally, with ensembles in which instruments and chorus join together. This is genuine orchestration, in which the composer takes into account tone color in laying out his composition and is no longer willing to depend on tradition and the whims of interpreters. All this, however, took place in another aesthetic climate, that of the Baroque.

The Romantics succeeded in implanting for a long time the notion that the ideal of sixteenth-century music was choral music sung strictly *a cappella,* a term still in use today for choral singing without accompaniment. However, it was the seventeenth and not the sixteenth century that took to speaking of *a cappella* music and at the very moment when rigorous polyphonic writing was becoming outmoded, when the current style was monody with instrumental accompaniment. At that time, the old style (*stylus antiquus*) and severe style (*stylus gravis*) were also called church style (*ecclesiasticus*) or chapel style (*a cappella*) and this meant counterpoint in the manner of Palestrina and the Flemish. In a quite artificial attempt to enhance the dignity of such music at a time when instrumental accompaniment had become a matter of course in every kind of music, it was insisted that such contrapuntal music was purely choral, meant for voices alone. The sixteenth century itself seems to have been much more liberal in the matter, sometimes performing polyphonic religious works with unaccompanied chorus, sometimes with balanced ensembles in which instruments either doubled the voices or even substituted for them.

In profane music also, the evolution of musical language after the end of the fifteenth century was responsible for an equilibrium among the contrapuntal parts, and chansons came to be interpreted by voices alone, without instruments. As for the Italian madrigal, its ideal seems to have been vocal performance pure and simple. Unlike religious music, there was never any question of using a chorus to sing madrigals. Secular music was music for soloists, performed only by small groups of amateurs or professionals.

Thus, interpreters were allowed certain possibilities of choice, and the indications in publications of the time prove this without question : *Songs apt as much to voices as to instruments,* said Susato in 1543, and *Most pleasant to sing and play on all musical instruments* in 1551; *Songs ... suitable to all musical instruments* were advertised by Attaingnant in 1549; *Joyful music fitting both for the human voice and to learn how to play spinets, violins and flutes,* announced Jacques Moderne in 1550; *Songs ... delightful to sing and useful for all instruments* were put out by the Nuremberg publisher Formschneider in 1536; and *Lovely, charming German songs, not only for singing but also for playing on all manner of instruments* were sold by J. vom Berg and Neuber in Nuremberg in 1563. And while instruments were not used in Italian madrigals, it is interesting to note that voices could be introduced into pieces like the *ricercari* and *fantasias,* which seem specifically instrumental, as is indicated by the title of a collection published by Gardane in Venice in 1551, *Fantasies, ricercari, counterpoints for three voices ... to sing and play on all sorts of instruments.*

The instruments most often used were the flute and lute, as we see in the trio of young ladies by the Master of the Half-Length Figures in the Harrach Museum, Vienna, and in the erotic scene by an anonymous Flemish master in the Musée Carnavalet, Paris. Performances could be by voices alone, with women participating in profane music, or by an ensemble of instruments of the same family, such as viols or flutes, or by instruments of different kinds, or finally by a mixture of voices and instruments. Further, it must not be forgotten that arrangements of polyphonic chansons were played on the lute or harpsichord and also that a voice could sing accompanied by a lute or harpsichord which played all the other polyphonic parts.

FACTS AND FANCIES

Despite all efforts to rediscover the actual sound of early music, many aspects of it still remain obscure. In these pages we have been able to do no more than stress a few things known for certain and to show what doubts remain as to the size of groups employed and the participation of instruments in an essentially vocal repertory.

The problems become more numerous as soon as one tries to reconstitute the works of the past in present-day performances which aim at authenticity. Today instruments of the past are either constructed on the model of a few rare examples which have survived or else after pictorial images, so that now we have lutes, spinets, clavichords, viols, recorders, cornets and organs. But how can we be sure that they have the same timbre as instruments once had ? And do not performers today too often employ modern techniques unfaithful to the nature of the instruments ?

And the human voice ? We should like to think it has not changed over the years, but that ignores the fact that vocal technique also is subject to changing aesthetic criteria. We know from gramophone records that Flamenco singing has nothing in common with the singing style of Negro spirituals or with that of Neapolitan *bel canto.* The standards that define beautiful voices or fine vocal style vary from one type of music to another. After all, we know that no fifteenth-century singer ever used his voice in the style used today for operas or lieder. But that does not mean that all early music must be sung in a style diametrically opposed to *bel canto,* for that too would be an arbitrary convention without basis in fact. The real situation in the past was more complex, far more varied.

If there is any positive conclusion to be drawn from these difficult problems, it is that, despite a certain unity of language, polyphony had many facets. There was not a single early music but many early musics, and they varied in aesthetic and technique at different times, in different places and according to their different functions. One of the most urgent tasks of musicology today is to try to rediscover the actual sound of works of the past in all their mobility and in all their possible variants. This is a particularly delicate undertaking since the evidence is contradictory and full of traps for the unwary. To reconstruct that reality, we must call not only on a rigorously historical critical method but even more on a heightened artistic sensibility : it is in fact the latter which, in the final analysis, must bring about that creative synthesis which is a musical performance.

No certainty rewards such great efforts. Quite the contrary. We know that we can never achieve more than an approximation of past realities. And this approximation must be ceaselessly corrected as our knowledge of the past grows and as our own sensibilities become more acute.

Chapter 8

81. The Three Ages of Man.
Giorgione (?).

The Flemings in Italy

It does not suffice to say that Flemish musicians were appreciated in Italy, that they were sought after for princely chapels and city churches. The fact is that it was Italy which crowned their merits, which spread their fame throughout Europe. And at the same time, the Flemings came under Italian influence and developed an art of profound originality thanks to their uninterrupted contact with that country.

THE FIRST NORTHERN MUSICIANS IN ITALY

This fruitful contact began at the end of the fourteenth century with a canon from Liège, Johannes Ciconia. His international career started in Avignon, where many clerics from the principality of Liège were busy at the pontifical court, though it does not appear that he was a member of the papal chapel, which included at that time only seven choirboys and a few cantors. It was in 1358 that he went for the first time to Italy, in the service of Cardinal Albornoz, who was charged with a military mission there. After the death of the Cardinal, in 1368, Ciconia must have returned to his native city for a long spell, but he finally went back to Italy, to Padua, where he became a canon and where he died in 1411.

At the start, Ciconia practiced the technique of the *ars nova* in its French manner, but after having composed *madrigali* and *ballate* completely Italian in form and spirit, and after having celebrated in his motets the splendor of Venise of the glory of the bishop of Padua, he developed a manner which is best described as a compromise between French *subtilitas* and Italian *dulcedo*. In this way, he contributed to the creation of a new style which turned its back on the mannerism of Machaut's successors and which sought after architectonic simplicity and effectiveness.

After the exile in Avignon, when the popes returned to Italy, first to Florence and then to Rome, they brought with them many northern musicians and continued to call in men from Liège, from Hainaut and from France. The chapel of Martin V in 1417 included only northern musicians, not a single Italian. Among those who have left evidence of activity as composers, there were Pierre Fontaine of Rouen, who was later to become chaplain of the dukes of Burgundy, the Parisian Nicolas Grenon, who had been attached to the cathedrals of Laon and Cambrai, Philippe Foliot of Cambrai, later in the service of Philip the Good, and Jean Brassart and Arnold de Lantins from the diocese of Liège.

If natives of Liège were so numerous among the first generation of northern musicians in Italy, the reasons without doubt had nothing to do with their art as such : the presence in Liège of a prince-bishop whose political support was desired by the Pope explains why so many clerics native to Liège, and

221

among them musicians, should have been taken on at the papal court. From such an elect position they were able to spread out to one or another of the princely courts or to important city churches. Such was the case with Hugo de Lantins, Johannes de Lymburgia, Johannes de Sarto, Johannes Franchois de Gemblaco (from Gembloux near Liège), Henri Battre of Ciney in the county of Namur, and also Reginald Liebert. Their compositions – motets, mass sections, *canzoni*, French chansons – are numerous in Italian manuscripts of the second third of the century, such as the codices 37 of the Liceo Musicale of Bologna, L. 471 of Modena, Canonici 213 of the Bodleian Library, Oxford, 87 to 93 of Trent and many others. These manuscripts also include works by Burgundian, French and English composers who must have worked in Italy, and they supply valuable evidence of the stylistic melting-pot from which was to come a new international language made famous by Guillaume Dufay.

If Dufay's Italian years gave him the leisure to compose works for special occasions for various cities and princely families, they permitted him above all to master progressively the essential elements of his language. Besseler has shown very well that it was during his Roman period around 1430 that Dufay integrated into his style those innovations characteristic of it : a flowing and supple rhythm in which the meter is often of the type called perfect-diminished and which rejects the use of imperfect meter with major prolation, a tonal harmony in which the lowest voice, solidly based on the tonic and dominant, begins to play a specific role and to sustain the entire edifice, a less rigorous counterpoint whose dissonances are introduced without shocking and acquire an expressive character.

To this must be added the fact that it was really Italy which established Dufay's fame as a composer. He remained in close contact with the Italians even after having given up his position as chapel master for the dukes of Savoy and even after his return to Cambrai.

NORTHERNERS AS SINGERS

It was perhaps not at first for their gifts as composers that northern musicians were first appreciated across the Alps but rather for their skill as singers. In the Renaissance, Italy had not yet acquired its reputation as the land of *bel canto*. When the wealthiest churches and courts began to wish to have polyphonic music as a regular part of their services, they organized choirs for which they needed good singers. For these, they called on musicians from the North, since what was needed was singers trained in the new art of mensural notation, one more proof that a fine voice is less a gift of nature than the product of training according to certain aesthetic standards.

In Florence, when polyphony was being introduced into the cathedral and baptistery, singers were first recruited from nearby Ferrara, but when higher standards of performance were sought after, it was from the Burgundian states that singers were brought. The Medici arranged for their bankers in Bruges to pay the expenses of special envoys charged with ferreting out good voices. Documents show them in 1448 on the hunt at Antwerp, where they engaged a *tenorista* and a *soprano*, in 1467 at Cambrai and Douai. Dufay himself procured singers from Cambrai, and in a letter the Florentine organist Squarcialupi thanked him for having sent the best musicians of his church : *They are excellent, as much for the sweetness of their voices as for the skill in singing they acquired under your direction.*

In 1474, Duke Galeazzo Sforza of Milan sent one of his Flemish cantors, the composer Gaspar van Weerbecke, into Picardy and Flanders with the mission of bringing back ten good *soprani*, two tenors and two basses. A few years later, an envoy of the Duke of Ferrara, Bartholomio de Fiandria, reported from a similar mission that he had engaged at the cathedral of Antwerp three tenors, two contraltos and a fine bass and found also a contralto at the church of Notre-Dame in Bruges and two good sopranos at Thérouanne in Picardy.

It was young choristers who were sought after, since boys were needed to sing the top voices in polyphonic pieces, and the Flemings enjoyed a high reputation in this, since in the chapel schools boys were trained early in a certain type of voice production and in a certain style. When their voices changed, some of these youngsters returned home, but others, whose adult voices remained good, stayed on to continue their careers abroad.

In the first half of the fifteenth century, northern musicians were not yet very numerous in Italy. It was only after 1460 that they were recruited in numbers, and this coincides with the time when the practice of polyphony seems to have become widespread in Italy. Cities and princes then competed to engage the best singers. It was no longer enough merely to seek them out in their native lands. Now they were lured from one city to another, from one court to another, and there was a constant scurrying back and forth of singers between Milan, Ferrara, Florence and Venice as the great families – the Estes, Sforzas, Visconti and Medici – strove to outbid each other.

THE GENERATION OF JOSQUIN DESPREZ

If mere singers received so much attention, outstanding professionals were even more sought after, those who could direct a chapel and give to it a distinctive style in performance and who could compose an entire repertory of motets and masses for their patrons.

A report sent to the Duke of Ferrara in 1502 illustrates these concerns. It is a question of which should be engaged, Josquin Desprez or Heinrich Isaac : *Isaac the cantor is at the moment in Ferrara. He took only two days to compose an excellent motet, a sure sign of how rapid he is in the art of composing. He is gentlemanly and has good manners and might very well please the Duke. I was charged with asking him if he would agree to enter the Duke's service, and he replied that while he would not decline the offer he would like a month* *to think over his answer. He was promised ten ducats a month if the Duke agreed. He would seem to me more apt than Josquin to serve the Duke since he is of more sociable character and would compose more. Not that Josquin is not perhaps the better composer, but he writes only when he feels like it. Besides, he wants two hundred ducats in payment, and Isaac will settle for one hundred and twenty.*

In the generation after Dufay, many good musicians had not yet been seduced across the Alps. This was the case of Ockeghem and Busnois although their works figure prominently in Italian manuscripts. Only the generation following, that of Josquin, really felt the call of Italy.

Johannes Tinctoris was never a prolific composer – from him we have only four masses, two motets, some lamentations and a few secular works – but he was certainly the most important theorist of the fifteenth century. He must have arrived in Italy from Brabant between 1471 and 1475, and until his death in 1511 he lived in Naples as chaplain to King Ferdinand of Aragon. His theoretical works constitute a systematic account of the teaching of music as practiced in the chapel schools of the North. The rules he lays down and the advice he gives are based on the compositions of Ockeghem, Busnois and the best of their contemporaries. It was he who was largely responsible for spreading throughout Italy the principles of perfection of the art as he understood them from the most representative masters of the time.

Josquin Desprez likewise had a career which was essentially Italian. Born around 1440 in Hainaut, apparently, it is in Italy that he turns up for the first time in any document. In 1459 he was still young but already a *biscantor,* that is, a cantor at the cathedral of Milan, but he left this modest position in 1473 to enter the private chapel of Duke Galeazzo Sforza, still as a cantor of the lowest category and with a humble salary. He left Milan in 1479 for Rome and the service of Cardinal Ascanio Sforza and the papal chapel, where he appears in

IOSQVINVS PRATENSIS.

82. Portrait of Josquin Desprez.
Woodcut.

the lists of cantors from 1486 to 1494. It was in Rome that he acquired his reputation as composer, a reputation which grew with startling rapidity. Already at the beginning of the new century, he was considered one of the best composers of his time and many saw in him the veritable master of them all. For some time he may have been in the service of King Louis XII of France, for whom he wrote several works, but in 1503 he was again in Italy. After serving as chapel master for Duke Ercole d'Este in Ferrara, he seems to have been able to live on the commissions he received and on certain canonical prebends. He was, as a matter of fact, also canon of the collegiate church of Sainte-Gudule in Brussels and provost of the chapter at the church in Condé-sur-l'Escaut, where he died in 1521, having returned to his native land to spend his last years despite his deeply Italian character. Just how important his contribution was has already been considered in this book.

Heinrich Isaac was born around 1450. Italian sources of the second half of the sixteenth century attribute a German origin to him, naming him Arrigo Tedesco, which may be explained by certain phases in his career; he himself, in his testament, says he was the son of a certain Ugo de Flandria. He lived for a long time in Florence, where he was cantor at the cathedral and at the baptistery from 1484 on and where he married a Florentine woman. Favorite musician of Lorenzo the Magnificent, he tutored the latter's sons in music, especially the future Pope Leo X. After the fall of the Medici and the rise to power of Savonarola, he became the official composer for Emperor Maximilian, but in 1509 he returned to Florence and died there in 1517.

Besides the *Choralis Constantinus*, he composed polyphonic Ordinaries, motets, secular songs in French, Italian and German, and a few purely instrumental fantasies. A master of international status and character, he generally remained faithful to the most austere contrapuntal art.

Gaspar van Weerbecke must have been born around 1440 in Audenarde. Arriving in Milan in 1471, fresh from Flanders, he was assigned the task of organizing the ducal chapel. Duke Galeazzo had had a French education, and *loving singers more than any prince in the world*, as Molinet put it, he could be content only with musicians from across the Alps. Not only did he have numerous singers recruited in Flanders and Artois, but he also blithely transferred to his private chapel all the foreigners previously engaged by the cathedral. Among his eighteen *cantori da camera* and his twenty-two *cantori da cappella*, alongside Josquin Desprez, Agricola, Compère and Martini, other less famous names betray their French or Flemish origins : Victore de Bruges, Rugiero de Flandria, Antonio de Cambray, Cornelio Svagher di Fiandra, Antonio Baerd de Bruges, Michele de Tours, Jacheto de Rohanno (Rouen), Enrico Knoep, Johannes Cordier (from Louvain), Du Bois, and so on. This splendid chapel was very much reduced after the assassination of the Duke in December, 1476. Thus, the rest of the career of Weerbecke passed mostly in Rome, where he was cantor in the pontifical chapel from 1481 to 1489 and from 1500 to 1515 and where he must have died soon after the latter date. Between these two sojourns in Rome he renewed his relations with the Sforzas and was also attached to the Burgundian chapel under Philip the Handsome.

If we stop confusing the few chansons by "Gaspart" with the much more numerous ones by a certain "Jaspart," a Flemish contemporary working as cantor at the court of Ferrara, it is evident that Weerbecke was above all a composer of religious music. He composed many motets of which some, according to a practice peculiar to northern Italy, were

225

organized in cycles to replace the sections of the Ordinary of the mass, and in addition there are lamentations, Magnificats and masses.

We know little about the origins of Alexander Agricola. Certain documents describe him as *ex Alamania,* but according to his epitaph he was *Belga.* It is most likely that he was Flemish. Born in 1446, he is to be found in Florence in 1470, when he married. From 1472 to 1474 he was at the court of the Sforzas in Milan. Then he seems to have been cantor at the cathedral of Cambrai but once again returned to Italy before entering the chapel of Philip the Handsome in 1500. Like his last master, he died of the plague at Valladolid in 1506. His surviving works comprise nine masses – of which one uses as *cantus firmus* a Flemish chanson, *In minen zin,* about twenty-five motets and almost a hundred chansons, most of them French but a few on Italian or Flemish texts. Agricola remained faithful to the tradition of Ockeghem, writing a tightly woven counterpoint built up by the superposition of dynamic lines which seem to preserve a large measure of independence. Except in his *canti carnascialeschi,* he was rather less willing than many others to lighten his style of writing and to practice the harmonic style occasionally indulged in by northern musicians in contact with Italy.

Loyset Compère seems to have been born around 1450, perhaps in Saint-Omer. It has been claimed that he was a pupil of Ockeghem, but that has been said of the best musicians of his generation – Josquin, Weerbecke, Agricola, Brumel – simply because they are mentioned in the *Déploration sur le trépas d'Ockeghem,* the memorial ode by Guillaume Crétin in which the phrase calling on them all *pour lamenter nostre maistre et bon père* is undoubtedly no more than a rhetorical formula. Compère probably began his musical studies in some church in northern France or in the duchy of Burgundy before leaving for Italy, where, in 1474, he was cantor at the ducal chapel in Milan. Later he became *chantre ordinaire* of King Charles VIII in Paris,

dean of the church of Saint-Géry in Cambrai, provost of the collegiate church of Saint-Pierre in Douai and canon in Saint-Quentin. His death occurred in 1518. It is obvious that his direct contacts with Italy were not many, and yet he is most extensively represented in Italian manuscripts with religious works including masses, motets, *motteti-missales,* Magnificats and the like and a great many of his chansons were printed by Petrucci in the *Odhecaton, Canti B* and *Canti C.* It is not impossible that certain years in his life which are not documented may have been spent in Italy.

Jacob Obrecht spent most of his life in the Low Countries. It has been presumed that he was born in Bergen-op-Zoom around 1450, but we know that from 1452 on his father Willem was trumpeter for the city of Ghent. He himself was in turn singing master at Bergen-op-Zoom, at the cathedral of Cambrai, at Saint-Donatien in Bruges, at the Antwerp cathedral, and then again in Bruges. But on the specific invitation of Duke Ercole I d'Este he spent some months in Ferrara in 1487 and 1488 and returned there in 1504 to be struck down by the plague in the following year. His music was known in Italy through numerous manuscripts and publications, and his masses, motets and chansons won for him there more than elsewhere his reputation as one of the greatest composers of the time.

On a somewhat lower level of excellence there was Johannes Martini, a Fleming so thoroughly assimilated into his adopted country that we know him only by this obviously Italianized name. From 1475 to 1489 at least, he was in the service of Ercole d'Este before joining the court of Francesco Gonzaga, husband of Isabella d'Este, in Mantua. There was also Johannes Prioris, organist at Saint Peter's in Rome in 1490 before becoming chapel master of King Louis XII of France. Marbriano de Orto was cantor in the pontifical chapel from 1484 to 1494 and in this period held benefices as canon at Comines and dean of Sainte-Gertrude in Nivelles, which permits us to make certain guesses about his origins. Later he joined the chapel of Philip the Handsome and of the future Charles V and died in Nivelles in 1529. Jean Ghiselin, known also as Jean Verbonnet, is mentioned at the court of Ferrara in 1491, 1503 and 1535. Johannes Stokhem of Liège, friend of Tinctoris, was a cantor in the pontifical chapel from 1486 to 1489, after having been in the service of the Queen of Hungary, Beatrice of Aragon from Naples. For his part, Antoine Brumel was French – he held various charges in the churches of Chartres, Laon and Paris – but in 1513 he was at the court of Pope Leo X and in 1520 in Ferrara.

This summary listing shows that the first generation of northern musicians really to be attracted to Italy was that of Josquin. From 1460 or 1470 on, not only the papal chapel but also princes and cities regularly recruited their musicians from the North. The organization of Italy into small principalities or rich and powerful cities favored a competitiveness from which musicians, like other artists, did not fail to profit. For the taste for Flemish counterpoint was also a matter of fashion. Every prince of quality, every church of any importance had to have Flemish singers. Italy thereby became a privileged market which stimulated musical creation, and excellent working conditions there encouraged many musicians to go on to composing who might have remained no more than humble cantors in one or another church of the Low Countries.

THE BEGINNINGS OF MUSIC PRINTING

The development of music printing helped to further the reputation of composers and to make their works known more widely. The first printed book to contain music was the *Psalterium latinum* published in Mainz in 1475 by Faust and Schöffer, Gutenberg's associates. But real music publishing occurred somewhat later and involved liturgical books – missals, graduals, antiphonaries and psalters – in Gregorian notation, which was either Gothic, that is, with lozenge-shaped notes, or Roman, with square notes. A missal printed in Rome by Ulrich Hahn

dates from 1476 and there is a gradual from Constance from a few years before. From then until the end of the century, some two hundred and seventy printed liturgical books have survived.

What was difficult in printing music was the placing at the right height on the horizontal lines of the various kinds of notes, whether isolated or grouped, and to co-ordinate them with the text. Usually the lines and the text were printed first and then were over-printed with all the notes belonging on a staff, which were assembled together. This type of double-printing was slow and expensive, which doubtless explains why in some books only the notes were printed, the lines of the staff being added later by hand.

Musical examples were also printed in theoretical works. There is a full page of printed music in the *Grammatica* of Francesco Nigro published in Venice in 1480 by Theodor von Würzburg; this includes both mensural music and plain-chant, but the lines of the staves were still added by hand. The first complete printing of polyphonic music appeared in 1487 in the *Musices opusculum* of Burtius published in Bologna. In the second part of the *Practica musicæ* by Gafurius published at Milan in 1496 there are numerous examples of polyphonic music. Up to that time, however, printed polyphonic music was limited to such examples in theoretical works.

In 1498 Ottaviano de' Petrucci in Venice obtained exclusive rights for twenty years to publish polyphonic music, whether vocal works or organ and lute tablatures. Petrucci used a three-stage process, printing first the staff, then the text, clefs and signatures, and finally the notes. He was able to apply the techniques then known to printing complete works in mensural notation and besides was the first to print lute tablatures. All the products of his press have remarkable formal beauty.

But Petrucci was much more than a printer. He was also an editor who, by putting on the market a great number of polyphonic works, contributed greatly to making their performance more widespread and to broadening the public for them.

In his first publications, the *Harmonice musices Odhecaton* (1501), the *Canti B* (1502) and the *Canti C* (1504), almost all the pieces are secular and by Flemish or French composers. They include all the composers from beyond the Alps who worked in Italy – Josquin, Isaac, Brumel, Compère, Weerbecke, Martini and the others – as well as many known in Italy only by reputation, such as Ockeghem, Busnois, Hayne van Ghizeghem, Pierre de la Rue and Regis. When Petrucci began to publish religious music – anthologies of motets and masses and volumes devoted to a single composer – he chose almost exclusively Flemings and a few French; Italians appear only in collections of Lamentations, written in a less highly developed style than that of the motets. On the other hand, in the books of *frottole*, secular pieces in a much lighter style, which he published from 1504 on, it is the Italians who predominate, thanks to certain composers who specialized in the genre, notably Tromboncino and Cara. In these, the Flemish appear only exceptionally, and this is true also of the collections of *laude*, religious hymns in a very simple style faithful to a specifically Italian tradition.

Thus there are two clearly distinguished currents in Petrucci's publications. On the one hand, high art, which is essentially religious but may include also chansons and which is the special province of the northern musicians, and on the other hand a light, unpretentious music, mostly secular but also sacred, which is a local product.

Other publishers took to imitating Petrucci in the following years. His most considerable rival was Andrea Antico. Working in Rome, Antico brought out in 1510 a book of *Canzoni nove* and in 1515 a *Liber quindecim missarum* and his subsequent publications along the same lines show that he followed the same policy as Petrucci of reserving the facile Italian pieces to local composers while calling on the French and Flemish for masses and motets.

Up to 1520, when his activity ceased, Petrucci remained the most important publisher of polyphonic music. By that date he had brought out fifty-nine volumes – thirty-two of religious music and twenty-seven of secular – while his competitors in Rome, Siena, Naples and Venice had published no more than seven in all.

Anne-Marie Bautier-Regnier has worked out highly instructive statistics on the first Italian publications. Between 1501 and 1510, fifty northern musicians and forty-four Italians had been printed, while between 1511 and 1520 the proportion became, respectively, thirty-three to thirty. Up to 1520 Italians appear in only four of the thirty-three volumes devoted to religious music; out of forty-three collections of secular music, the Flemings are responsible for only eight books of chansons.

Without in any way corresponding to their intrinsic value, the relative importance of various composers can also be glimpsed from such figures. Between 1501 and 1510, Josquin has a total of sixty-nine pieces published or re-published in twelve collections, Compère fifty-seven, Agricola forty-seven, Obrecht twenty-eight, Japart twenty-seven, Brumel twenty-five, Weerbecke twenty-three, Ghiselin eighteen, Busnois and Stokhem fifteen each, Isaac fourteen, Pierre de la Rue nine, and these same names reappear with Josquin in the lead in collections of masses. For the period between 1511 and 1520, new names appear in the wake of Josquin, those of a new generation, with Jean Mouton represented by twenty-three works and Antoine de Févin by seventeen; Josquin is still prominent, with twenty-one pieces, but musicians like Agricola, Isaac, Obrecht are relegated to secondary places.

Thus the first Italian music publications reveal most convincingly a situation which had existed ever since around 1470 : the predominance of Flemings and a few Frenchmen wherever the austere art of counterpoint was practiced, whether in the mass, the motet or the chanson.

ITALIAN INFLUENCE ON FLEMISH MUSIC
Alongside the high art of international quality, less learned techniques survived locally in a more traditional style, and these more typically Italian manifestations could easily in turn influence the men from the North. Within the religious repertory there were certain works with no ambition to be anything more than functional, written in a simpler style, easier to perform, with all four polyphonic voices moving along together in harmonies which follow the melody of the topmost voice. This style was used in Lamentations, Passions and, in general, for all texts too lengthy to be set without difficulty in the motet technique, as well as for *laude*, which were generally hymns of praise to the Virgin on poetic texts, always in the vernacular, which were modeled after the patterns of secular poetry. At the outset the music used for the *laude* was monodic, although in manuscripts from the fifteenth century there are polyphonic *laude* for two or three voices in a very simple style. In 1507 and 1508 Petrucci published two collections of *laude* for four or, exceptionally, for five voices. These are brief pieces composed in a style which can be called harmonic since the top voice with its flowing line has almost always all the melodic interest while the other voices merely support it, very seldom indulging in any contrapuntal activity and with the most rare and discreet imitations. Not that this was truly what could be called a popular art, but it was certainly a simpler art than that of the Flemings. *Laude* were written by specialists like Innocentius Dammonis, to whom Petrucci's first collection is devoted, or to composers of *frottole* like Tromboncino, Cara or Luprano, and it was not infrequent

that music initially written for a love ditty was later adapted to a canticle in praise of the Virgin.

But what was most typically Italian expressed itself best in the secular sphere. The tradition of *ballate* and *madrigali* which had produced so many masterworks had declined in the course of the Quattrocento but not disappeared, living on in a few courts. In the first half of the fifteenth century, the Venetian poet Leonardo Giustiniani sang amorous verses accompanying himself on the lute or lira da braccio, thereby giving rise to a genre of little pieces known as *Justiniane* or *Viniziane*. Using certain formulas as a basis, the music was largely improvised. But at times the melody was noted down along with the two accompanying voices intended for instruments, and there are even a few pieces with all their ornaments written out. In those cases we find the old tradition of the Italian *ars nova* still operating in these long coloraturas alternating with fragments of verse sung in a virtually syllabic manner. The old style lived on in this way into the fifteenth century, but was forced to lead a rather discreet existence in the face of the rousing success of rondeaux and ballades on French texts in the manner of Dufay.

When northern composers composed on Italian texts, they tried to instill into their melodies the spirit of this style, as we can hear it in *O rosa bella*, one of Giustiniani's *ballate* set to music by both Ciconia and Dunstable. Dufay too seems to have been sensitive to the charm of such highly ornate phrases in pieces like *Quel fronte signorille* and *Vergine bella*, the latter a setting of a poem of Petrarch, but he strove above all to integrate these elements into his own idiom, to assimilate them into his own learned style.

It was only at the end of the fifteenth century, at the very time the Flemish were most dominant on the musical scene, that certain courts aimed to restore to Italian songs their lost prestige. Thus Lorenzo de' Medici had songs written for the Florentine carnival when he had transformed it into a triumphal cortège to celebrate the greatness of the city and of its leaders. These were pieces for three or four voices in a very homophonic style and often on quite obscene subjects. Far from having the refinement of the *ballata,* they deliberately sought to be a stylization of a folk art. Some of these *canti carnascialeschi* were composed by Flemings like Isaac and Agricola.

In Mantua, Isabella d'Este, the very intellectual wife of Marquis Francesco Gonzaga, likewise helped restore the prestige of polyphonic songs on Italian texts in a style distinct from that of the Flemish, and their success was such that soon they were written and sung in Verona, Ferrara, Urbino and Venice and then in Rome and Naples. Under the general designation of *frottole,* these Italian songs became enthusiastically accepted from 1504 on, thanks to the publications of Petrucci, which were imitated and plagiarized by other editors.

The favorite theme of the frottola was love, treated most often in a rather precious way but sometimes also with a dash of wit. Some frottolas even indulged in outright obscenities, and they must be understood as a stylized parody of a popular entertainment served up in fancier form for the delight of aristocratic salons. At the beginning of the sixteenth century the frottola was generally written for four parts with the upper voice clearly dominating the others. The lowest voice moved along in leaps of a fourth or fifth and provided something like a functional bass while the inner voices merely filled in the framework. Often the frottola must have been sung by a solo voice accompanied on the lute or, as Castiglione indicates, by a viol, but also each of the parts could be played on a different instrument or all four voices could be sung. A rapid and syllabic melody, a frank and direct rhythm, a dancelike character – all conspired to make the frottola seem, however factitiously, a kind of popular music in marked contrast with the sophistication of that composed in counterpoint. In the more serious type, the *strambotti,* improvisation was used, and it

was precisely among the authors of frottolas that was perpetuated the old tradition of poet-improvisers such as Giustiniani had been. The most famous of them, and the most prolific, Bartolomeo Tromboncino and Marco Cara, were *cantori al liuto* who interpreted their own works at Mantua and in various courts. Their success was considerably helped by the publications of Petrucci and the others. There were many of these frottolists, and we know of something like forty of them who seem to have written nothing else. They were never musicians trained in either the one or the other church school, but rather specialists, at one and the same time singers, improvisers, lutenists, often poets also and always courtiers.

The success of the new genre could not fail to attract the interest of the Flemings, if only occasionally. Isaac wrote excellent strambotti, Josquin went so far in the way of pleasantry as to imitate a chirping cricket in *El grillo,* and Compère indulged his wit in *Scaramella fa la galla.*

But if the northerners came under Italian influence at that time, it was less in terms of adopting these native genres than of assimilating into their own contrapuntal style certain procedures inspired by local practice. To Italian influence may be ascribed the lightening of contrapuntal texture typical of Josquin's contemporaries. From their time on, composition was no longer conceived of as the mere superimposition of different melodic lines. The bond which linked all the voices in a polyphonic construction often led to the alternation of episodes in imitative style with others of homorhythmic character in which harmonic writing prevailed. In their secular music, the Flemings took to using those forthright and dancelike rhythms favored by the Italians, and like their hosts, they began to supply a tonal basis to their harmony. The formal equilibrium which from then on dominated their works was likewise, perhaps, learned from the Italians, as also the greater care used in setting texts, in terms of both declamation and expression.

231

84. Garden of Delights.
Cristoforo de' Predis or school.

Prolonged contact with Italy came in this way to give a new character to the music of the men from the North. Josquin was not alone in achieving a harmonious synthesis in which the contrapuntal tradition was revivified, and others such as Brumel and Weerbecke were similarly affected, though to a minor degree.

ADRIAN WILLAERT

The great transmigration of musicians from the North into Italy did not slacken in the first half of the sixteenth century. In the papal chapel the Italians were still not numerous, and among the foreign singers there were, along with the Flemings, many Frenchmen and Spaniards. And after Josquin, another Fleming came to represent what was perfection in music for Italy : Adrian Willaert.

Willaert was born between 1480 and 1490 in Bruges, it is thought. He must have had his first training in some church in the Low Countries and then studied law in Paris. There is some possibility that he may have been a pupil of Mouton. He did not turn up in Italy until around 1520, when he appeared at the court of Alfonso I in Ferrara. From 1525 to 1527 he was cantor in the chapel of Archbishop Ippolito d'Este — one of the sons of the Duke — in Milan. But, at the end of 1527 he succeeded Petrus de Fossis, another Fleming, as chapel master of Saint Mark's in Venice. By remaining in this position until his death in 1562, he was able to make of Venice one of the most active centers of musical creation of the period. He composed prolifically in all the genres, often giving them a novel orientation, and he trained a great number of students of real worth, both Flemish and Italian, who for long continued to sing his praises.

It was at first by his religious music that Willaert aroused the enthusiasm of his contemporaries. We do not have many masses from his pen but there are a great many motets and these were often reprinted. As early as 1539, Scotto in Venice published a volume of motets for four voices by the *famosissimus Adrianus Willaert.* In that same year there appeared another volume of motets, this one for five voices, and in 1549 a volume for six voices was almost entirely devoted to him. Finally, in 1559, his *Musica nova* appeared with thirty-three motets for from four to seven voices together with twenty-five of his secular madrigals, all of them works which must have been composed before 1545. If they still deserved to be called *musica nova*, it was because Willaert appeared to his contemporaries as an audacious musician not content to rework the old formulas of Flemish counterpoint that had been inherited from Josquin.

Two Italian pupils of Willaert, Vincentino and Zarlino, both of them important theorists, accord to him the glory of having restored to honor the use of chromaticism. In the Greek and Latin theoretical writings on music, the Humanists had discovered that Antiquity had known three melodic genera : diatonic, chromatic and enharmonic. For them, Willaert was among the first composers to enrich music with the resources of chromaticism, by coloring it with accidentals — sharps and flats — and by broadening the use of *musica ficta.*

Even before 1520 Willaert had made a great impact by composing a brief piece for two voices without words to which he gave the title *Quidnam ebrietas* (more correctly, according to certain sources *Quid non ebrietas*), a title taken from Horace's Fifth Epistle and justified by the bizarre character of the counterpoint : below a perfectly normal soprano line, a tenor seems to wander about aimlessly, stumbling into apparently weird contrapuntal contradictions, and finally concluding on the dissonance of a seventh without resolution. This piece was discussed and commented on by erudite theorists who, either to justify it or attack it, called on the respective systems of Pythagoras or Ptolemy. Composers especially engaged in passionate controversy over it, since obviously it was plunging music into the uncharted and troublesome paths of chromaticism. And yet, to look at the piece, Willaert

233

seems to have made only a quite discreet use of chromaticism : the two voices use a single flat in the signature, the tenor has only a few passing accidentals and the soprano none. But that was where the rub lay : those passing accidentals had to be interpreted according to the principles of *musica ficta,* that is, in conformity with the practice of solmization. Every flattened note was sung as *fa* whatever its real name was in the hexachord and this promptly plunged all the following notes into a new hexachord. In this way the rules of solfeggio led singers quite unconsciously into multiplying the accidentals : soon every note in Willaert's little piece had a flat attached to it and there was nothing left except to go in for double-flats. Thus, when a complete cycle of fifths had been run through, the last note of the piece, which – on paper at least – was an E in the tenor, actually was to be sung as an E-double-flat, in other words as a D, and this gave a perfectly consonant octave with the soprano and resolved all difficulties. What the theorists argued about was whether this E-double-flat really was a D or differed from it by a comma, a minute difference in pitch. Willaert himself was not concerned with scientific demonstration but merely wished to write a work which, in appearance, would be traditional but which would, in fact, be profoundly revolutionary in actual sound : so-called chromatic accidents would no longer merely give a passing coloration to a melody but would now plunge music into the discovery of a new world, thanks to the hazards of modulation; further, a correct performance of these accidents made it necessary to adopt the system of tuning the instruments in equal temperament, which was to triumph only much later.

Other composers in the sixteenth century were to exploit chromaticism in a more consistent manner than Willaert did in most of his works, but by proposing a convincing and provocative demonstration of new possibilities the Venetian Fleming once and for all established his reputation as an innovator. It was, in fact, neither archaeological in-

85. Frontispiece to the *Musica nova* of Adrian Willaert. Woodcut.

terests nor a perverse taste for complications which led many others after him to indulge in chromaticism : their aim was to render their music more expressive. This concern likewise throws light on Willaert's modernism. It is not true, as Zarlino claimed, that Willaert was the first to accord great importance to the relations between text and music. Music's independence from its texts, an independence characteristic of medieval notions, had been progressively lessening : isorhythm had virtually disappeared from the motet, and chansons were no longer based on fixed forms. Already with Josquin the musical idea often sprang from the suggestive power of the words. Willaert's merit lies in having systematized the application of a procedure, in having deduced from it rules of composition.

According to Zarlino, who codified the teaching principles of Willaert, music could no longer be satisfied with evoking an atmosphere corresponding only to the general character of a text. It must accompany and underline every word by those melodies, harmonies and rhythms which would best express its inner meaning, and must also respect the internal rhythm of phrases, the accentuation of words, the length of syllables. Such precepts, it is true, tended to produce illustrations which were no more than picturesque, but they also laid down profoundly creative principles of composition. Musicians were thereby led to construct on the basis of their texts totally unpredictable forms created anew for each poem. Such forms were of value only if they also achieved purely musical coherence, and for the best composers subordination of music to text was only apparent, for in fact it provided a profound stimulus to musical invention.

SEPTIMA PARS
MVSICA NOVA DI
ADRIANO VVILLAERT
ALL'ILLVSTRISSIMO ET ECCEL-
LENTISSIMO SIGNOR IL SI-
GNOR DONNO ALFONSO
D'ESTE PRENCIPE
DI FERRARA.

The same concern with expression impelled certain composers to introduce unusual tensions, to exploit dissonances, rendering them constantly more subtle, here bitter, there sweet, and to this end utilizing all the resources offered by chromaticism.

In addition, Willaert has been hailed as responsible for that bi-choral music which was later to undergo significant developments in Venice in the hands of the two Gabrielis, uncle and nephew, and which was to lead to the polychoral style of the Baroque. Willaert, however, did not himself invent this technique based on the alternation of two choral groups. It had always existed in plain-chant for certain pieces in the repertory, and on the basis of this liturgical convention it was later extended to alternation between a group singing in polyphony and another in plain-chant, and eventually between two polyphonic groups. Certain Italian manuscripts of the fifteenth century – codices *Estense lat.* 454-455 – contain hymns and psalms in which two choirs alternate from verse to verse in a chordal type of polyphony and sometimes in simple fauxbourdon. In 1542 Willaert published a set of hymns calling for alternation between polyphony and chant. In each verse set in polyphony, the forces used vary from two to six voices according to an overall architectonic scheme. The Gregorian melody is always present but sometimes it is merely set out by the upper voice, sometimes it gives rise to a rigorous canon between two inner voices, at others it is paraphrased and ornamented, and, in all cases, it impregnates all the other contrapuntal voices with its material. Both technically and spiritually, these works are at the origin of the great choral art which was to flower in Lutheran countries and to achieve its climax in the works of Johann Sebastian Bach.

In psalms, the antiphonal effects can be presented in various ways. Willaert wrote *Salmi a versi senza risposte,* in which verses are sung alternately by a four-voice choir and in plain-chant, but he also wrote *Salmi a versi con le sue risposte,* in which two complete polyphonic choirs alternate; as a matter of fact, in 1550 he published a collection of these in which the even-numbered verses were set by him, the odd by Jachet of Mantua. Finally, he composed *Salmi spezzati,* with divided choirs and conceived as an integral work : two four-voice choirs alternate and, at times, unite in an eight-voice ensemble. It is in this that Willaert's originality is seen : he was able to revivify a traditional practice by taking advantage of certain practical, functional factors to achieve purely artistic ends. At Saint Mark's, the two choirs occupied facing tribunes, and alternation could create echo effects or else contrasts in timbre if instruments were used along with the voices, or then again the two choirs could be united to produce a fullness of sound such as had never before been heard anywhere. Music was thereby oriented toward aesthetic perspectives quite remote from those of contrapuntal orthodoxy. In the final analysis, it is no error to consider Willaert as the innovator in the use of antiphonal choirs. The technique he devised for the psalms proved to be a compositional device applicable elsewhere – to the motet, mass, chanson and even instrumental music – where there was no functional, liturgical necessity for what was in essence an aesthetic principle.

And yet, in his French chansons Willaert most often remained attached to an austere counterpoint. In the *chanzoni franciose* which he published in 1520 and which really brought him to the notice of the Italian public, almost all of the pieces are written in double canon. However, as more and more Italian influence touched him, he began to turn occasionally to a chordal style and a concern with the expression of the text. The same rigor, nevertheless, appears in the *ricercari* for three voices and the *fantasie* he published in 1549 and 1559, which are contrapuntal pieces for instruments, pure music composed on the model of motets and chansons. His synthesis between Flemish art and the new Italian tendencies is most marked in his madrigals. Without giving up contrapuntal subtleties, in these he introduces a chordal style here and there for

236

expressive purposes, ventures into chromaticism, and strives for an intimate fusion between text and music. It was these characteristics that made Willaert a "modern" musician for his contemporaries, a musician not content to follow tradition but determined instead to explore ways still unknown.

THE MADRIGAL AND THE NORTHERNERS

Around 1530 a new genre appeared in Italy : the *madrigal*. The name at least was not new : along with the *ballata* and the *caccia*, the madrigal had been one of the favorite forms of the Trecento, but the new madrigal had nothing in common with the old one. It derived from the frottola, or rather from the most serious pieces grouped under that name, for example the *canzoni* on poems by Petrarch. From the musical point of view, the madrigal marked the introduction into profane music of the compositional procedures used in the motet by the northern musicians, tempered, however, by the wish to make music the handmaiden of the text.

Like the frottola, the madrigal was quite willing to use *poesia per musica*, poems dashed off to be set to music. What it was not interested in were the fixed forms once held in honor, preferring forms with no preconceived limitations on the number of lines or on rhyme schemes; what it liked best was a short poem more or less corresponding to a verse of the old *canzone*. In spirit, the madrigal is less varied than the frottola, rejecting witty or bawdy texts in popular style in favor of love poems in which the sentiments are expressed in subtle, often epigrammatic manner.

The finest examples of refined amorous poetry were to be found in Petrarch, who, almost two centuries after his death, underwent a veritable resurrection : hundreds and hundreds of madrigals use poems from the *Canzoniere*, and an infinite number of imitations of them gave rise to a Petrarchism often rather remote from the quality of the original. Musicians also appropriated poems from those that Sannazaro inserted into his pastoral novel *Arcadia*

as well as fragments from Ariosto's *Orlando furioso* and later from Tasso's *Gerusalemme liberata* and Guarini's pastoral play *Il pastor fido,* and this was poetry of considerable originality.

The success of the madrigal in the sixteenth century was considerable : twenty-four collections were published before 1540, seventy-six between 1540 and 1550, and then, counting by decades, 81, 172, 135, 241, 225 in 1600, 137 in 1610 and 137 in 1620, after which it declined in favor. Its success went hand in hand with the important development of music publication in Rome, Ferrara, Bologna and especially in Venice, where Gardane, musician and publisher of French origin, put out beginning in 1538 and continuing for some forty years collections of every sort and where the dynasty of the Scottos was also active from 1535 on and throughout the century. Madrigals were also extensively published outside of Italy.

At the outset the madrigal developed in the aristocratic atmosphere of the Italian courts, where composers wrote them at the request of a prince or some great lady, sometimes of a courtesan, but very soon it reached a middle-class public of music lovers. The number of volumes published in the sixteenth century is a sufficient index of the broadness of the public involved. Whatever obstacles there were to an even wider popularity must have been due to difficulties in performance, for the madrigal is essentially a polyphonic work of vocal soloists. True, madrigals came to be transcribed for a solo voice with lute accompaniment or even to be played entirely on a lute or keyboard instrument, but much more often than the French chanson the madrigal must have been interpreted by voices alone. Since its very subtle polyphony is based on an equilibrium between all the parts, only an exclusively vocal performance is, in fact, really satisfactory. The notation itself presented no particular difficulties, but there were often problems in keeping on pitch, particularly when there were chromatic complications. Initially composed for three or four voices, the madrigal achieved its classic character when composed for five voices, but in the second half of the century it was at times written for six, seven or even eight voices. At the very beginning, the ensembles seem to have used men's voices only, but soon women participated in them as a matter of course. It is quite possible that certain works may have required the services of real professionals but most often they were sung by amateurs. In any event, this was not music for a concert, music to be listened to, but rather music to be sung in a group. At times ensembles of amateurs were formed whose common aim was to sing madrigals together. Italy in the sixteenth century had many so-called academies where artists, poets and men of culture met to share their humanistic or artistic interests, and it was in this spirit that in Verona, in 1543, was founded an *Accademia filarmonica* whose members assembled after a good meal to sing madrigals under the direction of a professional musician who also gave them lessons and chose the repertory.

The most important composers appearing in 1530 in the first publications of madrigals were Festa, Verdelot and Arcadelt – one Italian and two northerners. The Italian, Costanzo Festa, was not a court musician like Tromboncino or Cara but was cantor in the papal chapel from 1517 until his death in 1545, and this at a time when the choir included very few of his countrymen. He had therefore been trained in the contrapuntal discipline and, moreover, his sacred music was written in the Flemish style. Philippe Verdelot was doubtless of French origin. From 1523 to 1530 he was first cantor, then chapel master at the baptistery of San Giovanni in Florence and died before 1539, leaving masses and motets of high quality. Jacques Arcadelt, likewise most probably a Frenchman, had been *magister puerorum* in the Cappella Giulia in Rome in 1539 and then cantor in the papal chapel between 1540 and 1552, after which he returned to France. He too composed masses and motets. It is obvious from these three instances that the first composers of madri-

gals were no longer improvisers, virtuosos, specialists in secular music but, instead, learned musicians who were able to transplant into the new genre all the skill acquired in the course of their training.

Among the first madrigalists there were, along with Festa, the Florentine Francesco Corteccia as well as Verdelot, Arcadelt and Willaert, who not only wrote original works but also transcribed madrigals by Verdelot for voice and lute, and there were also Maistre Jhan of Verona (called Giovanni Nasco by the Italians), Jhan Gero, Jachet Berchem, Hermann Mathias Werrecore, all of them natives of the Low Countries. In the succeeding generation one finds Italians like Domenico Ferrabosco, Nicolò Vincentino and Palestrina, but the outstanding composer was still a Fleming, Cipriano de Rore.

Born in 1516, probably in Malines, Rore was the foremost disciple of Willaert; master of the chapel at the court of Ferrara and then at Parma and even, for a few months, at Saint Mark's in Venice, where he succeeded Willaert, he died in 1565. He left 125 madrigals and, in addition, Latin odes, sixty-five motets plus masses, psalms and Magnificats. In his madrigals he made it a rule to write for five voices although he continued to turn out pieces for three or four voices. Often he dedicated his works to women, either anonymous like *"la bella Greca"* or *"alma Susanna"* or *"alta Isabella"* or princesses of repute such as Margaret of Parma, Governess of the Low Countries. One indication of the new high status of the madrigal is the fact that his texts were not always love poems but instead, sometimes, pieces written for specific occasions, often political, such as, for one, the rebellions of the Protestant princes against Charles V. His third book of madrigals, dating from 1548, contains eleven *stanze* by Petrarch in honor of the Virgin, and these are spiritual madrigals of an austere grandeur, somber and impressive in sonority.

Musically, the madrigals of Cipriano de Rore are characterized by their dramatic intensity and expressive power. In each of the polyphonic voices the words are clearly brought out and give rise to musical equivalents of constantly renewed interest. In the title of his first book of 1544, he announces that it contains *madrigali cromatici,* but these are not chromatic in the modern sense of the word, the word *cromatico* here referring rather to a new way of writing with black notes, *a note nere,* which marks a forward step in the conquest of rhythmic flexibility.

There can be no doubt that Rore was, in every sense, a modern musician. Indeed, later, Monteverdi himself hailed him as the inventor, *il primo rinovatore,* of the musical language, a forerunner of Monteverdi's own new *seconda prattica.* Often in the latter half of his career, after 1550, he introduced unexpected harmonies achieved through the skillful use of sharps and flats. Like his master Willaert, he too composed a Latin ode, the *Calami sonum ferentes,* out of which he made an experimental work which ventured into a cycle of rarely used tonalities.

After Rore, three other Netherlanders continued to dominate the production of madrigals : Giaches de Wert, Roland de Lassus and Philippe de Monte. Giaches de Wert was probably born in Antwerp in 1535 but lived a good part of his life in Mantua. At his death in 1596 he left eleven books of madrigals for four and five voices. His was a resolutely modernist style in the line of Willaert and Rore, often employing chromaticism and augmented or diminished intervals, with unexpected dissonances and startling modulations. To bring out the text, he often assigns the words of a poem to all the voices simultaneously in a vertical alignment which nevertheless preserves the melodic independence of all the parts. Beginning with his eighth book of madrigals, he most often set aside the notion of equality between all five voices and instead pitted the three upper voices against the two lower. At the same time, he abandoned almost entirely all pretense of imitative writing, transforming the character of his melodic lines into something approaching a true

recitative style in which voices were accompanied by other voices. He thereby anticipated the dramatic madrigal, paved the way for the audacities of Monteverdi and, still within the context of polyphony, made possible the triumph of the *stile nuovo* which was to destroy it.

Neither Lassus nor Monte was as daring, but they were the most successful composers of the last quarter of the century. Only their youth was spent in Italy, the rest of their careers in Germany mostly, but they were both prolific composers of Italian madrigals.

Early in his career, Lassus wrote madrigals of considerable audacity, inspired no doubt by those of Rore. Later he utilized all the compositional procedures and, indeed, all the formulas of his contemporaries but he revitalized them always thanks to his unflagging invention. Some of his works were composed for particular occasions, others for the academies which were becoming gathering-places for musical amateurs. In his last years, in preference to conventional love poems he set to music the *Trionfi* of Petrarch or the *rime spirituali* of a canon of the Lateran, Gabriele Fiamma. His last work, the *Lagrime di San Pietro* (The Tears of Saint Peter), is a cycle of vast proportions made up of twenty spiritual madrigals.

Like Roland de Lassus, Philippe de Monte was affected by the spirit of Counter Reformation. He too wrote spiritual madrigals, which have their place in an enormous production comprising almost eleven hundred pieces, for the most part non-religious. This incredibly large group of works maintains a consistently high level, although perhaps they tend to be somewhat conventional, lacking in spontaneity.

The great success of Roland de Lassus and Philippe de Monte masks the profound transformation which had taken place in the last third of the sixteenth century : Flemish musicians were no longer playing the principal roles. Contrary to what had occurred around 1530, Italian composers had finally come to surpass the Flemish in the favor of the

239

publishers. Moreover, by using the same idiom in novel and subtle ways, certain among them already were writing music superior in quality to that of the foreigners. The works written at that time by Andrea Gabrieli, Claudio Merulo and, above all, by Luca Marenzio, Carlo Gesualdo and Claudio Monteverdi constitute the highest point reached by the genre. Nothing can approach them in refinement of writing, harmonic daring and expressive intensity. After Lassus and Monte, the Flemish had no more than minor masters to pit against the Italians : René de Mel and Jean de Macque. Under Italian influence, there came about also a late but extraordinary flowering of the English madrigal with Morley, Weelkes and Wilbye.

It was in the madrigal that was applied in the most systematic manner the attempt to render the text supremely expressive by musical means. The notion that music must *imitare le parole* – imitate the words – often gave rise to a rhetoric which may strike one as a little oversimplified. It was held that joy must be expressed by major consonances and rapid notes, sorrow by minor chords, dissonances and a slower movement. When the text spoke of going together, it was thought that all of the voices should express the union implied by holding a long note; if it was a question of going up in the text, then the melody must rise; if the text spoke of a hard heart – *aspro cuore* – dissonances must appear in the music.

It cannot be denied that such musical-poetic equivalents threaten to become rather childish when on the word *sol* – alone – one hears a solo voice singing the note *sol,* and they become quite absurd when the musician neglects the negation specifically expressed in a phrase and, to illustrate a verse of Ariosto which says that no sound was heard of drums, no blare of trumpets, the music promptly gets busy imitating them both. They become no more than a kind of game when words like *night* and *obscurity* are set to black notes, an audible-visual pun of which only the singer is aware. And yet this rhetoric

was used so consistently in the genre that it has been given the name of *madrigalism*. Obviously such a compositional device called forth no more than conventional works from composers lacking inspiration. However, it helped the best of the musicians to revivify contrapuntal writing by suggesting melodies of unusual shape, by calling for more and more subtle harmonies, and by opening to them the new world of chromaticism.

THE RISE AND FALL OF NORTHERN MUSICIANS

The madrigal was a learned art form which demanded of the composer a perfect mastery of counterpoint. Such skill, however, could only be acquired in the chapel schools and at the cost of a long apprenticeship, so it was quite natural that the great madrigal composers should also have written religious music; on the other hand, few musicians devoted themselves entirely to music for the church.

During the first half of the sixteenth century, the papal chapel remained the special province of the French and Flemish. In Rome, the most important composer of religious music was Arcadelt, but it would not be fair to overlook the Provençal Elzéar Genet (ca. 1475-1548), who became known under the name of his birthplace, Carpentras. Cantor and master of the papal chapel, he wrote masses, Lamentations, hymns, Magnificats and a few frottolas which, in their severity, presage the madrigal; he died at Avignon in 1548. Jean Lhéritier was chapel master of the church of San Luigi dei Francesi, the French church of Rome, and wrote motets, a mass and chansons, while Ghiselin Danckerts, a native of Zeeland and cantor in the papal chapel from

CYPRIANVS DE RORE MVSICVS

1538 to 1565, is known mostly because of a polemical work he wrote against the theorist Vicentino.

In Florence, Philippe Verdelot wrote masses and motets which were published in the most successful editions of the time in Italy, France and Germany, and there is some suspicion, based on internal evidence in his works, that he was a partisan of Savonarola's reform movement. Jacobus Collebaudi, a Breton born in Vitré around 1500, was master of the chapel of the Cardinal of Mantua, Ercole Gonzaga. He, for one, wrote religious music only : masses, motets, psalms for double choir (these in collaboration with Willaert), hymns and Magnificats. Better known as Jachet de Mantua than under his own name, he has often been confused with Jachet Berchem, who came from around Antwerp according to Guicciardini, and who was above all a composer of chansons and madrigals. In Ferrara, a certain Maistre Jhan, a Fleming, author of a Passion according to Saint Matthew, must not be confused with another Fleming, the Maistre Jhan who came to be called Giovanni Nasco when he worked in Verona and at the cathedral of Treviso. In Milan there was Hermann Matthias Werrecorre (d. ca. 1558), who composed motets and a *Bataglia Taliana*, an Italian counterpart to Janequin's *Bataille de Marignan*. In Venice, Jacob Buus, a native of Ghent and pupil of Willaert, wrote motets and lengthy instrumental *ricercari*; he died in Vienna in 1565. There was also Cipriano de Rore, who composed remarkable masses, motets and a Passion according to Saint John.

The statistical analysis of Italian publications prepared by A.-M. Bautier-Regnier reveals the pattern of Flemish influence in mid-century. Beginning in the years that marked the rise of the madrigal, publishing activity was concentrated in Venice, where, thanks to the competition between Scotto and Gardane as well as a few lesser firms, nine-tenths of the entire Italian production was printed. Out of 149 volumes published from 1536 to 1545, ninety-three were of secular music, fifty-six of religious. The religious works are virtually entirely due to northern composers. In the composition of masses, only the Spaniard Morales takes a place among them, but he has the leading position with three volumes of twenty masses and with thirteen masses included in seven anthologies. After him came Jachet of Mantua with eleven masses, Gombert with eight, Pierre Colin with six, Jachet Berchem with five. These same names, along with a few others, figure prominently among the composers of motets, but in a different order.

In secular music also the northerners predominated. The learned art of the madrigal promptly reversed the situation as it had stood at the time of the frottola. The most successful composer was Arcadelt with twenty volumes entirely devoted to his own work and with seventy-four pieces in twenty-three different collective publications. Then came Verdelot with nine volumes of his own and forty-five pieces in thirteen collections, Willaert with three volumes of his own and fifty-eight pieces in twenty-three collections, followed by Jachet Berchem, Gombert, Jhan Gero, and Maistre Jhan. Only two Italians achieved anything like this : Festa with two volumes of his own and forty-eight pieces in twenty-three collections and Corteccia with one volume of his own and thirty-one pieces in not less than ten collections.

Beginning in 1545 things began to change. For the first time, in that year, there were more secular works by Italians published than by northerners, and this new development became even more marked in the years following : in the ten years between 1546 and 1555 ninety-six volumes by Italians were published as against only sixty by the foreigners. Nevertheless, the most favored composers remained Arcadelt, Willaert, Gombert and Rore. Still, even in religious music, where the prominent composers were Gombert, Jachet of Mantua and the Spaniard Morales, the Italians became increasingly important, appearing in thirteen volumes out of fifty-three, and it was at this time that Palestrina was beginning to publish his masses. In any event, religious music already no longer counted for more than twenty-five per cent of all publications.

In the course of the following years these trends were confirmed. In religious music – now no more than ten to fifteen per cent of the total production – the Italians succeeded in coming even with the northerners, and in secular music in surpassing them decisively. Nevertheless, the musicians who continued right up to the end of the century to gather the most laurels were still northerners : Roland de Lassus and Philippe de Monte. However, both of them lived in Germany, and their Italian triumphs were no more than a part of their international glory. In Italy itself, the number of northern musicians resident there continued to diminish throughout the last third of the century, and Jean de Macque, of Hainaut, was quite exceptional in remaining at his post as chapel master to the Viceroy of Naples up to his death in 1614.

The explanation lies, of course, in the fact that the Italians had progressively absorbed the lessons of the Flemish. Even as early as the end of the fifteenth century, some of them contributed notably to the spread of these techniques by writing theoretical works. Franchino Gafori, for example, master of the chapel at the cathedral of Milan and himself a composer, carried further in his treatises the work of Tinctoris : his *Theorica musicæ* of 1492 and his *Practica musicæ* of four years later are among the first theoretical works to be printed. The introduction the Italians proposed to mensural music and counterpoint is based on a solid acquaintance with Flemish music, and the principles of polyphony were presented by Gafurius according to the precepts of the Flemish masters. After him, Pietro Aron employed the vernacular, Italian, for four of his five treatises, so there can be no doubt that it was exclusively for Italian musicians and not for an international audience that he intended his *Toscanello in musica* of 1523, a general manual in which the practical problems of music are treated from the

87. Portrait of Roland de Lassus at the Age of Twenty-eight.
Hans Muelich.

point of view of the men of the North. The other Italian theorists of the sixteenth century were often Humanists who drew their science from ancient texts, at the same time relating this ancient lore to the *ars perfecta* that Flemish music represented for them. This was the case with Nicolò Vicentino, who in his *L'antica musica ridotta alla moderna prattica* of 1555 proclaimed himself a disciple of "Willaert the unique," and also of Gioseffo Zarlino, whose *Istitutioni harmoniche* of 1558 is based on the teaching of his master, this same Willaert.

But thanks to these theorists, more and more Italians were trained in the techniques of the northerners. Palestrina, for one, was a composer who assimilated those techniques with such perfection and used them with such mastery that for long he has been considered the ideal representative of the art of counterpoint. The bulk of his career was passed in Rome at the Cappella Giulia and Cappella Sistina of Saint Peter's, at San Giovanni Laterano, or at Santa Maria Maggiore, and it was at Rome he died in 1594. Thus it was in the very same papal centers which until then had been the exclusive fief of musicians from across the Alps that Palestrina succeeded in imposing himself to the point of becoming virtually a symbol of the Catholic composer. The predominance of his works in the pontifical chapel coincided with the Counter Reformation and the adoption of certain new principles on the part of the Council of Trent, and this has led to making of Palestrina some sort of mythical figure, the savior of sacred music. The fact, however, is that his *Missa Papæ Marcelli* never had the influence on the decisions of the Council that has been attributed to it and, furthermore, Palestrina played no notable role in any reform of Gregorian chant. But his madrigals, including the spiritual madrigals, are only a tiny part of a production which includes 105 masses, 202 motets, hymns for the entire liturgical year, Magnificats and litanies. If Palestrina was so highly regarded in the pontifical chapel – a chapel which was highly reactionary from the artistic

point of view – it was precisely because of his conservative tendencies, because he condemned the modernist audacities of the disciples of Willaert, and because he strove to augment the rigor of an already severe art in order to adapt it to the spirit of the Counter Reformation. When he wrote masses on a *cantus firmus,* he chose his basic theme from the Gregorian repertory rather than from profane songs; when he wrote parody-masses, he shaped them most often on motets rather than on madrigals. In all of his work Palestrina seems to have established a harmonious bond with the art of Josquin Desprez, with the latter's balanced structures, his serenity and austerity. However, Palestrina was able to adapt to the spirit of the Council of Trent the concern with expression which preoccupied his contemporaries : he was constantly alert to the need to bring out the text without drowning it in a too elaborate polyphony, and he presented it with clarity of declamation. His counterpoint is characterized by a manner of treating dissonances which avoids any kind of shock, sweetening and effacing them. It was on the basis of the works of Palestrina that Fux, in 1725, in his *Gradus ad Parnassum* codified the classical rules of counterpoint, and it was thus, through Palestrina, that the counterpoint of the sixteenth century – Flemish counterpoint – finally was handed down to posterity.

We see then how, in the second half of the sixteenth century, there came about progressively a complete assimilation of Italians and northerners; it was so thoroughgoing that, henceforth, the latter no longer seemed indispensable. Princes and churches no longer thought it obligatory to place a foreigner in charge of their chapels. When an old Flemish master died, it was one of his Italian disciples who replaced him : in Venice, Zarlino held the post of chapel master at Saint Mark's after Willaert and the brief interim of Cipriano de Rore.

Only the greatest masters, secure in their international fame, a Roland de Lassus, for example, could resist this new current. But Lassus, who had

AMPLISSIMO HOC APPARATV ET PVLCHRO ORDINE
POMPA FVNEBRIS BRVXELLIS A PALATIO AD DIVÆ
GVDVLÆ TEMPLM PROCESSIT CVM REX HISPANIARVM
PHILIPPVS CAROLO.V. ROM . IMP. PARETI MŒSTISSIMVS
IVSTA SOLVER'ET

88. The Funeral Ceremony of Charles V at Brussels.
Jean and Lucas Duatecum after Jerome Wellens de Cock.

come to Italy at the age of twelve and who had received most of his musical training there, is surely himself a good example of the evolution which was taking place in his lifetime. It was as an Italianized prodigal son that he was hailed when he returned to the Low Countries. In a meaningful reversal of the situation, in the following years the publishers of the Low Countries – Susato, Phalèse, Waelrant – printed many works by the Flemish in Italy such as Willaert and Rore.

In Italy, in the last third of the sixteenth century, counterpoint was so profoundly assimilated by everyone who composed that it was no longer associated with the musicians from the North. It became the normal language in which everyone expressed his own temperament and his personal genius. Certain Italians such as Anerio, Nanino and Soriano in Rome continued to exploit a Palestrina tradition which already was on the way to becoming academic, while others, in Venice, showed more daring and invention : following Willaert, Andrea and Giovanni Gabrieli developed the polychoral technique, writing a sumptuous music which delighted in extraordinary effects of sonority. Elsewhere, Vecchi, Striggio and Banchieri oriented the madrigal toward a kind of dramatized entertainment which seemed to call for staging, and Gesualdo and Monteverdi revealed themselves in all their modernist audacity, sweeping everything before their genius.

But it was in Italy also that the first criticisms of the contrapuntal art were made, and it was in Italy that, simultaneously with the last flowering of polyphony, a new style was developing which aimed to liberate music from a technique considered too erudite, too unnatural, inadequately expressive, archaic. The death of Flemish art was being prepared. With this *stile nuovo,* Italy was making itself ready to take over the leadership of the international musical movement.

In summary, then, the history of counterpoint never ceased to be profoundly linked to Italy throughout the fifteenth and sixteenth centuries. In imposing their technique, the numerous musicians from across the Alps who had settled in Italy underwent at the same time the persistent and refining influence of a less learned music, of a music more sensitive to harmonic consonance than to contrapuntal complexities. It was through his contact with Italy that Dufay first worked out his new style and succeeded in implanting it. The originality of Josquin Desprez was certainly linked to the artistic climate of Italy, where he passed most of his life. The madrigal is the best example of a native Italian genre entirely won over by the contrapuntal style, but, in return, the madrigal taught to counterpoint certain expressive devices which were then applied elsewhere. Musicians like Andrea and Giovanni Gabrieli, like Monteverdi, show the culmination of the evolution : thanks to them, Flemish counterpoint finally came to know a life entirely independent of those who had given it birth. It became truly an international language.

Chapter 9

89. The Concert Within the Egg (copy).
Hieronymus Bosch.

The Flemings in Europe

It was not only in Italy but also throughout Europe that Flemish music made itself known in the fifteenth and sixteenth centuries. Even before the general exodus, works of the best musicians were known abroad through manuscripts that were copied and re-copied from one chapel to another.

MUSICIANS IN THE LOW COUNTRIES

Cantor for Philip the Good, Gilles Binchois was famed throughout Europe for his chansons and his religious music. After him, Antoine Busnois, favorite musician first of Charles the Bold and then of Mary of Burgundy, was hailed as a model in the art of counterpoint by Tinctoris in Naples and by Adam von Fulda in Wittenberg. This was a dignity he earned for his learnedly constructed large motets, but above all for his chansons, which express courtly charm and noble melancholy with elegance and in a highly refined technique. Pierre de la Rue served in turn Maximilian, Philip the Handsome, Margaret of Austria and Charles V and was, in addition, canon at Courtrai. His works figure prominently in German and Italian manuscripts and were printed by Petrucci as early as 1503 and then by Antico in Venice and Giunta in Rome and later, in Germany, by Wyrsung, Ott, Rhaw, Petreius, Kriesstein and Berg. In his *Table Talks*, Martin Luther cited Pierre de la Rue together with Josquin and Finck as among the *feine Musici* he particularly appreciated.

Throughout his work Pierre de la Rue reveals himself to be a learned composer. Of the musicians of his generation, he is among those who, like Isaac and Josquin, most often employ the canon. Indeed, certain of his masses are entirely based on that procedure. In the *Missa Ave sanctissima Maria*, a riddle canon requires six voices to be spun out of the three written out; elsewhere, five voices are to be built out of four written out, or even four out of a single voice. Most of the other masses include at least a few sections in canon form, and the same technique is used often in his motets and chansons. In all of these cases, Pierre de la Rue displays extraordinary virtuosity and unfailing invention.

Except for brief journeys into Italy, Jacob Obrecht seldom left the Low Countries. This, however, did not prevent his works from being known and appreciated abroad. More frequently than most of his contemporaries he wrote songs on Flemish texts : *Ic en hebbe gheen ghelt, Ic hoerde des cloeskins luden* or *'t Saat een meskin,* for instance, but he also wrote chansons on French or Italian texts, either in fixed forms such as the rondeau or in free

249

forms. Nevertheless, his religious works are more important than his secular ones. This is true above all of his motets, in which he reveals conservative traits – the use of a *cantus firmus* in long note-values, multiple texts and only a modest indulgence in imitative procedures – but also, at the same time, shows certain progressive tendencies in his insistence on imposing formal unity on the work. His masses constitute the major part of his production. They often use a monodic *cantus firmus* : a fragment of plain-chant, as in the *Missa Caput* and *Missa sub tuum presidium*; a chanson tune, as in the *Missa super Maria zart* and the *Missa L'Homme armé*; or a melody borrowed from a contemporary polyphonic piece, as in the *Missa Malheur me bat,* which is based on a chanson probably by Ockeghem. Sometimes he used several borrowed melodies in a single work : various pieces of plain-chant in the *Missa diversorum tenorum*; several chansons in the *Missa carminum;* different voices from some polyphonic composition, as in the *Missa Fortuna desperata,* based on a work by Busnois, or in the *Missa Si dedero,* on a work by Agricola. However, it was only exceptionally that Obrecht used the parody technique; the polyphonic fragments are rarely taken over as a homogeneous unit but are rather employed one after the other, thereby splitting up the original composition from which they are borrowed. Whatever might be its source, the *cantus firmus* is divided into segments and reworked to provide a structural basis for the form of a work of large dimensions and to impregnate the entire work with its material.

Charles van den Borren considers Obrecht the antithesis of Josquin Desprez : where Josquin seems always to be seeking equilibrium and striving for an entirely classical serenity, Obrecht pours out new ideas in such number as to burst apart the framework and to permit his restless lyrical temperament to express itself without restraint. But Obrecht was also gifted with a constructive spirit : he makes systematic use of devices such as the repetition of sequences and the ostinato which have rhetorical power and which also became fundamental procedures in the musical vocabulary.

Other musicians of less remarkable merit also gained international repute without leaving the Low Countries. Jacobus Barbireau, singing master at Notre-Dame in Antwerp from 1447 to 1491, was largely responsible for the fame of that city's singers and musical performances. Johannes Regis, a disciple of Dufay, lived in Cambrai, Antwerp and Soignies, and certain of his works appeared in Italian manuscripts while others were printed by Petrucci. Hayne van Ghizeghem, cantor and personal valet of Charles the Bold, composed nothing but chansons, but his works were copied into many manuscripts and published in Petrucci's *Odhecaton* of 1501 and *Canti B* of 1502 as well as in a publication by Formschneider from as late as 1538. His chanson *De tous biens playne* was especially popular; it was used as a *cantus firmus* in motets by Compère and Josquin, in a mass by Isaac, in German and Italian instrumental works, and even adapted for a *Souterliedeken*. Around 1500, Mathieu Pipelare, probably a native of Louvain, was *sangmeester voor die jongen* at 's Hertogenbosch and, in a style like that of Obrecht, composed some ten masses, motets and chansons in French, German and Flemish which are found in the great Burgundian, Italian and German manuscripts or in the editions of Petrucci, Antico, Giunta and the others. Jean Richafort, singing master at Malines from 1507 to 1509, entered the service of the Governess Mary of Hungary in 1531 and was also chapel master at Bruges; his contemporaries praised him highly as a perfect disciple of Josquin.

If it is true that beginning with the end of the fifteenth century the most important composers lived outside of the Low Countries – Ockeghem in France, Josquin, Willaert, Rore in Italy, Monte and Lassus in Germany – a great number of excellent musicians never left their native soil but continued to work in some church or other or at the court of the governesses Margaret of Austria and Mary of

250

Hungary. They preserved the authentic, rigorous contrapuntal tradition thanks to a more complex, more seemingly erudite style than that of the composers who came under Italian influence.

Nicolas Gombert cannot be relegated among those who never left the Low Countries, since from 1526 to 1539 he was attached to the chapel of Charles V and must therefore have traveled much, because the chapel followed the Emperor in all of his voyages. But most of his life was spent there : in Courtrai in his youth, in Tournai, where he was canon near the end of his life, his death occurring in 1557. Gombert's style seems to have had deep influence on the musicians who did not go abroad. It was based on tightly interwoven imitation and was applied first to the motet and mass, later to profane chansons. Initially, it involved a limited number of voices – three or four – but later went beyond this. But while Josquin isolated the voices in pairs and pitted them against the ensemble, and while the Italianized musicians alternated episodes in imitative style with others in homorhythm, Gombert kept up a perpetual use of all the voices at once, which inevitably creates a certain opacity of texture. On the other hand, he eschews certain tonal bases often used by Josquin, and he favored the diversity of Gregorian modes, their mobility, their functional indecision in harmony. All of this often gives to his works – ten masses, eight Magnificats, a hundred and fifty motets, and fifty chansons – an appearance of austerity.

This style triumphed in the Low Countries in the second quarter of the sixteenth century. It is perfectly true that in the hands of less gifted musicians it can end up heavy and wearying to listen to, but this is certainly not true of Clemens non Papa, whose life is as mysterious as his name is bizarre. His right name was Jacques Clément, and it has been supposed that he may have added non Papa to his name to distinguish himself from Pope Clement VII or from a certain Jacobus Papa who lived, as did he, at Ypres, but who did not compose music. In 1544

he was attached to the church of Saint Donatien in Bruges, and in 1550 he was in 's Hertogenbosch. His first chansons were published by Attaingnant in 1538, and later his works appeared in Germany, Italy and the Low Countries. In his masses and motets he employs a most rigorous style based on sustained imitations, but his chansons are often lightened, in the French manner, as much by chordal writing as in the choice of rather licentious or bawdy texts. Likewise, his *Souterliedekens*, spiritual chansons on Flemish texts, are in a deliberately simplified style.

Thomas Crecquillon followed Gombert in 1540 as master of the choirboys in the chapel of Charles V, and was canon at Namur, Termonde and Bethune and died before 1566. From 1545 to as late as 1636 – a date which proves his success – his works were frequently printed in Germany, in Nuremberg, Wittenberg and Augsburg, as well as in Venice, France and the Low Countries. His chansons, like his motets, reveal the supremacy of a severe counterpoint.

A SECRET CHROMATIC ART ?

Gombert, Clemens non Papa and Crecquillon were, in the sixteenth century, the foremost among the composers who did not leave the Low Countries. Certain scholars have raised the question as to whether, to the obvious characteristics of their style, there should not be added another, more mysterious but not less significant. Edward Lowinsky has written a most ingenious book in which he tries to show that these composers indulged in what can only be called a secret chromatic art. This esoteric technique was actually applied to only a handful of works, Lowinsky himself extending it only to a half-dozen motets by Clemens non Papa, one motet each by Crecquillon and Gombert, and eleven works by Hubert Waelrant, the Antwerp composer-publisher of a younger generation who had lived in Italy and who employed a much lighter style with greater attention to the text.

251

As we know, in the fifteenth and sixteenth centuries not all chromatic accidentals were noted down. *Musica ficta* was added by the singer according to certain rules of solmization and counterpoint, but it affected only certain notes of the melody, particularly at characteristic points such as the cadence. According to Lowinsky, in certain motets of the middle of the sixteenth century a systematic form of chromaticism, in no way indicated by the notation, was applied during performance itself, and this was not limited to a few notes but instead plunged the music into a cycle of remote modulations. Nothing prevented the work's being sung in its diatonic version, using the notes as they stood, unaltered, but the initiate knew that at certain moments the notation could be interpreted chromatically in a way that would profoundly alter the entire character of the piece. These moments which constituted pivot-points between diatonicism and chromaticism were determined by the text itself, to which chromaticism brought a much more powerful expressive significance.

Lowinsky believes that this secret chromatic art was practiced by Catholic musicians who had certain inclinations toward Protestantism. It is a fact that in Antwerp, more than in other cities, part of the bourgeoisie which was in contact with Germany was much troubled by the Reformation. Some of them actually joined the movement, but others, and they were more numerous, may have been impressed by the new doctrines without, for all that, formally renouncing their Catholic ties. It seems possible that Clemens non Papa may have had Protestant sympathies, but his *Souterliedekens* do not in any way prove this since these spiritual songs were perfectly acceptable to Catholics in general. As for Waelrant, his publications of psalms by Marot, his composition of spiritual songs, and his regular relations with Germany all go to make his adherence to the new cult seem more probable.

But, for Lowinsky's hypothesis to be valid, would it not be necessary to show that the Church had itself banned chromaticism? Its secret practice would then become a manifestation of resistance against the rigors of the Inquisition. But the fact is that written-out chromaticism was widely practiced in Catholic Italy and not only in madrigals but in motets too, and this is easily verified by certain motets by Willaert which are contemporary with those of Clemens non Papa. It is true that the religious authorities have never encouraged modernisms of any type, and the Council of Trent directed sacred music into the most undisturbing of channels, but even at the most harassing periods of the Inquisition the Church never forbade chromaticism or even formally condemned it. Further, the motets studied by Lowinsky were liturgical works which figured normally in the Proper of the mass or in one of the offices, and it is difficult to imagine that they might have been sung in a diatonic form in church and in a chromatic guise in clandestine assemblies where Protestant sympathizers would have manifested in this way their spiritual unity.

According to contemporary evidence, both Catholics and persecuted Protestants expressed their faith in a much less devious manner in the course of family or friendly gatherings : they sang psalms to strengthen their courage and their will to resist. These psalms acquired a symbolic importance in the period : outside of religious services, they were frequently sung in family circles sympathetic to the Reformation, as well they could be, since the texts were quite unequivocal and the music was easily performed. This is certainly not true of the motets by Clemens or Waelrant, whose Latin texts and mensural notation, further complicated by an unwritten chromaticism, made them accessible only to professional performance. One may even point out that chromatic subtleties were in contradiction to that desire for simplicity which most often the Protestants called for when they wished to oppose the Catholics by means of music. It is for these reasons that the historical, theological and artistic arguments of Lowinsky have not been widely accepted.

However, during that same period, theorists, musicians and amateurs all spoke of *musica reservata,* which Lowinsky does not neglect to relate to his secret chromaticism. Documentary evidence for *musica reservata* is not rare, but the term has been debated back and forth by numerous musicologists without ever becoming really clear. It was used for the first time in 1552 by Adriaen Petit Coclico in the preface to his *Compendium musices* and as the title for a collection of motets; then by Dr. Seld, a German diplomat at the court of Brussels, who used it in speaking of a singer and a composer, and also by Samuel Quickelberg of Antwerp but living in Munich, who applied it to the *Penitential Psalms* of Lassus, and, in 1559, by a Humanist from Hainaut, Jean Taisnier. It has been suggested that *musica reservata* must have been a matter either of music which strives to bring out the full expression of the text or else of compositions in which singers added improvised ornamentation to the written notes. In fact, it really seems that the term was used in Germany and the Low Countries to describe what the Italians called more simply *musica nova.*

That new music was characterized by a greater concern with the text, sometimes by improvisations on the part of the singers, and often by the use of chromaticism. It did not respect the traditional rules passed down from Josquin and it was a more difficult kind of music to perform and to understand. If it was *reservata,* it was not because it was practiced in secret for religious reasons but simply because it required particularly experienced singers to perform it and well-informed audiences to appreciate it. It was often music for soloists. When they became known in the Low Countries in 1555, the new Italian works of Roland de Lassus may well have seemed to be a *musica reservata* just like his *Penitential Psalms* composed in Munich some five years later. Thus we see that *musica reservata* was the new music : it corresponded to the mannerist current which was to prevail until the end of the century and to lead to the Baroque.

The best of the Flemish musicians who practiced this style, in which the art of counterpoint renewed itself, all lived abroad. After Clemens non Papa, those who were content to limit their careers to the home country were no more than musicians of second rank. One may mention Antoine Barbé, singing master at Antwerp from 1527 to 1562, Severin Cornet (1530-1582), a native of Valenciennes who worked mostly in Malines and Antwerp, Andries Pevernage (1543-1591), singing master at Bruges, Courtrai and Antwerp, who wrote motets, chansons and madrigals, and finally Corneille Verdonck (1563-1625), who lived mostly in Antwerp.

At the beginning of the century, in 1506, a Venetian ambassador to the Low Countries, Vincenzo Quirini, paid Flemish music the highest compliment in declaring it to be equal in perfection to paintings in Holland and tapestries in Brabant : *in detto paese tre cose sono di somma eccellenza : tele sottilissime e belle in copia in Olanda; tapezzerie bellissime in figure in Brabante; la terza è la musica, la quale certamente si puo dire che sia perfetta.*

In 1567, in the *Descrittione di tutti i Paesi Bassi* published in Antwerp, Lodovico Guicciardini was still able to acclaim the universal superiority of Flemish musicians : *Questi sono i veri maestri della musica e quelli che l'hanno restaurata e ridotta a perfezione, perchè l'hanno tanto propria e naturale che uomini e donne cantan naturalmente a misura con grandissima grazia e melodia; onde, avendo poi congiunta l'arte alla natura fanno e di voce e di tutti gli strumenti quella pruova e armonia che si vede e ode, talchè se ne truova sempre per tutte le corti de' principi cristiani.* (It is they who are the true masters of music, they who revived it and brought it to perfection; it is for them so natural and normal a thing that men and women sing instinctively measured music with utmost grace and melody. Having in this way wedded nature to art, they display both in singing and playing that skill and that harmony which you can see and hear and which is such as graces all the courts of Christian princes).

Desperando spero ⁒

ADRIAN PETIT
COCLICO MVSICO.
ÆTAT: LII,

90. Portrait of Adriaen Petit Coclico.
Woodcut.

The prestige of Flemish musicians was so great that travelers like Guicciardini included in their admiration both those masters actually living in the Low Countries and those others – certainly far more numerous – whose careers were made abroad.

During this period, Antwerp seems to have had a virtual monopoly on musical activity in the Low Countries, and it was quite natural that Antwerp should have become an important center of music publishing.

MUSIC PUBLISHING IN THE LOW COUNTRIES
The first book of polyphonic music to appear in the Low Countries was the volume with two motets by Benedictus de Opitiis published in 1515 on the occasion of the Joyous Entry into Antwerp of Emperor Maximilian and his grandson Charles V. A certain Jan De Gheet, of whom nothing more than the name is known, printed the work in a primitive and complicated technique, engraving every page of music as a wood-block as if it were an illustration.

The first printer to employ for music more fitting typographical procedures already in use elsewhere was Christophe van Remunde, a native of Eindhoven settled in Antwerp since 1524, but he used them only for books of plain-chant. The first publication of non-liturgical music was *Een devoot ende profitelijck boeckxken, inhoudende veel gheestelijcke liedekens ende leysenen,* put out in Antwerp in 1539 by Simon Cock and still utilizing for these spiritual songs a notation without rhythmic precision quite similar to that of plain-chant. The collection of *Souterliedekens* published by Cock in 1540 and frequently reprinted throughout the century still used this limited type of notation and, what is more, was still printed in the traditional two-stage technique.

However, for a dozen years already a new procedure was being used : each note was printed together with a fragment of the staff line to which it belonged. This invention has been attributed to the Parisian printer Pierre Haultin, and it was in fact employed for the first time by Attaingnant in the first book of chansons he brought out in 1528. A new epoch began in the history of music publishing : printing all the elements of music in a single operation made possible lowering prices and thus contributed to diffusing printed music more widely. The procedure was adopted by all the important Flemish publishers of the sixteenth century, including Susato, Phalèse and Plantin.

The first to publish polyphonic music in the Low Countries was Tielman Susato, who came from around Cologne to establish himself in Antwerp in 1529 as music copyist and instrumentalist until, in 1543, he secured authorization to print music. His *Premier Livre de Chansons* came out in that year and was followed, up to 1560, by numerous anthologies of the same type, collections of motets and *Musyckboexkens* with dance pieces, Flemish chansons and *Souterliedekens*. Susato's success was quite remarkable. Antwerp was a thriving commercial center, and the many foreign merchants who came

255

91. The Publisher Tielman Susato Presents One of His Works to Mary of Hungary, Governess of the Netherlands.
Woodcut.

A TRESILLVSTRE ET TRESVERTVEVSE DAME, DAME MARIE ROYNE
Et Douaigiere D'hongrie. & ce. Thylman Susato son Treshumble seruiteur Felicite prosperite & valitude.

Long temps ya, tresillustre Princesse,
   Que mon vouloir a iamais na prins cesse.
De s'emploier a trouuer la practicque
Et le moien d'imprimer la Musicque
Or est ainsi, qu' appres grant diligence
Non sans trauail, non sans cost & despence

Paruenu suis au chief de mon entente
Dont touteffois encoir ne me contente.
Iusques a ce qu'il plaira a fortune
De m'octroier saison bien opportune
Pour humblement en toute obeissance
Me presenter de toute ma puissance

to the bustling city guaranteed a wide diffusion for musical publications intended especially for amateurs. The repertory was essentially drawn from local sources, which means it was composed almost exclusively by musicians living in the Low Countries, but this was perfectly normal since many of them also enjoyed considerable repute abroad. After Josquin, a master who belonged already to the past with his rigorous contrapuntal idiom and who — doubtless for that very reason — returned to favor a quarter-century after his death, the composers most frequently published by Susato were Gombert, Clemens non Papa, Crecquillon, Manchicourt, along with musicians of lesser fame but some talent such as Roger Pathie, Corneille Canis, Nicolas Payen and Susato himself. The generally severe style lent to these chansons a tone quite different from that of the chansons being published in France at the same time by Attaingnant or Jacques Moderne. As for the works in Flemish in the *Musyckboexkens*, by their very nature they were intended basically for a regional clientele, the local bourgeoisie. The collections of motets, dominated by the names of Gombert, Clemens, Crecquillon and Manchicourt, exploit the imitative-syntactic technique. Susato gave no sign of any confidence in more modern currents until he published the first works of Lassus, which explicitly showed Italian influence.

256

Beginning in 1545 Susato acquired a formidable competitor in the person of Pierre Phalèse, a bookseller of Louvain who published lute tablatures, books of French and Flemish chansons and collections of motets or *cantiones sacræ*. After having for long profited from the same authors as Susato, Phalèse gave a larger place to the great Flemings settled out of the country – to Lassus, Rore, Monte – and even to foreigners like the Spaniard Francisco Guerrero. After the death of Pierre Phalèse, the establishment continued its activity under his sons Corneille and Pierre, the latter of whom left to set up a press in Antwerp in association with Jean Bellère which, from 1575 on, drew on a completely international repertory including not only Willaert, Lassus, Monte and Rore but also Marenzio, Gabrieli, Nanino and Palestrina. Even the Italian titles of his madrigal volumes – *Il paradiso musicale, Il vago alboreto* – reveal his desire to bring the repertory up to date, but Phalèse, like most other publishers of his time, was often content merely to republish works which had appeared in Italy. Sometimes he brought out an entire anthology which had already been successful elsewhere : *Il lauro verde* of 1591 adds only a few new pieces to the madrigals published under that title by V. Baldini in Ferrara in 1583, and *Il trionfo di Dori* of 1595 was simply the same collection put out by Gardane in Venice three years before. The same cosmopolitan tendencies showed themselves in collections specially assembled for Phalèse and Bellère. In the *Livre de meslanges contenant un recueil de chansons à quatre parties,* for which the choice was made by Jean de Castro from Liège, who had settled in Germany, the only local musicians represented were Severin Cornet and Waelrant, and along with them appear Costeley, Le Jeune, Arcadelt, Rore and Monte. In the *Harmonia celeste* of 1583, only Pevernage is there to represent the local musicians – and he was the editor of the anthology; otherwise there were expatriate Flemings like Lassus, Macque, Monte and Wert and, especially, Italians. The same tendency held in the *Musica divina*

published the same year, in the *Symphonia angelica* assembled in 1585 by Hubert Waelrant, in which the only local composers were René de Mel, Verdonck and Waelrant himself, and in the *Melodia Olympica,* a collection of madrigals chosen this time by Peter Philips, an English composer settled in Antwerp.

In this way a marked change came about. The publications of Susato, the first books brought out by Phalèse and those published from 1554 on by the composer Hubert Waelrant in association with the printer Jan Laet had all exploited a local repertory, and in all the genres there prevailed a rather old-fashioned style which was constantly severe and sometimes rather too weighty. At the end of the century, however, the Antwerp publishers seem to have had little use for the local musicians, among whom, it must be confessed, there were no longer any outstanding figures. Concurrently, they more or less neglected the religious repertory in favor of secular works and particularly of anthologies of madrigals, and the composers they chose were mostly Italians or Flemings settled abroad. This change illustrates very well the changes coming about in music itself : in the last quarter of the sixteenth century, the style of the Flemish composers had been so thoroughly absorbed and imitated throughout Europe that it had lost the distinction of exceptional superiority it had so long enjoyed. On their own terrain, the Flemish henceforth had to compete with a great number of musicians of other countries.

Christophe Plantin represents a rather special case among publishers in Antwerp. He put out liturgical books, missals, graduals and antiphonaries, but only rarely ventured into the field of polyphonic music. Composers published by him were obliged to share the expenses. What he specialized in were large choir books, luxuriously presented models of typography. His first polyphonic publication was a volume of masses by Georges de la Hèle, and this was followed by masses or motets by Philippe de Monte, Jacobus de Kerle, Alard du Gaucquier, Jacques de Brouck – all of them settled in Germany – and the

Mélanges of Claude Le Jeune plus chansons or madrigals by Cornet and Pevernage.

Other luxurious editions, but even more exceptional, were the engravings made between 1584 and 1590 by Jan Sadeler and published for the most part in Antwerp. In these, in the midst of various scenes showing the Virgin and Child, angel musicians or King David, appears an open choir book on which one can read clearly the music of a motet. These are not illustrations of a musical work but an engraving in which the music, always religious, is integrated into the subject depicted, always with some sort of link between the theme of the work and the subject of the engraving. These *picture-motets* obviously were not intended for practical use. Nor were they numerous. In a series of only ten engravings there are no more than a few works by Pevernage, Verdonck, Lassus and others, to which must be added an eleventh piece, a six-voice motet by Pevernage used as the title page for the *Encomium musices,* a series of eighteen engravings illustrating biblical scenes published in Antwerp by Philippe Galle.

Thanks to Susato, Phalèse, Plantin and a few more modest houses, sixteenth-century music publishing in the Low Countries achieved some admirable realizations. And yet, in terms of the history of Flemish music, its contribution was less than that of German and Italian publishers, for the international importance of that music was manifested more significantly in editions published outside the Netherlands. The fact is, at the time when Flemish music was triumphing, its foremost representatives lived abroad : it was in Italy, in Germany and in Spain that fame and glory came to them.

FRANCO-FLEMISH COUNTERPOINT

France too was part of this field of expansion. However it is not to France that one must look to learn the importance of Flemish music in Europe. Flemish influence is difficult to make out there because it was intimately linked to the essence of French music.

If the art of Dufay was readily assimilated in France, it was because it was able to give a completely new turn to certain French traditions. Later, Ockeghem spent the major part of his life in France as cantor for the Duke of Bourbon and then as cantor and music master in the royal chapel, and he helped introduce into the French scene a polyphony in the style of the masters of the Burgundian States. At the royal chapel in Paris, the prestige of Charles the Bold and Philip the Handsome was such that musicians were recruited from Flanders, Hainaut and Artois. Antonius Divitis of Louvain and Jean Braconnier, also known as Lourdault, both of them cantors for Louis XII, had previously served Philip the Handsome. Louis van Pulaer, chapel master at Notre-Dame in Paris from 1507 to 1527, was born in Cambrai and had previously been attached to the cathedral of Cambrai and to the collegiate church of Saint-Denis in Liège.

The foremost composers in France at the beginning of the sixteenth century, Jean Mouton and Antoine de Févin, came from the North. Mouton was born near Boulogne in 1470, and after a brief spell as *magister puerorum* at the cathedral of Amiens entered the service of the kings of France, later becoming canon at Saint-Quentin; he died in 1522. He wrote religious music especially. His contemporaries saw in him a disciple of Josquin. Like Josquin, but with greater austerity, he alternated canons and rigorous counterpoint with homophonic passages, massive ensembles with more airy episodes using only two voices. As for Antoine de Févin, born in Arras at about the same time as Mouton, he too was attached to the royal chapel of France, and, except for a few chansons, he seems to have written nothing but religious music – masses, motets, Magnificats and Lamentations – in a style close to that of Josquin.

Févin and Mouton were well known in Italy, where their works were often printed by the first Italian publishers. Antoine Brumel, Elzéar Genet, Philippe Verdelot, Jacques Arcadelt and others who

92. Ornamental letters.
Engraving.

⟨Secundus liber tres missas continet,

Cum gratia et priuilegio christianissimi Francorum Regis ad sexenniũ vt patet primo libro.

M.v.xxxij

Regiſtrũ Ꮐ.Ᏸ.Ꭵ.Ꮶ.Ꮮ.Ꮇ.oẽs ſunt terni ꝑter Ꮇ.ꝗ eſt quatern⁹   19

93. Mass at the Court of Francis I of France.
Master of the Monogram F.I.

were French were appreciated in Italy and made their careers there. The truth is, the French were very much involved in the Flemish artistic conquest of Italy, and their music scarcely differed in any way from that of the best of the Flemings. Indeed, they were so very much alike that most often no distinction was made : to the Italians, all these musicians from across the Alps were *fiamminghi*.

In certain works, however, in particular the chansons, sixteenth-century French musicians displayed such originality that it was no longer possible to confuse them with the Flemish. Be that as it may, in other genres, especially motets and masses, traditional counterpoint – which was essentially Flemish – continued to be the rule.

If Flemings were called upon to organize and direct chapels in France less often than elsewhere, it is because the music practiced in that country was, on the whole, so very similar to theirs. The type of counterpoint which prevailed throughout Europe in the second half of the fifteenth century owes, from the historical standpoint, much to France, but it was composers from the North who gave it its most characteristic traits. When one studies the diffusion throughout Europe of this style, it becomes evident that the musicians who propagated it came from the Low Countries more than from France. This was true of the greatest among them, of Dufay, Ockeghem, Josquin, Willaert, Monte and Lassus, and it was no less true of those often little-known singers and composers who made up the chapels for cathedrals and princely courts.

THE FLEMINGS IN SPAIN

After having for long been subject to French influence, Spain in the fifteenth century did not ignore the new currents represented by the Flemings. The proof is to be found among their theorists. An anonymous manuscript from Seville, the *Ars mensurabilis et immensurabilis cantus,* seems to have been influenced by Tinctoris. The composers cited as examples are Dufay, Dunstable, Binchois, Busnois, Ockeghem and Faugues – all of these cited by Tinctoris also – and Constans, a musician in the service of Charles the Bold, Pullois, Johannes Martini, a certain Enricus, and Johannes Urrede. These are all Burgundians, except for the Englishman Dunstable. As for Johannes Urrede, he came from Bruges and his name was really Wreede; settled in Spain, he entered the service of the Duke of Alba in 1476 and later became chapel master for Ferdinand V of Aragon. The most famous Spanish theorist of the fifteenth century, Bartolomé Ramos de Pareja, lived much in Italy, and it was in Bologna that he published his *Musica practica* in 1482. The rules of counterpoint he proposes are drawn from the works of the great composers of the time, consequently the Flemings, but he mentions also Spaniards and on the basis of Spanish music urges greater flexibility in standards of writing. Guillermo Despuig was no less familiar with the dominant tendencies in European music in his *Ars musicorum,* published in Valencia in 1495, although he never left Spain.

Encouraged by their theorists, Spanish composers sought models in Flemish polyphony. The first composers whose names have come down to us worked for the kings of Aragon who, ever since 1443, had also reigned over Naples, Sicily and Sardinia. A musician like Johannes Cornago lived for many years in Naples at the time of Tinctoris, and the same is true of Bernardo Ycart, who was, without doubt, a Fleming who had become, to all intents and purposes, Spanish. Moreover, many Flemings and Frenchmen were employed as cantors in the chapel of Aragon at Naples.

Juan de Anchieta, who was chapel master for Johanna the Mad, used the melody of *L'Homme armé* as *cantus firmus*. Francisco de Peñalosa used as *cantus firmus* the tenor of the famous chanson *De tous biens playne* by Hayne van Ghizeghem. In the *Cancionero* of the Biblioteca Colombina, Seville, the first great collection of secular polyphonic music in Spain, prepared before 1490, are found the well-known *Petite camusette* and *Le pauvre amant,* both of them chansons by Ockeghem, as well as *Qu'es mi vida preguntays,* a *cancion* attributed to a collaboration between Ockeghem and Cornago, and three *villancicos* by the Fleming Urrede. One of these *villancicos, Nunca fué pena mayor,* was so successful as to be included in Petrucci's *Odhecaton* and *Canti C,* and was also used in masses by Pierre de la Rue and Peñalosa. The slightly later *Cancionero musical de Palacio* includes a frottola by Josquin copied from one of Petrucci's volumes, a few other Italian frottolas, and a piece by Robert Morton, the Englishman working at the court of Charles the Bold. Besides these, the two *cancioneros* contain *romances* and *villancicos* by Spanish composers.

Remote as they were from the most active centers of European polyphony, fifteenth-century Spanish composers seem rather provincial. This is not meant to be derogatory. It means that if these musicians are perfectly well acquainted with the rules of counterpoint, they do not hesitate to apply them with a certain independence. Their music is less complex than that of the Flemish and of greater harmonic clarity because of the use of cadences which underline the tonality. But the specific character of Spanish chansons was a matter of temperament rath-

er than of technique, and the same holds for their religious music. The Spaniards reveal themselves to be particularly inspired when the texts possess some dramatic vitality.

Historic events created close bonds between Flanders and Spain. Philip the Handsome married Johanna the Mad, daughter of the Catholic King. During his sojourns in Spain in 1502 and 1506 he was accompanied by his chapel, which included musicians like Agricola, Weerbecke, Orto and Pierre de la Rue. When Charles V set up a chapel with Flemish musicians only – master, cantors and choirboys, all of them Flemish – he did no more than perpetuate the Burgundian chapel, but at the same time he obeyed certain aesthetic requirements, since Flemish artistic superiority in sacred music was generally conceded. While for secular entertainments Charles maintained Spanish minstrels, no Spaniards were ever taken into the chapel which followed him on his voyages. Whenever recruits were needed, they were engaged in groups of boys or men from the churches of the Low Countries. Nicolas Gombert, Thomas Crecquillon, Corneille Canis of Ghent and Nicolas Payen of Soignies were each in turn masters

HORTVS MVSARVM

IN QVO TANQVAM FLOSCVLI

quidam selectissimorum carminum collecti sunt ex optimis
quibusq́ autoribus.

Et primo ordine continentur αὐτόματα, quæ Fantasiæ dicuntur.

Deinde cantica quatuor uocum.

Post, carmina grauiora, quæ Muteta appellantur, eaq́ quatuor,
quinq́, ac sex uocum.

Demum addita sunt carmina longe elegantissima duabus testudinibus
canenda, hactenus nunquam impressa.

COLLECTORE
Petro Phalæsio.

Concessum est Petro Phalesio Cæ. Ma. priuilegio ad triennium, ne quis hunc librum imprimat,
aut alibi impressum diuendat, sub pœna uigintiquinque florenorum,
ut latius patet in literis illi concessis.
Signato, à Philippo de Lens.

LOVANII

apud Petrum Phale-
sium bibliopolam
iuratum,
M. D. LII.

of the chapel of Charles V, where they maintained a strict discipline in the performance of sacred polyphony, for which they provided compositions of great austerity.

However, the wife of Charles V, Isabella of Portugal, had her own chapel, which included Spaniards and a few Portuguese, and at her death these singers were taken into the service of Prince Philip and his sisters Mary and Johanna. When Philip succeeded his father, he therefore already had a chapel with Spanish musicians but nevertheless re-engaged his father's singers, without, however, combining the two institutions. He maintained separately a *Capilla española,* with Spanish singers and players as the financial charges of the Casa de Castilla, as well as a *Capilla flamenca,* with Flemish singers only, under the direction of a master from the Low Countries, this one included in the budget of the Casa de Borgoña.

As director of Philip's Flemish chapel, there was at first Pierre de Manchicourt, a native of Béthune. He had been *phonascus* – singing master – at the cathedral of Tournai and canon at Arras before entering the service of Philip II when the latter left for Spain in 1559. He was a composer of worth whose works – chansons, masses and motets – were printed in Germany, France and the Low Countries. He belonged to the most conservative wing of the Flemish school, perpetuating the style of Gombert and Crecquillon. After his death in 1564, his successors were first Jean Bonmarché of Douai, who had directed the choir in Cambrai, then after 1571 Gerardus van Turnhout, who had previously been singing master at the cathedral of Antwerp, and, after the latter's death in 1580, Georges de la Hèle.

The *Capilla flamenca* was a truly imposing institution in that period. Often it included as many as twenty *niños* – choirboys – twenty-four *cantores,* an *organista* and about ten *capellanes.* Lacking his father's wandering habits, Philip II never left Spain after 1559, and his chapel remained there. However, voyages between the Low Countries and Spain

were always frequent. Trained in the churches of the North, youngsters of seven to twelve years were taken off to Spain, but they returned home to continue their studies when their voices changed; later, some may have returned to Spain as cantors, and toward the close of their lives those among them who were priests sought to obtain prebends which would permit them to finish their days in the Low Countries.

Georges de la Hèle, born in Antwerp in 1547, did his first apprenticeship there at the cathedral of Our Lady, and then, from 1562 to 1570, was falsettist in the royal chapel at Madrid. Returned to the North, he attended the University of Louvain before becoming, in 1572, singing master at Saint-Rombaut in Malines and the singing master and canon of the cathedral at Tournai. Appointed master of the royal chapel in 1580, he did not actually assume the function until two years later and died in 1586. His best-known work is the luxurious collection of masses published by Plantin in 1578. His successor, Philippe Rogier, had his entire career in Spain. Born in Namur, he was recruited as choirboy as early as 1572 while still a student in Antwerp. In Madrid he became cantor in 1580, assistant master in 1582 and died, still young, in 1596. Before him, all

OCTO
MISSAE,
QVINQVE, SEX,
ET SEPTEM
VOCVM,

Auctore
GEORGIO DE LA HELE,

Apud insignem Cathed. Tornacensem
Ecclesiam PHONASCO;

IAM *primùm in lucem edita.*

ANTVERPIÆ,
EX OFFICINA CHRISTOPHORI
PLANTINI TYPOGRAPHI REGII.
M. D. LXXVIII.

LABORE, ET CONSTANTIA.

the Netherlandish musicians seem to have wished to spend as little time as possible in Spain, and whether in Madrid or at home, they composed the same masses, the same motets in the same style. Rogier, however, spent all of his life in Spain and wrote *villancicos*, a Spanish genre rather like the madrigal, in a precise musical and poetic form which often had a popular character. In his religious music, Rogier wrote motets and parody-masses based on works of Gombert, Clemens non Papa, Morales, Palestrina and Lassus – a clear indication of his own preferences – as well as masses for two or three choirs which reveal Venetian influence. The five most important masses by Rogier were published after his death by Géry Ghersem at the Typographia Regia at the expense of the King through the initiative of a Flemish printer settled in Madrid known as Johannes Flander or Juan Flamenco.

Whereas in Italy the influx of Flemish musicians became more and more limited in the second half of the sixteenth century, in the Spain of Philip II it increased considerably in importance. So true was this that it has been said that musicians arrived from the Low Countries in squads. In the diplomatic post, the letters exchanged between the King and his governor-general in the Low Countries were often taken up not with grave problems of policy but, rather, with the engagement of a singer, an organist or a dozen *little boys having attained the age of seven and up to twelve, but not more ... as long as they have good voices and are of good intelligence.* Right up to the end of the century, Flemish musicians continued to form a unified body in Madrid and maintained an unbroken tradition.

The last great recruitment of singers and boys in the Low Countries was in 1594. Thereafter, only individuals were engaged, and less and less frequently, until in the second half of the seventeenth century this policy ceased completely. At the death of Philip II, his successor Philip III continued to maintain the Flemish chapel. The composers active in it continued to be Netherlanders: Géry de Ghersem of Tournai and Jean Dufon of Namur, who were assistant masters, Philippe Dubois of Soignies, Martin Buset and Nicolas Dupont, who were cantors, and all of them began as choirboys in Madrid and pupils of Philippe Rogier.

As for the chapel master who succeeded Rogier, it was long thought that he was a Spaniard. But the name of Mateo Romero, by which he is generally known, is deceiving: he was actually from Liège, though he came to Spain very young and became completely assimilated; his right name was Mathieu Rosmarin. Favorite musician of Philip III and Philip IV, he was awarded most honorable titles such as Clerk of the Order of the Golden Fleece. In his compositions, Rosmarin-Romero abandoned the Flemish tradition to write in the new thorough-bass style. It is of some significance that this man from Liège, profoundly integrated into his Spanish environment, should have been mistakenly considered to be of Spanish origin. Under his direction, the Flemish chapel frequently called on Spanish singers and at last became less important than the Spanish chapel, with which, finally, it fused.

Thus, in Spain as elsewhere, the new style which rejected counterpoint as something archaic finally cost the Flemish their supremacy. The political ties between the Low Countries and Spain helped to maintain the Netherlanders in their privileged position a little longer than in Italy, but as soon as the style they represented had passed out of fashion this advantage was of no help.

On the other hand, it must be recognized that while Flemish musicians were particularly numerous in Madrid in the sixteenth century, in the other cities of Spain they never played a role comparable to that played in most Italian cities and courts: they never succeeded in taking over the chapels of the many cathedrals in the various provinces of Spain. Spain was a poor country and could not offer Flemish singers and composers sufficient advantages to attract and hold them. Not that musical activity was not intense in Andalusia, in Old and New

Castille and in a few other provinces, but whether in Toledo, Avila, Salamanca, Burgos, Cordova, Malaga or Seville, wherever they sang polyphonic music, the singers and chapel masters were Spanish.

Spanish composers did not need to become direct disciples of the Flemings to learn from them. Josquin Desprez and later Gombert were the models they chose for their religious works, and still later it was Palestrina they considered the perfect master. When they wrote *cantus firmus* or parody masses, motets, hymns, Magnificats and Lamentations, they preserved something indubitably their own by respecting local traditions, but they were able also to master all the stylistic subtleties of international polyphony. Musicians like Morales, Victoria and Guerrero succeeded in gaining a place on the European scene by practicing to perfection the Flemish contrapuntal style, which they were able to infuse with great dramatic intensity by a highly expressive alternation between sweetness and violence.

A few very eminent theorists such as Bermudo, Salinas and Cerone likewise demonstrate that counterpoint, an international language, was profoundly assimilated by the Spaniards, who, from a common technical base, were able to develop personal and original analyses and reflections.

THE FLEMINGS IN GERMANY AND ELSEWHERE
We can not possibly follow all the traces left by Flemish music in all the countries of Europe, but we can at least recall that in Portugal King John IV assembled, in the first half of the seventeenth century, a very rich collection of musical manuscripts, publications and theoretical works in which the Flemings, and particularly those who had lived in Spain, were in the majority. Unfortunately, this library was destroyed in the earthquake which ravaged Lisbon in 1755, and only the catalogue, published in 1649, remains to tell us of the extraordinary riches lost thereby.

Other countries, some of them remote from the most active musical centers, adopted the international polyphonic style insofar as their royal and princely courts cared about what was considered good tone elsewhere and to the extent that their churches wished to have music like that practiced abroad for their own solemn occasions.

In Hungary at the end of the fifteenth century, the chapel master of King Matthias Corvinus and his Queen, Beatrice of Aragon, was Johannes Stokhem of Liège. In the following century, the lutenist Valentin Bakfark, who lived in Poland and Vienna also, put into tablature chansons, madrigals and motets by Josquin, Gombert, Clemens non Papa and Lassus and composed fantasies in a contrapuntal style directly derived from the Flemish.

In Poland, works of Ciconia are found in manuscripts of the first half of the fifteenth century. At the beginning of the following century, theorists like Sebastian de Felstin and Stephanus Monetarius taught the principles of mensural notation and counterpoint, composers like Waclaw Szamotulczyk and Martin Lwowczyk (Martin of Lwow) wrote in an imitative style close to that of Gombert, and in the keyboard tablature of Jan of Lublin and in that of Cracow, both from before 1550, are to be found instrumental adaptations of works by Josquin, Janequin, Gombert and Verdelot.

We need not insist again on the close relationships which existed at the beginning of the fifteenth century between English musicians such as Dunstable and the Flemings Dufay and Binchois. Later, Flemish musicians do not seem to have been called into England as they were elsewhere, but their works were well known and even profoundly assimilated. Nevertheless, great English composers such as Fayrfax, Taverner, Tallis, Byrd and many others were able to maintain an authentic originality in spirit and language even when they submitted to the general rules of counterpoint.

It was Germany which, with Italy, was most open to Flemish influence. As early as the fifteenth century, works of Burgundian composers began to appear frequently in German manuscripts. Manuscript 222 C 22 of the library of Strasbourg (destroyed in the war of 1870 but preserved in part thanks to a copy made by Coussemaker) came from the Alsatian region from the first half of the fifteenth century. Along with works of Vitry and Machaut, by that time archaic, it contained pieces by Grenon, Binchois, Dufay and chansons in Flemish. The Trent manuscripts were assembled in an Italian-speaking region belonging to the Empire. They count among the most important sources for the first half of the fifteenth century, with an abundant representation of composers from Liège and Burgundy. Works by these same composers appear in the three great *Liederbücher* of the fifteenth century along with German monodic and polyphonic pieces. The *Lochamer Liederbuch,* assembled in Nuremberg between 1452 and 1460, contains a three-voice Flemish chanson and also, under the odd-looking title *Geloymors,* a well-known ballade by Binchois, *Je loe amours.* In the *Schedelsches Liederbuch,* written out around 1460 by the Humanist Hartmann Schädel during his student years in Leipzig, Padua and Nuremberg, there are works by Dufay, Ockeghem, Busnois and Pullois. The *Glogauer Liederbuch* contains, either with new Latin texts or in instrumental versions, pieces which originally were chansons by Dufay, Ghizeghem, Ockeghem, Busnois, Caron and Tinctoris. Most of the German pieces in these collections are anonymous, and the only names given are of obscure musicians, obviously much impressed by the prestige of the Flemish masters, whom they attempt to imitate, although rather clumsily.

The most interesting, most original music written in Germany in the fifteenth century is found in the organ tablatures. The most important of these, the *Buxheimer Orgelbuch,* dates from around 1460 and includes some two hundred pieces, among which are ornamented arrangements for the organ of secular chansons by those musicians found also in the *Liederbücher*: Dufay, Binchois, Johannes Franchois, Arnold de Lantins, and the Englishmen Dunstable,

Frye and Bedingham. Their chansons and motets first served the German organists as a basis for their instrumental versions and then as a model for completely instrumental contrapuntal fantasies.

In the middle of the fifteenth century, Flemish musicians settled only rarely in Germany. Jean Brassart of Liège, who had been in the pontifical chapel in 1431, seems to have been one of the first to work in the Imperial chapel. Under Albert II and Frederick III, in 1439 and 1443, he was first cantor, then *cantor principalis,* that is, master of the chapel, and he wrote ceremonial motets in honor of the emperors.

A half-century later, Heinrich Isaac was to become one of the glories of that chapel. He is mentioned for the first time in 1484 at the court of the Archduke of Austria in Innsbruck, but he was there only briefly. It was only after Maximilian came to the Imperial throne that Isaac entered his service, to be precise, in 1496, and the following year he was named *Hofkomponist* (court composer a title he kept until his death in 1517. In Maximilian's service, Isaac seems to have had no obligations other than to compose, which probably explains why he was able to travel about at will, making frequent visits to Italy and passing his last years in Florence, all this obviously with the consent of the Emperor. However, his relations with Germany must have been close enough to lead to his being considered a German not only by certain of his contemporaries but also by some of the theorists of the sixteenth century as well as by nineteenth-century historians. As is known, it was for Vienna and Constance that he composed his *Choralis Constantinus,* a monumental but unfinished work containing polyphonic versions in motet-style of ninety-six Propers of the mass. In the second part of it, he took as basis for his composition plain-chant melodies in the version of the Gradual of Constance. He also wrote a motet in honor of the Emperor Maximilian. In several of his masses he used German songs as *cantus firmus,* and he composed polyphonic *lieder* on German texts, among which one, *Innsbruck, ich muss dich lassen,* has enjoyed particular success. Isaac therefore appears as a composer open to quite diverse influences : Italian frottolas and German lieder each in turn attracted him, and he profited from these influences in his compositions while remaining above all faithful to the Flemish contrapuntal tradition.

Some historians have claimed to recognize a portrait of Isaac in the altarpiece painted by Jörg Breu for the church of Sankt Anna in Augsburg : the aged man writing is said to be Isaac, the master, and the young man at the organ, Senfl, his disciple. This is an entirely gratuitous hypothesis, but it is true that the sojourns of Isaac in Vienna, Innsbruck and other German cities permitted him to exert a deep influence on the local musicians who adopted as an ideal of composition the procedures of Flemish counterpoint. The most remarkable of his pupils, Ludwig Senfl, a native of Zurich, was one of Maximilian's composers and one of the leading musicians of the chapel of the dukes of Bavaria at Munich. It was he who completed the *Choralis Constantinus,* and he wrote *cantus firmus* masses and parody-masses in a style in no way distinct from that of the best Flemish composers. Another important pupil, Balthasar Resinarius, became a Lutheran and helped to maintain music in the contrapuntal tradition in the Reformed cult.

Another composer of Isaac's generation, Alexander Agricola, was often considered *Germanus* although he was probably Flemish. It is certain that some of his works were written for German churches, since several times he used plain-chant melodies in strictly local versions. At a time when Flemings had generally given up writing them, he composed hymns such as the *Ave maris stella* and *A solis ortus* using the Gregorian melody in long note-values, a technique particularly favored in Germany. Also, he composed a *Missa paschalis* on several plain-chant melodies found only in Germany and Central Europe. Finally, his works are especially well represented in German manuscripts. All this tends to convince us that the Fleming Agricola must have worked in Germany between his sojourns in Italy and before rejoining the chapel of Philip the Fair. Together with Isaac, he contributed to implanting into that country a solid contrapuntal practice in accord with Flemish principles.

It must not be forgotten that in 1477 Maximilian of Austria married Mary of Burgundy, daughter of Charles the Bold, and lived with her in the Low Countries and also that, after her death in 1482, he was regent for Philip the Handsome, who was only four years old. Thus he was able to come to know and appreciate the qualities of the Burgundian chapel and of its musicians. It is not surprising to learn that later he demanded of his German chapel that they should *brabantisch diskantieren,* which may be translated as "to sing counterpoint in the manner of Brabant." However, with a few exceptions, his own musicians were all German.

At the death of Maximilian in 1519, his chapel was dispersed. His successor was his grandson Charles V, but Charles had been reigning over the Low Countries ever since the death of Philip the Fair in 1506, over Spain since the death of his maternal grandfather Ferdinand of Aragon in 1516, and thenceforth over Austria, all this by the time he succeeded to the Empire. Contrary to the opinion of certain historians, Charles V did not maintain separate musical chapels in Spain, Germany and the Low Countries but had only one. That chapel accompanied him on his incessant travels and was a continuation of the Burgundian chapel with its cantors, chaplains and choristers, the same chapel left to him by Philip the Fair. As we already know, this chapel included Flemings exclusively. Charles's personal prestige probably induced many princely courts in Germany to call on Flemish musicians. Their emigration in that direction occurred later than to Italy, not becoming intense until the sixteenth century and especially during the second half of that century, but it was no less definite. Whereas in Italy there were many Frenchmen among

Les Chantres de l'Empereur accompagnés d'une saquebute & d'une flûte executent à grand chœur un concert de voix. George Slakonia Evèque de Vienne, Directeur de la Musique de S.M.I. y preside : un personnage est assis à ses côtés, & l'on ne peut guere douter que ce ne soit le Maitre de Musique.

APOLLO

MELPOMENE
TALIA
TERPSICOR
CALLIOPE
POLYMNIA
URANIA
ERATO
EVTERPE

96. The Cantors of Emperor Maximilian.
Hans Burgkmair.

the Flemings and all were considered *Oltramontani,* in Germany the newcomers came almost entirely from the Low Countries and the principality of Liège.

A separate chapel was set up by Ferdinand, the younger brother of Charles V, who governed the Germanic lands and became Emperor in 1555. After Arnold von Bruck — and it is not known if he was a native of Bruges in Flanders or of Bruck in Austria — all the heads of the Imperial chapel were Flemish.

First there was Peter Maessins, born in Ghent around 1505. He began as choirboy in the chapel of Margaret of Austria, Regent of the Netherlands, and led an adventurous life as a *condottiere* before becoming singing master of the church of Notre-Dame in Courtrai, assistant master of the Imperial chapel from 1543 to 1545, and master of the chapel from 1546 to 1560. Of his compositions there survive masses, motets, secular works and a few teaching pieces.

He was succeeded by Jean Guyot (1512-1588), often called Castileti from the name of his native town, Châtelet, which at that time belonged to the principality of Liège. Guyot studied at the University of Louvain, where he obtained the degree of *magister artium,* and became associated with vari-

ous churches in Liège, publishing in 1554, under the title of *Minervalia,* a piece of Latin rhetoric. His connection with the Imperial chapel lasted only one year and he seems to have passed the rest of his life in Liège. He left a mass for eight voices, motets and chansons.

Jacob Vaet (1529-1567) began his apprenticeship in Courtrai, his native city. From 1554 on, he was in the service of the Archduke of Austria, where he remained when, ten years later, his master was elected Emperor under the name of Maximilian II. Vaet belongs to the line of Gombert in the severity of his counterpoint and his rigorous application of the procedures of syntactic imitation in works which were almost entirely religious : ten masses, eight Magnificats, seventy-six motets, several hymns but no more than three chansons.

Philippe de Monte of Malines followed Vaet in the position in 1568. As master of the chapel until his death in 1603, he played a principal role in German musical life, and his work made an impact all over Europe. His importance will be discussed later, together with that of Roland de Lassus. He was succeeded in the chapel by one of his pupils, Lambert de Sayve of Liège, who had been choirboy in the Imperial chapel and had occupied important functions at the court of the archdukes of Austria in Graz. He was deeply influenced by the Venetian School, writing masses for ensembles of from eight to fourteen voices, Magnificats for eight voices and motets for from four to sixteen voices. In their echo effects and generally chordal character, these works are quite remote from the contrapuntal tradition. There is in them already a profoundly Italianate tendency, sure signs of the style which was to mark the end of Flemish hegemony.

In fact, after Lambert de Sayve, no other Liégeois, no other Fleming was ever again to direct the Imperial chapel. The music which was preferred in the seventeenth century was the new art with thorough-bass, and this was Italian. A quite different epoch had begun.

271

Other musicians from Liège or the Low Countries occupied various positions in the Imperial chapel in the sixteenth century. It would be quite impossible here to enumerate all the singers, but the names of a few of them suffice to reveal their origins : Jesse Wautters, Gerard Meert, Andreas Cornet, Simon Straels, Alard du Gaucquier, Wilhelm de la Fontaine, Nicolas le Febure. There is more profit in singling out those who distinguished themselves as composers. In the first place must come Jacob Buus of Ghent, who lived for a long time in Italy, where he was organist at Saint Mark's in Venice from 1541 to 1550 before occupying the same post in the Imperial chapel from 1551 to his death in 1564. Besides motets and *canzoni francesi*, he wrote *ricercari* for instrumental ensembles or organ. These *ricercari* borrow their imitative procedures from the motet, developing at length different themes one after the other. Monothematic *ricercari* in particular have attracted the attention of music historians since they are an important step on the way to the fugue, a form which was to enrich instrumental music throughout the next two centuries. In Vienna as in Venice, Buus implanted a most severe organ style which was an adaptation of contrapuntal technique to the possibilities of the instrument.

Two other talented Flemings were organists in the Imperial chapel : from 1570 to 1593 Paul de Winde, a native of Malines who had been organist there at Saint-Rombaut, and, especially, Charles Luython, born in Antwerp around 1557, who was in turn choirboy (and as such a pupil of Jacob Vaet and Philippe de Monte), chamber musician, organist and court composer and who died at Prague in 1620. He wrote motets, masses, Lamentations and madrigals in which the contrapuntal style is often made less severe through homophonic episodes; besides these, he composed excellent fantasies, *ricercari* and *canzoni* for organ.

For the same period one can add Jacques Regnard (d. 1599) of Douai, where he had been assistant master, Jacobus de Kerle (1531-1591) of Ypres, who was *Hofkaplan* (court chaplain), Christian Hollander (d. 1568) from Audenaerde, who was a cantor, Franciscus Sale (d. 1599), a tenor from Namur, and Alexander Utendal (d. 1581), formerly in the service of Mary of Hungary, Governess of the Low Countries, and then assistant master of the Imperial chapel. Worthy of special note is another assistant master, Jean de Castro of Liège (ca. 1540-ca. 1600). This minor but prolific composer was one of the most popular composers of his time. His polyphonic chansons went through innumerable editions in every country, and as late as 1634 Phalèse published two volumes of his *Sonnets, chansons, danses et épigrammes*. All of these composers wrote a vast number of religious or secular works which are still little known because few of them have been published in modern editions.

The Imperial chapel was not the only attraction in Germany for musicians from the Low Countries or Liège. At the beginning of the sixteenth century, Adam Rener of Liège, who, in 1498, had been choirboy and later cantor in Maximilian's chapel, led a double career as historiographer and composer at the court of the Prince-Elector of Saxony, Frederick the Wise, in Torgau. His masses for four voices, fragments of the Proper, motets and polyphonic lieder reveal him as one of the best foreign musicians settled in Germany at the time of Isaac. It is thought that Noël Bauldewijn of Antwerp, who from 1509 to 1513 was singing master at the cathedral of Malines, must have lived in Germany since his works are known mostly in manuscripts or publications in that country. Anton Gosswin (ca. 1540-1594) belonged to the chapel in Munich and held posts as organist or chapel master in Landshut, Freising and Bonn. Rogier Michael (1554-1619) of Mons was a member of the chapel at Graz and later chapel master at the court of Saxony in Dresden. Samuel Mareschall (1554-1640), a native of Tournai, was organist and professor at the University of Basel.

But, of course, the most important Netherlandish musician settled in Germany was Roland de Lassus. From 1564 until his death in 1594 he directed the chapel of Bavaria, of which he had been a member since 1556. From Munich his fame spread throughout Europe.

Printed editions were the principal means of diffusion of Flemish music in Germany. Isaac, Josquin, Pierre de la Rue, Obrecht, Mouton appear alongside Senfl and Hofhaimer in the first polyphonic collections published in Germany beginning in 1512. Subsequently there were always a great many Flemish works included in the volumes published by Formschneider, Petreius and Grapheus in Nuremberg, by Egenolf in Frankfurt, and by Rhaw in Wittenberg. Certain names continue to appear for many years, those of Josquin and Isaac among them, while others appeared and disappeared as fashions changed.

When Johann vom Berg of Ghent, better known by his Latinized name Montanus, became associated with Ulrich Neuber to publish in Nuremberg, his anthologies made an even larger place for the Flemish. The Flemish are in the majority among composers of the two-voice pieces *Biphona amœna et florida,* published in 1549 as well as in the psalm collections of 1553, the *Novum et insigne opus musicum* of 1558, and the *Thesaurus musicus* of 1564. In all these collections, the musicians of the beginning of the century – Josquin and Isaac – are still included, but the masters of the generation following are more numerous, among them Mouton, Willaert, Arcadelt, Clemens non Papa, Crecquillon, Manchicourt and Gombert, as well as the younger group around Philippe de Monte and Roland de Lassus. Thus all the varieties of Flemish counterpoint are represented : archaizing tendencies by works based on a *cantus firmus,* the imitative-syntactic style by motets with highly elaborate counterpoint, and the new orientation of chordal polyphony by motets for eight voices and double choir.

As for the Germans included in these publications, they had adopted and assimilated the various styles of Flemish counterpoint.

For their part, the theorists also played an active role in fostering Flemish music and its techniques. Ever since the end of the fifteenth century they had chosen their examples from the best Flemish composers. In his *De musica* of 1490, Adam von Fulda, who lived at Torgau and Wittenberg, named Busnois as his favorite musician. Martin Agricola (not to be confused with the composer Alexander Agricola) took Josquin as his model in his treatises in German published by Rhaw at Wittenberg from 1529 on, as did Lampadius in his *Compendium musices,* which came out in Berne in 1537. For them, the standards of *ars perfecta* were determined by music in the manner of Josquin. The preferences of Glareanus are apparent in the choice of examples in his *Dodecachordon* of 1547 : twenty-five fragments from works by Josquin, five by Isaac, four each by Brumel and Mouton, and three each by Obrecht and Ockeghem, while among the Germans Gregor Meyer is cited ten times, Sixtus Dietrich five and Ludwig Senfl three. Adriaen Petit Coclico claimed to be a direct disciple of Josquin, and the conceptions he expounds in his *Compendium musices,* published in Nuremberg in 1552, are entirely in accord with the norms of Flemish counterpoint. In his *Practica musica,* published in 1556 at Wittenberg, Hermann Finck took Gombert as his model of perfection. The numerous treatises written for Lutheran schools included among material to be taught mensural music and polyphony as conceived by Flemish composers. Solmization and counterpoint were learned from collections of *bicinia* and *tricinia,* pieces for two or three voices taken from masses and motets.

LUTHERANS AND CATHOLICS
It might be thought that the Lutheran reforms would have put an end to the development of Flemish music in Germany. Flemish cantors and com-

posers were, after all, most often Catholic, and the most significant of their works were intended for the Church. As part of his reforms, Luther aimed to reorganize the church service, to condense it into a smaller number of offices, and to encourage participation on the part of the congregation by the use of the vernacular. To this end he introduced spiritual songs – the *chorales* – into the service, but in this he was less radical than Calvin, who restricted church music to the singing of psalms. Luther did not reject the traditional liturgical forms and even urged the development of local practices. He had deep love for music and the greatest admiration for that of Josquin. Thus plain-chant was in part retained as well as Latin motets and even fragments of the Ordinary of the mass. Certain churches continued even to use chants in honor of the Virgin or of some saints, and at Vespers Marian antiphons and Magnificats were occasionally sung. Differing in various places and periods, services might contain a variable number of polyphonic pieces in Latin which could be doubled or replaced by German chorales. Luther considered that Latin motets were particularly appropriate to solemn occasions in churches which disposed of a well-trained choir, and it was in this way that works by Catholic musicians continued to be employed. It was for Lutheran choirs in particular that were intended the collections of motets published in Nuremberg by editors like Ott, Petreius, Gerlach, Berg and Neuber, collections which included many works written by Catholics. When Lutheran composers came to write motets, they adopted a style which differed in no way from that used for Catholic motets.

But at the same time Luther encouraged the singing of German chorales. In its text, the chorale was a canticle which served as commentary on the Gospel reading for the day. Musically, it might derive from a Gregorian hymn, from a spiritual song of the Middle Ages, from a profane song or, sometimes, from an original melody. It could be sung in unison or polyphonically. In the latter case, the composer

97. A Chamber Concert at the Court of Bavaria in Munich.
Hans Muelich.

had recourse to the well-known technique of *cantus firmus* by placing the melody in long note-values in the tenor and surrounding it with contrapuntal variations in the other voices. Thus, it was procedures borrowed from Flemish masters which were utilized in this first phase of the polyphonic chorale, and the basic model was the lied, such as Isaac's *Innsbruck, ich muss dich lassen.*

Few Netherlanders wrote for the Lutheran Church, and they composed very few polyphonic chorales. However, Mathieu Le Maistre of Liège, *Kapellmeister* for the Elector of Saxony in Dresden, published in 1577 his *Schöne und auserlesene teutsche und lateinische Gesänge zu 3 Stimmen,* in which one finds Latin and German pieces in the same style as the chorales by Johann Walter and Georg Rhaw, who had worked in close collaboration with Luther.

On the other hand, Lutheran composers wrote motets on German texts in no way different from other motets of the period as well as chorales in a chordal style with the melody clearly exposed, a style more easily mastered by amateur choirs of little training. However, the chordal-style chorale was not to triumph until the end of the century, and when it did it contributed to the decline of Flemish counterpoint.

274

Two Flemish musicians brought counterpoint to its supreme height in sixteenth-century Germany. Philippe de Monte was born in Malines in 1521 and undoubtedly received his first training in that city at the cathedral. He was very young when he left for Italy, living in Naples from 1542 to 1544 and then in Rome. After a brief stay in Antwerp in 1554 and in England as a member of the chapel of Philip II, who had married Mary Tudor, he returned to live in Italy, in Florence, Rome and Genoa, where, apparently, he was in the service of various noble families. In 1568 he was summoned by Maximilian II to succeed Vaet as master of the Imperial chapel, a function he retained until his death in 1603, never leaving Vienna and Prague except for occasional voyages to the Low Countries to recruit young musicians. He was an extraordinarily prolific composer : beside 45 chansons, 319 motets and 38 masses, he left 1073 secular madrigals and 144 spiritual madrigals.

In recommending Monte to the Duke of Bavaria as chapel master, Dr. Seld, vice-chancellor of the court of Vienna on mission in Brussels, described him in 1555 as a quiet man, timid and gentle as a young girl – *ein stiller eingezogener züchtiger Mensch, wie ein Junkfrau.* This charm infuses his music and explains perhaps the abundance of his production. Monte is a musician without problems and without passion. He avoids all excess of pathos and dramatic effects and is not interested in chromatic experiments. His particular forte is the expression of lyrical, serene sentiments. And yet, he was not a reactionary. In his religious music he did not indulge in archaicisms, was not preoccupied by erudite constructions, rhythmic complexities and contrapuntal subtleties, and his great concern was with bringing out the text. All this leads to a certain variety in his music, which, in essence, however, remains unchanged throughout his many works, preserving always the same atmosphere and, with minor modifications in the course of the years, the

same style, in which counterpoint is lightened by episodes in a more harmonic style.

Roland de Lassus and Philippe de Monte have nothing more in common than the general line of their careers and the abundance of their production, for they differ as much in personal character as in the spirit of their works. As for the composer known to the Italians as Orlando di Lasso and whose right name is Roland de Lassus, despite what one might expect the *de* in *de Lassus* is not an indication of noble birth and *Lassus* is not some name Latinized through the whim of a Humanist : it means nothing more than *de là-dessus* – from up there – and appears in French or Walloon regions more often in the form *Delahaut.* Lassus was born in the Walloon town of Mons in 1532, it is believed, and must have been choirboy in the church of Saint-Nicolas of his native city. He was no more than twelve years old when he was engaged because of his fine voice by Ferdinand Gonzaga, Viceroy of Sicily, who at that time was in command of an army of Charles V and was campaigning in France. The youngster followed his new master to Palermo and then to Milan. Toward

98. The Chapel Choir at Munich Under the Direction of Roland de Lassus.
Hans Muelich.

276

1549, he was in the service of a Neapolitan noble, and in 1553 he became chapel master at the basilica of the Lateran in Rome at the very early age of twenty-one. It was thus in Italy that he acquired almost all of his musical training. When he returned to the Low Countries in 1554 because of the death of his parents, he settled in Antwerp and there it was his Italianism which fascinated those with whom he came into contact. That Italianism was particularly marked in his first collections of madrigals, chansons and motets, which Susato published in the following year. Soon after, he was engaged as tenor by Duke Albert V of Bavaria and settled in Munich in the autumn of 1556. Promoted to chapel master in 1563, he never left the ducal court until his death in 1594 except for professional voyages to the Low Countries to recruit cantors and choristers and, more frequently, to Italy. He married the daughter of a lady-in-waiting of the court and had two sons, Ferdinand and Rudolph, who, like their father, were to become musicians. In the last years of his life, this jovial man, whose correspondence is larded with plays on words in a half-dozen languages and with burlesque inventions, fell into a profound depressive melancholy.

Beginning in 1555, the leading publishers of Italy, France, the Low Countries and Germany put out regularly each year his many collections of works in every genre. The Duke of Bavaria treated him most generously, often adding to his wages gifts in money, precious objects and property. Lassus was well compensated for the dedications he made of his works to queens, princes and wealthy bankers, and the publishers paid him well. Thus, he was able to live in lordly style. He seems to have been the most universally admired musician of the sixteenth century, and poets and Humanists celebrated his merits in verse and prose, in Latin, French, Italian and German.

Prefacing the *Meslanges d'Orlande de Lassus*, published in 1576 by Le Roy and Ballard, was this sonnet by Régnier, which is typical of many, hailing Lassus as the most perfect master of the great line of Flemish musicians, an opinion which seems to have been general:

Le bon père Josquin de la musique informe
Ebaucha le premier le dur et rude corps;
Le grave et doux Willaert secondant ses efforts
Cet œuvre commencé plus doctement réforme.

L'inventif Cyprien pour se rendre conforme
Au travail de ces deux qui seuls estoyent alors
L'enrichit d'ornemens par ces nouveaux accords,
Donnant à cette pièce une notable forme.

Orlande à ce labeur avec eux s'estant joinct
A poli puis après l'ouvrage de tout poinct,
De sorte qu'après luy n'y faut plus la main mettre.

Josquin aura la palme, ayant esté premier;
Willaert le myrte aura; Cyprien le laurier;
Orlande emportera les trois comme le maistre.

(Good father Josquin from music was first / To hew out a rough and rude shape; / Grave, gentle Willaert then lent a hand / To polish and form the work thus begun. / Inventive Cipriano, to match their deeds, / To the work of those two – alone in their time – / Brought rich ornament of new harmonies / And gave to the piece a shape and a form. / Orlando to their labors then brought all his skill, / Polished the work in finest detail, / So that after him no more need be done. / To Josquin the palm, for he was the first; / To Willaert the myrtle, to Cipriano the laurel; / To Orlando all three : the master is he.)

Lassus was placed at the head of all his contemporaries in the preface Ronsard wrote to a *Livre des meslanges* published in 1560 by the same editors: *And at present, the more than divine Orlando, who like a honey-bee has sipped from the most beautiful flowers of the Ancients, and besides seems to have been alone in robbing Heaven of its harmony to rejoice us on earth, surpassing the Ancients to become the unique marvel of our time.*

There can be no doubt that with Lassus music once and for all ceased to be a field for artisans and became truly an art. Ronsard expressed this in the same text, declaring that *the divine furies of music, of poetry and of painting do not come by degrees of perfection as in the other sciences, but by sudden bursts and like lightning flashes* and that artists of genius are exceptional beings to whom it is proper to pay homage; addressing himself to King Francis II, Ronsard insists: *And for this reason, Sire, when there is revealed some excellent worker in this art, you should cherish him with care as something the more excellent for being so rare.*

All possible honor was paid to Lassus. He was welcomed everywhere as the "prince of musicians": by Pope Gregory XIII in 1574 as well as by the King of France, Charles IX, in 1571, who urged him to enter his service, and the Emperor, Maximilian II, granted him letters of nobility. The Duke of Bavaria chose a most splendid way of honoring his favorite composer when, between 1573 and 1576, he had published an important selection of religious works by Lassus. The five volumes of the *Patrocinium musices* are distinguished from the hundreds of other editions of Lassus not only by their luxurious presentation but also by the concern with offering a coherent and representative sampling of his production. In the same spirit, after the composer's death, his sons published the *Magnum opus musicum,* which contains his most significant works.

Roland de Lassus is surely the musician who best expressed his epoch through his art, a universal genius who handled every type of music with equal mastery.

It was, without doubt, his chansons which won him widest popularity, for they represent the most facile and immediately attractive aspect of his work. Thanks to them, his music entered into bourgeois dwellings as easily as into princely palaces, and they are most diverse in character and style. In rustic or refined verses, Lassus sang of the vines of Margot or the mythological fancies of a Ronsard, and, al-

ways in tune with the verses being set, he could in turn be witty and bawdy or elegant and tender, sometimes writing music that was light and direct, sometimes composing in a learned but expressive idiom. The same diversity appears in his Italian works. Lassus wrote, on the one hand, madrigals which conform to the stylistic subtleties required by the genre and, on the other, villanelles and moresques in a popular manner with dancing rhythms and simplified counterpoint. Like all the musicians from the Low Countries who worked in Germany, he also wrote polyphonic lieder of all kinds : drinking songs, burlesque ditties, love songs, moralizing and spiritual pieces.

But despite the abundance and quality of his secular production, Lassus was above all a composer of sacred music, writing 53 masses, more than 100 Magnificats, over 500 motets and various pieces such as Lamentations, psalms and the like in motet-style. In his masses, Lassus did not choose to employ a *cantus firmus* but was partial to the parody technique based on a motet, chanson or madrigal. The directives of the Council of Trent did not prevent him from writing a mass on suggestive songs such as *Je ne mange point de porcq* and *Le Berger et la bergère,* but the original melodies are so profoundly integrated into the substance of the work and so greatly modified that not even the most touchy listener could take offense. He often applied the same parody technique to the Magnificat, using especially his own compositions as a basis. However, it was certainly in the motet that he found the finest field for his extraordinary invention. He set to music specially written texts for public and private ceremonies as well as liturgical texts without ever concerning himself as to whether or not they lent themselves to musical illustration. These included fragments from the Gospels, Epistles, Psalms, the Song of Songs, the Book of Job and the Lamentations of Jeremiah as well as Marian antiphons and hymns. He was often preoccupied with bringing out all the dramatic intensity of the text in hand

PATROCINIVM. MVSICES.

LAVDATE DOMINVM OMNES GENTES

MISSÆ
ALIQVOT QVINQVE VOCVM.
ORLANDI DE LASSO
Sereniss: Ducis Bauariæ, Chori Magistri.

Monachii excudebat Adamus Berg.
M. D. L XXXIX.

and sought always to find the perfect musical expression for both the general meaning and all the nuances of the words. In his great cycles – the *Psalmi Davidis pœnitentiales* (Penitential Psalms), *Lectiones sacræ novem ex libris Hiob* (Lessons of Job) and *Prophetiæ Sibyllarum* (Prophecies of the Sibyls) – he achieved veritable perfection.

It was only at the beginning of his career that Lassus was what can be considered a modernist. In the *Prophetiæ Sibyllarum* he had recourse to systematic chromaticism, but later he used it only occasionally and never again with the same audacity. For his contemporaries in the Low Countries at the start of his career, his modernism must also have been found in his rejection of the imitative-syntactic style, his "Italian manner," which Willaert and a few others had already fostered and which was later to impose its newly won freedom everywhere. What characterizes Lassus is that in all the genres he gave up all use of a priori schemes of construction, using neither the *cantus firmus* nor any systematic, continuous imitation. In line with the principles then winning out in Italy, especially in the madrigal, Lassus always allowed the text to be the source of his inspiration.

It is this concern with expression which best explains the transformations Lassus brought about in melodic style. He rejects those ample melodic lines with their infinite melismas which, scarcely coming to rest at cadence points, constantly flow off into new curves. These he replaces with briefer motifs more closely related to each phrase of the text and to the key words which must be brought out. Deliberately renouncing an aesthetic derived from the Gregorian, he does not hesitate to launch his melodic phrases into unexpected leaps, to break them up with silences which themselves have an expressive function. He constantly strives for contrast. There are only brief imitations of small melodic motifs, which are well characterized and based on well-defined rhythms, and this counterpoint liberated from conventional weightiness often alternates with episodes in homophonic style. In certain works, the chordal style dominates, along with quite rapid syllabic declamation. All of the expressive procedures favored by the madrigalists were employed by Lassus so regularly and so consistently that, at the beginning of the seventeenth century, his work could provide a theorist like Burmeister with the basis for his catalogue of figures in musical rhetoric. Despite all this, music never sacrifices its own rights to the text. It is in response to suggestions from the text and without any preconceptions that Lassus sometimes had recourse to archaicisms such as rigorous counterpoint, fauxbourdon, and chords without the third, while at other times he used modernisms such as chromaticism and piled-up dissonances. Everything for him was conditioned by his striving for expression, and toward that end he did not hesitate to use the most dramatic effects.

While still respecting the norms of contrapuntal style, Lassus employed different techniques and even different idioms which vary according to the

281

genres, the works, and the effects sought after. Often musical instruments must have contributed their richer sonorities to vocal works, lending to them a color quite unlike that grave austerity which musicologists for a long time thought proper to them. Unlike what has often been said by those who ill-advisedly apply the notion to all sixteenth-century music, Lassus was not a "classical" composer. Without creating a revolution in language, remaining always within the norms of counterpoint although forcing them to co-operate in his quest for expressiveness, Lassus led Flemish music to a renewal in depth which was in line with the aesthetic transformations of the end of the sixteenth century and which corresponded to what is called mannerism in the visual arts.

Epilogue

100. Fall of the Rebel Angels.
Pieter Bruegel.

Decline and Fall

In the fifteenth and sixteenth centuries, a single style was used in all genres, whether sacred or profane. Not that there were not variants : the polyphonic voices might function with a high degree of independence or, on the other hand, be marshaled into a more or less rigorous homophony; there might be preconceived formal schemes or free structures which strove to follow the text and bring out its meaning; there might be an overall modal climate or, instead, something approaching a tonal basis. Contrapuntal writing, the fundamental technique of all composition of the time, was flexible enough to permit the most diverse tendencies, above all in secular music. Through their use of Italian, Spanish, German or English texts, musicians seem to have been led to concern themselves with local traditions, to profit more from certain popular practices which had preserved a certain autonomy in idiom. Italian villanellas, Spanish villancicos and Parisian chansons all have their own character, their own typical stylistic traits, and even in religious music local usages gave rise to original conceptions.

But on the whole it was Flemish counterpoint which set for all Europe its models of style. In all the choir schools, the correct way to sing polyphony was taught according to Flemish principles, and composition was learned by studying and imitating Flemish examples. This universal acceptance was possible because the Flemish had no ambitions to create a specific national art. From the outset they were open to outside influences which they transformed and assimilated as they wished. From Guillaume Dufay to Roland de Lassus, this open-mindedness led to a constantly renewed art which nevertheless never questioned a certain number of basic principles.

It was, however, these very principles that were challenged at the end of the sixteenth century. The sharpest criticisms of counterpoint were, at that time, formulated in Italian Humanist circles, which sought support for their arguments from the Greek philosophers. According to Vincenzo Galilei in his *Dialogo della musica antica e della moderna* of 1581, all those who practiced counterpoint were nothing more than barbarians, and it was against them that it was necessary to struggle in order to regenerate music, to restore to it its lost power and its beauty.

For the adversaries of counterpoint, the essential flaw in the technique was its complexity, which prevented it from attaining efficacity in expression : all polyphony contains contradictory elements because the pitches, melodies and rhythms that it jumbles together each have, of necessity, diverse expressive meanings. In order to bring out sentiments in

285

their full intensity, to penetrate the soul of the listener, music must turn its back on this anarchy in which all expressive effects cancel each other out; it must return to that monodic style which already in Antiquity had proved its superiority. But this was not to be mere archaeological reconstruction. No one really took the Humanists seriously when they claimed that the ancient monody *promoted modesty, tamed wild beasts, calmed dissensions between nations, restored hearing to the deaf, drove away plague, made sorrow-wracked souls gay, healed serpent bites, quieted drunkards and madmen and, even, could liberate men from death.* But these were convenient arguments in the struggle to pit a new style against counterpoint.

Within the technique of counterpoint itself, an internal evolution had increasingly fostered chordal writing to the detriment of the independence of voices. A simplified polyphony often brought about the predominance of the topmost voice, which acquired even more importance when it was sung as a solo. This apparent accompanied monody became even more marked when the lower parts were all confided to a single instrument, a lute, for instance, which could play all the polyphonic voices in simplified version. In the Italian courts, certain singers had built up a repertory of villanelles or *canzoni* which they sang solo with lute accompaniment, and in these the principal melody, that of the upper voice, predominated completely.

Thus certain tendencies indigenous to counterpoint led to the making of pseudo-monodies which departed radically from the spirit of polyphony without yet breaking with it. The definite split occurred when a singer and lutenist like Giulio Caccini composed around 1590 madrigals for solo voice accompanied by the chitarrone (a bass lute) and published them in 1602 under the title of *Nuove musiche*. This was, in fact, a new music, for it no longer depended on a voice which stood out against a complex polyphonic background, but instead was written for a solo voice, completely liberated from any polyphonic ties, which could thereby achieve the utmost in vivacity, spontaneity and flexibility in delivery and a more intense variety and veracity in expression. Supporting it there was only a relatively immobile bass line from which, guided by a system of ciphers, the accompanist was to reconstruct the harmonies desired by the composer, fill in the inner parts and proceed in a series of long-held chords with some melodic embroidery.

At first the new style, the *stile nuovo*, was above all dramatic and in recitative, and, thus, it made possible the birth of opera, a genre which explored and exploited all of its expressive possibilities. Beginning in 1605, Monteverdi gave the style the stamp of approval of an artist of great reputation by applying it to the noble genre that was the madrigal. Thus, on the basis of a minor tendency within counterpoint itself and by a metamorphosis in which collaborated great musicians such as Caccini, Peri and Monteverdi, an entirely new language was created.

The *stile nuovo* did not in a single blow write finis to the contrapuntal idiom. In reply to criticisms of his harmonic audacity, Monteverdi explained that monody accompanied by thorough-bass, by *basso continuo*, was in fact a *seconda prattica*, a second manner, which did not in itself obviate the first manner, that of counterpoint, and Monteverdi did not fail to express his admiration for musicians like Josquin Desprez, Mouton, Gombert and, above all, Willaert. But, he maintained, the contrapuntal technique was not adaptable to all ends, for, even when it employed chromaticism, as the *moderns* – Rore, Marenzio, Wert – had done, it could no longer provide satisfactory expression to the essential artistic principle which held that the text was more important than the music. The *stile nuovo* was preferable, according to Monteverdi, because with it one could express all the passions in all their violence, with all their contrasts in feeling and with fullest dramatic tension, whereas counterpoint could give satisfaction only in those genres which did not demand such intensity of expression.

This was not the first time in the history of Western music that a new kind of music, an *ars nova*, was pitted against an older style. But in the past such conflicts had always been settled by the definitive consignment of the older style to extinction. At the beginning of the seventeenth century, the struggle was settled by the bursting asunder of the musical language : the unity of style which had always prevailed until then simply ceased to exist. The *stile nuovo* triumphed first in the secular genres, while counterpoint continued to be used in religious music and was thought of as fitting for such solemn, impersonal music immune to outbursts of passion. The Baroque period insisted on classifying music according to its functions. Thenceforth there would be one kind of music for the church, another for chamber diversions, another for the theater, and, from the point of view of style, there would be a *prima* and a *seconda prattica,* which would be adopted or rejected in line with their respective functions.

However, the *stile nuovo* was not limited to that exaggerated opposition to counterpoint that recitative represented with its total subjection to the text. In becoming Baroque music, the new style preserved many stylistic elements of its predecessor but renewed and revivified them, becoming steadily more rich in its own right and ending finally as a quite different kind of music, entirely distinct from that of the Renaissance in its melodic character, its rhythm and its harmonic principles.

Counterpoint lived on, but as something archaic called *stylus antiquus, stylus gravis.* It was thought of as more austere than it had ever in fact been. It was sung slowly and solemnly to enhance its nobility, and was performed *a cappella* (by a choir alone, without instruments). All this tended to confer on it an ideal and unreal purity which placed it beyond the normal contingencies of life. It was made into something fixed and frozen and, in truth, dull and boring. Diminished and caricatured in this way, it was called for whenever it was desired to create an exaggeratedly austere atmosphere in religious music.

The rules of sixteenth-century counterpoint continued to be taught. Palestrina was taken as the model, because Palestrina seemed to be the ideal church musician and because his cautious style, without audacities, seemed to demand the most rigorous restraint. In Fux's *Gradus ad Parnassum* of 1725, in which he set down a pedagogy of musical technique, the rules of counterpoint *alla Palestrina* were virtually disembodied, no longer corresponding to any music that had ever lived, reduced to no more than dreary school exercises in a system of teaching entirely cut off from reality.

What of the Flemish ? It was their style which thus lived on embalmed and inert, but their music itself was no longer sung, not even in church. No more of it was known than a few rare examples, included for didactic reasons, in works on history or theory.

It was at the precise moment when the *stile nuovo* triumphed that the spread of Flemish music throughout Europe came to an end. The new style had first appeared in Italy and was at the outset considered as essentially Italian. But soon other national styles competed with it : French taste challenged Italian, and the Germans tried to promote a tendency in which the two of them would be reconciled. In the entire history of Baroque music, the Flemings had no role whatsoever to play. Not that music was not still made in the Low Countries, but it merely followed the fashion, imitating the Italians or the French. It was as if the genius of the Flemish had been linked with a particular language, counterpoint, without which it could only wither away.

The fact is that this decadence can already be discerned in the last third of the sixteenth century : then, there were no longer any but musicians of minor rank left in the Low Countries, and the best composers were educated abroad; then, also, national schools took root in Italy, Spain, Germany and England, and it became apparent that local composers could often use counterpoint with more skill and invention than their masters. Still, as if by ingrained

101 and 102. Four Angel Musicians.
Hans Memling.

habit, all Europe continued to call on the Flemings as long as counterpoint continued to be the international language.

If the Flemish were totally eliminated from the international scene when the new style triumphed, it was, without doubt, because they were too closely associated with counterpoint. They were rejected and condemned at the same time as was their own style.

And then, for a long time, the contrapuntalists of the Renaissance were forgotten. Whatever it may have claimed, the Baroque did not truly tolerate a genuine aesthetic pluralism. It was only slowly, in the Romantic age, that Flemish musicians of the fifteenth and sixteenth centuries were rediscovered. Even today they do not truly live again except among those by whom their language is no longer thought of as archaic, who welcome them with something other than the coldly indifferent respect due their venerable age. And yet, their masses, motets, chansons and madrigals can and do touch us – at last – as works of art with their own high qualities.

Guillaume Dufay, Josquin Desprez, Roland de Lassus are all part of our present. Thanks partly to them, we know that the world of music is not confined to Beethoven with his nine symphonies and Bach with his *Brandenburg Concertos*. The Flemish polyphonists have made for themselves a special place, and a choice one, in our universal museum of sound. They have returned to life and will not, cannot, ever again fall back into undeserved obscurity.

Appendixes

A Critical Bibliography

GENERAL CONSIDERATIONS.

It is, of course, beyond the scope and intent of this book to propose an exhaustive reading list for the history of Flemish music in the fifteenth and sixteenth centuries. Much has been written on the subject ever since the *Mémoires* prepared simultaneously in 1829 by two pioneers of musicology in the Romantic era, F.-J. Fétis and R.G. Kiesewetter, in reply to a question posed by the Académie des Pays-Bas. The first over-all study to present the material in a satisfactory manner was the *Geschichte der Musik*, vol. III, Breslau, 1868, and vol. IV, Leipzig, 1881, by A.W. Ambros. For many years this work served as a basic source for more detailed studies, and its best chapters were often borrowed from liberally.

In all justice this bibliography must give first place to a few musicologists who, in the course of the past half-century, have contributed most to our understanding of Flemish music of the Renaissance.

The work of Charles van den Borren has been of particular significance for all subsequent research. The year 1964 was noteworthy for us since it marked his ninetieth birthday. Throughout his very active career he has poured forth studies on individual musicians (notably on Dufay and Lassus), on periods (*Etudes sur le XVe siècle musical*, Antwerp, 1941), and on problems of aesthetics and style. He has published musical texts of the period (*Polyphonia Sacra, A Continental Miscellany of the Fifteenth Century*, Burnham, 1932; *Pièces polyphoniques profanes de provenance liégeoise (XVe siècle)*, Brussels, 1950). He has written all-embracing studies whose special merit is that they are entirely based on first-hand knowledge. Vast as is the field, Charles van den Borren speaks always of works he has studied directly from the texts, often at the cost of himself transcribing compositions which do not exist in modern editions. There is, in the first place, an important chapter, *Van Hucbald tot Dufay*, in the *Algemeene muziekgeschiedenis* edited by A. Smijers, Utrecht, 1938, pp. 37-106, which was followed by chapters II to IV, *Le Moyen Age et la Renaissance*, in the collective publication *La Musique en Belgique du Moyen Age à nos jours*, Brussels, 1950, and, above all, by his *Geschiedenis van de muziek in de Nederlanden*, vol. I, Antwerp, 1948. Moreover, Charles van den Borren has been unsparing of time and counsel in guiding the work of the many scholars throughout the world who never cease to have recourse to his encyclopedic knowledge.

It is fitting also to single out the work of Heinrich Besseler. After *Die Musik des Mittelalters und der Renaissance*, Potsdam, 1931, a general study in which the Flemish are accorded a leading place, he re-oriented our knowledge of fifteenth-century music by a series of profoundly original works in which he analyzed with great subtlety the stylistic traits of various Flemish composers. Of his many writings, we must at least mention *Bourdon und Fauxbourdon : Studien zum Ursprung der niederländischen Musik*, Leipzig, 1950.

Likewise, André Pirro produced an over-all study on fifteenth- and sixteenth-century music in which Flemish musicians are given their due, his *Histoire de la musique de la fin du XIVe siècle à la fin du XVIe*, Paris, 1940.

Less personal in approach than the works cited above, the book by Gustave Reese, *Music in the Renaissance*, New York, 1954, is a veritable model for academic manuals. In a highly analytic manner, it provides the most precise and detailed information about composers, genres and forms. It is a book which must be consulted before undertaking any serious research, a veritable vade mecum for all study of the music of the fifteenth and sixteenth centuries.

To these outstanding names must be added that of Manfred Bukofzer. While he wrote no over-all book on Flemish music, he contributed a few penetrating studies on certain special problems of its history.

There have been some recent general studies which deserve mention, that of Helmuth Christian Wolff, *Die Musik der alten Niederländer (XV. und XVI. Jahrhundert)*, Leipzig, 1956, and the first volume, *Des origines à Jean-Sébastien Bach*, of the *Histoire de la musique*, Paris, 1960, which forms part of the *Encyclopédie de la Pléiade*, the latter being especially noteworthy since, alongside minor contributions, there are some excellent chapters on various special aspects which will be mentioned later in this bibliography. Further, there is the third volume, *Ars Nova and the Renaissance, 1300-1540*, edited by Dom Anselm Hughes and Gerald Abraham, London, 1960, in the *New Oxford History of Music*, as well as the second volume, *Renaissance and Baroque*, edited by Alec Robertson and Denis Stevens, London, 1963, of the *Pelican History of Music*, the latter a handy little volume with the rare distinction of taking into consideration the social aspects of music. These various general works on music of the fifteenth and sixteenth centuries all give generous place to Flemish music in accordance with the determining role it played in the period.

The encyclopedia *Die Musik in Geschichte und Gegenwart* which is still in course of publication has already become an indispensable reference work. It includes a clear and concise article on *Niederländische Musik* with a good bibliography in vol. IX, columns 1461-1507, and it is an excellent source for information about forms, genres, stylistic factors and various composers.

The history of music must be based in the first place on the music itself. Important collections were published in the nineteenth century, and still worthy of mention are those edited by K. PROSKE, by F. COMMER and by R. VAN MALDEGHEM, although they no longer satisfy present-day scientific criteria. Since these, many compositions have been published, some in special works, some in general collections such as the *Denkmäler der Tonkunst in Österreich*, Vienna, 1894–, or *Das Chorwerk*, Wolfenbüttel, 1929–, and others in complete editions of the works of composers like Jacob Obrecht, Josquin Desprez, Roland de Lassus and Philippe de Monte. Especially praiseworthy is the activity of the American Institute of Musicology which is currently concerned with publishing the works of Dufay, Willaert, Clemens non Papa, Brumel, Gombert, Barbireau, Regis, Rore, Compère, Tinctoris, Agricola, Ghiselin-Verbonnet, and Wert.

If our present-day acquaintance with music of the centuries which concern us here is becoming ever more precise and more sensitive, it is due to the publication of the music itself. The number of works available for study in satisfactorily authentic editions has increased considerably in the last fifteen years. Much, however, remains to be done. Many composers are still known only through too few works to permit us to place them accurately within the history of genres and forms. R. LENAERTS has published a small anthology of value for teaching purposes which helps to show the style of Flemish musicians in their most characteristic phases; this is *Die Kunst der Niederländer*, Cologne, 1962. This approach was anticipated by A. SMIJERS in the seven volumes of an anthology published in fascicles between 1939 and 1956 under the title *Van Ockeghem tot Sweelinck : Nederlandsche muziekgeschiedenis in voorbeelden*. In its series of *Musicological Studies and Documents*, the American Institute of Musicology, under the direction of A. CARAPETYAN, publishes critical editions of important theoretical works of the Middle Ages and the Renaissance.

But most of all, music is made to be heard. It is not irrelevant to scientific research that alongside synthetic and analytic studies or editions of musical texts and theoretical writings there have been produced phonograph recordings which make it possible for the public to become acquainted directly with this music of the past and for musicologists to verify by ear that which they have studied from books and manuscripts. For this reason, a brief list of available recordings has been appended to this book.

The bibliography which follows is arranged according to the plan of the book itself. It mentions only basic works, recent studies which provide new orientations, and those books and articles which were of particular help in preparing this book.

PROLOGUE : A QUESTION AND SOME PROPOSALS.

In two highly trenchant articles entitled *Introduction à l'histoire de la musique en Belgique*, in *Revue belge de musicologie*, vol. V, 1951, pp. 2-22 and 114-131, SUZANNE CLERCX not only threw open the whole question of terminology but also proposed that there might, in fact, be a music which was, to all intents and purposes, specifically Flemish or Netherlandish in the fifteenth and sixteenth centuries. The rest of this study has never appeared, but the first part elicited several replies of diverse character : R. LENAERTS, *Contribution à l'histoire de la musique belge de la Renaissance*, in *Revue belge de musicologie*, 1955, pp. 103-121; A. VAN DER LINDEN, *Comment désigner la nationalité des artistes des provinces du Nord à l'époque de la Renaissance*, in *La Renaissance dans les provinces du Nord (Picardie - Artois - Flandres - Brabant - Hainaut)*, ed. FRANÇOIS LESURE, Paris, 1956, pp. 11-17; FL. VAN DER MUEREN, *Ecole bourguignonne, école néerlandaise au début de la Renaissance*, in *Revue belge de musicologie*, 1958, pp. 53-66.

In the as yet unpublished doctoral dissertation of J. STENGERS, *Les Fondements historiques de la nationalité belge : Etude critique*, University of Brussels, 1948, there is presented the historical evidence for the political and spiritual cohesion of the Burgundian states and the Low Countries in the fifteenth and sixteenth centuries. As for the fundamental question as to whether there was a specifically Flemish music, a partial answer can be found in H. BESSELER, *Bourdon und Fauxbourdon*. The problem is also treated, at least implicitly, in the various studies on the leading masters of the period.

CHAPTER 1. TALKING ABOUT MUSIC.

On music in classical Antiquity, see C. SACHS, *Die Musik der Antike*, Potsdam, 1928, and by the same author, *The Rise of Music in the Ancient World East and West*, New York, 1943. H.-I. MARROU, *Histoire de l'éducation dans l'Antiquité*, Paris, 1948, treats very competently the role of music in ancient pedagogy. See also P. BOYANCÉ, *Le Culte des Muses chez les philosophes grecs*, Paris, 1937.

A remarkable book on music in the Christian church up to the tenth century is SOLANGE CORBIN, *L'Eglise à la conquête de sa musique*, Paris, 1960. See also G. REESE, *Music in the Middle Ages*, New York, 1940, and J. CHAILLEY, *Histoire musicale du Moyen Age*, Paris, 1950. The musical conceptions of the end of Antiquity and of the Middle Ages were studied rather superficially by T. GÉROLD, *Les Pères de l'Eglise et la musique*, Paris, 1931. Of more value are H.-I. MARROU, *Saint Augustin et la fin de la culture antique*, Paris, 1949, and also G. PIETZSCH, *Die Klassifikation der Musik von Boethius bis Ugolino von Orvieto*, Halle (Saale), 1929, as well as his *Die Musik im Erziehungs- und Bildungsideal des ausgehenden Altertums und frühen Mittelalters*, Halle (Saale), 1932. On Boethius, consult L. SCHRADE, *Music in the Philosophy of Boethius*, in *The Musical Quarterly*, 1949, pp. 188-200, and H. POTIRON, *Boèce, théoricien de la musique grecque*, Paris, 1961.

Considerations about music are integrated into the entire field of medieval aesthetics in E. DE BRUYNE, *Etudes d'esthétique médiévale*, Ghent, 1946, 3 vols.

Medieval musical pedagogy is treated in J. SMITS VAN WAESBERGHE, *School en muziek in de Middeleeuwen. De muziekdidactiek van de vroegere Middeleeuwen*, Amsterdam, 1949.

For Hucbald, see R. WEAKLAND, *Hucbald as Musician and Theorist*, in *The Musical Quarterly*, 1956, pp. 66-84, and for Jacques de Liège, R. BRAGARD, *Le Speculum musicæ du compilateur Jacques de Liège*, in *Musica Disciplina*, 1953, pp. 59-104 and 1954, pp. 2-17.

Everything concerning the teaching of music in the universities has been collected by NAN C. CARPENTER, *Music in the Medieval and Renaissance Universities*, Norman (Oklahoma), 1958.

For the musical conceptions of Humanism, see D.P. WALKER, *Musical Humanism in the 16th and early 17th Centuries*, in *The Music Review*, 1941, pp. 1-13, 111-121, 220-227, 288-308, and 1942, pp. 55-71. For Zarlino, one of the most important theorists of the sixteenth century, consult H. ZENCK, *Zarlino's "Istitutioni harmoniche" als Quelle zur Musikanschauung der italienischen Renaissance*, in *Zeitschrift für Musikwissenschaft*, 1929-30, pp. 540-578.

CHAPTER 2. MUSICA PRACTICA.

The treatises of Johannes Tinctoris were published in E. DE COUSSEMAKER, *Œuvres théoriques de Jean Tinctoris*, Lille, 1875. Since then, the *Diffinitorium* has been re-edited with a French translation by A. MACHABEY, *Johannis Tinctoris terminorum musicæ Diffinitorium : Lexique de la musique*, Paris, 1951. Another treatise has benefited by re-edition with an English translation prepared by A. SEAY, *The Art of Counterpoint (Liber de arte contrapuncti)*, American Institute of Musicology, 1961. About Tinctoris himself, see CH. VAN DEN BORREN, *Johannes Tinctoris*, in *Biographie nationale*, Brussels, 1930-32, vol. XXV, cols. 288-316.

For more information about plain-chant, consult W. APEL, *Gregorian Chant*, Bloomington, 1958. The use of Gregorian modes in fifteenth-century polyphony is examined by R.W. WIENPAHL, *Modal Usage in Masses of the Fifteenth Century*, in *Journal of the American Musicological Society*, 1952, pp. 37-52, and see also L. BALMER, *Tonsystem und Kirchentöne bei Johannes Tinctoris*, Strasbourg, 1935.

Mensural music is treated in J. WOLF, *Geschichte der Mensural-Notation von 1250-1460*, Leipzig, 1904, 3 vols., and also in his *Handbuch der Notationskunde*, Leipzig, 1913, 2 vols. (republished Hildesheim, 1963), as well as in W. APEL, *The Notation of Polyphonic Music*, 900-1500, Cambridge (Massachusetts), 1949.

An article by G. DE VAN, *La Pédagogie musicale à la fin du Moyen Age*, in *Musica Disciplina*, 1948, pp. 75-97, attempts to show that mensural notation aimed at a veritable esoterism. "Singing from the book" and improvisation have been studied by E. FERAND in *Die Improvisation in der Musik*, Zürich, 1938, as well as in *"Sodaine and unexpected" Music in the Renaissance*, in *The Musical Quarterly*, 1951, pp. 10-27, and in *Improvised Vocal Counterpoint in the Late Renaissance and Early Baroque*, in *Annales musicologiques*, vol. IV, 1956, pp. 129-174.

For the practice of *musica ficta*, see E. LOWINSKY, *The Function of Conflicting Signatures in Early Polyphonic Music*, in *The Musical Quarterly*, 1945, pp. 227-259, and also *Conflicting Views on Conflicting Signatures*, in *Journal of the American Musicological Society*, 1954, pp. 181-204; also consult G. REESE, *Music in the Renaissance*, pp. 44-48.

The principles of sixteenth-century counterpoint have been analyzed by K. JEPPESEN in *Counterpoint, the Polyphonic Vocal Style of the Sixteenth Century*, London, 1950. As for the first musical scores, E. LOWINSKY has written penetrating studies on the evolution of compositional procedures in counterpoint in *On the Use of Scores by Sixteenth-Century Musicians*, in *Journal of the American Musicological Society*, 1948, pp. 17-23, and especially in *Early Scores in Manuscript*, *ibid.*, 1960, pp. 126-173.

CHAPTER 3. A PERFECT ART.

On the appearance of polyphony in the principalities of the future Netherlands, interesting details are to be found in EDM. VAN DER STRAETEN, *La Musique aux Pays-Bas avant le XIXe siècle*, Brussels, 1867-1888, 8 vols. See also L. DE BURBURE, *La Musique à Anvers aux XIVe, XVe et XVIe siècles*, in *Annales de l'Académie royale d'archéologie de Belgique*, 1906, pp. 159-256; G. VAN DOORSELAER, *La Maîtrise de Saint-Rombaut à Malines jusqu'en 1580*, in *Musica Sacra*, 1936, pp. 162-185; R. WANGERMÉE, *Notes sur la vie musicale à Bruxelles au XVe siècle*, in *Bruxelles au XVe siècle*, Brussels, 1953, pp. 299-311; and for the principality of Liège, A. AUDA, *La Musique et les musiciens de l'ancien pays de Liège*, Paris-Brussels-Liège, n.d.

Concerning the Burgundian chapel, consult J. MARIX, *Histoire de la musique et des musiciens de la cour de Bourgogne sous le règne de Philippe le Bon*, 1420-1467, Strasbourg, 1939, and G. VAN DOORSELAER, *La Chapelle musicale de Philippe le Beau*, in *Revue belge d'archéologie et d'histoire de l'art*, 1934, pp. 21-57 and 139-161. EDM. VAN DER STRAETEN, *op. cit.*, provides various information on the chapel in the fifteenth and sixteenth centuries. J. SCHMIDT-GÖRG in *Nicolas Gombert, Kapellmeister Kaiser Karls V. : Leben und Werk*, Bonn, 1938, has very well elucidated the much debated question of the chapel of Charles V, his single but itinerant chapel.

For music in the fourteenth century, there is *L'Ars nova, Recueil d'études sur la musique du XIVe siècle*, in *Les Colloques de Wégimont*, II, 1955, Liège, 1959. Works of the end of the century have been published by W. APEL in *French Secular Music of the Late Fourteenth Century*, Cambridge (Massachusetts), 1950, in which the author proposes for this period a useful classification which distinguishes one style deriving directly from Machaut, another which is mannerist and in which all the traits of the *Ars nova* are carried to extremes, and finally a modern style tending toward greater simplicity, whose representative composer was Matteo da Perusio.

Concerning the appearance of a new spirit in Ciconia, read H. BESSELER, *Johannes Ciconia, Begründer der Chorpolyphonie*, in *Atti del Congresso internazionale di musica sacra (Roma,*

1950), Rome-Tournai-Paris, 1952, pp. 280-283, and above all S. CLERCX, *Johannes Ciconia : Un musicien liégeois et son temps (vers 1335-1411)*, Brussels (Académie royale de Belgique), 1960-1961, 2 vols.

The works of musicians of the beginning of the fifteenth century prior to Dufay have been published by G. REANEY, *Early Fifteenth-Century Music* (American Institute of Musicology : *Corpus Mensurabilis Musicæ*), New York, 1955-1960, 2 vols.

On the notion of "Renaissance" in the visual arts, see E. PANOFSKY, *Renaissance and Renascences in Western Art*, Stockholm, 1960. The concept of "renovatio" in music has been analyzed and its application to the benefit of Flemish musicians well brought out by L. SCHRADE, *Renaissance : the Historical Conception of an Epoch*, in *Kongress-Bericht, Internationale Gesellschaft für Musikwissenschaft, fünfter Kongress, Utrecht, 1952*, Amsterdam, 1953, pp. 19-43, as well as in the first two chapters of the same author's *Monteverdi, Creator of Modern Music*, New York, 1950; see also H.C. WOLFF, *Der Stilbegriff der "Renaissance" in der musik der alten Niederländer* in the above-mentioned Utrecht congress report, pp. 450-455, and especially the article *Renaissance* by F. BLUME in *Die Musik in Geschichte und Gegenwart*, vol. XI, cols. 224-280. E. LOWINSKY, *Music in the Culture of the Renaissance*, in *Journal of the History of Ideas*, 1954, pp. 509-553, is a penetrating and original study which locates music admirably within the ensemble of cultural concerns of the Renaissance, and see also the study of R.E. WOLF, *The Aesthetic Problem of the "Renaissance,"* in *Revue belge de musicologie*, 1955, pp. 83-102. The article by BLUME appears in his *Renaissance and Baroque Music*, New York, 1967.

The profound renewal of style brought in by Dufay has been admirably analyzed by H. BESSELER in various studies, in particular in *Bourdon und Fauxbourdon*, Leipzig, 1950, and in *Das Neue in der Musik des 15. Jahrhunderts*, in *Acta Musicologica*, 1957, pp. 75-84. The problem of fauxbourdon, the characteristic element of the new style, has given rise to an extensive literature. The state of the question is well summed up by S. CLERCX, *Aux origines du fauxbourdon*, in *Revue de musicologie*, 1957, pp. 151-165, in which the author holds out for Italian rather than English influences. MANFRED BUKOFZER treated the problem at various times, studying especially English music and its influence on that of the Continent, notably in *John Dunstable, a Quincentenary Report*, in *The Musical Quarterly*, 1954, pp. 29-49, in *John Dunstable : Complete Works (Musica Britannica, VIII)*, London, 1953, and in *Studies in Medieval and Renaissance Music*, New York, 1950.

F.L. HARRISON in *Music in Medieval Britain*, London, 1958, gives a picture of the specific traits of English music in both its liturgy and aesthetics, thereby making it possible to measure more clearly the possible influence of that music on the Continent. On the other hand, by proving that English *discant* did not differ from the Continental form, S. KENNEY, *"English Discant" and Discant in England*, in *The Musical Quarterly*, 1959, pp. 26-48, helps clear up some traditional errors in the question of fauxbourdon.

It is in the work of the various composers – Ockeghem, Josquin, Willaert, Gombert, Lassus – that the subsequent evolution of counterpoint must be studied. On a characteristic aspect of this style in the sixteenth century, see CH. VAN DEN BORREN, *Quelques réflexions à propos du style imitatif syntaxique*, in *Revue belge de musicologie* 1946, pp. 14-20. See also, in the *New Oxford History of Music*, in the third volume, *Ars Nova and the Renaissance, 1300-1540*, London, 1960, chapter VII, *Dufay and his School* by CH. VAN DEN BORREN, and chapter VIII, *the Age of Ockeghem and Josquin*, by N. BRIDGMAN.

CHAPTER 4. MUSIC IN THE CHURCH.

The work of P. WAGNER, *Geschichte der Messe, I.Teil, Bis 1600*, Leipzig, 1913 (re-edition, Hildesheim, 1963) remains the only over-all study on the polyphonic mass; it is still useful and retains its qualities of clarity, but must be corrected and completed on various points.

For the mass in the fourteenth century, consult H. STÄBLEIN-HARDER, *Fourteenth-Century Mass Music in France*, 2 vols., published by the American Institute of Musicology in 1962 and containing works and critical texts.

On Dufay, see CH. VAN DEN BORREN, *Guilllaume Dufay. Son importance dans l'évolution de la musique au XVᵉ siècle*, Brussels (Académie Royale de Belgique), 1925, and also his *Polyphonia Sacra*, London, 1932, in which he presents an important selection of works of the first half of the fifteenth century; in his *Etudes sur le XVᵉ siècle musical*, Antwerp, 1941, the same author first demonstrates the stylistic development of the Ordinary of the mass in the first half of the fifteenth century and the elaboration of the cycle mass by Arnold de Lantins and Dufay, and then studies the traits of the mass in Ockeghem. For his part, R. BOCKHOLDT, *Die frühen Messenkompositionen von Guillaume Dufay*, Tutzing, 1960, 2 vols., does not succeed in handing this difficult subject. On the other hand, the prefaces by H. BESSELER for the various volumes of *Opera omnia* of Dufay, published by the American Institute of Musicology from 1948 on, are remarkably informative in detail and full of original conceptions. For the entire period of Dufay, we can only refer the reader over and over again to *Bourdon und Fauxbourdon* by BESSELER.

M. BUKOFZER, *Caput : A Liturgico-musical Study*, in his book, *Studies in Medieval and Renaissance Music*, New York, 1950, pp. 216-310, is a model of musicological research drawing on the most diverse sources. To this must be added, by the same author, *"Caput redivivum" : a New Source for Dufay's "Missa Caput,"* in *Journal of the American Musicological Society*, 1951, pp. 97-110, as well as B. MEIER, *Caput, Bemerkungen zur Messe Dufays und Ockeghems*, in *Die Musikforschung*, 1954, pp. 268-276. L. FEININGER has published ten masses on *L'Homme armé* in *Monumenta polyphoniae liturgicae Sanctae Ecclesiae Romanae*, Series I, Rome, 1948. The masses of Ockeghem have been published by D. PLAMENAC in *Johannes Ockeghem : Sämtliche Werke*, vol. I, Leipzig, 1927, and *Johannes Ockeghem : Collected Works*, vol. II, 1949 (publications of the American Musicological Society). For Pierre de la Rue, read J. ROBYNS, *Pierre de la Rue (circa 1460-1518) : Een bio-bibliographische Studie*, Brussels, 1954.

The preface by M. VAN CREVEL for his edition of Obrecht's *Missa sub tuum presidium* (in *Opera Omnia : Missæ*, vol. VI, Amsterdam, 1959) cannot be accepted in all of its mathematical and esoteric speculations, but it provides an invaluable analysis of the architecture of an important Renaissance mass. On Obrecht, O. GOMBOSI, *Jacob Obrecht, ein stilkritische Studie*, Leipzig, 1925, remains indispensable.

The first volume of H. OSTHOFF, *Josquin Desprez*, Tutzing, 1962 (the only volume as yet published) is entirely devoted to a biography of the composer and a study of his masses. On the parody mass of the sixteenth century, see R.B. LENAERTS, *The 16th-Century Parody Mass in the Netherlands*, in *The Musical Quarterly*, 1950, pp. 410-421.

The history of the Proper of the mass has not yet been adequately studied. One can refer to a not thorough study by W. LIPPHARDT, *Die Geschichte des mehrstimmigen Proprium Missæ*, Heidelberg, 1950. Fortunately the *Choralis Constantinus* of Heinrich Isaac is available in a modern edition, the first and second parts published in 1898 and 1909 in Vienna in the *Denkmäler der Tonkunst in Österreich*, the third part in 1950 at Ann Arbor (Michigan) ; it is a matter of some interest that the transcription of the second part of this major work was made by the great composer Anton Webern.

For the history of the motet, one can only refer to the not very satisfactory work by H. LEICHTENTRITT, *Geschichte der Motette*, Leipzig, 1908. Because of this, one must take as a basis the article *Motette* in the encyclopedia *Die Musik in Geschichte und Gegenwart* which provides a good over-all picture as well as bibliographical information. See also E. DANNEMANN, *Die spätgotische Musiktradition in Frankreich und Burgund vor dem Auftreten Dufays*, Strasbourg, 1936; W. STEPHAN, *Die Burgundisch-Niederländische Motette zur Zeit Ockeghems*, Kassel, 1937; R. DAMMAN, *Spätformen der isorythmischen Mottete im XVI. Jahrhundert*, in *Archiv für Musikwissenschaft*, 1953, pp. 16-40, and by the same author, *Geschichte der Begriffstimmung Motette*, ibid., 1959, pp. 337-377; E.H. SPARKS, *The Motets of Antoine Busnois*, in *Journal of the American Musicological Society*, 1953, pp. 216-226; J.A. MATTFIELD, *Some Relationships between Texts and Cantus Firmi in the Liturgical Motets of Josquin des Prés*, ibid., 1961, pp. 159-183.

It is important to consult the articles *Lamentatio, Magnificat, Passion, Psalm* and *Requiem* in *Die Musik in Geschichte und Gegenwart*. For the polyphonic passion, see O. KADE, *Die älteren Passionskompositionen bis zum Jahre 1633*, Gütersloh, 1893, and A. SCHMIT, *Zur motettischen Passion des 16. Jahrhunderts*, in *Archiv für Musikwissenschaft*, 1959, pp. 232-245. For the magnificat, read C.H. ILLING, *Zur Technik der Magnificat-Kompositionen des 16. Jahrhunderts*, Wolfenbüttel, 1946, and E.R. LERNER, *The Polyphonic Magnificat in 15th-Century Italy*, in *The Musical Quarterly*, 1964, pp. 44-58. In the first volume of the *Histoire de la Musique (Encyclopé-*

die de la Pléiade), the chapters written by M. BUKOFZER, L. SCHRADE, G. BIRKNER, N. BRIDGMAN can be consulted with profit.

For a brief summary of the decisions of the Council of Trent in relation to music, see K.G. FELLERER, *Church Music and the Council of Trent*, in *The Musical Quarterly*, 1953, pp. 576-594.

H. BESSELER in *Die Musik des Mittelalters und der Renaissance*, Potsdam, 1931, proposed a connection of the religious music of Ockeghem with the *Devotio moderna* movement, and later, in 1950, in *Bourdon und Fauxbourdon*, he suggested the same relationship for that of Dufay. He was supported in this by M. BUKOFZER in *Studies in Medieval und Renaissance Music* in 1950 and by still others, but serious objections were formulated by L. SCHRADE in the *Encyclopédie de la Pléiade*.

For the history of the *Devotio moderna*, see S. AXTERS, *La Spiritualité des Pays-Bas. L'évolution d'une doctrine mystique*, Louvain-Paris, 1948, and also the same author's *Geschiedenis van de Vroomheid in de Nederlanden*, the third volume, *De moderne Devotie, 1380-1550*, Antwerp, 1956; in addition, R.R. POST, *De moderne Devotie : Geert Grote en zijn stichtingen*, Amsterdam, 1950. However, these works should be read in the light of the very lucid and systematically de-mystifying analyses of J. TOUSSAERT, *Le Sentiment religieux en Flandre à la fin du Moyen Age*, Paris, 1963.

CHAPTER 5. MUSIC OF COURT AND CITY : THE CHANSON.

No one has yet written a complete history of the polyphonic chanson. For an initial acquaintance, consult the article *Chanson* in the encyclopedia *Die Musik in Geschichte und Gegenwart* and also the chapters by G. THIBAULT, P. CHAILLON and F. LESURE in the *Encyclopédie de la Pléiade, Histoire de la musique*, vol. I, and in *A History of Song*, edited by D. STEVENS, London, 1960, the chapters devoted to the Middle Ages by G. REANEY and to the Renaissance by D. STEVENS.

The article by H. BESSELER, *Umgangsmusik und Darbietungsmusik im 16. Jahrhundert*, in *Archiv für Musikwissenschaft*, 1959, pp. 21-43, is one of the few musicological studies taking into account social factors; it makes large use of pictorial evidence.

For the fifteenth century, see especially E. DROZ and G. THIBAULT, *Poètes et musiciens du XVᵉ siècle*, Paris, 1924; A. PIRRO, E. DROZ, Y. ROKSETH and G. THIBAULT, *Trois chansonniers français du XVᵉ siècle*, Paris, 1927; the work on Guillaume Dufay by CH. VAN DEN BORREN already cited above; J. MARIX, *Les musiciens de la cour de Bourgogne au XVᵉ siècle*, Paris, 1937 (a collection of musical texts); *Die "Chansons" von Gilles Binchois (1400-1460)*, ed. W. REHM, Mainz, 1957 (musical texts preceded by an introduction); H. BESSELER, *Die Besetzung der Chansons im 15. Jahrhundert*, in *Kongress-Bericht, Internationale Gesellschaft für Musikwissenschaft*,

Utrecht 1952, Amsterdam, 1953, pp. 65-72; CH. VAN DEN BORREN, *Pièces polyphoniques profanes de provenance liégeoise (XVᵉ siècle)*, Brussels, 1950 (musical texts).

For the chanson at the court of Margaret of Austria, see M. FRANÇON, *Albums poétiques de Marguerite d'Autriche*, Cambridge (Massachusetts)-Paris, 1934, also CH. VAN DEN BORREN, *A propos d'un album musical de Marguerite d'Autriche*, in *Mélanges d'histoire et d'esthétique musicales offerts à Paul-Marie Masson*, vol. I, Paris, 1955.

The edition by HELEN HEWITT of *Harmonice musices Odhecaton A*, Cambridge (Massachusetts), 1942, contains a remarkable introduction which is certainly the most serious study yet written on the chanson at the end of the fifteenth century. The same subject is treated in C.L.W. BOER, *Chansonvormen op het einde van de XVᵉ eeuw*, Amsterdam, 1938.

Many of the poems used by fifteenth-century composers can be found in *Le Jardin de plaisance et fleurs de rhétorique*, facsimile edition with introduction and notes by E. DROZ and A. PIAGET, Paris, 1910-1925, 2 vols.

As for the use of theatre songs by polyphonic composers, consult H.M. BROWN, *Music in the French Secular Theater, 1400-1550*, Cambridge (Massachusetts), 1963, a study accompanied by an anthology entitled *Theatrical Chansons of the Fifteenth and Early Sixteenth Centuries*.

On the chanson in the sixteenth century, see D. VON BARTHA, *Probleme der Chansongeschichte im 16. Jahrhundert : Nicolas Gombert, Benedictus Appenzeller*, in *Zeitschrift für Musikwissenschaft*, 1930-31, pp. 507-530; K.J. LEVY, *Vaudeville, vers mesurés et airs de cour*, in *Musique et poésie au XVIᵉ siècle*, Paris, 1954 (this entire volume, containing the papers read at an international congress organized by the Centre National de la Recherche Scientifique of Paris, should be consulted); F. LESURE, *Musicians and Poets of the French Renaissance*, New York, 1955.

In regard to music publishing in the sixteenth century, see A. GOOVAERTS, *Histoire et bibliographie de la typographie musicale dans les Pays-Bas*, Brussels, 1880; F. LESURE and G. THIBAULT, *Bibliographie des éditions d'Adrian Le Roy et Robert Ballard (1551-1598)*, Paris, 1955, and by the same authors, *Bibliographie des éditions musicales publiées par Nicolas du Chemin (1549-1576)*, in *Annales musicologiques*, vol. I, Paris, 1953, pp. 269-373; and the *Répertoire international des sources musicales, Recueils imprimés, XVIᵉ-XVIIᵉ siècles* (under the direction of F. LESURE), Munich-Duisburg, 1960.

On Clément Marot and music, see J. ROLLIN, *Les Chansons de Clément Marot : Etude historique et bibliographique*, Paris, 1951, and F. LESURE, *Autour de Clément Marot et de ses musiciens*, in *Revue de musicologie*, 1951, pp. 109-119.

For Ronsard, consult G. THIBAULT and L. PERCEAU, *Bibliographie des chansons de P. de Ronsard mises en musique au XVIᵉ siècle*, Paris, 1941, and R. LEBÈGUE, *Ronsard et la musique*, in *Musique et poésie au XVIᵉ siècle*, pp. 105-119.

Further information is contained in studies devoted to particular composers, notably E. HERTZMANN, *Adrian Willaert in der weltlichen Vokalmusik seiner Zeit*, Leipzig, 1931; CH. VAN DEN BORREN, *Orlande de Lassus*, Paris, 1920, and also his *Roland de Lassus*, Brussels, 1944; W. BOETTICHER, *Orlando di Lasso und seine Zeit, 1532-1594*, Kassel-Basel, 1958.

The chanson on Flemish texts has been studied by R. LENAERTS, *Het nederlands polifonies lied in de zestiende eeuw*, Malines-Amsterdam, 1933, which includes notably some curious selections from manuals of conversation which are useful as documents for a social study of the chanson. See also F. NOSKE, *The Linköping-Faignent Manuscript* in *Acta Musicologica*, 1964, pp. 152-155.

For the *Souterliedekens*, see K.P. BERNET KEMPERS, *Die "Souterliedekens" des Jacobus Clemens non Papa*, in *Tijdschrift der Vereeniging voor Nederlandsche muziekgeschiedenis*, 1928, 1929, 1931.

CHAPTER 6. MUSIC AND LIFE.

The book by J. HUIZINGA, *Herfsttij der middeleeuwen*, Haarlem, 1919, has been many times reprinted in English under the title *The Waning of the Middle Ages*; it provides an admirable picture of the psychological and cultural climate of the fifteenth century.

On the festivities at the Burgundian court, see O. CARTELLIERI, *Am Hofe der Herzöge von Burgund*, Basel, 1926, and more especially for the music, the book already cited by J. MARIX, *Histoire de la musique et des musiciens de la cour de Bourgogne*, Strasbourg, 1936.

For the Banquet of the Oath of the Pheasant, consult G. DOUTREPONT, *La Littérature française à la cour des ducs de Bourgogne*, Brussels, 1909, and the various contemporary chronicles.

The fêtes of the Renaissance have recently aroused the interest of scholars in several fields and were studied in the course of two congresses organized through the initiative of J. JACQUOT by the Centre National de la Recherche Scientifique in Paris, the various papers of which are printed in two volumes of great interest : *Les Fêtes de la Renaissance*, vol. I, 1956, and *Fêtes et cérémonies au temps de Charles-Quint*, Paris, 1960. The latter volume especially is rich in information about the festivities in the Low Countries; in particular, read the contributions of D. DEVOTO, *Folklore et politique au Château Ténébreux*, pp. 311-328, and of D. HEARTZ, *Un Divertissement de palais pour Charles-Quint à Binche*, pp. 329-342. Important also are the articles of P. DU COLOMBIER, *Les Triomphes en images de l'empereur Maximilien Iᵉʳ*, pp. 99-112; N. BRIDGMAN, *La Participation musicale à l'entrée de Charles-Quint à Cambrai, le 20 janvier 1546*, pp. 235-255; and especially J. JACQUOT, *Panorama des fêtes et cérémonies du règne*, pp. 413-492.

The motets sung at Antwerp in 1515 in honour of Emperor Maximilian I and of Charles V have been published in G. and B. DE OPITIIS, *Lofzangen ter eere van Keizer Maximiliaan en sijn zoon Karel den vijfde, 1515*, facsimile edition, The Hague, 1925.

On the dance, consult C. SACHS, *Eine Weltgeschichte des Tanzes*, Berlin, 1933, available in English as *World History of the Dance*, New York, 1937. For the basse dance in particular, see E. CLOSSON, *Le Manuscrit dit des basses danses de la Bibliothèque de Bourgogne*, Brussels, 1912. In an "Annexe" to a motion on Ernest Closson, in *Mélanges Ernest Closson*, Brussels, 1948, pp. 14-17, CH. VAN DEN BORREN gave a bibliography for the question of basses dances and for the identification of the themes in the Brussels manuscript. The musical problems involved in the basse dance were treated by O. GOMBOSI, *About Dance and Dance Music in the Late Middle Ages*, in *The Musical Quarterly*, 1941, pp. 289-305, and by M. BUKOFZER, *A Polyphonic Basse Dance of the Renaissance*, in *Studies in Medieval and Renaissance Music*, pp. 190-216. On the forms of dance music of the sixteenth century, see F. BLUME, *Studien zur Vorgeschichte der Orchestersuite im 15. und 16. Jahrhundert*, Leipzig, 1925. It is indispensable to consult that picturesque and precise document, the *Orchésographie* by THOINOT ARBEAU, whose full title is *Orchésographie traité en forme de dialogue par lequel toutes personnes peuvent facilement apprendre à pratiquer l'honnête exercice des danses*, Langres, 1589. It was reprinted by L. FONTA in 1888, and there are English translations by C.W. BEAUMONT, 1925, and by M.S. EVANS, 1948.

G. COHEN in his *Histoire de la mise en scène dans le théâtre religieux du Moyen Age*, Paris, 1926, grants some place to music, but the most valuable material on the role of music in the performance of a mystery is found in his *Le Livre de conduite du régisseur et le compte des dépenses pour le Mystère de la Passion joué à Mons en 1501*, Strasbourg, 1925. For the chanson in the French theatre, consult the study already cited by H.M. BROWN, *Music in the French Secular Theater, 1400-1550*.

The popular song has never been studied satisfactorily except for a few aspects, but one can consult T. GÉROLD, *Chansons populaires des XVe et XVIe siècles avec leurs mélodies*, Strasbourg, 1913; E. MONTELLIER, *Quatorze chansons du XVe siècle extraites des Archives namuroises*, Antwerp, 1938; F. LESURE, *Eléments populaires dans la chanson française au début du XVIe siècle*, in *Musique et poésie au XVIe siècle*, pp. 169-184.

On the minstrels, see W. SALMEN, *Der fahrende Musiker im europäischen Mittelalter*, Kassel, 1960; F. LESURE, *La Communauté des "joueurs d'instruments" au XVIe siècle*, in *Revue historique de droit français et étranger*, 1953, pp. 79-109; E. BOWLES, *Tower Musicians in the Middle Ages*, in *The Brass Quarterly*, 1962, pp. 91-103. On the minstrels in the Low Countries, see E. VAN DER STRAETEN, *La Musique dans les Pays-Bas*, vols. II and IV, and R. VAN AERDE, *Ménestrels communaux et instrumentistes divers établis ou de passage à Malines de 1311 à 1790*, Malines, 1911.

CHAPTER 7. THE SOUND OF THE PAST.

Much pictorial material relating to music in the fifteenth and sixteenth centuries can be found in general works such as G. KINSKY, *A History of Music in Pictures*, New York, 1930, and P. COLLAER and A. VAN DER LINDEN, *Atlas historique de la musique*, Paris, 1960.

On the contribution of the visual arts to the understanding of music of the past, E. WINTERNITZ, *The Visual Arts as a Source for the Historian of Music*, in *International Musicological Society, Report of the Eighth Congress*, New York, 1961, pp. 109-120, is a study in methodology of great value.

R. HAMMERSTEIN, *Die Musik der Engel, Untersuchen zur Musikanschauung des Mittelalters*, Berne-Munich, 1962, is an important contribution to our knowledge of medieval conceptions of music, making excellent use of material from the liturgy, from literature and from art history. On pictorial representations of musical instruments, see V. DENIS, *De muziekinstrumenten in de Nederlanden en in Italie naar hun afbeelding in de 15e eeuwsche kunst*, Antwerp, 1944. Attempts have been made to go one step farther and to draw conclusions about musical practice from pictorial evidence; for these, see G. THIBAULT, *Le Concert instrumental dans l'art flamand au XVe siècle et au début du XVIe*, in *La Renaissance dans les provinces du Nord*, Paris, 1956, pp. 197-206; P. EGAN, *"Concert" Scenes in Musical Paintings of the Italian Renaissance*, in *Journal of the American Musicological Society*, 1961, pp. 184-195; E. WINTERNITZ, *On Angel Concerts in the 15th Century : A Critical Approach to Realism and Symbolism in Sacred Painting*, in *The Musical Quarterly*, 1963, pp. 450-463 (the articles by Winternitz are particularly important for their critical method).

The most serious studies on instruments are often confined to their technical aspects, but three books by C. SACHS are outstanding : *Real-Lexikon der Musikinstrumente*, Berlin, 1913; *Handbuch der Instrumentenkunde*, Leipzig, 1920; *The History of Musical Instruments*, New York, 1940. The small volume *Musical Instruments through the Ages*, edited by A. BAINES, London - New York, 1966, prepared collectively by members of the Galpin Society, is a useful book for the non-professional. On the manufacture of harpsichords in Flanders, see the small volume by A.M. POLS, *De Ruckers en de klavierbouw in Vlaanderen*, Antwerp, 1942.

The studies by E. BOWLES link the history of instruments to social factors and to performance practice; they include *Instruments at the Court of Burgundy (1363-1467)*, in *The Galpin Society Journal*, 1953, pp. 41-51; *Haut and bas : the Grouping of Musical Instruments in the Middle Ages*, in *Musica Disciplina*, 1954, pp. 115-140; *La Hiérarchie des instruments de musique dans l'Europe féodale*, in *Revue de musicologie*, 1958, pp. 115-169; *Musical Instruments in Civic Processions during the Middle Ages*, in *Acta Musicologica*, 1961, pp. 147-161.

The article devoted to the trombone by H. BESSELER, *Die Entstehung der Posaune*, in *Acta Musicologica*, 1950, pp. 8-35, utilizes with rare skill information gleaned from archive documents, literary texts, pictorial evidence, and the analysis of certain musical works. See also C. SACHS, *Chromatic Trumpets in the Renaissance,* in *The Musical Quarterly,* 1950, pp. 62-66.

On problems in the interpretation of music of the past, there is a book of somewhat general character, R. HAAS, *Aufführungspraxis der Musik,* Potsdam, 1931; an interesting study by A. SCHERING, *Aufführungspraxis alter Musik,* Leipzig, 1931; and an excellent small manual by T. DART, *The interpretation of Music,* London, 1954. On special problems, see M. BUKOFZER, *The Beginnings of Choral Polyphony,* in his *Studies in Medieval and Renaissance Music,* New York, 1950, pp. 176-189; E. BOWLES, *Were Musical Instruments Used in the Liturgical Service during the Middle Ages?,* in *The Galpin Society Journal,* 1959, pp. 40-56. On the controversial problem of the *tactus,* there is a partisan but interesting study by A. AUDA, *Le Tactus, principe générateur de l'interprétation de la musique polyphonique classique,* in *Scriptorium,* vol. IV, pp. 43-66. The same author is currently preparing a book on the subject, *Théorie et pratique du tactus.*

CHAPTER 8. THE FLEMINGS IN ITALY.

The musicians of the Pontifical Chapel have been studied on the basis of documents from the archives by F.W. HABERL, *Die römische "schola cantorum" und die päpstlichen Kapellsänger bis zur Mitte des 16. Jahrhunderts,* in *Vierteljahrschrift für Musikwissenschaft,* 1887, pp. 189-296 (published also as *Bausteine zur Musikgeschichte,* vol. III, Leipzig, 1888).

For Flemish musicians in Italy, see in the first place G. VAN DER STRAETEN, *La Musique aux Pays-Bas avant le XIXᵉ siècle,* and, of course, G. REESE, *Music in the Renaissance,* both previously cited in this reading list. For the most important of them in the fifteenth century, see C. SARTORI, *Josquin des Prés, cantore del Duomo di Milano (1459-1472),* in *Annales musicologiques,* IV, Paris, 1956, pp. 55-83; H. OSTHOFF, *Josquin Desprez,* Tutzing, 1962, vol. I; G. CROLL, *Gaspar van Weerbeke : An Outline of His Life and Works,* in *Musica Disciplina,* 1952, pp. 67-81; L. FINSCHER, *Loyset Compère and His Works,* in *Musica Disciplina,* 1958, pp. 105-143; B. MURRAY, *New Light on Jacob Obrecht's Development : A Bibliographical Study,* in *The Musical Quarterly,* 1957, pp. 500-516.

A concise introduction to the history of music publishing can be found in A. HYATT KING, *Four Hundred Years of Music Printing,* London, 1964.

On Italian publications of music, consult C. SARTORI, *Bibliografia delle opere musicali stampate da Ottaviano Petrucci,* Florence, 1948; A.-M. BAUTIER-REGNIER, *L'Edition musicale italienne et les musiciens d'Outremonts au XVIᵉ siècle (1501-1563),* in *La Renaissance dans les provinces du Nord,* Paris, 1956, pp. 27-49.

On cross-influences in Flemish and Italian music, see CH. VAN DEN BORREN, *Considérations générales sur la conjonction de la polyphonie italienne et de la polyphonie du Nord pendant la première moitié du XVᵉ siècle,* in *Bulletin de l'Institut historique belge de Rome,* 1938, pp. 175-187, and also his *Actions et réactions de la polyphonie néerlandaise et de la polyphonie italienne aux environs de 1500,* in *Revue belge d'archéologie et d'histoire de l'art,* 1936, pp. 51-61.

For Italian music, see K. JEPPESEN, *Die mehrstimmige italienische Laude um 1500,* Leipzig-Copenhagen, 1935; W. RUBSAMEN, *The Justiniane or Viniziane of the 15th Century,* in *Acta Musicologica,* 1957, pp. 172-184. For Florentine carnival music, consult F. GHISI, *I canti carnascialeschi nelle fonti del XV e XVI secolo,* Florence-Rome, 1937. For the frottola and the madrigal, a good groundwork can be found in the articles on those subjects in the encyclopedia *Die Musik in Geschichte und Gegenwart,* and see also N. BRIDGMAN, *La Frottola et la transition de la frottola au madrigal,* in *Musique et poésie au XVIᵉ siècle,* pp. 63-77.

The madrigal has been studied excellently in all its aspects in A. EINSTEIN, *The Italian Madrigal,* Princeton, 1949, 3 vols., but this should be supplemented by H. ENGEL, *Die Entstehung des italienische Madrigals und die Niederländer,* in *Kongress-Bericht, Internationale Gesellschaft für Musikwissenschaft, fünfter Kongress, Utrecht, 1952,* Amsterdam, 1953, pp. 166-180, and by the same author, *Werden und Wesen des Madrigals,* in *Internationale Gesellschaft für Musikwissenschaft, Berich über den siebenten ... Kongress, Köln, 1958,* Kassel, 1959, pp. 39-52.

On Willaert, read J.S. LEVITAN, *Adrian Willaert's Famous Duo Quidnam Ebrietas,* in *Tijdschritf der Vereeniging voor Nederlandsche Muziekgeschiedenis,* 1938, pp. 166-233; A. CARAPETYAN, *The Musica Nova of Adriano Willaert,* in *Journal of Renaissance and Baroque Music,* 1946, pp. 200-221; H. ZENCK, *Adrian Willaert's "Salmi spezzati" (1550),* in *Die Musikforschung,* 1949, pp. 97-107; G. D'ALESSI, *Precursors of Adriano Willaert in the Practice of Coro Spezzato,* in *Journal of the American Musicological Society,* 1952, pp. 187 ff. N. BRIDGMAN, *La Vie musicale au Quattrocento et jusqu'à la naissance du madrigal (1400-1530),* Paris, 1964, is an excellent over-all study of music in the cultural life of the Italian Renaissance and does not fail to show the relationship of Flemish Musicians with Italy.

CHAPTER 9. THE FLEMINGS IN EUROPE.

For music publishing in the Netherlands, consult A. GOOVAERTS, *Histoire et bibliographie de la typographie musicale dans les Pays-Bas,* Antwerp, 1880; P. BERGMANS, *La Typographie musicale en Belgique au XVIᵉ siècle,* in *Histoire du livre et de l'imprimerie en Belgique,* Brussels, 1930, vol. V; J.A. STELLFELD, *Bibliographie des éditions musicales plantiniennes,* Brussels (Académie royale de Belgique), 1949; S. CLERCX, *Les Editions musicales anversoises du XVIᵉ siècle et leur rôle dans la vie musicale des Pays-Bas,* in *De Gulden Passer,* 1956, pp. 238-249. See also the exhibition catalogue, *Muziekdrukken van de zestiende eeuw. De ontwikkeling van de muziek naar handschrift, prent en druk, voornamelijk in de Nederlanden,* Antwerp, 1963. Picture-motets have been studied by M. SEIFFERT, *Bildzeugnisse des 16. Jahrhunderts,* in *Archiv für Musikwissenschaft*, 1919, pp. 49 ff, and the principal works have been edited by the same author in *Niederländische Bildmotetten (Series Organum, erste Reihe)*, 1920, 2 vols.

The inexhaustible work of E. VAN DER STRAETEN, *La Musique aux Pays-Bas avant le XIXᵉ siècle*, often cited in these pages, contains many documents concerning Flemish musicians who lived in one or another European country or who remained in the Low Countries. See also J. SCHMIDT-GÖRG, *Nicolas Gombert, Kapellmeister Karls V : Leben und Werk*, Bonn, 1938.

On the state of music in the Netherlands in the middle of the sixteenth century, read the remarkable analyses of E. LOWIN-SKY, *Das Antwerpener Motettenbuch Orlando di Lasso's und seine Beziehungen zum Motettenschaffen der niederländischen Zeitgenossen*, in *Tijdschrift der Vereeniging voor Nederland-sche Muziekgeschiedenis*, 1932-35, pp. 185-229; 1936-39, pp. 1-43 and 94-105 (also published separately in 1937).

The very ingenious work by E. LOWINSKY, *Secret Chromatic Art in the Netherlands Motet*, New York, 1946, is exciting to read and full of brilliant deductions but errs in applying too systematically to music the precepts of Panofsky drawn from pictorial iconology, and has been severely criticized by M. VAN CREVEL, *Secret Chromatic Art in the Netherlands Motet?*, in *Tijdschrift der Vereeniging voor Nederlandsche Muziekgeschie-denis*, 1946, pp. 253-304, and by L. SCHRADE, *A Secret Chro-matic Art*, in *Journal of Renaissance and Baroque Music*, 1946, pp. 159-167.

On *musica reservata*, there is a good summary of the state of the question as of 1954 in G. REESE, *Music in the Renais-sance*, pp. 511-517, to which must be added B. MEYER, *Reser-vata-Probleme, ein Bericht*, in *Acta Musicologica*, 1958, pp. 77-81, and by the same author, *The Musica Reservata of Adrianus Petit Coclico and Its Relationship to Josquin*, in *Musica Disciplina*, 1956, pp. 67-105, and especially C.V. PA-LISCA, *A Clarification of "Musica Reservata" in Jean Taisnier's Astrologica*, *1559*, in *Acta Musicologica*, 1959, pp. 133-161. See also M. VAN CREVEL, *Adrianus Petit Coclico : Leben und Beziehungen eines nach Deutschland emigrierten Josquinschü-lers*, The Hague, 1940.

The chapter by N. BRIDGMAN, *The Age of Ockeghem and Josquin*, in the *New Oxford History of Music*, vol. III, shows the diffusion of Flemish music throughout Europe at the end of the fifteenth century and the beginning of the sixteenth.

Secular works in German composed by Flemings have been studied by H. OSTHOFF, *Die Niederländer und das deutsche Lied (1400-1640)*, Berlin, 1938.

Spanish music has recently been given remarkable treatment in R. STEVENSON, *Spanish Music in the Age of Columbus*, The Hague, 1960, and by the same author, *Spanish Cathedral Music in the Golden Age*, Berkeley-Los Angeles, 1961. On the relationships of the Flemings with Spain, see H. ANGLÈS, *Les Musiciens flamands en Espagne et leur influence sur la polyphonie espagnole*, in *Kongress-Bericht, Internationale Ge-sellschaft für Musikwissenschaft, fünfter Kongress, Utrecht, 1952, Amsterdam*, 1953, pp. 47-54; N. BRIDGMAN, *Les Echan-ges musicaux entre l'Espagne et les Pays-Bas au temps de Phi-lippe le Beau et de Charles-Quint*, in *La Renaissance dans les provinces du Nord*, Paris, 1956, pp. 51-61. The unpublished thesis by P. BECQUART, *Musiciens néerlandais en Espagne, Philippe Rogier et son école à la cour de Madrid (1560-1647)*, Louvain, 1963, is a very thorough biographical and biblio-graphical study of a great many Flemish musicians who worked in Spain from 1560 on, particularly Rogier, Ghersem and Romero.

For Germany, consult A. SMIJERS, *Die kaiserliche Hofmusik-Kapelle von 1543-1619*, in *Denkmäler der Tonkunst in Öster-reich*, 1919-22; L. VON KÖCHEL, *Die kaiserliche Hof-Musik-kapelle in Wien von 1543 bis 1867 nach urkündlichen For-schungen*, Vienna, 1869; E.R. LERNER, *The "German" Works of Alexander Agricola*, in *The Musical Quarterly*, 1960, pp. 56-66; W. RUBSAMEN, *The International "Catholic" Reper-toire of a Lutheran Church in Nürnberg (1574-1597)*, in *Annales Musicologiques*, V, 1957, pp. 229-327.

On Philippe de Monte, see G. VAN DOORSLAER, *La Vie et les œuvres de Philippe de Monte*, Brussels, 1921, and P. NUTEN, *De Madrigali Spirituali van F. de Monte*, Brussels, 1958.

On Roland de Lassus, read the excellent study by CH. VAN DEN BORREN, *Orlande de Lassus*, Paris, 1920, or the massive monograph by W. BOETTICHER, *Orlando di Lasso und seine Zeit, 1532-1594*, Kassel-Basel, 1958.

EPILOGUE : DECLINE AND FALL.

R.E. WOLF, *The Aesthetic Problem of the "Renaissance,"* in *Revue belge de musicologie*, 1955, pp. 83-102, has proposed an interesting theory of Mannerism as a term relevant to late sixteenth-century music; he has developed further his argu-ment in a more extensive study, *Renaissance, Mannerism, Ba-roque : Three Styles, Three Periods*, in *Le "Baroque" musical (Les Colloques de Wégimont, IV, 1957)*, Paris, 1963, pp. 35-59.

On the conflict between *Ars perfecta* of the Flemish musicians and the *stile nuovo*, read L. SCHRADE, *Monteverdi, Creator of Modern Music*, New York, 1950.

Notes on the Illustrations

These pages have been prepared in collaboration with PIERRE BAUDSON, Master in Philosophy and Letters.

1
Concert in the Country.
Tapestry in wool with linen thread, 25 5/8 x 55 1/8 in.
Nuremberg, Germanisches Nationalmuseum, no. 813.
Authorized reproduction.

The theme of this tapestry, made in Brussels around 1500, is similar to that of the "Gardens of Love," but the conventional aspects are tempered by a concern with realism in this depiction of lords and ladies enjoying a musical entertainment out of doors. From left to right, the first man holds a lute in his right hand, a woman plays a rebec, a man a bombard, a woman plays a harp, another a dulcimer, a man plays a lute, and a man standing holds a lute in his left hand. The three other figures do not have instruments.

Lit.: B. KURTH, *Die deutschen Bildteppiche des Mittelalters,* Vienna, 1926, vol. I, p. 266.

2
Tree of Jesse.
Miniature, page area 10 19/32 x 8 25/64 in.; picture area 5 33/64 x 5 7/16 in.
Breviary of Philip the Good, vol. I, fol. 15.
Brussels, Bibliothèque Royale de Belgique, Manuscript collection, no. 9511.
Authorized reproduction.

This breviary according to the rite of Paris, copied from a previous breviary, was executed in Flanders around 1455-60. Most of the miniatures are by Guillaume Vrelant, but the *Tree of Jesse* and the *Nativity* – the first two illustrations of the section for winter – are by an unidentified painter. The iconography of the *Tree of Jesse* goes far back in time, but it was especially popular toward the middle of the fifteenth century. Often the Kings of Judah have musical instruments on which they sound praises of God. From top to bottom and from left to right, there are in the hands of the kings, seated within crowns of flowers, a triangle, a double flute, a bombard, a harp, a lute, a fife and drum, bagpipes, a hurdy-gurdy, a trumpet, a portative organ; then, a king who holds no instrument but appears to be conducting the ensemble; finally, there is a dulcimer player.

Lit.: P. DURRIEU, *La Miniature flamande au temps de la Cour de Bourgogne (1415-1530)*, Brussels-Paris, 1921, p. 44-45. – V. LEROQUAIS, *Le Bréviaire de Philippe le Bon*, Paris-Brussels-New York, 1929. – L.-M.-J. DELAISSÉ, *Miniatures médiévales*, Brussels, 1958, pl. 29.

3
JAN VAN EYCK, *Singing Angels.*
Oil on wood, 64 53/64 x 28 1/8 in.
Polyptych of the Adoration of the Mystic Lamb.
Ghent, Church of St. Bavon.
Authorized reproduction.

It is generally agreed that the polyptych was executed between 1425 – the year in which van Eyck entered the service of Philip the Good – and 1432. On the modern frame there is a Latin inscription which is probably a copy of the inscription on the original frame: *Melos Deo laus perhennis gratiorum actio.*

Lit.: L. VON BALDASS, *Jan van Eyck*, London, 1952. – E. PANOFSKY, *Early Netherlandish Painting*, Cambridge, Massachusetts, 1953. – L. VAN PUYVELDE, *L'Agneau Mystique*, Brussels, 1959.

4
JAN VAN EYCK, *Angel Musicians.*
Oil on wood, 64 5/8 x 28 3/4 in.
Polyptych of the Adoration of the Mystic Lamb.
Ghent, Church of St. Bavon.
Authorized reproduction.

On the modern frame, there is written a fragment of Psalm 150 : *Laudate eum cordis et organo.* The instruments are a positive organ, a harp, and a tenor fiddle.

Lit.: See no. 3.

5
Music and Her Attendants.
Miniature, 9 59/64 x 7 33/64 in.
Boethius, *De arithmetica*, fol. 47 r°.
Naples, Biblioteca Nazionale, MS V.A. 14.
Authorized reproduction.

Although the two miniatures in this fourteenth-century Italian manuscript were made for the Angevin court of Naples, they are not typical of Neapolitan art of the period. Salmi believes that the artist might have come from the Siennese-Avignonese circle around Matteo da Viterbo. Surrounding Music, who plays a portative organ, there are various instrumentalists who pay homage to her : above, players on fiddle, psaltery and lute; in the middle, to the left a tambourine player and to the right, a dancer; below, players on bagpipes, shawm, kettle-drums and trumpets.

Lit.: M. SALMI, *Italian Miniatures*, New York, 1954.

6

Orpheus Charming the Animals.
Miniature, 8 $^5/_{32}$ x 6 $^1/_2$ in.
REMI DU PUYS, *La tryumphante et solennelle entree faicte sur le Joyeulx advènement de Treshault et Trespuissant prince Monsr. Charles Prince des Espagnes, Archiduc daustrice etc. en sa ville de Bruges l'an quinze centz et quinze le dix-huictiesme jour dapvril apres Pasches*, fol. 39 v°.
Vienna, Österreichische Nationalbibliothek, Manuscript collection, no. 2591.
Authorized reproduction.

The historiographer Remi Du Puys recounted the Joyous Entry of Charles V into Bruges during the voyage he undertook when he came to the throne in 1515. The manuscript includes thirty-three miniatures by an unidentified Flemish artist depicting the triumphal arcs, tribunes, tableaux vivants, and mysteries associated with the festivity. In his account, Du Puys draws moral lessons concerning the duties and responsibilities of the young prince. The general theme of the Entry was a reminder of the prosperity Bruges had once known and the city's hopes that the prince would restore it.
The miniature reproduced here shows a *tableau vivant* prepared by the Spanish "Nation" of Bruges. Orpheus is seen playing a fiddle and charming the animals in a garden. Du Puys stresses that the garden symbolized the kingdom of the young prince who is urged to "tune the instrument of his conduct, that is to say, the institution of his reign, in perfect consonance and melodious harmony with all excellent virtues."
The account by Du Puys was printed in Paris in 1515 by Gilles de Gourmont with woodcuts similar to the miniatures of the manuscript. It was republished in 1850 by the Société d'Emulation of Bruges.

Lit. : GH. DE BOOM, *La Librairie de Marguerite d'Autriche*, in *Revue de l'Université de Bruxelles*, October-November, 1926, pp. 39-78. – F. UNTERKIRCHER, *Inventar der illuminierten Handschriften, Inkunabeln und Frühdrucke der Österreichischen Nationalbibliothek*, vol. I, Vienna, 1957. – J. JACQUOT, *Panorama des fêtes et cérémonies du règne*, in *Les Fêtes de la Renaissance*, vol. II : *Fêtes et cérémonies du temps de Charles-Quint*, Paris, 1960, pp. 413-491. – Exhibition catalogue, *Bibliothèque nationale d'Autriche, Manuscrits et livres imprimés concernant l'histoire des Pays-Bas, 1475-1600*, Brussels, 1962, pp. 63-64.

7

The Nine Muses.
Miniature, 1 $^{49}/_{64}$ x 3 $^{11}/_{32}$ in.
MARTIN LE FRANC, *Le Champion des dames*, fol. 109 v°.
Paris, Bibliothèque Nationale, mss. fr. no. 12476.
Authorized reproduction.

This manuscript of the long poem by Martin Le Franc, inspired by the *Roman de la Rose*, is a dedicatory copy prepared for Philip the Good, whose arms appear on it. The copyist, J. Boignan d'Arras, signed his work and dated it 1451 on fol. 147 v°.
The miniatures illustrate certain passages in the poem. The text specifies for the nine Muses that Euterpe plays the bom-

bard, Terpsichore the harp, Melpomene the *douchaines* (a low-pitched instrument like the bassoon), Calliope the great trumpet, Clio the fiddle (and she sings also), Erato the *cymbales* (actually here a triangle), Polyhymnia sings, Thalia plays *du flajol et de la pippe* (flageolet and pipe), and Urania the organ.

Lit. : Exhibition catalogue, *La musique française du Moyen Age à la Révolution*, Paris, Bibliothèque Nationale, 1934, no. 97.

8

Theorica musica.
Woodcut, 9 $^{27}/_{32}$ x 7 $^7/_8$ in.
FRANCHINO GAFFURIO, *Theorica musica Franchini Gafuri Laudensis*, Milan, 1492, at end of Book I.
Brussels, Bibliothèque Royale de Belgique, Fonds Fétis, no. 5278.
Authorized reproduction.

Gaffurio (1451-1522) was singing master at the cathedral of Milan and a composer of much merit but, above all, one of the most important theorists of music at the end of the fifteenth century. The *Theorica musica* is a re-edition in 1492 at Milan of a work which appeared in 1480 in Naples under the title *Theoricum opus musicæ disciplinæ* and which has been lost. This engraving presents the mythical or historical figures Jubal, Pythagoras and Philolaos to whom medieval theorists traditionally ascribed the origin of the science of music.

Lit. : A. CARETTA, L. CREMASCOLI and L. SALAMINA, *Franchino Gaffurio*, Lodi, 1951. – C. SARTORI, *Gaffurius*, in *Die Musik in Geschichte und Gegenwart*, vol. IV, cols. 1237-1243. A facsimile edition of the *Theorica musica* was issued in Rome in 1934.

9

King David at Prayer.
Miniature, 7 $^{23}/_{64}$ x 5 $^5/_{16}$ in.
From a *Book of Hours*, fol. 128 r°.
Vienna, Österreichische Nationalbibliothek, Manuscript collection, no. 1857.
Authorized reproduction.

This *Book of Hours*, which includes a great many miniatures, twenty of them full-page, must have been executed around 1470-1480. Up to fol. 34, the text is transcribed in gold and silver letters on black parchment. The miniatures were made by unidentified artists who, for the most part, must have belonged to the older generation that had worked under Philip the Good and Charles the Bold. Four of the miniatures (*King David at Prayer* is not among them) are by a younger artist sometimes called the Master of Mary of Burgundy.

Lit. : P. DURRIEU, *La Miniature flamande au temps de la Cour de Bourgogne, 1415-1530*, Brussels-Paris, 1921, pl. XLII. – F. WINKLER, *Die flämische Buchmalerei des XV. und XVI. Jahrhunderts*, Leipzig, 1925, pp. 103-113, 203-204. – F. UNTERKIRCHER, *Inventar der illuminierten Handschriften, Inkunabeln und Frühdrucke der Österreichischen Nationalbibliothek*, vol. I, Vienna, 1957, p. 53. – Exhibition catalogue, *Bibliothèque nationale d'Autriche, Manuscrits et livres concernant l'histoire des Pays-Bas, 1475-1600*, Brussels, 1962, no. 1. A facsimile edition of the manuscript was issued in Graz in 1968.

10

An Aubade.

Colored woodcut, 3 $^{13}/_{16}$ x 5 $^{15}/_{64}$ in.

L'Iſtoire du tresvaillant chevalier Paris et de la belle Vienne, fille du dauphin, Antwerp.

GERARD LEEU, Antwerp, May 15 1487, fol. a 3 r°.

Vienna, Öſterreichische Nationalbibliothek, Ink. 11 F 27.

Authorized reproduction.

The woodcut is entitled "How Paris and Edward Offered *Aubades* Before the Chamber of Vienne", but more accurately it is a serenade, since the text itself says, "... many times they went together at night in greateſt secrecy to the place where they knew the bedchamber of Vienne lay and there they sang moſt sweetly and played diverse inſtruments, and so pleasant and sweet was the melody of their playing and singing that it surpassed all other pleasures."
The musicians have a lute and a harp.
In moſt of the other known copies of this early printed book, the engravings are not coloured.

Lit. : M.F. CAMPBELL, *Annales de la typographie néerlandaise au XVe siècle,* The Hague, 1874. – Exhibition catalogue, *Bibliothèque nationale d'Autriche, Manuscrits et livres imprimés concernant l'hiſtoire des Pays-Bas, 1475-1600,* Brussels, 1962, pp. 26-27.

11

JUSTUS OF GHENT, *Music.*

Oil on wood, 61 $^3/_8$ x 38 $^3/_8$ in.

London, National Gallery, no. 756.

Reproduced by courtesy of the Truſtees, The National Gallery, London.

Joos van Wassenhove – Juſtus of Ghent – was maſter in the guild of painters of Antwerp in 1460. From 1464 to 1469 he lived in Ghent, and then went to Italy, firſt to Rome, and then to Urbino where he entered the service of Federigo da Montefeltro. It is thought that the panel depicting Music was part of a series devoted to the Liberal Arts intended for one of the palaces of the Duke, either at Urbino or at Gubbio. It is dated around 1476. Music is symbolized by a young woman seated on a throne on the ſteps of which kneels a young knight, believed to be Coſtanzo Sforza, brother-in-law of Federigo. Her left hand points to a portative organ of unusual form : the double row of pipes is arranged so that the longeſt of them are in the center, unlike the usual plan. This balanced arrangement is not due to a whim of the painter; similar organs are depicted elsewhere in Italy at the same time and seem to be typical of Italian organs at the end of the fifteenth century.

Lit. : J. LAVALEYE, *Juſte de Gand, peintre de Frédéric de Montefeltre,* Louvain, 1936. – V. DENIS, *De muziekinſtrumenten in de Nederlanden en in Italië naar hun afbeelding in de 15e eeuwsche kunſt,* Antwerp, 1944, pp. 176-177. – M. DAVIES, *Corpus de la peinture des anciens Pays-Bas méridionaux au XVe siècle. Les Primitifs flamands. The National Gallery,* London, vol. II, Anvers, 1954, n° 49. – IDEM, *National Gallery Catalogues, Early Netherlandish School,* 2nd ed., London, 1955.

12

JEHAN DE NIZIÈRES, *Music and Measure.*

Miniature, 6 $^{31}/_{32}$ x 7 $^{31}/_{64}$ in.

JEAN CORBICHON, *Livre des propriétés des choses,* fol. 336, French translation of *Liber de proprietatibus rerum* by Barthélemy Glanville.

Paris, Bibliothèque Nationale, mss. fr. no. 22532.

Authorized reproduction.

This volume belonged to Charles, Duke of Orleans, father of King Louis XII of France. On fol. 12 is found the signature of the author of the miniatures : "Jehan de Nizières, enlumineur." The miniature reproduced here illuſtrates a chapter devoted to "the differences between numbers, measures, weights and sounds." In the choir of a church there are five singers ſtanding before a lectern and surrounded by inſtrumentaliſts who cannot be said to conſtitute a realiſtic ensemble but are there only to underline the importance of music in the realm of number. From left to right, a player of fife and drum, players on trumpet, hurdy-gurdy, lute, harp, portative organ, shawm; on the other side of the lectern, performers on dulcimer, fiddle, cymbals, horn and yet another fiddle.

Lit. : H. MARTIN, *La Miniature française du XIIIe au XVe siècle,* Paris-Brussels, 1923. – Exhibition catalogue, *La Musique française du Moyen Age à la Révolution,* Paris, Bibliothèque Nationale, 1934, no. 96.

13

THE BROTHERS MOLA, *Musical Symbols.*

Marquetry.

Mantua, Ducal Palace, the Studiolo of Isabella d'Eſte.

Authorized reproduction.

In the fifteenth century and the early sixteenth, many Italian princes had their private ſtudies decorated in marquetry. In that of Federigo da Montefeltro in Urbino there are numerous musical inſtruments thus depicted, and with great concern for realism. One of the chambers of Isabella d'Eſte, formerly in the Palazzo San Giorgio and now in the ducal palace at Mantua, similarly employs music as a decorative motif. On one of the panels there is a ſtaff with five lines, a C-clef, four mensural signs superimposed, and signs for reſts of various values arranged in an ornamental fashion. The mensural signs recall the *Missa prolationum* of Ockeghem which is entirely conſtructed on the four fundamental mensural types. The association is particularly suggeſtive since in the same private ſtudy there is another panel in which the chanson in canon form by Ockeghem, *Prenez sur moi,* has been worked in intarsia. The marquetry-work was executed in 1505 by the Mola brothers.

Lit. : E. WINTERNITZ, *Quattrocento-Intarsien als Quelle der Inſtrumentengeschichte,* in *Report of the International Society for Musicology, Seventh Congress,* Cologne, 1959, pp. 300-302. – L. OZZÒLA, *Il Museo d'arte medievale e moderno del Palazzo ducale di Mantova,* Mantua, n.d.

Lit. : See notes on plate 14.

14

MASTER OF JAMES IV OF SCOTLAND (?).
Kyrie of the Mass Ave maris stella *by Josquin Desprez.*
Miniature and musical calligraphy, page area 15 x 10 $^{53}/_{64}$ in.,
picture area 13 $^5/_8$ x 9 $^{27}/_{32}$ in.
Brussels, Bibliothèque Royale de Belgique, Manuscript collection,
no. 9126, fol. 1 v°.
Authorized reproduction.

This manuscript is part of an abundant production of choir
books executed in the Netherlands between 1480 and 1520.
Winkler ascribes the style of the miniatures to the workshop
of the Master of the *Hortulus animæ*, but this manuscript is
not considered to be by the Master himself but by one of his
disciples, the Master of James IV of Scotland, who was, perhaps, Gerard Horenbout. According to Van Doorslaer, the
calligraphy of the music is due to Martin Bourgeois. The
manuscript must have been completed between 1504 and 1506 :
intended for the Archduke Philip the Handsome and his wife
Joanna of Aragon, it contains a mass by Josquin entitled
Philippus Rex Castilliæ, and Philip was not proclaimed king
of Castile until 1504, and he died in September, 1506.

Lit. : F. WINKLER, *Die flämische Buchmalerei des XV. und
XVI. Jahrhunderts*, Leipzig, 1925. – G. VAN DOORSLAER,
Calligraphes de musique à Malines au XVIᵉ siècle, in *Bulletin
du Cercle archéologique de Malines*, 1928. – IDEM, *La Chapelle musicale de Philippe le Beau*, in *Revue belge d'archéologie
et d'histoire de l'art*, 1934. – H. KELLMANN, *The Origins of
the Chigi Codex*, in *Journal of the American Musicological
Society*, 1958, pp. 6-19.

15

A Chapel Choir.
Woodcut, 8 $^{27}/_{64}$ x 6 $^3/_8$ in.
Practica musicæ utriusque cantus excellenti Franchini Gaffori...,
Venice, 1512, in-fol., title-page.
Brussels, Bibliothèque Royale de Belgique, Fonds Fétis, no. 5280.
Authorized reproduction.

This is from the fifth edition of a work first published at
Milan in 1496. Of all the treatises by Gaffurio, the *Practica*
is the most original, aiming to confront the student with all
sorts of practical problems and providing examples borrowed
mostly from the Flemish masters of the period. Here we see
a choir of about twenty singers, both boys and adults,
gathered around a lectern on which rests a very large choir
book. The master, in black, beats the *tactus* as does also one
of the cantors. The music being sung must therefore be
mensural, although the *Benedicamus Domino* in the choir
book shows only a single voice-part which is, however, written in rhythmic notation and on a staff of five lines.

Lit. : See notes for plate 8.

16

A Chapel Choir.
Woodcut, 3 $^5/_{32}$ x 3 $^{21}/_{32}$ in.

HERMANN FINCK, *Practica musica*, title-page.
Brussels, Bibliothèque Royale de Belgique, Fonds Fétis, no. 5322.
Authorized reproduction.

This engraving is taken from a treatise published in 1556 at
Wittenberg by the heirs of Georg Rhaw. Hermann Finck
(1527-1558) should not be confused with Heinrich Finck
(ca. 1445-1527), his great-uncle who was master of music
at the Imperial chapel and a distinguished composer. Hermann
Finck taught music at Wittenberg and owes his fame to the
Practica musica, a major treatise whose five books consider all
the aspects of music of the time, the fifth being especially
devoted to the art of singing with a detailed description of
musical practice in Germany at that period. The engraving
shows a chapel choir at work. Around a large choir book is
gathered a four-voiced choir, with six boys, nine adult cantors
and three instrumentalists (two cornet players and one sackbut player).

Lit. : H. ALBRECHT, *Finck*, in *Die Musik in Geschichte und
Gegenwart*, vol. IV, cols. 214-216.

17

GHERARDO and MONTE DI GIOVANNI DEL FORA, *Circular
Canon by Ramos de Pareja.*
Miniature, 9 $^{29}/_{64}$ x 6 $^{11}/_{16}$ in.
From a musical manuscript, fol. C III D.
Florence, Biblioteca Nazionale, Banco Rari no. 229 (Magl.
XIX, 59).
Authorized reproduction.

Bartolomé Ramos de Pareja was a theorist of Spanish origin.
In his *De Musica tractatus sive Musica practica*, published in
Bologna in 1482, he appears as an audacious innovator who
attempted to adapt theory to the realities of music of his time
and who foresaw the coming developments in music with a
clarity which did not fail to stir up violent disputes among
his contemporaries. This circular canon is his only known
composition and is actually a scholastic exercise in the spirit
and technique of the Flemish masters.
The miniaturist has symbolized this perpetual canon – which
can continue as long as the singers have breath left to sing
it – by putting the musical staff into the form of a circle. The
successive entries of the four voices are indicated by the four
winds blowing from the four cardinal points onto the notes.
The legend at the bottom of the miniature is an ironical phrase
which announces that "all singers have the fault of not
deigning to sing when they are begged to and refusing to stop
when no one has asked them to sing." The authors of the
miniatures of this manuscript are Gherardo (1445-1497) and
Monte (1448-1528) di Giovanni del Fora.

Lit. : S. VAGAGGINI, *La Miniature florentine aux XIVᵉ et XVᵉ
siècles*, Milan-Florence, 1952, pl. 61. – A. SEAY, *Florence : The
City of Hothby and Ramos*, in *Journal of the American Musicological Society*, 1956, p. 195. – B. BECCHERINI, *Catalogo
dei manoscritti musicali della Biblioteca Nazionale di Firenze*,
Kassel, 1959. – R. STEVENSON, *Spanish Music in the Age of
Columbus*, The Hague, 1960, p. 62.

18

PUPIL OF JEAN LE TAVERNIER (?). *Philip the Good Attends a Mass in Music Sung by the Burgundian Chapel Choir.*
Miniature, page area 15 5/8 x 11 19/64 in., picture area 6 29/64 x 6 19/64 in.
Traité sur l'oraison dominicale, translated by Jean Miélot, fol. 9.
Brussels, Bibliothèque Royale de Belgique, Manuscript Collection, no. 9092.
Authorized reproduction.

L.-M.-J. Delaissé believes that the three miniatures in this splendid manuscript are by a pupil of Jean le Tavernier. The manuscript was copied between 1457, date of the translation, and 1467 when it is known to have been in the Burgundian library. Here we see the Duke attending mass in his private chapel. The choir of the chapel is closed off by red hangings stretched from one pillar to another. The Duke kneels in a separate oratory, and a few noblemen stand behind their master.

The cantors are gathered before a lectern which holds a choir book of modest dimensions, and there are seven of them who actually sing, two others being seated to the side.

There seems to be much concern with realistic depiction in this miniature and it is probably a trustworthy depiction of such a service. For that reason, it is especially interesting that there are no instrumentalists, which may be a significant clue to the interpretation of music of the period. On the other hand, there are also no boy choristers, and this is surprising since they are mentioned in all the documents of the archives and must have been used to sing the upper parts.

Lit. : L.-M.-J. DELAISSÉ, *La Miniature flamande à l'époque de Philippe le Bon,* Milan, 1956. – IDEM, *Miniatures médiévales de la librairie de Bourgogne au cabinet des manuscrits de la Bilbliothèque royale de Belgique,* Brussels, 1958. – IDEM, exhibition catalogue, *La Miniature flamande : Le mécénat de Philippe le Bon,* Brussels, 1959.

19
Johannes Ockeghem and His Cantors.
Miniature, 12 9/32 x 7 7/8 in.
Recueil de chants royaux, fol. 58 v°.
Paris, Bibliothèque Nationale, mss. franç., no. 1537.
Authorized reproduction.

This manuscript is a collection of royal songs crowned at the poetry and music tourneys of the Puy de la Conception at Rouen from 1519 to 1528 and must have been written out around 1530. The miniatures are excellent examples of the fine illumination done in Rouen at that time.

One of the poems was composed in 1523 in honour of Ockeghem (fols. 59 v° and 60 r°) :

Okhem très docte en art mathématique
Aritmétique aussy géométrie
Astrologie et mesmement musique
Qui fantastique ennuy chasse et maistrise
Par industrie en fleurtys et deschant...

(Ockeghem most learned in the mathematical arts, / Arithmetic as well as geometry, / Astrology and likewise music / Which drives away melancholy care and masters it / By skilful play with ornament and discant...).
The miniature which illustrates this poem therefore postdates Ockeghem's death by some thirty years. It appears realistic, but one hesitates to consider it a faithful representation unless, perhaps, it was itself inspired by an earlier document. In any event, the choir of nine cantors around a lectern is a quite convincing depiction. One can make out clearly on the choir book the words *Gloria in excelsis Deo et in terra pax hominibus bonæ voluntatis.*

Lit. : A. BLUM and P. LAUER, *La Miniature française aux XVe et XVIe siècles,* Paris-Brussels, 1930, 2 vols. – D. PLAMENAC, *Autour d'Ockeghem,* in *La Revue Musicale,* February, 1928, pp. 26-47. – IDEM, *Ockeghem,* in *Die Musik in Geschichte und Gegenwart,* vol. IX, col. 1830.

20
The Emperor Maximilian Confides the Regency of the Netherlands to Margaret of Austria.
Miniature, 26 3/4 x 20 1/2 in.
From a large choir book, fol. 1 v°.
Malines, Communal Archives.
Authorized reproduction.

This large choir book appears to have been offered by Maximilian to his daughter Margaret of Austria. Like several other collections of the same period, it was copied by Pierre Alamire, a celebrated calligrapher of music. In style, the miniatures are close to those of the *Hortulus animæ,* and similar ones, especially in the marginal decorations and the grotesque ornamental letters, are found in various choir books of the time which must have been executed in Flanders or Brabant.

This miniature, from the first page of the volume, shows Maximilian in all his imperial majesty seated on a throne, holding scepter and sword, wearing the order of the Golden Fleece and the crown of the Holy Roman Empire surmounted by the two-headed eagle adopted as a symbol by Maximilian in 1508. At his feet, at the right, his heir, the future Charles V; at the left, Margaret of Austria; in the center, three sisters of Charles V, the princesses Eleanor, Mary and Isabella.

Present also are representatives of the clergy, the nobility and the bourgeoisie. The event thus commemorated, the regency of Margaret of Austria, occurred in 1507.

The book must have been written out before 1511, since it is mentioned in that year in the accounts of payment to Pierre Alamire, and the miniatures may have been done a little later.

Lit. : V. HERMANS, *Le Livre de chant de Marguerite d'Autriche (1507-1511),* in *Bulletin du Cercle archéologique, littéraire et artistique de Malines,* 1904, pp. 211-226. – GH. DE BOOM, *La Librairie de Marguerite d'Autriche,* in *Revue de l'Université de Bruxelles,* 1926, pp. 39-78. – Exhibition catalogue, *La Bibliothèque de Marguerite d'Autriche, Bibliothèque royale,* p. 49.

21

BAUDE CORDIER, *Belle, bonne...*, Rondeau.
Page of music, 15 1/4 x 11 17/64 in.
Chantilly, Musée Condé, ms. no. 1047, fol. 11 v°.
Authorized reproduction.

This manuscript is thought to be an Italian copy made around
the beginning of the fifteenth century from a French original
written around 1390. It includes rondeaux, virelais and ballades for three or four voices by composers who are either
anonymous or little known (Solage, Trebor, Vaillant among
them). Most of the works belong to the period between the
death of Machaut and the end of the fourteenth century. The
most characteristic of them are of an extreme complexity in
writing and in a style which has been called "mannered." The
two works by Baude Cordier found on folios 11 v° and 12 r°
are later than the others. In them, the musical notation takes
the form of a heart, as in the rondeau here illustrated, or of a
circle, as in the three-voiced canon *Tout par compas suis
composé*, but in style they are less extravagant.

Lit. : G. DE VAN, *La Pédagogie musicale à la fin du Moyen
Age*, in *Musica Disciplina*, 1948, pp. 75-97. – W. APEL, *The
Notation of Polyphonic Music, 900-1600*, Cambridge, Massa-
chusetts, 4th ed., 1949. – IDEM, *French Secular Music of the
Late Fourteenth Century*, Cambridge, Massachusetts, 1950. –
H. BESSELER, *Chantilly*, in *Die Musik in Geschichte und Ge-
genwart*, vol. II, cols. 1085-1090.

22

MARTIN DE VOS, *Musica*.
Drawing in pen and bistre wash on paper, 12 7/8 x 5 29/32 in.
Antwerp, Municipal print collection, inv. no. 44.
Authorized reproduction.

Martin De Vos did sixty-six pen drawings depicting allegorical
figures which were used in preparing the Joyous Entry of
Archduke Ernest of Austria into Antwerp on June 15, 1594.
These included the parts of the world, the ages, the virtues,
the liberal arts and the like, all depicted as young women.
During the festivities, the platforms, chariots and triumphal
arches set up along the route of the procession were decorated
either with painted figures or allegories represented by girls in
postures and costumes based on the drawings by De Vos. The
Seven Liberal Arts, including Musica, adorned the seating area
of the Theater of Peace erected at the bridge over the Meir.

Lit. : A. DOUTREPONT, *Martin De Vos et l'entrée triomphale
de l'Archiduc Ernest d'Autriche à Anvers en 1594*, in *Bulletin
de l'Institut historique belge de Rome*, 1937, pp. 125-198. –
L. VAN PUYVELDE, *La Peinture flamande au siècle de Bosch
et Brueghel*, Paris, 1962, pp. 381-383. – Exhibition catalogue,
Le Siècle de Brueghel : La Peinture en Belgique au XVIe siècle,
Brussels, 1963, no. 304.

23

Dufay and Binchois.
Miniature, 2 29/32 x 2 63/64 in.

MARTIN LE FRANC, *Le Champion des dames*, fol. 98 r°.
Paris, Bibliothèque Nationale, mss. no. 12476.
Authorized reproduction.

For this manuscript, see notes for plate 7.
This miniature illustrates the famous text in which Martin Le
Franc insists on the novelty of the style of Dufay and Binchois (see page 70). Master Guillaume Dufay is dressed in a
blue robe of clerical cut, and beside him there is a small portative organ. Binchois wears a red tunic fastened at the waist
by a leather belt with a metal buckle, and he holds a harp.
The choice of costume seems to have been intended to symbolize the importance of Dufay in sacred music and of Binchois in the secular forms.

Lit. : CH. VAN DEN BORREN, *Guillaume Dufay : Son importance dans l'évolution de la musique au XVe siècle*, Brussels,
1926, p. 34. – E. PANOFSKY, *Who is Jan van Eyck's "Tymotheos" ?*, in *Journal of the Warburg and Courtauld Institutes*,
1949, pp. 80-90.

24

Portrait of Adrian Willaert.
Woodcut, 7 31/64 x 4 23/32 in.
Musica nova di Adriano Willaert, Septima pars.
Paris, Bibliothèque Sainte-Geneviève, Vm 25.
Authorized reproduction.

This collection of motets and madrigals published by Gardane
in Venice in 1559 is an especially significant anthology of the
work of Willaert. At that time, Willaert was famous throughout Europe as both composer and teacher. Despite the many
years he spent in Venice, the Flemish origins of the master are
always stressed : *Effigies Adriani Willaert Flandrii*.

Lit. : A. CARAPETYAN, *The Musica Nova of Adriano Willaert*,
in *Journal of Renaissance and Baroque Music*, 1946, pp. 200-
221.

25

PUPIL OR FOLLOWER OF JAN VAN EYCK. *The Triumph of the
Church over the Synagogue* (detail).
Painting on wood, 71 1/4 x 45 5/8 in.
Madrid, Prado, no. 1511.
Authorized reproduction.

This is certainly not by van Eyck himself but may be a copy
of a lost work or, more probably, a work by a painter influenced by van Eyck : the style of the *Mystic Lamb* is
especially evident in the figure of God the Father. The work
may date from around 1430.
The angel musicians to the left play fiddle, portative organ
and marine trumpet; those to the right, psaltery, lute and
harp.

Lit. : L. VON BALDASS, *Jan van Eyck*, London, 1952, no. 65.

26
Musicians in the Square Before a Church.
Miniature, 4 $^9/_{64}$ x 4 $^{47}/_{64}$ in.
From the manuscript known as *The Isabella Book*, fol. 184 v°.
London, British Museum, ms. add. 18851.
Reproduced by courtesy of the Trustees, British Museum, London.

This manuscript is a breviary according to Spanish Dominican usage. It was offered by Francisco de Rojas to the Queen of Castile, Isabella the Catholic, probably around 1497 on the occasion of the marriage of the Infante Don Juan, her son, to Margaret of Austria, daughter of Emperor Maximilian and Marie of Burgundy, a marriage which Francisco de Rojas had helped to arrange.
The manuscript includes a great many miniatures by various Flemish artists, but they do not all sustain the same high level. The following instruments are being played, from left to right : fife and drum, triangle, shawm, straight trumpet, harp, two lutes, three shawms, psaltery and another shawm, and the seated musician plays a small portative organ. The various instruments are depicted realistically, as are the musicians themselves, but the grouping of these particular instruments does not really seem probable.

Lit. : P. Durrieu, *La Miniature flamande au temps de la cour de Bourgogne (1415-1530)*, Brussels-Paris, 1921.

27
Jean Colombe (?). *Mass on Christmas Day.*
Miniature, 6 $^1/_2$ x 4 $^{21}/_{64}$ in.
Les Très Riches Heures de Jean de France, duc de Berry, fol. 158 r°.
Chantilly, Musée Condé, ms. no. 1284.
Authorized reproduction.

This famous manuscript was commissioned by Jean, Duke of Berry, brother of King Charles V of France and of Philip the Hardy, Duke of Burgundy. The illustration was begun by the brothers Limbourg but was not completed at the death of the Duke in 1416, and was not continued until many years later, between 1485 and 1489, probably by Jean Colombe. The *Mass on Christmas Day* belongs to the latter series. According to Durrieu, Colombe seems to have utilized sketches made during the lifetime of the Duke, particularly for the architecture of the church. Of musical interest are the great organ on the rood-screen and the five singers bent over the lectern. The foliated scrolls in the margins date from the time of the Duke.

Lit. : P. Durrieu, *Les Très Riches Heures de Jean de France, duc de Berry*, Paris, 1904. – Gh. De Boom, *La Librairie de Marguerite d'Autriche*, in *Revue de l'Université de Bruxelles*, 1926, pp. 39-78. – J. Meurgey, *Les principaux Manuscrits à peinture du Musée Condé à Chantilly*, Paris, 1930.

28
Master of James IV of Scotland (?). *Kyrie of the Mass*
Ave maris stella *by Josquin Desprez.*
Miniature, page area 15 x 10 $^{53}/_{64}$ in., picture area 13 $^5/_8$ x 9 $^{27}/_{32}$ in.

Brussels, Bibliothèque Royale de Belgique, Manuscript collection, no. 9126, fol. 2 r°.
Authorized reproduction.

This choir book was prepared for Philip the Handsome and his spouse Johanna of Aragon, who figure in the miniatures on the first page of the manuscript.
See notes for plate 14.

29
Philippe Galle after Pieter Bruegel. *Temperance.*
Copperplate engraving, 8 $^{25}/_{32}$ x 11 $^{27}/_{64}$ in.
Brussels, Bibliothèque Royale de Belgique, Print Collection.
Authorized reproduction.

Engraved after a drawing now in the Boymans Museum of Rotterdam and dated 1560, this engraving is part of a series of *The Seven Virtues* published by Hieronymus Cock from 1559 to 1561 as a companion set to his *Seven Deadly Sins*. According to Van Bastelaer and Lebeer, the series was engraved by Philippe Galle; however, Hollstein attributes it to P. Van der Heyden.
Surrounding the central allegorical figure of *Temperantia*, various small scenes symbolize the Liberal Arts. Religious music is particularly stressed : an organist plays a positive organ while an assistant works the large bellows; before a lectern stands a group of singers including children; behind them are players of sackbut, bassoon and cornett. Secular music, however, is present also : seated on the ground is a lutenist, and scattered about are various instruments, a lute, a harp and a book of profane chansons.

Lit. : R. van Bastelaer, *Les Estampes de Peter Bruegel l'ancien*, Brussels, 1908, no. 138. – L. Lebeer, *Annales de la Société royale d'archéologie de Bruxelles*, 1941, pp. 175-176. – F.W.H. Hollstein, *Dutch and Flemish Etchings, Engravings and Woodcuts*, vol. IX, p. 18, nos. 37-43. – C. de Tolnay, *The Drawings of Peter Bruegel the Elder*, London, 1952.

30
Philippe Galle after Johannes Stradanus. *Harmony, Music and Measure.*
Copperplate engraving, 9 $^{19}/_{64}$ x 11 $^{17}/_{64}$ in.
Title-page of *Encomium musices.*
Brussels, Bibliothèque Royale de Belgique, Print collection.
Authorized reproduction.

Born in Haarlem in 1537, Philippe Galle spent most of his life in Antwerp where in 1557 he began to print engravings. He first worked for the editor Hieronymus Cock, but later, when he had become a citizen of Antwerp and dean of the Guild of St. Luke, he set himself up as engraver and publisher. His workshop, "At the sign of the White Lily", was most productive and highly prosperous.
The *Encomium musices* is a series of eighteen engravings related to music. They were designed by Johannes Stradanus – Jan van der Straat – who was born in Bruges in 1523 and died in Florence in 1605, having spent a good part of his career in Italy. Most of the engravings in the *Encomium musices*

309

are inspired by the Bible, and, in depicting musical instruments, the artist attempted archeological reconstructions which are often merely fanciful. In the present engraving, first of the series, Harmony, Music and Measure hold an open choir book in which can be read a six-voiced motet by Andries Pevernage, *Nata et grata polo vocum discordia*. The motet is intended to illustrate Psalm 150.

The names of two burgomasters of Antwerp mentioned on the engraving – Edward van der Dilft and Charles Malineus – permit dating the *Encomium musices* in the years in which they held office, between May 14, 1589 and May 18, 1591, or else between May 1, 1594 and April 11, 1598.

Lit.: A.-J.-J. DELEN, *Histoire de la gravure dans les anciens Pays-Bas et dans les provinces belges, des origines jusqu'à la fin du XVIIIᵉ siècle*, Paris, 1924-1935, vol. II, 2.

31

HUGO VAN DER GOES. *Sir Edward Bonkil, Provost of Trinity College, Kneeling Before an Angel Who Plays the Organ.*
Back of the right wing of an altarpiece, 85 x 45 ¼ in.
Edinburgh, Holyrood Palace.
Authorized reproduction.

This painting is thought to have been executed around 1480. Bonkil visited the Netherlands, and it was there that he must have commissioned this altarpiece as a gift for King James III of Scotland. A positive organ in a church is shown with a music book which is not an organ tablature but, instead, a volume of plain-chant. This is not necessarily due to error or carelessness, since organists improvised on Gregorian melodies or accompanied the chant with other polyphonic lines.

Lit.: M.J. FRIEDLÄNDER, *Die altniederländische Malerei*, Leyden, 1934, vol. IV, no. 12. – M. DAVIES, *National Gallery Catalogues. Early Netherlandish School*, 2nd ed., London, 1955, p. 44.

32

Virgin and Child.
Miniature, 7 ⁹/₃₂ x 5 ¹³/₆₄ in.
From a Book of Hours, fol. 35 v°.
Vienna, Österreichische Nationalbibliothek, Manuscript collection, no. 1857.
Authorized reproduction.

See no. 9. Like *King David*, this miniature was made by one of the older masters who worked on the manuscript. Around the Virgin, angels play the harp and lute, and in the decorative frame there are three angels who, from top to bottom, play the trumpet, triangle and fiddle.

33

ISRAËL VAN MECKENEM. *Acanthus with Musicians and Dancers.*
Engraving, 4 ⁴¹/₆₄ x 10 ⁷/₁₆ in.
Paris, Bibliothèque Nationale, Print collection, Ea 48b, Rés., B 201.
Authorized reproduction.

Within the intertwining fronds, one finds a woman surrounded by six men, all dancing, while at her feet a musician plays fife and drum and a court fool entertains.

34

ADRIAEN VAN WESEL. *Three Angel Musicians and Saint Joseph.*
Carved oak with traces of polychrome, 17 ½ x 14 ¾ in.
Fragment of the altarpiece of the *Illustre Lieve Vrouwe-Broederschap* executed for the Church of Sint-Jan, 's Hertogenbosch.
Amsterdam, Rijksmuseum.
Authorized reproduction.

Adriaen van Wesel, born around 1420, died about 1480, having lived mostly at Utrecht, where he had several times been dean of the guild. He did sculpture for the cathedral of Utrecht and for churches in Delft and 's Hertogenbosch. The altarpiece in the latter city was sculpted between 1475 and 1477. The three angel musicians play respectively a fiddle, lute and clavichord, and this is the oldest depiction known of the latter instrument.

Lit.: W. VOGELSANG, *Die Holzskulpturen in den Niederländen*, Utrecht, 1912, vol. II; exhibition catalogue, *Le Siècle de Bourgogne*, Brussels, 1951, no. 201.

35

JAN SADELER THE ELDER. *Madonna and Angel Musicians.*
Engraving with music, 8 ¹/₃₂ x 11 ³/₈ in.
Paris, Bibliothèque Nationale, Print collection, Cc 20 fol., no. 118.
Authorized reproduction.

Jan Sadeler the Elder, who was born in Brussels in 1550 and died in Venice in 1600, worked as an engraver at Antwerp, Cologne, Frankfurt, Munich and Venice. Between 1584 and 1590 he published in Antwerp, Frankfurt and Mainz a series of curious engravings, each of which has a complete piece of polyphonic music surrounded by various personages. Here one sees, around the Madonna, four angel musicians (bass viol, cornett, flute and another bass viol) and two other angels holding two panels on which one can read without difficulty a *Magnificat* for four voices by Cornelis Verdonck.

Lit.: M. SEIFFERT, *Bildzeugnisse des 16. Jahrhunderts*, in *Archiv für Musikwissenschaft*, 1920, pp. 49 ff. – IDEM, *Niederländische Bildmotetten*, in *Organum*, Erste Reihe, nos. 19-20, 2 vols., 1920. – A.-J.-J. DELEN, *Histoire de la gravure dans les anciens Pays-Bas et dans les provinces belges*, Paris, 1924-1935, vol. II, 2, p. 127.

36

PHILIPPE GALLE after JOHANNES STRADANUS. *A Religious Service.*
Copperplate engraving, 8 ⁵/₈ x 11 ³/₁₆ in.
Encomium musices, plate 17.
Brussels, Bibliothèque Royale de Belgique, Print collection.
Authorized reproduction.

For the *Encomium musices*, see no. 30.
Numerous musicians take part in the service. Before the lectern there are singers and players on sackbut and cornett; to the right, another lectern with more singers and instrumentalists. Apparently what is being performed is music for two choirs. In his Biblical scenes, Stradanus often indulged in fantastic archeological reconstructions of instruments, but there is no reason to doubt this depiction of a contemporary ceremony, although it does seem excessively sumptuous with what may be an exaggerated number of musicians.

37
SIMON MARMION (?). *Angelic Choir.*
Oil on wood, 22 ⁵/₈ x 8 ⁵/₆₄ in.
London, National Gallery, no. 1303.
Reproduced by courtesy of the Trustees, The National Gallery, London.

This is the upper panel of a wing of the altarpiece from the Abbey of Saint-Bertin at Saint-Omer; its companion-piece, showing the soul of St. Bertin ascending to God, is also in the National Gallery, while the lower sections are in Berlin and the central panel, a large Crucifixion, has disappeared. The altarpiece was painted between 1455 and 1459 and is generally attributed, although without definite proof, to Simon Marmion, miniaturist and painter, born probably around 1425, who worked at Amiens, Valenciennes and Tournai.
Three angels play oboes, two sing from a large scroll of music.

Lit. : C. GASPAR and F. LYNA, *Philippe le Bon et ses beaux livres*, Brussels, 1942. – M. DAVIES, *National Gallery Catalogues, Early Netherlandish School*, 2nd edition, London, 1955, pp. 66-67. – L.-M.-J. DELAISSÉ, *La Miniature flamande : Le Mécénat de Philippe le Bon*, Brussels, 1959, p. 60 ff.

38
De ce que fol pense...
Tapestry in wool, silk and gold, 61 ³/₄ x 72 ⁷/₈ in.
Paris, Musée des Arts Décoratifs.
Authorized reproduction.

This tapestry from an Arras workshop dates from the first third of the fifteenth century and is part of a series of five devoted to scenes from court life. A woman plays a harp while before her a gentleman unrolls a scroll on which one can make out notes of music, unfortunately impossible to decipher, and the words *De ce que fol pense...* There is a ballade for three voices by Pierre des Molins beginning with these words, but it is earlier by a half-century than this tapestry.

Lit. : R.-A. WEIGERT, *La Tapisserie française*, Paris, 1956, p. 47.

39
WORKSHOP OF THE MASTER OF WAVRIN. *An Aubade.*
Miniature : pen drawing with watercolor, 3 ⁴⁷/₆₄ x 5 ³³/₆₄ in.
L'Histoire du chevalier Paris, fol. 1 r°.

Brussels, Bibliothèque Royale de Belgique, Manuscript collection, no. 9632-33.
Authorized reproduction.

The three miniatures from this manuscript, which relates the story of the knight Sir Paris, come from the workshop of the Master of Wavrin who worked in Lille. The same artist, a skilled caricaturist, illustrated around 1465 other manuscripts, written on paper, containing chivalric romances and intended for Jean de Wavrin. Here one sees the two heroes of the romance, Paris and Edward, playing lute and harp as they offer an aubade to the fair Vienne. The same scene is depicted in an engraving in the early Antwerp edition of this book (see plate 10).

Lit. : P. DURRIEU, *La Miniature flamande au temps de la cour de Bourgogne, 1415-1530*, Brussels-Paris, 1921. – C. GASPAR and F. LYNA, *Philippe le Bon et ses beaux livres*, Brussels, 1944. – Exhibition catalogue, *La Miniature flamande : Le Mécénat de Philippe le Bon*, Brussels, 1959, pp. 76-77 and 82.

40
FOLLOWER OF JAN VAN EYCK (?). *The Hunt of Philip the Good.*
Painting on wood, 63 ³/₈ x 46 ¹/₈ in.
Versailles, Musée, M V 5423.
Authorized reproduction.

This is a sixteenth-century copy of a lost original once in the Palace of the Prado near Madrid but destroyed in 1608. The original has often been attributed to Jan van Eyck, and various details – the type of coat-of-arms, the fact that the Duke does not wear the order of the Golden Fleece – suggest the date of 1430-1431. Two groups are particularly interesting for the hints they give us as to the musical practice of the time : the singers close to the Duke, and the three instrumentalists (sackbut and two shawms) to the left; at the bottom of the painting, in front of the musicians, four couples dance.

Lit. : P. POST, *Ein verschollenes Jagdbild Jan van Eycks*, in *Jahrbuch der Preussischen Kunstsammlungen*, Berlin, 1931, pp. 120-132. – L. VON BALDASS, *Jan van Eyck*, London, 1952, p. 82. – H. BESSELER, *Umgangsmusik und Darbietungsmusik im 16. Jahrhundert*, in *Archiv für Musikwissenschaft*, 1959, pp. 21-43.

41
ISRAËL VAN MECKENEM. *Two Musicians : Lutenist and Singer.*
Engraving, 6 ⁷/₃₂ x 4 ²³/₃₂ in.
Paris, Bibliothèque Nationale, Print collection. Ea 48 b, Rés., B 174.
Authorized reproduction.
See notes on plate 73.

42
JAN VAN EYCK. *Tymotheos. Portrait of Gilles Binchois (?).*
Oil-tempera on oak panel, 13 ¹/₈ x 7 ¹³/₃₂ in.
London, National Gallery, no. 290.
Reproduced by courtesy of the Trustees, The National Gallery, London.

311

This painting, signed and dated October 10, 1432 by van Eyck, bears an inscription, which appears almost as if engraved in stone, consisting of the words *Tymotheos* and *Léal Souvenir*. It is on the basis of the name Tymotheos that Erwin Panofsky believes that this may be a portrait of Gilles Binchois. Timotheos was virtually unknown as a Christian name in the Netherlands before the Reformation, but it could have been used as a complimentary surname, an allusion to Timotheos of Miletos, a musician contemporary with Plato whose fame survived from Antiquity to make of him a legendary figure in the Middle Ages. It is therefore presumed that this may be a portrait of a famous musician. The Burgundian style of dressing suggests that the sitter may have belonged to the household of Philip the Good, and it so happens that at the time of the painting Binchois was probably the outstanding musician of that court, Dufay being in Italy and Dunstable in England. Panofsky's arguments are not entirely convincing, but it may very well be that some prominent musician is portrayed here. Perhaps the puzzle could be solved if we were able to track down the meaning of *Léal Souvenir*.

Lit.: E. PANOFSKY, *Who is Jan van Eyck's "Timotheos"?*, in *Journal of the Warburg and Courtauld Institutes*, vol. XII, 1949, pp. 80-90. – M. DAVIES, *Corpus de la peinture des anciens Pays-Bas méridionaux au XVe siècle. Les Primitifs flamands. The National Gallery, London*, vol. II, Anvers, 1954, no. 49. – IDEM, *National Gallery Catalogues, Early Netherlandish School*, 2nd ed., London, 1955, no. 290, p. 41.

43
HANS MEMLING. *Portrait of Canon Gilles Joye.*
Painting on oak panel, 12 1/64 x 8 13/16 in.
Williamstown, Massachusetts, Sterling and Francine Clark Art Institute, Inv. no. 943.
Reproduced by courtesy of the Trustees, Sterling and Francine Clark Art Institute, Williamstown.

This portrait was for long a problem, but it has recently been identified by an old inscription glued to the back of the panel, which was revealed by ultra-violet examination : it dates from 1472 and depicts Gilles Joye at the age of forty-seven. A native of the diocese of Tournai, Joye had first been canon at the church of Our Lady in Cleves before obtaining a prebend at the church of St. Donatian in Bruges in 1463. At the same period, he entered the chapel of Philip the Good, first as cleric, then as chaplain, and remained there until 1469, dying in Bruges in 1483. A few secular compositions of some merit are known to be by him.

Lit.: J. MARIX, *Les Musiciens de la cour de Bourgogne au XVe siècle (1420-1467)*, Paris, 1937. – FR. VAN MOLLE, *Identification d'un portrait de Gilles Joye attribué à Memling*, Brussels, 1960.

44
Garden of Love.
Miniature, 8 3/16 x 7 19/32 in.
London, British Museum, mss. Harley, no. 4425, fol. 12 v°.
Reproduced by courtesy of the Trustees, British Museum, London.

Our illustration comes from one of the best known manuscripts of the *Roman de la Rose*, whose numerous miniatures are of Flemish origin and can be dated around 1500. Winkler attributes them to a minor master who also illuminated many Books of Hours.
Traditionally, the Gardens of Love take the form of stylized scenes with music-making. Here there is a quartet of musicians : two women, two men, doubtless aristocratic amateurs. One woman sings, standing, reading from a sheet of music, while the three others remain seated, one of the men playing the lute, the other couple singing (the young woman holds a sheet of music in her hands).

Lit. : E. LANGLOIS, *Les Manuscrits du Roman de la Rose : Description et classement*, Lille-Paris, 1910. – A. KUHN, *Die Illustration des Rosenromans*, in *Jahrbuch des Kunsthistorischen Sammlungen des allerhöchsten Kaisershauses*, 1912. – P. DURRIEU, *La Miniature flamande au temps de la cour de Bourgogne, 1415-1530*, Brussels-Paris, 1921, pl. LXXII. – F. WINKLER, *Die flämische Buchmalerei des XV. und XVI. Jahrhunderts*, Leipzig, 1925, p. 179.

45
ISRAËL VAN MECKENEM. *An Organist and His Wife.*
Engraving, 6 39/64 x 4 23/32 in.
Paris, Bibliothèque Nationale, Print collection, Ea 48b, Rés. B 175.
Authorized reproduction.

The positive organ was not only used in church but could also have a place in a domestic interior. The performer here is a burgher who has placed a small organ on his dining-room table. His wife works the bellows.

46
SIMON BENING (?). *Promenade on the Canals in the Month of May.*
Miniature, 4 17/32 x 3 11/32 in.
Heures de Notre-Dame (also known as *Les Heures de Hennessy*), fol. 5 v°.
Brussels, Bibliothèque Royale de Belgique, Manuscript collection, no. II 158.
Authorized reproduction.

This manuscript takes its name from an Irish family who settled in Belgium in the seventeenth century and to whom it belonged. The miniatures are in a style typical of Ghent and Bruges, and are attributed to Simon Bening and dated around 1540. In the small boat, a man – a rich burgher, perhaps, or a nobleman – plays the flute and a young woman a lute, while in the town itself men and women dance, suggesting a scene from some popular festivity. A very similar miniature, from the same workshop no doubt, is found in the incomplete *Book of Hours* known as the *Golf Book* in the British Museum (ms. add. 24098, fol. 22 v°).

Lit. : J. DESTRÉE, *Les Heures de Notre-Dame dites de Hennessy*, Brussels, 1895. – P. DURRIEU, *La Miniature flamande au temps de la cour de Bourgogne, 1415-1530*, Brussels-Paris,

1921, pl. LXXXIX. – Exhibition catalogue, *Trésors de la Bibliothèque royale de Belgique*, Brussels, 1958.

47
SIMON BENING (?). *A Woman Standing at the Spinet.*
Miniature, 7 $\frac{1}{64}$ x 4 $\frac{23}{32}$ in.
Hortulus animæ, fol. 1 v°.
Vienna, Österreichische Nationalbibliothek, Manuscript collection, no. 2706.
Authorized reproduction.

The *Hortulus animæ* is considered one of the masterworks of late Flemish miniature painting. It was executed between 1510 and 1520, and the text is merely copied from that of a printed book, the German translation published in Strasbourg in 1510 of a very popular devotional book. The author of the miniatures has not been identified, but he is thought to be Simon Bening. The same style is found in various important manuscripts and notably in the choir books made for Philip the Handsome or Margaret of Austria.
In this miniature, which surrounds a calendar, one sees a middle-class dwelling with a woman playing the spinet in a standing position which might strike us as odd but which reappears often in pictures of the sixteenth and seventeenth centuries.

Lit.: F. DÖRNHÖFFER, *Hortulus animæ*, Amsterdam, 1907. – P. DURRIEU, *La Miniature flamande au temps de la cour de Bourgogne, 1415-1530*, Brussels-Paris, 1921. – GH. DE BOOM, *La Librairie de Marguerite d'Autriche*, in *Revue de l'Université de Bruxelles*, 1926, pp. 39-78. – Exhibition catalogue, *Bibliothèque nationale d'Autriche. Manuscrits et livres imprimés concernant l'histoire des Pays-Bas, 1475-1600*, Brussels, 1962, pp. 37-40.

48 and 49
Chansonnier of Tournai.
Pages illustrated with miniatures, 3 $\frac{5}{64}$ x 4 $\frac{21}{64}$ in.
Brussels, Bibliothèque Royale de Belgique, Manuscript collection, no. IV, 90, fol. 11 v° - 12 r° and fol. 4 v° - 5 r°.
Authorized reproduction.

In the library of the city of Tournai there is an oblong-shaped song-book of unusually small size with only three staves on each page. For long it has intrigued historians of music. Most of the manuscript chansonniers of the time have the various voices of polyphonic compositions laid out on two facing pages, but in the Tournai song-book there is only a single voice, as was to be the case usually in printed collections of chansons in the sixteenth century. This led to the conclusion that the Tournai volume was a collection of monodic songs. However, recently a manuscript has been found which turned out to have fragments of another voice part for the Tournai songs, and the pages here presented are from that manuscript. Thus we now know the Tournai song-book to be, in fact, a collection of polyphonic chansons, although it remains incomplete. The chansons are by well-known composers such as Hayne van Ghizeghem, Compère, Obrecht, Josquin, Ockeghem, and Pipelare and are in French or Flemish with a few pieces in Latin. The date of 1511 written in the ornamental letter on fol. 21 r° of the Tournai volume applies equally to the Brussels manuscript. Both are decorated with miniatures which are most often confined to the outer margin of each page and depict flowers, insects, allegories, human figures and tiny love scenes which at times are some way related to the songs.

Lit.: CH. VAN DEN BORREN, *Inventaire des manuscrits de musique polyphonique qui se trouvent en Belgique*, in *Acta Musicologica*, 1934, pp. 119-121. – P. FAIDER and P. VAN SINT JAN, *Catalogue des manuscrits conservés à Tournai (Bibliothèque de la ville et du séminaire)*, Gembloux, 1950, vol. VI, p. 96.

50
The Planets : Mercury (detail).
Tapestry in wool, silk, and gold and silver thread, 165 $\frac{3}{8}$ x 214 $\frac{3}{8}$ in.
Munich, Bayerisches Nationalmuseum.
Authorized reproduction.

In the last third of the sixteenth century, the Brussels workshops turned out a series of seven tapestries on the theme of the planets. Mercury was considered to be the planet which confers genius on men and which arouses interest in the arts and sciences. In the foreground of the composition, as its principal subject, there is a woman personifying Music who plays a positive organ.

Lit.: R.-A. D'HULST, *Tapisseries flamandes du XIVe au XVIIIe siècle*, Brussels, 1960.

51
MASTER OF THE JUVÉNAL DES URSINS (?). *Carole in the Orchard.*
Miniature, 6 $\frac{3}{8}$ x 5 $\frac{15}{32}$ in.
Roman de la Rose, fol. 7.
Paris, Bibliothèque Nationale, Ms. franç. no. 19153.
Authorized reproduction.

This comes from a luxurious manuscript of the *Roman de la Rose* whose miniatures are attributed to the Master of the Juvénal des Ursins and are dated around 1460. Three oboists play for this carole danced by eight gentlemen and their ladies.

Lit.: E. LANGLOIS, *Les Manuscrits du Roman de la Rose : Description et classement*, Lille-Paris, 1910. – A. KUHN, *Die Illustration des Rosenromans*, in *Jahrbuch der Kunsthistorischen Sammlungen des allerhöchsten Kaiserhauses*, vol. I, Vienna, 1912. – Exhibition catalogue, *Les Manuscripts à peinture en France du XIIIe au XVIe siècle*, Paris, Bilbiothèque Nationale, 1955, p. 134, no. 285.

52
ISRAËL VAN MECKENEM. *Ornamental Foliage with a Tree of Jesse.*
Engraving, 4 $\frac{41}{64}$ x 10 $\frac{35}{64}$ in.
Paris, Bibliothèque Nationale, Print collection, Ea 48 b, Rés., B. 202.
Authorized reproduction.

David alone among the kings plays an instrument, the harp.

53
JEAN DREUX. *A Tourney.*
Miniature in grisaille, 5 $^3/_{64}$ x 7 $^1/_8$ in.
Composition de la Sainte Écriture, fol. 240.
Brussels, Bibliothèque Royale de Belgique, Manuscript collection, no. 9017.
Authorized reproduction.

The manuscript of the *Composition de la Sainte Écriture* was executed in 1462 for Philip the Good by David Aubert, with miniatures by Jean Dreux, the French valet of the Duke of Burgundy who had recently left Bruges to settle in Brussels. In a box there are three musicians playing "high" instruments: two straight trumpets and a sackbut.

Lit.: C. GASPAR and F. LYNA, *Philippe le Bon et ses beaux livres*, Brussels, 1944. – L.-M.-J. DELAISSÉ, *Miniatures médiévales*, Brussels, 1958. – Exhibition catalogue, *La Miniature flamande. Le Mécénat de Philippe le Bon*, Brussels, 1959.

54
Philip the Good Preceded by His Trumpeters Is Welcomed at His Entry into Dijon by a Procession of Burghers.
Miniature.
Manuscrit du Saint-Esprit, fol. 18.
Dijon, the Hôtel-Dieu.
Authorized reproduction.

The chroniclers report that on solemn occasions the Duke was always preceded by his trumpeters mounted on horses, especially when he made an entry into a city.

55
PIETER COECKE VAN AELST (?). *The Festivities at Binche.*
Drawing with wash.
Cadland (England), Collection of Mrs. Mildred Quinnell.
Authorized reproduction.

The drawing depicts the dance of the knights, ladies and wild men at the festivities organized at Binche by Mary of Hungary in honor of Charles V on August 28, 1549. We see at the back of the hall the Emperor seated between his two sisters, Eleanor, the Dowager-Queen of France, and Mary of Hungary. Beside the latter is Prince Philip, the future Philip II, along with courtiers who watch the spectacle. It has been conjectured that the author of the drawing may have been Pieter Coecke van Aelst.

Lit.: A. VAN DER PUT, *Two Drawings of the Fêtes at Binche*, in *Journal of the Warburg and Courtauld Institutes*, 1939-40, pp. 49-55. – A.E. POPHAM, *The Authorship of the Drawings of Binche, ibid.*, pp. 55-57. – D. HEARTZ, *Un Divertissement de palais pour Charles-Quint à Binche*, in *Les Fêtes de la Renaissance, II, Fêtes et cérémonies au temps de Charles-Quint*, Paris, 1960, pp. 329-357.

56
FOLLOWER OF SIMON BENING (?). *The Tidings Brought to the Shepherds.*
Miniature, 4 $^{13}/_{32}$ x 2 $^{29}/_{32}$ in.

From a *Book of Hours* in Latin, fol. 95 v°.
Vienna, Österreichische Nationalbibliothek, Manuscript collection, no. 1984.
Authorized reproduction.

This very luxurious Latin manuscript was written out and illustrated around 1510-1520. The author of the miniatures copied from excellent models but not without a certain awkwardness, and he seems to have been well acquainted with the miniatures produced by the workshop of Simon Bening. Note especially the dance here in which peasants hold hands and follow a bagpiper.

Lit.: F. WINKLER, *Die flämische Buchmalerei des XV. und XVI. Jahrhunderts*, Leipzig, 1920. – Exhibition catalogue, *Bilbiothèque nationale d'Autriche. Manuscrits et livres imprimés concernant l'histoire des Pays-Bas, 1475-1600*, Brussels, 1962, p. 46, no. 72.

57 and 58
Basses Dances.
Musical manuscript, 5 $^3/_{64}$ x 8 $^{17}/_{64}$ in.
Basses Danses de Marguerite d'Autriche, fols. 20 v° and 12 r°.
Brussels, Bibliothèque Royale de Belgique, Manuscript collection, no. 9085.
Authorized reproduction.

Although this volume belonged to the Regent of the Low Countries, it actually dates from the last third of the fifteenth century. It is a small oblong manuscript on black paper with musical notation and texts in gold and silver, and is, in fact, a manual of dancing. It begins with five pages of theoretical instructions, followed by fifty-nine pieces with their titles and indications, by means of letters, of the steps to be used. The pieces are most often notated without specific rhythm, and this has raised difficult problems for musicologists.

Lit.: E. CLOSSON, *Le Manuscrit dit des basses danses de la Bibliothèque de Bourgogne*, Brussels, 1912. – Exhibition catalogue, *La Bibliothèque de Marguerite d'Autriche*, Brussels, 1940. – M. BUKOFZER, *A Polyphonic Basse Dance of the Renaissance*, in *Studies in Medieval and Renaissance Music*, New York, 1950, p. 190-216. – Exhibition catalogue, *Trésors de la Bibliothèque royale de Belgique*, Brussels, 1958, no. 46.

59
LOYSET LIÉDET or WORKSHOP (?). *Ball at the Court of King Yon of Gascony Before the Betrothal of His Daughter Clarissa with Renaud de Montauban, Eldest of the Four Sons of Aymon.*
Miniature, 5 $^{15}/_{64}$ x 6 $^{17}/_{32}$ in.
Histoire de Renaud de Montauban, fol. 117 v°.
Paris, Bibliothèque de l'Arsenal, mss. franç. 5073.
Authorized reproduction.

The story of Renaud de Montauban is contained in five volumes which were among the most beautiful in the library of Philip the Good. This transcription of a prose tale was made by David Aubert in 1462, and the miniatures, which were commissioned by the Duke but not executed until after his death, were done between 1468 and January 1470 by Loyset Liédet or by his workshop.

The miniature here reproduced illustrates the following text : "After supper, when the tables were removed, there came into the hall minstrels and jongleurs with divers instruments of many kinds, and all expert in the science of minstrelsy and music, and when they had entered everyone of joyful heart thought only of sounds and notes, and such was the gaiety that little by little all entered into the festivities... Regnault then led Clarissa into the dance, and she followed him without hesitation, like one who enjoys a happiness beyond all telling."

Lit. : H. MARTIN and P. LAUER, *Les principaux Manuscrits à peintures de la Bibliothèque de l'Arsenal à Paris*, Paris, 1929, p. 49. – C. GASPAR and F. LYNA, *Philippe le Bon et ses beaux livres*, Brussels, 1944.

60
MASTER M.Z. (MARTIN ZASINGER). *The Great Ball.*
Copperplate engraving, 8 $47/64$ x 12 $23/64$ in.
Brussels, Bibliothèque Royale de Belgique, Print collection, S. II no. 63149.
Authorized reproduction.

In the background, Duke Albert IV of Bavaria, seated at a table, plays cards with the Duchess. To the left, on a platform, two musicians play flute and drum, while on another platform, to the right, four trumpeters and drummers await their cue to juin in. Four couples dance "the great ball," a ceremonious pavane. Above the head of the Duke is engraved the date 1500.

Lit. : M. LEHRS, *Geschichte und kritischer Katalog des deutschen, niederländischen und französischen Kupferstichs im XV. Jahrhundert*, Vienna, 1908-1934, 9 vols., vol. VIII, p. 367.

61
PIETER BRUEGEL. Peasant Dance.
Painting on panel, 44 $7/8$ x 64 $5/8$ in.
Vienna, Kunsthistorisches Museum, no. 719.
Authorized reproduction.

Like the *Wedding Feast*, its companion piece of the same dimensions, the *Peasant Dance* dates from the last years of the artist's life, around 1568. The usual folk instrument, the bagpipes, plays for this dance in which the peasants, two by two, hold hands.

Lit. : R.-L. DELEVOY, *Bruegel*, Geneva, 1959. – V. DENIS, *All the Paintings of Pieter Brueghel*, London, 1961. – L. VAN PUYVELDE, *La Peinture flamande au siècle de Bosch et Brueghel*, Paris, 1962.

62
HANS BURGKMAIR. *A Masque.*
Woodcut, 8 $37/64$ x 7 $43/64$ in.
Der Weißkunig, volume of proofs, fol. 147 v°.

Vienna, Österreichische Nationalbibliothek, Manuscript collection, no. 3032.
Authorized reproduction.

Der Weißkunig – The White King – is a fanciful autobiography by Emperor Maximilian I. Begun in 1505, it was finished by 1516 but never published during the lifetime of the monarch. The text was actually written by Marx Treitzsauerwein, privy secretary of Maximilian, who followed the plan and information provided by the Emperor. The work was illustrated by 251 woodcuts of which 118 were by Hans Burgkmair. Before the definitive edition, a volume of proofs was made up including first printings of the engravings and sometimes the original drawings themselves. The work was not published until 1775.

Here, in a hall of a palace, before a table at which sit several ladies, among them Mary of Burgundy, there are dancers who are masked with birds' beaks and plumes and bearing clubs, and they are welcomed by the young White King – Maximilian himself. To the left, there is a group of musicians with several instruments lying on a table before them.

Lit. : F.W.H. HOLLSTEIN, *German Engravings, Etchings, Woodcuts, 1400-1700*, vol. V, pp. 116-119. – P. DU COLOMBIER, *Les Triomphes en images de l'Empereur Maximilien Ier*, in *Les Fêtes de la Renaissance, II, Fêtes et cérémonies au temps de Charles-Quint*, Paris, 1960, pp. 99-112. – H.T. MUSPER, *Kaiser Maximilians Weißkunig*, Stuttgart, 1955-56, 2 vols.

63
WORKSHOP OF THE MASTER OF WAVRIN. A Moresque.
Miniature, 2 $1/4$ x 5 $45/64$ in., pen drawing with water color.
Histoire du chevalier Paris, fol. 168 r°.
Brussels, Bibliothèque Royale de Belgique, Manuscript collection, nos. 9632-33.
Authorized reproduction.

See plate 39.

64
Young Charles V Enthroned.
Miniature on parchment, 12 $3/64$ x 8 $21/32$ in.
REMI DU PUYS, *La truymphante et solennelle entree faicte sur le Joyeulx advènement de Treshault et trespuissant prince Monsr. Charles...*, fol. 44 r°.
Vienna, Österreichische Nationalbibliothek, Manuscript collection, no. 2591.
Authorized reproduction.

For the account by Remi Du Puys of the Joyous Entry of Charles V into Bruges, see no. 6.

The miniature shows a *tableau vivant* arranged by the Italian merchants in Bruges and presented in a sort of covered gallery : Solomon, as an adolescent, is on his throne surrounded by his court with, at his feet, "four virgins beautiful as goddesses, attired and bedecked in Italian fashion" who praise his glory

and his wisdom – a flattering allegory for young Charles. To
the left there are three musicians with oboe and cornetts.
See notes for plate 6.

65
HEINRICH ALDEGREVER. *Town Minstrels.*
Engraving, 4 $\frac{39}{64}$ x 3 $\frac{5}{64}$ in.
Paris, Bibliothèque Nationale, Print collection, EC 5, Rés. fol.
B 171.
Authorized reproduction.

Part of a series dating from 1538, this engraving shows three
sackbut players.

Lit.: F.W.H. HOLLSTEIN, *German Engravings, Etchings and
Woodcuts, 1450-1700, 1954*, vol. I, pp. 68-72.

66
HANS BURGKMAIR. *Oboists and Sackbut Players.*
Woodcut, 15 $\frac{5}{8}$ x 15 in.
Triomphe de l'Empereur Maximilien, 18th-century re-edition
after the original, fol. 92, pl. 78.
Paris, Bibliothèque Nationale, Print collection, Pd 23, Rés.
fol. obl.
Authorized reproduction.

The Emperor Maximilian died on January 12, 1519. The
Triumphal Procession in the form of a volume of woodcuts
which he had commissioned was not yet finished at that date.
The first edition, which was incomplete, was not printed until
1526 and included 135 woodcuts of which 67 were by Burgkmair. The edition employed here dates from the eighteenth
century but uses the original wood blocks and occasionally
interpolates explanatory comments in French.

Lit.: P. DU COLOMBIER, *Les Triomphes en images de l'Empereur Maximilien Ier*, in *Fêtes de la Renaissance, II. Fêtes et
cérémonies au temps de Charles-Quint*, Paris, 1960, pp. 99-112.

67
The Prodigal Son Among the Courtesans.
Oil on wood, 32 $\frac{5}{8}$ x 51 $\frac{1}{8}$ in.
Paris, Musée Carnavalet, no. P. 619.
Authorized reproduction.

This painting has sometimes also been known as *A Pleasure-
Garden near the Quai Saint-Bernard During the Reign of
Francis I* and also *Amorous Party on the Outskirts of Paris*,
but the two subordinate scenes in the background – the Prodigal Son driven away by the courtesans and the Prodigal Son
tending the swine – prove that it was meant to depict one of
those "gallant gatherings" which were understood to refer to
the parable of the Prodigal Son. In the Budapest Museum there
is a similar painting attributed to the Monogrammist of Bruns-
wick, an Antwerp painter of the sixteenth century, but it
may be that this painting is by a Frenchman.
In the midst of the wanton gathering, four people make music:
a man and three women, one of whom is a servant. One of

the women plays the flute, another the lute. These musicians
are doubtless amateurs. Before them are music books and they
are apparently about to perform a polyphonic chanson.

Lit.: G. MARLIER, *Erasme et la peinture flamande de son
temps*, Damme, 1954. – L. VAN PUYVELDE, *La Peinture flamande au siècle de Bosch et Brueghel*, Paris, 1962. – Exhibition catalogue, *Le Siècle de Bruegel. La Peinture en Belgique
au XVIe siècle*, Brussels, 1963, p. 175, no. 252.

68 and 69
HANS MEMLING. *Angel Musicians.*
Oil on wood, each panel, 65 x 90 $\frac{1}{2}$ in.
Left and right wings of the so-called *Najera Triptych.*
Antwerp, Musée des Beaux-Arts, nos. 779-780.
Authorized reproduction.

The panels of this triptych once decorated the organ case in
the church of Santa Maria la Real at Najera in Castile. They
were painted around 1480. On the central panel, next to the
Lord, there are singing angels, while the lateral panels have
instrumentalists : on the left-hand panel, psaltery, marine
trumpet, lute, trumpet, bombard; on the right-hand panel,
two trumpets, portative organ, harp and fiddle.

Lit.: G. MARLIER, *Memlinc*, Brussels, 1934. – L. VON BALDASS,
Hans Memling, Vienna, 1942. – E. WINTERNITZ, *On Angel
Concerts in the 15th Century : A Critical Approach to Realism
and Symbolism in Sacred Painting*, in *The Musical Quarterly*,
1963, pp. 450-463.

70
JAN MANDYN. *The Trials of Job.*
Painting on wood, 26 $\frac{3}{8}$ x 55 $\frac{1}{2}$ in.
Douai, Musée, no. 145.
Authorized reproduction.

This painting was attributed by Friedländer to Peter Huys
and by Demmler to Jan Mandyn. After an examination of all
the signed pictures of Mandyn, the latter seems in fact to be
the author of this as well as of the *Temptation of Saint
Anthony* in the museum at Haarlem. Influenced by Hieronymus
Bosch, Mandyn painted numerous pictures of diabolic torments.
Job on his dunghill mocked by his friends has often given
rise to satirical depictions in which music figures. Here, to the
left, we see a woman playing bagpipes, to the right a sorceress
playing kettle-drums placed on the ground like cauldrons, a
man blowing a trumpet, a woman beating a drum and holding
a long pipe like a flute, and a figure lying down who plays
the lute with his feet.

Lit.: L. VAN PUYVELDE, *La Peinture flamande au siècle de
Bosch et Brueghel*, Paris, 1962, pp. 69-72.

71
HANS MEMLING. *Virgin and Child.*
Oil on wood, 27 $\frac{3}{4}$ x 27 $\frac{3}{4}$ in.
Triptych of Sir John Donne, central panel.
London, National Gallery, no. 6275.

Surrounding the Virgin and Child are placed in the conventional manner the donors – Sir John Donne, his wife Elizabeth, and their daughter Anne, along with two female saints – Catherine and Barbara – and two angels. One angel offers an apple to the Child and holds in the right hand a fiddle and bow, while the other angel plays a portative organ. The painting can be dated around 1480.

Lit.: National Gallery Catalogues. Acquisitions 1953-62, London, n.d., pp. 60-64.

72
MASTER OF THE HALF-LENGTH FIGURES. *Young Girl Playing the Lute.*
Painting on oak panel, 10 ⁵³/₆₄ x 8 ⁵/₆₄ in.
Brussels, private collection.
Authorized reproduction.

The Master of the Half-Length Figures is an unidentified artist of the first half of the sixteenth century, presumably Flemish. He gets his name from a series of half-length portraits of women who are often depicted as musicians, playing the lute or clavichord, as in the most famous of his works, the *Three Female Musicians*, of the Harrach Museum, Vienna.
Young Girl Playing the Lute, like most works of the same type, represents a Mary Magdalene as is proved by the covered vase, her characteristic symbol in paintings of the time. Before the lutenist there are two hand-written sheets of music on which can be made out the word *Jouyssance*, the first word of a poem by Marot set to music by many composers and, in the first place, by Claudin de Sermisy, whose version is reproduced in the painting in a reduction to tablature. The same piece appears in the painting of the three musicians in Vienna. It was printed for the first time by Attaingnant in Paris in 1528 as a four-voiced polyphonic piece, and was often reprinted in various forms, including a version for keyboard instruments.

Lit.: J.A. PARKINSON, A Chanson by Claudin de Sermisy, in Music and Letters, 1958, pp. 118-122. – L. VAN PUYVELDE, *La Peinture flamande au siècle de Bosch et Brueghel*, Paris, 1962, pp. 363-364. – Exhibition catalogue, *Le Siècle de Brueghel. La Peinture en Belgique au XVIᵉ siècle*, Brussels, 1963, no. 245.

73
ISRAËL VAN MECKENEM. *Two Musicians near a Fountain.*
Engraving, 6 ³⁷/₆₄ in. in diameter.
Paris, Bibliothèque Nationale, Print collection, no. Ea 48 b, Rés. B. 203.
Authorized reproduction.

Israël van Meckenem was born about 1450 in the Netherlands and died in 1503, after having lived most of his life in Germany. His works are rich in glimpses of aristocratic and middle-class life of his time. In this music-making by a fountain, the man plays a lute and the woman a harp.

Lit.: A.-J.-J. DELEN, Histoire de la gravure dans les anciens Pays-Bas et dans les provinces belges des origines jusqu'à la fin du XVIIIᵉ siècle, Paris, 1924, vol. I.

74
A Woman Playing the Portative Organ.
Drawing, 6 ¹¹/₁₆ x 7 ¹/₆₄ in.
Paris, Musée du Louvre, Drawing collection, no. 20676.
Authorized reproduction.

The headdress and clothing of the woman indicate a date around 1440.
The instrument is depicted with great precision, and all eighteen pipes are clearly visible.

Lit.: Y. ROKSETH, La Musique d'orgue au XVᵉ siècle et au début du XVIᵉ, Paris, 1930, p. 22.

75
RUCKERS. *Spinet-Harpsichord.*
Total length 86 ⁵/₈ in., maximum width 32 ¹/₄ in., height 49 ¹/₄ in.
Brussels, Musée du Conservatoire, no. 2935.
Authorized reproduction.

This instrument, made in the late sixteenth century by the famous Ruckers of Antwerp, is most unusual. By means of three keyboards, it combines a harpsichord and a spinet. Two superimposed keyboards for the harpsichord are placed on the narrow side of the rectangle while a third keyboard, for the spinet, is set up on one of the long sides. The painting on the inside of the lid is a modern copy of a painting by Martin De Vos (see plate 76).

Lit.: V.C. MAHILLON, Catalogue du Musée instrumental du Conservatoire de Bruxelles, Ghent, 1912, vol. IV, pp. 440-441.

76
MARTIN DE VOS. *Apollo and the Muses.*
Painting on oak panel, 17 ¹/₂ x 25 in.
Brussels, Musées Royaux des Beaux-Arts de Belgique, no. 3882.
Authorized reproduction.

Martin De Vos (1532-1605) was a painter of Antwerp who studied in Italy. There is no doubt that this panel was once the lid of a spinet. On it, Euterpe, the muse of music, stands before a spinet directing an ensemble of voices and instruments formed by the other muses and Apollo. Just as the costumes introduce antique details into the elegance typical of the end of the sixteenth century, so too there are certain instruments – spinet, fiddle, lute, cornett – which belong to that century, while others – Apollo's lyre and Terpsichore's harp – are vaguely archeological reconstructions. A curious note is the lid of the spinet painted by the artist which itself is decorated with a painting.

Lit. : L. van Puyvelde, *La Peinture flamande au siècle de Bosch et Brueghel*, Brussels, 1962, p. 283. – Exhibition catalogue, *Le Siècle de Bruegel. La Peinture en Belgique au XVIe siècle*, Brussels, 1963, p. 165, no. 236.

77
Hieronymus Bosch. *Garden of Delights.*
Oil on wood, fragment of the right wing of a triptych, 86 ⁵/₈ x 38 ¹/₄ in.
Madrid, Prado.
Authorized reproduction.

This famous painting is a highly moralistic work. The musical instruments – lute, harp, hurdy-gurdy, bombard, fife and drum, cornett – become here instruments of torture, punishing in Hell those who in life gave themselves too much to the pursuit of music or used it for immoral purposes.

Lit. : P. Fierens, *Le Fantastique dans l'art flamand*, Brussels, 1947, pp. 55-56. – L. van Puyvelde, *La Peinture flamande au siècle de Bosch et Brueghel*, Brussels, 1962, pp. 48-49.

78
Jan Cornelisz. Vermeyen. *Lady at a Clavichord.*
Preparatory drawing for an engraving, in pen and bister, 10 ²⁹/₃₂ x 8 ⁵/₃₂ in.
Berlin, Staatliches Museum, Engraving collection, K. d. z. 516.
Authorized reproduction.

Born in Beverwijk near Haarlem, Vermeyen died in Brussels in 1559, having first been in the service of Margaret of Austria and then worked for Charles V.

Lit. : A.-J.-J. Delen, *Histoire de la gravure dans les anciens Pays-Bas et dans les provinces belges jusqu'à la fin du XVIIIe siècle*, Paris, 1924-1935, 3 vols. – M. Davies, *National Gallery Catalogues. Early Netherlandish School*, 2nd ed., London, 1955. – Exhibition catalogue, *Charles-Quint et son temps*, Ghent, 1955, no. 202, pl. 104.

79
The Master of the Petrarch. *Emperor Maximilian Attends Mass at Augsburg.*
Woodcut, 11 ³/₁₆ x 8 ¹⁷/₆₄ in.
Vienna, Albertina, no. 1949/416.
Authorized reproduction.

Röttinger identifies the Master of the Petrarch as Hans Weiditz, an engraver who worked at Augsburg and Strasbourg and died in 1537.
On this engraving, which dates from around 1518, Maximilian is seen kneeling at mass. His chapel choir sings in polyphony, with six choirboys and four or five cantors gathered around a lectern which holds a large choir book. The only instrument in use is a regal – a small organ with reed pipes only – which is probably being played by Paul Hofhaimer, the court organist.

Lit. : H. Röttinger, *Hans Weiditz der Petrarcameister*, Strassburg, 1904, p. 13. – T. Musper, *Die Holzschnitte des Petrarcameisters*, Munich, 1927, p. 576. – M. Geisberg, *Der deutsche Einblatt-Holzschnitt in der ersten Hälfte des 16. Jahrhunderts*, Munich, 1930, p. 1524. – Exhibition catalogue, *Maximilian I, 1459-1519*, Vienna, 1959. – Exhibition catalogue, *Die Kunst der Graphik. Das Zeitalter Albrecht Dürers-Werke aus dem Besitz der Albertina*, Vienna, 1964, p. 59.

80
Hans Burgkmair. *Maximilian with His Musicians.*
Woodcut, 8 ³⁷/₆₄ x 7 ⁴³/₆₄ in.
Der Weißkunig, volume of proofs, fol. 142 v°.
Vienna, Österreichische Nationalbibliothek, Manuscript collection, no. 3032.
For *Der Weißkunig*, see notes on plate 62.
Authorized reproduction.

In the left background, there is a group of four singers bent over a music book and a cornett player. In the foreground, a man at the positive organ with another working the bellows, while one man plays the harp and another a spinet placed on a table. On the table, there are a fiddle, flutes, a cornett and music books, and on the ground a marine trumpet, a sackbut, a lute, a drum and a kettledrum.

81
Giorgione (?). *The Three Ages of Man.*
Oil on wood, 24 ³/₈ x 30 ³/₈ in.
Florence, Galleria Pitti.
Authorized reproduction.

This work has posed fascinating and difficult problems for art historians. It has been attributed in turn to Lorenzo Lotto, Sebastiano del Piombo, Giovanni Bellini and, most recently, to Giorgione.
The identification of the personages portrayed has been no less controversial. According to Vasari, the mature man to the right is the composer Verdelot (*Verdelotto Franzese musico eccelentissimo, che era allora maestro di cappella in S. Marco*) and the aged man is *Uberto suo compagno cantore*. It has been claimed that this refers to Jacob Obrecht, but this is not likely, and according to another hypothesis it is the young boy in the middle who is *Uberto* and who would be the musician from Liège Hubert Naich who lived in Italy and composed madrigals. All these hypotheses, however, are fragile, since it is not absolutely certain that Vasari's text refers to this particular painting.

Lit. : H. Prunières, *Un Portrait de Hobrecht et de Verdelot par Sebastiano del Piombo*, in *Revue musicale*, 1922. – A. Einstein, *The Italian Madrigal*, Princeton, 1949, vol. I, p. 155. – Exhibition catalogue, *Giorgione e i Giorgioneschi*, ed. P. Zampetti, Venice, 1955, no. 41. – P. Della Pergola, *Giorgione*, Milan, 1955, p. 64. – E. Sindona, *E Hubert Naich e non Jacob Hobrecht il compagno cantore del Verdelot nel quadro della Galleria Pitti*, in *Acta musicologica*, 1957, pp. 1-9. – J. Quitin, *A propos de Hubert Naich de Liège et d'un tableau de la Galleria Pitti à Florence*, in *Revue belge de musicologie*, 1957, pp. 134-140.

82
Portrait of Josquin Desprez.
Woodcut, 2 $^9/_{16}$ in. in diameter.
PETRUS OPMEER, *Opus chronographicum orbis universi*, Antwerp, 1611, p. 440.
Paris, Bibliothèque Nationale.
Authorized reproduction.

According to Opmeer, this engraving copies a portrait of Josquin Desprez which was on an altar in the choir of the Church of Sainte-Gudule in Brussels. This late and clumsy effigy is the only portrait known of the composer.

Lit.: H. OSTHOFF, *Josquin Desprez*, Tutzing, 1962, vol. I, pp. 75, 87, 237.

83
Tubal-cain.
Miniature, 9 $^{29}/_{64}$ x 6 $^{11}/_{16}$ in.
From a choir book, fol. C. IVb.
Florence, Biblioteca Nazionale, Banco Rari no. 229 (Magl. XIX 59.)
Authorized reproduction.

This miniature from an early sixteenth-century Florentine manuscript depicts Tubal-cain striking an anvil and thereby discovering the principle of the relationship between different pitches. The musical work on the page is by the Flemish composer Johannes Martini.
See notes for plate 17.

84
CRISTOFORO DE' PREDIS or SCHOOL. *Garden of Delights.*
Miniature, 6 $^{57}/_{64}$ x 5 $^{15}/_{32}$ in.
Codice "De Sphaera," fol. C 10 r°.
Modena, Biblioteca Estense, ms. 209.
Authorized reproduction.

This manuscript is of Lombard origin. Its miniatures may be dated before 1470 and are attributed to a Northern Italian artist influenced by the Flemish, often identified with Cristoforo de' Predis or his school.
Around the Fountain of Youth, people eat, drink, make love and make music. In the foreground there is a lutenist; at the back of the garden to the left two men and a boy unroll a scroll of music and sing, apparently in polyphony; in another group, to the right, there are three players of shawms and one of sackbut, the typical ensemble for music out-of-doors, and a little to the side a fifth instrumentalist plays fife and drum.

Lit.: Exhibition catalogue, *Arte lombarda dai Visconti agli Sforza*, Milan, 1958. – P. PULIATTI, *Il libra illustrato dal XIV al XVIII secolo nella Biblioteca Estense*, Modena, 1961. – S. SAMEK LUDOVICI, *Il "De Sphaera" estense e l'iconografia astrologica*, Milan, 1958.

85
Frontispiece to the Musica nova *of Adrian Willaert.*
Woodcut, 7 $^7/_8$ x 5 $^{33}/_{64}$ in.

Musica nova di Adriano Willaert, septima pars, title-page.
Paris, Bibliothèque Sainte-Geneviève, Vm 25.
Authorized reproduction.

This is the edition published by Gardane in 1559 at Venice.
See notes for plate 24.

86
HANS MUELICH. *Portrait of Cipriano de Rore.*
Miniature, 24 $^3/_8$ x 17 $^3/_8$ in.
From a musical manuscript, fol. 304.
Munich, Bayerische Staatsbibliothek, Mus. ms. B.
Authorized reproduction.

This splendid large manuscript was prepared for the chapel of the Duke of Bavaria. A native of Flanders, Cipriano de Rore lived mostly in Italy but returned to the Low Countries in 1558-59 and may have passed through Munich on the return voyage, at which time he may have sat for this very lifelike and realistic portrait. The same manuscript contains twenty-six of his motets ornamented by miniatures by Muelich.

Lit.: A.H. JOHNSON, *Rore*, in *Die Musik in Geschichte und Gegenwart*, vol. XI, cols. 897-901.

87
HANS MUELICH. *Portrait of Roland de Lassus at the Age of Twenty-eight.*
Gouache, 5 $^3/_{64}$ x 4 $^1/_4$ in.
From a musical manuscript, end of tenor part, fol. 36 r°.
Vienna, Österreichische Nationalbibliothek, Music collection, ms. mus. no. 18774.
Authorized reproduction.

The collection contains in four fascicles the soprano, alto, tenor and bass parts of two important works by Lassus, the *Prophetiæ Sibyllarum* and the *Lectiones ex propheta Job*. These are in the composer's own hand and are ornamented with numerous miniatures. At the end of each volume there is a portrait: *Orlandus de Lasso ætatis suæ XXVIII* (however, the portrait has been removed from the soprano part). The volume was prepared for the ducal chapel of Bavaria at Munich and must date from 1560 if the true birth date of Lassus is 1532.

Lit.: W. BOETTICHER, *Orlando di Lasso und seine Zeit*, Kassel-Basel, 1958, pp. 72, 836.

88
JEAN and LUCAS DUATECUM after JEROME WELLENS DE COCK.
The Funeral Ceremony of Charles V at Brussels.
Copperplate engraving and etching, 10 $^7/_{16}$ x 14 $^1/_4$ in.
La magnifique et sumptueuse pompe funèbre faite aux obsèques et funérailles du très grand et très victorieus empereur Charles cinquième, célébrées en la ville de Bruxelles le XXIX jour du mois de décembre. M.D.L. VIII par Philipe, roy catho-

319

lique d'Espaigne, son fils. A Anvers, de l'Imprimerie de Christophe Plantin, M.D.L.IX., page 6.
Brussels, Bibliothèque Royale de Belgique, no. II 8052 C.
Authorized reproduction.

The death of Charles V was the occasion for many ceremonies of which numerous accounts have survived. This work, published by Plantin in 1559, is devoted to the funeral service held in Brussels in December 1558. The various plates in the volume were designed by Jerome Wellens de Cock, and engraved by the Duatecum brothers. They depict the procession which went to the church of Sainte-Gudule. Following the clergy, come the musicians of the royal chapel with trumpeters and drummers.

Lit.: A.-J.-J. DELEN, Histoire de la gravure dans les anciens Pays-Bas et dans les provinces belges, Paris, 1924-1934, vol. II, 1. – J. JACQUOT, Panorama des fêtes et cérémonies du règne, in Les Fêtes de la Renaissance, II, Fêtes et cérémonies au temps de Charles-Quint, Paris, 1960, pp. 413-491.

89
HIERONYMUS BOSCH. The Concert Within the Egg (copy).
Oil on canvas, 42 3/4 x 49 13/16 in.
Lille, Musée des Beaux-Arts, no. 1020.
Authorized reproduction.

This is a sixteenth-century copy of a lost original. Inside an enormous egg shell, some ten personages sing under the direction of a monk and play the trumpet, harp and lute. However, on the open choir book one can read the text and music not of a mass or motet but of a profane song for four voices: Toutes les nuicts que sans vous je me couche, pensant à vous ("All the nights I go to bed without you, thinking of you"), an amorous song which thereby suggests satire and mockery. Moreover, the choristers wear headdresses and are surrounded by objects which symbolize heresy, deceit, licentiousness, and the egg itself suggests an alchemist's crucible. In other works, for instance the Ship of Fools and the Hay Wain, Bosch likewise gives to music a similar equivocal or diabolic significance.

Lit.: CH. DE TOLNAY, Hieronymus Bosch, Basel, 1937. – J. DION, Le Concert dans l'œuf, in Amis du Musée de Lille, 1954, no. 12. – J. COMBE, Jheronimus Bosch, Paris, 1957. – Exhibition catalogue, Le Siècle de Brueghel. La Peinture en Belgique au XVIe siècle, Brussels, 1963, no. 40.

90
Portrait of Adriaen Petit Coclico.
Woodcut, 6 7/64 x 4 23/32 in.
Compendium musices, fol. A 4 v°.
Authorized reproduction.

This portrait comes from the Compendium musices which Coclico published in Nuremberg in 1552, at which time, it is precisely stated, the author was fifty-two years old. He must have been born around 1500 in Flanders. He claimed to be a pupil of Josquin and to have been in the service of the kings of France and England, but none of this seems likely. It is known that he lived in Germany and was converted to Protestantism.

The Compendium musices is a short treatise full of practical information ignored by most other authors, notably about improvisation and musica reservata. On this engraved portrait, Coclico is depicted curiously like a gnome; there is also a brief perpetual canon on the words Desperando spero, the musician's personal motto.

Lit.: M. VAN CREVEL, Adrianus Petit Coclico, Leben und Beziehungen eines nach Deutschland emigrierten Josquinschülers, The Hague, 1940. – Facsimile edition of the Compendium musices edited by M. Bukofzer as vol. IX in the series of Documenta musicologica published by the International Association of Music Libraries, Kassel-Basel, 1954.

91
The Publisher Tielman Susato Presents One of His Works to Mary of Hungary, Governess of the Netherlands.
Woodcut, 2 3/4 x 2 31/64 in.
Vingt et six chansons musicales et nouvelles à cincq parties, convenables tant à la voix comme aussi propices à jouer de divers instrumens. Nouvellement imprimées en Anvers par Tielman Susato, correcteur et imprimeur de musique, Antwerp, 1543, reverse of title-page of tenor part.
Brussels, Bibliothèque Royale de Belgique, Fonds Fétis, no. 2310.
Authorized reproduction.

This collection is printed in four fascicles: superius, tenor, counter-tenor and bassus, the fifth voice being printed facing one of the other parts. On the back of the tenor part, there is a dedication to Mary of Hungary together with this woodcut on which one sees Mary of Hungary in her palace, seated on a throne and surrounded by courtiers, musicians and musical instruments (a harpsichord and a lute), with Tielman Susato offering to her his latest collection of chansons.

92
Ornamental letters.
Engraving, 3 11/32 x 3 11/32 in.
GEORGES DE LA HÈLE. Octo missæ quinque, sex et septem vocum, Antwerp, Christophe Plantin, 1578, fol. 67.
See No. 95.
Authorized reproduction.

Within the ornamental letters there are tiny angels playing various instruments: organ, harp, bagpipes, sackbut and shawm.

93
MASTER OF THE MONOGRAM F.I. Mass at the Court of Francis I of France.
Woodcut, 16 3/8 x 11 39/64 in.
PIERRE ATTAINGNANT. Secundus liber tres missas continet, Paris, 1532, title-page.
Vienna, Österreichische Nationalbibliothek.
Authorized reproduction.

This important publication by Pierre Attaingnant contains three polyphonic masses by Mouton, Sermisy and Manchicourt. The title-page shows a mass at the court of the King of

France, Francis I. Eight singers gather around a lectern to read from a large choir book. The engraving is marked with the monogram "F.I."

94

Hortus musarum.
Engraving, 12 $^9/_{32}$ x 7 $^7/_8$ in.
Hortus musarum in quo tanquam flosculi quidam selectissimorum carminum collecti sunt ex optimis quibusque auctoribus... Collectore Petro Phalesio..., Louvain, Pierre Phalèse, 1552, title-page.
Brussels, Bibliothèque du Conservatoire.
Authorized reproduction.

The *Hortus musarum* is among the most important of Pierre Phalèse's publications, containing in lute tablature original fantasies, arrangements of well-known polyphonic chansons and even of motets, and some pieces for two lutes. The group of nine female musicians in this title-page should not be considered a realistic picture of a musical ensemble of the time; it is merely the printer's mark and meant to be symbolic. As is evident, the group consists of Apollo playing the lute while surrounded by the nine Muses who sing or play : those to the left playing cornett, shawm, transverse flute, recorder, bass viol; those to the right, the harp and recorder.

Lit. : A. GOOVAERTS, *Histoire et bibliographie de la typographie musicale aux Pays-Bas*, Antwerp, 1880. – P. BERGMANS, *La Typographie musicale en Belgique au XVIe siècle*, Brussels, 1930.

95

Title-page for a Book of Music.
Engraving, 21 $^1/_4$ x 16 $^1/_8$ in.
GEORGES DE LA HÈLE. *Octo missæ quinque, sex et septem vocum*, Antwerp, Christophe Plantin, 1578, title-page.
Brussels, Bibliothèque Royale de Belgique, 7e cl., V. K. Dele, gr. fol.
Authorized reproduction.

While Plantin did not often publish polyphonic music, he occasionally produced an especially lavish volume of it, as in this collection of masses by Georges de la Hèle, his first such venture. The same title-page was employed for other works of the same type, notably for the masses by Alard du Gaucquier in 1581 and those by Philippe de Monte in 1587.

Lit. : J.A. STELLFELD, *Bibliographie des éditions musicales plantiniennes*, Brussels, 1949.

96

HANS BURGKMAIR. *The Cantors of Emperor Maximilian.*
Woodcut, 15 $^5/_8$ x 15 in.
Triomphe de l'Empereur Maximilien, fol. 29 v°, pl. 20.
Paris, Bibliothèque Nationale, Print collection, Pd 23, Rés., fol. obl.
Authorized reproduction.
See notes for plate 66.

97

HANS MUELICH. *A Chamber Concert at the Court of Bavaria in Munich.*
Miniature, 23 $^5/_8$ x 17 $^3/_4$ in.
From a large choir book, fol. 187.
Munich, Bayerische Staatsbibliothek, Mus. ms. A II.
Authorized reproduction.

The entire musical chapel of Munich is seen here in a hall of the palace. The vocal and instrumental ensemble is not directed by Roland de Lassus, who, instead, is pictured as a listener by the side of the Duke in the far left foreground. The director is probably the chapel organist, who is seen seated before a spinet set on a table. Around him there are some fifteen musicians with a large bass viol played standing, a viola da gamba of smaller size, a tenor viol held crosswise like a lute by the seated performer, four arm viols (viole da braccio) of which two are played by seated musicians seen here from the back and the others by two men standing, a lute, two cornetts, a bassoon, a transverse flute, a trombone, a shawm, and a recorder. There are three choirboys behind the spinet and some fifteen singers behind the instrumentalists. On the frame, there is a list of famous composers, which concludes with "Orlando di Lasus."
See notes for plate 98.

98

HANS MUELICH. *The Chapel Choir at Munich Under the Direction of Roland de Lassus.*
Miniature, 23 $^5/_6$ x 17 $^3/_4$ in.
From a large choir book, fol. 186.
Munich, Bayerische Staatsbibliothek, Mus. ms. A II.
Authorized reproduction.

This extremely lavish large choir book contains the *Penitential Psalms* by Roland de Lassus. The first volume was finished in 1565, the second, from which this miniature comes, in 1570. The musical chapel is gathered in the church of Sankt Lorenz in the ducal court. There are no instrumentalists, but about thirty singers and a half-dozen boy choristers gather around a lectern which holds a large choir book. Lassus stands to the left of the lectern and seems to be beating the tactus.

Lit. : W. BOETTICHER, *Orlando di Lasso und seine Zeit*, Kassel-Basel, 1958, pp. 342, 380-382.

99

JOHANN NEL. *Frontispiece for a Volume of Masses by Roland de Lassus.*
Engraving, 17 $^3/_4$ x 12 $^{19}/_{32}$ in.
Patrocinium musices : Missæ aliquot quinque vocum Orlandi de Lasso, Munich, Adam Berg, title-page.
Brussels, Bibliothèque Royale de Belgique, Fonds Fétis, no. 1649.
Authorized reproduction.

This is from the sixth volume of a collection of the works of Lassus undertaken by Adam Berg of which the first volume appeared in 1573, the next three in 1574, and the fifth in

1576. The same engraving is used for the title-pages of all the volumes. It depicts a concert of secular music, although this particular volume is devoted to religious works. The musicians are seated around a large table in a salon. There is a spinet set on the table, a viola da gamba to the left, a viola da braccio to the right, a lute, two trombones, a transverse flute, two shawms, and in the background three singers with two children who sing also near the table. This scene was a publisher's mark for Adam Berg and should not be taken literally as a guide to the interpretation of religious works by Lassus.

100
PIETER BRUEGEL. *Fall of the Rebel Angels.*
Oil on oak panel, 46 $^1/_8$ x 63 $^3/_4$ in.
Brussels, Musées Royaux des Beaux-Arts de Belgique, no. 584.
Authorized reproduction.

The painting is signed and dated "M.D.LXII. BRUEGEL." The theme is a familiar one, found as far back as miniatures in old manuscripts. In this general catastrophe in which all the vices are symbolized, musical instruments are thrown down together with monsters, beasts, fish, reptiles, birds, insects, plants, and a diversity of objects.

Lit.: R. GENAILLE, *Pierre Bruegel l'ancien*, Paris, 1953. – R.-L. DELEVOY, *Bruegel*, Geneva, 1959. – L. VAN PUYVELDE, *La Peinture flamande au siècle de Bosch et Brueghel*, Paris,

1962. – Exhibition catalogue, *Le Siècle de Bruegel. La Peinture en Belgique au XVIᵉ siècle*, Brussels, 1963, no. 52.

101 and 102
HANS MEMLING. *Four Angel Musicians.*
Gilded and polychromed oak, diameter of the medallions 4 $^{17}/_{32}$ in.
Reliquary of Saint Ursula, lunettes from the cover.
Bruges, Hôpital Saint-Jean.
Authorized reproduction.

The translation of the relics of Saint Ursula into this reliquary took place on October 21, 1489 at the Hôpital Saint-Jean in Bruges and in the presence of the Bishop of Tournai. The reliquary must therefore have been executed before that date. The angel musicians surround, on the one hand, Saint Ursula bearing the arrow of her martyrdom, on the other hand, the glorification of the Virgin. The four angels play respectively the portative organ, the lute, the fiddle and the psaltery. It is generally admitted that the painting of the cover was not done by Memling himself but by his pupils.

Lit.: G. MARLIER, *Memlinc*, Brussels, 1934. – L. LAMBOTTE, *Hans Memlinc, le Maître de la Châsse de Sainte-Ursule*, Antwerp-Amsterdam, 1939. – Exhibition catalogue, *Memlinc*, Bruges, 1939. – Exhibition catalogue, *Le Siècle des primitifs flamands*, Bruges, 1960.

A Glossary of Technical Terms

These definitions have been made deliberately as concise and simple as possible. They are intended to provide the reader who is not a professional musician with a brief guide to a vocabulary which, by nature, involves certain technicalities. The most important terms are explained in detail in the body of this book.

A CAPPELLA – A purely vocal ensemble without any instrumental accompaniment.

ACCIDENTAL – The temporary alteration of a note in the course of a piece by addition of a sharp, flat, or natural sign.

ACCOMPANIMENT – The harmonic support of one or more principal parts in a composition.

ALLEMANDE – A dance in duple rhythm and moderate tempo whose popularity began around 1550.

ALTERATION – 1. In ternary rhythm in mensural notation, the procedure of doubling systematically the value of two notes of equal value that follow each other. 2. Modification of the pitch of a tone by a sharp, flat, or natural sign.

ANTIPHON – A chant in the Catholic liturgy; a brief melody that is isolated or serves as a refrain in a psalm.

ANTIPHONARY – A book containing the chants of the various offices of the liturgical hours.

ARS ANTIQUA – The name given to the Parisian school of polyphony in the thirteenth century (composers Leoninus, Perotinus).

ARS NOVA – Title of a treatise by Philippe de Vitry; by extension, it also refers to the new style of the fourteenth century in France and Italy.

AUGMENTATION – In counterpoint and in the proportions of mensural notation, the procedure of increasing the value of the notes of a theme.

AUGMENTED – Applied to an interval increased by a chromatic semitone beyond the major; refers also to a chord using such an interval.

AUTHENTIC – A Gregorian mode whose entire range is below its final tone.

BAGPIPE – A folk instrument made up of several reed-pipes attached to a windbag (French, *cornemuse, musette*; Italian, *piva, zampogna*; German, *Dudelsack*).

BALLADE – Poetic and musical form which, in the fourteenth and fifteenth centuries, inspired many polyphonic works of subtle technique and great refinement.

BALLATA – Poetic and musical form used in Italy in the fourteenth century for both monodic and polyphonic compositions.

BALLET DE COUR – A type of ballet presented at the court of the King of France in the sixteenth and seventeenth centuries, employing both singing and dancing.

BASSE DANCE – A court dance of ceremonious character used in the fifteenth and early sixteenth centuries.

BERGERETTE – Poetic and musical form very popular in the second half of the fifteenth century; it is basically a virelai reduced to a single verse.

BICINIUM – A two-voiced contrapuntal piece intended primarily for teaching purposes.

BOMBARDE – The bass shawm.

BRANLE – A dance of peasant origin very popular in the sixteenth century.

BUYSINE – The medieval trumpet.

CACCIA – Fourteenth-century Italian musical form with two voices in canon above a tenor, generally using as text a description of a hunt.

CADENCE – Melodic or harmonic formula used in musical phrases to mark a half or full close.

CANON – A polyphonic piece in rigorous imitation; in the enigmatic canon, the directions are given in the form of a riddle.

CANONICAL HOURS – In the Catholic church, liturgical offices other than the mass.

CANTI CARNASCIALESCHI – Carnival songs in Renaissance Florence.

CANTICLE — In Catholic liturgy, psalmlike chants not using psalm texts.

CANTILENA – The name generally given in the fifteenth century to any secular polyphonic piece entirely invented by the composer and set to a poetic text.

CANTILLATION – Recited declamation in the Catholic liturgy; its use derives from the Jewish service.

CANTOR – A church singer, but also an ecclesiastical dignitary who presides over the religious service.

CANTUS FIRMUS – A pre-existing melody – fragment of plainchant or chanson, etc. – which serves as a basis for contrapuntal development.

CANTUS SUPER LIBRUM — "Singing on the book," that is, counterpoint improvised on the basis of a pre-existing melody.

CANZONE – At the end of the fifteenth century, a type of frottola; a century later, the *canzone alla francese* became an instrumental genre modeled after the polyphonic chanson.

323

CAROLE – Medieval round dance done outdoors by partners holding hands and forming a chain.

CHANSON – A poem in any form set in either monodic or polyphonic style.

CHITARRONE – The large bass lute in Italy.

CHOIR – 1. A vocal ensemble. 2. The chancel, the space surrounding the altar reserved for the singers.

CHOIR BOOK – Manuscript in large format used in the fifteenth and sixteenth centuries for sacred polyphony. It was placed on a lectern in the middle of the choir and the singers gathered around it. The voice-parts were written out separately from the top to the bottom of each page.

CHORALE – A Lutheran hymn.

CHORD – The combination of several tones produced simultaneously.

CHROMATICISM – The use of tones foreign to the diatonic scale. Cf. ACCIDENTAL, ALTERATION 2.

CLAVICHORD – A small keyboard instrument whose strings are struck.

CLAVIER – The keyboard of an instrument such as the organ or harpsichord, also called MANUAL.

CLEF – Sign placed at the beginning of the musical staff to regulate the pitch of the notes.

COBLA – Folk-music orchestra in Catalonia.

COLORATION – 1. In mensural notation, the procedure by which a note loses a third of its value. 2. Ornamentation of a melody.

CONSONANCE – Harmonious simultaneous combination of tones. Based on acoustical principles, consonance is nevertheless essentially an aesthetic conception. It tends to give a sensation of repose. The Middle Ages distinguished between perfect consonances (unison, octave, fifth, sometimes fourth) and imperfect ones (third, sixth).

CONTRALTO – Today the lowest female voice, but in the Renaissance it could also be a man's voice, sometimes that of a castrato, corresponding to the highest tenor voice.

CORNETT – Wind instrument used from the fifteenth to the seventeenth century consisting of a straight or curved wooden tube, pierced with finger-holes and equipped with a mouthpiece.

COUNTERPOINT – Superimposition on a given melody of one or several other melodies in conformity with certain rules.

COUNTER-TENOR – In polyphonic compositions of the fourteenth and the early fifteenth century, the third voice in a polyphony, in the same range as the tenor; later, it often took the lowest part, in the bass register, and served as a harmonic foundation for the work.

COURANTE – A dance which originated in Italy in the sixteenth century; it was in rapid tempo and, according to Arbeau, demanded large movements and even leaps.

CROMORNE – Double-reed wind instrument of the oboe family, like a shawm but with a curved tube.

DIATONIC – Applies to a natural scale using no accidentals, either sharp or flat, that is, like C major, and also all transpositions of such a scale to other pitches.

DIMINISHED – Term used for intervals reduced by a chromatic semitone below the minor.

DIMINUTION – 1. In mensural notation, indicates a proportion in which the value of the notes is reduced. 2. Formula for melodic ornamentation.

DISCANT – 1. Note-against-note counterpoint as distinguished from the melismatic style of the organum. 2. The upper voice in polyphony.

DISSONANCE – Combination of two or more tones which produces a psychological sensation of tension.

DOLCIAN – Double-reed wind instrument of the shawm family, also known as dolcino, dulcian and douçaine.

DRUM – Percussion instrument generally made of one or two membranes stretched over a cylindrical frame.

DULCIMER – Instrument similar to the psaltery but in which the strings are struck by small hammers.

ENSALADA – Spanish name for the quodlibet.

ESTAMPIE – A favorite dance of the thirteenth and fourteenth centuries.

FALSO BORDONE – Four-voiced harmonizations of Gregorian chant in a style derived from the fauxbourdon.

FAUXBOURDON – A type of polyphonic composition practiced around 1430 by Dufay, Binchois and a few others, in which the upper voice uses a Gregorian cantus firmus forced into a rhythmic mold, the lowest voice follows it in note-against-note counterpoint, and between them a voice part, not written out, merely follows the upper voice in rigid parallel motion at the interval of a fourth.

FLAGEOLET – A small whistle-flute somewhat similar to the recorder.

FLAT – An alteration sign used to lower note by a semitone.

FLUTE – A wind instrument consisting of a cylindrical tube with finger-holes; the recorder is blown directly at the end through a mouthpiece in the form of a beak, whereas the transverse flute is played by blowing across a hole in the side of the head of the instrument.

FRETS – Raised lines to indicate the semitones on the finger boards of lutes, viols and some other stringed instruments.

FRICASSÉE – French name for the quodlibet.

FROTTOLA – A polyphonic piece on a secular text in Italian at the end of the fifteenth and the beginning of the sixteenth century; a general term covering various forms.

GALLIARD – A sixteenth-century dance in rapid tempo and triple rhythm (French, *gaillarde*; Italian, *gagliarda*).

GRADUAL – 1. A chant used in the Proper of the mass. 2. Liturgical book containing the chants of the Proper of the mass.

GREGORIAN CHANT — The musical repertory of the Roman Catholic liturgy which took its name from Pope Gregory the Great (590-604) who is believed to have had an important part in organizing and codifying the liturgy.

GUIDONIAN HAND — A mnemonic procedure said to have originated with Guido d'Arezzo which helps to memorize the names of the notes and to indicate the mutations in solmization.

HARMONY — 1. "An ordering of the parts of a whole in such fashion as to work toward the same end" (Littré). 2. Relationships which govern the hearing of tones produced simultaneously. 3. Art of linking chords in succession.

HARPSICHORD — Instrument with plucked strings arranged perpendicularly to a keyboard; it may have several registers and more than one keyboard (manual).

HEXACHORD — A scale with six tones; in the Middle Ages, this scale included only one semitone which was always placed between the third and fourth degrees.

HIGH INSTRUMENT — In the medieval classification, an instrument with powerful sonority such as the trumpet.

HOCKET — A procedure used in primitive polyphony and often employed in the thirteenth and fourteenth centuries in which a melodic line is split up between two or more voices which alternately sing tiny fragments of it.

HOMORHYTHM — The simultaneous use of the same rhythm in all the parts of a polyphonic piece.

HORN — Wind instrument consisting of a circular tube of conical bore provided with a mouthpiece.

HURDY-GURDY — A folk instrument with both bowed strings and a keyboard.

HYMN — In Christian liturgy, a piece of poetry divided into stanzas.

IMITATION — Procedure used in contrapuntal writing in which a melodic phrase announced by one voice is repeated by other voices at some other interval which may or may not be rigorously determined by the form used.

IMITATIVE-SYNTACTIC STYLE — A compositional procedure using imitation systematically, in a manner particularly favored by Gombert and his successors in the Netherlands.

IMPERFECTION — In mensural notation, indicates a binary unit of measure.

IMPROVISATION — Invention and performance without the use of written-out music.

INTERVAL — The distance which separates two tones, as tone, semitone, third, fourth, fifth, sixth, seventh, octave, etc.

INTROIT — A chant of the Proper of the mass.

ISORHYTHM — Compositional procedure employed especially in the fourteenth-century motet but which persisted until the sixteenth century : a rhythmic schema is imposed in advance on the *cantus firmus* and, sometimes, on the other contrapuntal voices.

KEY SIGNATURE — The group of accidentals noted at the beginning of the staff to indicate the overall tonality of the piece.

LAMENTATIONS OF JEREMIAH — Chants or polyphonic pieces sung during the Tenebrae services of Holy Week.

LAUDA — In Italy, a canticle in the vernacular which may be either monodic or polyphonic, in which latter case in a simple chordal style, and most often with a text in praise of the Virgin.

LAUDS — One of the canonical hours.

LEADING TONE — In music of the so-called classical period, the seventh degree of the scale which is never more than a semitone distant from the tonic; in medieval music, however, there are two leading-tones : not only the note immediately below the final tone (the tonic) but also the note immediately below the dominant (the fifth degree of the scale) which is converted into a semitone.

LIED — A chanson using a Flemish or German text.

LIGATURE — A notational sign first used in plain-chant and then in mensural music. It groups two or more notes under a single sign.

LIRA DA BRACCIO — An instrument belonging to the violin family used in Italy in the fifteenth and sixteenth centuries. It has supplementary strings which vibrate in sympathy with those bowed.

LOW INSTRUMENT — In the medieval classification, a musical instrument of soft sonority such as the lute or fiddle.

LUTE — An instrument with plucked strings stretched over a fretted neck and with a resonating body in the shape of a halved pear.

MADRIGAL — A musical form used in Italy in the fourteenth century whose structure is based on that of its text, always secular. It must be distinguished from the madrigal created around 1530 in Italy that became popular throughout Europe and has no fixed form whatsoever, its music being "a continuous composition without refrain or repetition of verses strictly adapted to the accents of the words and to the expression of the sentiments of the text" (Nanie Bridgman).

MADRIGALISM — A type of procedure used in sixteenth-century madrigals to bring out the meaning of the text through musical means.

MAGNIFICAT — Canticle of the Virgin sung at Vespers.

MAJOR — 1. Applied to the mode, in classical music it involves always semitones between the third and fourth and between the seventh and eighth degrees of the scale. 2. Applied to intervals, it indicates the interval which is a semitone larger than the minor interval.

MANICHORD or MANICORDION — Another name for the clavichord.

MASQUE — The English equivalent of the French ballet de cour.

MASS — Central liturgical ceremony of the Christian service which, musically, includes recitations (cantillations) and chants for the Ordinary and the Proper.

MATINS — One of the canonical hours.

325

MELISMA – An ornamented melodic formula sung to a single syllable of text.

MELODY – A series of tones organized in pitch and duration which can be perceived as a coherent whole.

MENSURAL MUSIC – In opposition to plain-chant, music whose rhythmic note-values are specified; generally refers to polyphonic music.

MINOR – 1. Applied to the mode, in classical music it is characterized by the position of the semitones between the second and third and the sixth and seventh degrees of the scale. 2. Applied to intervals, it indicates the interval smaller than the major.

MINSTREL – A musician who performed songs or dances and who was either independent or attached to a city or the court of a prince.

MISSAL – A volume containing all the texts recited and sung in the mass.

MODE – 1. In a general sense, it indicates the relative disposition of the intervals in relation to a basic tone in a musical scale; in plain-chant the mode is characterized by certain melodic formulas and also by the position of the intervals in relation to the final tone. 2. In mensural notation, the mode indicates how the longa is divided into breves : the mode is perfect when the longa contains three breves, imperfect when it contains only two.

MODULATION – Literally it should mean a change of mode, but in practice in classical harmony it designates the passage from one key to another.

MONOCHORD – A musical instrument with a single string and a movable fret, used only to measure intervals.

MONODY – A piece for a single voice, sung or played.

MORESQUE – A pantomimic dance which often took on a comic character.

MOTET – Type of polyphonic piece varying considerably in both content and form in various periods. Originally it was based on a *cantus firmus* and each of its voices had a different text whose subject might be profane, but in the fifteenth and sixteenth centuries it was most often a polyphonic work on a religious text.

MOTETTI MISSALES – Motets which could be used to replace certain chants of the mass.

MUSETTE – A kind of bagpipe.

MUSICA FICTA – In medieval and renaissance music, the practice of raising or lowering certain written-out notes of a melody by a semitone which is, itself, not written out but whose use naturally obeys strictly certain rules of solmization or counterpoint.

MUSICA PLANA – Plain-chant.

MUSICA RESERVATA – In mid-sixteenth century, in the Germanic countries, the term probably designated a music of new tendencies which made much use of chromaticism and which were particularly concerned with expressing the meaning of the text.

MUTATION – Passage from one hexachord to another in solmization.

MYSTERY – Medieval dramatic work on a religious subject such as some biblical episode or the life of Christ.

NAKERS – Small medieval kettle-drums.

NEUME – Originally designated a brief characteristic melody in Gregorian chant, and later came to mean the graphic representation of that melody by a sign; the name is used for the early primitive type of musical notation.

OBOE – Woodwind instrument of conical bore and double-reed mouthpiece.

OFFICE – The ensemble of chants and prayers imposed by the Catholic liturgy outside of the mass.

OLIPHANT – A horn made of ivory.

OMMEGANG – In the cities of Flanders and Brabant, a procession in which the religious and municipal authorities, the confraternities, corporations, etc., participated.

ORDINARY – Those chants in the mass whose texts are invariable : the Kyrie, Gloria, Credo, Sanctus, Agnus Dei, Ite, missa est or Benedicamus Domino; these are the sections most often composed in polyphony and together constitute, musically speaking, the mass.

ORGAN – A wind instrument made up of many pipes plus one or more keyboards. The portative organ (in Italian, *organetto*) was a very small instrument played with the right hand while the left operated the bellows. The positive organ was an instrument of moderate size placed on a table or on the floor; in the Middle Ages, it was often to be found in the choir of churches while the great organ was set up in a tribune or choir-loft.

ORGANUM – Primitive form of polyphony in which one or more melodies were added to a pre-existing melody, all of them using the same text.

PARODY – Compositional procedure used especially for the mass in the sixteenth century in which the work was constructed on the basis of a pre-existing polyphonic motet, madrigal or chanson.

PASSION – The solemn recitation of the Passion is part of the liturgy for Holy Week; polyphonic settings of all or part of the Passion were frequent.

PAVANE – A slow and ceremonious dance in duple rhythm which was very popular in the sixteenth century.

PERFECTION – In mensural notation, indicates a triple unit of measure, considered perfect because of the symbol of the Trinity.

PLAGAL – A Gregorian mode whose range extends below and above its final tone.

PLAIN-CHANT – Name given in the thirteenth century to Gregorian chant to distinguish it from mensural music.

POLYCHORALITY – Use of several choral ensembles within a single work.

326

POLYRHYTHM – Superposition of different rhythmic structures.

POSE – A musical interlude in a medieval mystery.

PROLATION – In mensural notation, the division of the semibreve into minims.

PROPER – All those chants in the mass whose texts vary according to the feast being celebrated : Introit, Gradual, Tract, Alleluia, Offertory, Communion; there is also a Proper for the liturgical offices.

PSALM – Principal prayer of the Synagogue, it entered into the Catholic liturgy with a Latin text. The Biblical Psalms were often given polyphonic settings, and during the Reformation were translated into the vernacular and, provided with simpler music, came to constitute the principal element in the liturgy of most Reformed churches.

PSALMODY – Recitation of the Psalms in the liturgy; its forms are infinitely more varied and richer than one would suppose from the association with monotonous recitation the word seems to have acquired.

PSALTER – Volume containing the Book of Psalms.

PSALTERY – A trapezoid-shaped instrument whose strings, stretched the length of a flat soundboard, are plucked with the fingers or a plectrum.

QUODLIBET – A polyphonic potpourri in which fragments of popular tunes were juxtaposed; known as Fricassée in France and Ensalada in Spain.

REBEC – Small pear-shaped instrument with bowed strings.

REED – A thin piece of reed or some other material used in the mouthpiece of certain wind instruments.

REGISTER – That part of the scale or range which has a homogeneous sonority.

REQUIEM – First word of the Introit of the mass for the dead, so by extension that mass itself.

RES FACTA – "The thing done" : applied to counterpoint entirely written out in contrast to *Cantus super librum*, that is, improvisation.

RESPOND or RESPONSORIUM – Piece in the liturgical repertory used in the mass (Gradual) and in the Nocturne of Matins and the early canonical hours.

RHYTHM – The organization of sound in time.

RICERCARE – Form of instrumental music using imitation and modeled after the motet.

RONDEAU – French poetic and musical form which, up to the fifteenth century, was used for many polyphonic compositions.

ROUND DANCE – Lively sixteenth-century dance in duple rhythm and of folk origin.

RUBATO – Expressive interpretation in which certain notes are accelerated, others slowed down, while maintaining the general movement of the phrase in its dynamic rigor.

SACKBUT – A bass trumpet with a slide, that is, the medieval trombone.

SCALE – Disposition of the sounds used according to their pitch.

SCORE – Notation of a musical work in which all the different voices are placed one above the other on staves on which the bar-lines are indicated.

SEQUENCE – A melody often provided with a poetic text which is added to an Alleluia in plain-chant; also designates the repetition of an easily recognizable melodic motif on different degrees of the scale; in the most general sense, the succession of characteristic motifs.

SHAWM – A kind of oboe (French, *chalumeau*; German, *Schalmei*; Italian, *cialamello*).

SILETE – A musical interlude in a medieval mystery.

SOLFEGGIO – In singing, the use of the mnemonic syllables do (ut), re, mi, fa, sol, la, si.

SOLMIZATION – System of solfeggio used in the Middle Ages and the Renaissance which was based on hexachords, that is, on six syllables only (ut, re, mi, fa, sol, la) and not on seven as was the later practice.

SOUTERLIEDEKENS – Psalms translated into Flemish and set to music.

SPINET – Instrument with plucked strings arranged parallel to the keyboard.

STABAT MATER – A strophic poem on the Seven Sorrows of the Virgin at the foot of the Cross.

STILE NUOVO – The style which dominated at the beginning of the seventeenth century in which accompanied monody won out over the older contrapuntal technique.

STRAMBOTTO – A variety of the frottola though of more serious character. The music is adapted to a poem with a fixed form of eight-line stanzas.

SUPERIUS – The highest part in a vocal ensemble.

SYNCOPATION – A rhythmic displacing of the regular beat by putting greater emphasis on a normally weak beat than on the strong beat which follows it.

TABLATURE – A notational system used for instruments like the lute and organ which instead of notes employs letters, numbers and other symbols.

TABOR – A small cylindrical drum with two membranes played with one hand while the other plays a flageolet or fife.

TACTUS – The rhythmic beat.

TEMPUS – In mensural notation, the division of the breve into semi-breves.

TENOR – 1. In plain-chant, the central note around which psalmodic recitation or cantillation gravitates. 2. A basic melody used as the point of departure for contrapuntal elaboration, either a pre-existing melody (*cantus firmus*) or a melody invented by the composer. 3. Later, the name was used for one of the voices in a polyphonic ensemble. 4. From this it came to be applied to the highest male voice which normally sang that part.

TESSITURA – The normal range of a voice or instrument.

THEME – Characteristic melodic or rhythmic fragment serving as a basis for the development of a composition.

TIMBRE – The characteristic "color" of a voice, an instrument or an ensemble.

TIMPANI – Percussion instruments made up of a membrane stretched over a hemispheric shell, usually of metal; generally known as kettledrums.

TONALITY – In Western music, the organized system of the degrees of the scale in function of the tonic (first degree) and the dominant (fifth degree).

TONARIUM or TONALE – Liturgical volume in which the pieces are classified according to their tones, that is, their musical modes.

TONE – 1. In Western music, interval determining the division of the scale. 2. In plain-chant, the liturgical tone used for psalmodic recitation is exactly equivalent to the mode.

TONIC – The fundamental note of a scale or mode, usually the first degree.

TRANSPOSITION – "Mutation by an identical change of pitch of all the elements of a musical ensemble" (E. Costère).

TRITONE – Interval of a fourth when made up of three full tones which, because of its harshness, was banned by the theorists from both melody and harmony.

TROMBA MARINA – Instrument generally made up of a single string stretched across a pyramidal soundbox which was bowed; literally, "marine trumpet."

TROMBONE – The bass trumpet.

TROPE – Ornamentation of a liturgical chant by interpolation, addition or amplification.

TRUMPET – Wind instrument made of a straight or curved metal tube with a mouthpiece.

TUTTI – The total ensemble of the forces used to perform a work.

UNISON – The absence of an interval between two notes; identity.

VARIATION – Modification of a musical theme affecting its melody, rhythm, harmony or instrumentation.

VESPERS – Constitutes with lauds one of the great canonical hours; it is sung at sunset, and from the standpoint of music the principal piece is the Magnificat.

VIÈLE – Instrument with a finger board and bowed strings; the medieval fiddle.

VILLANCICO – A Spanish musical and poetic genre.

VILLANELLA – A polyphonic piece of popular character in Italy in the sixteenth and seventeenth centuries.

VIOL – Family of bowed stringed instruments. The strings are more numerous than in the violin family and the finger board is equipped with frets. The viola da gamba is the largest of these and is held between the legs.

VIOLIN – Family of bowed stringed instruments whose four strings are stretched along a finger board without frets.

VIRELAI – Poetic and musical form used by the trouvères beginning in the thirteenth century, often employed for polyphonic compositions but declined in the course of the fifteenth century.

VIRGINAL – The English form of the spinet.

VOLTA – Dance of Italian origin often accused, in the sixteenth century, of being too daring and even indecent.

Discography

In our days, a book on the history of music is simply not complete without a list of phonograph records. The problem is to make it a practical and useful list. Record lending libraries are few, and recordings are dropped from current catalogues with no plans for re-pressing. On the other hand, each month brings a new crop of recordings onto the market, so that no matter how carefully a list has been compiled, it risks being out of date before it is printed.

The present list was originally prepared by Mr. Bernard Huys of the Bibliothèque Royale in Brussels. It shows at least what was available in 1968 of those works relevant to the history of Flemish music. In addition, it lists a few recordings now out of print but of such value that one can only hope for a re-edition.

The names, symbols or catalogue numbers of certain manufacturers vary among the Continent, Great Britain and the United States, but dealers should be able to identify the records on this list from the information given.

ABBREVIATIONS AND SYMBOLS USED :

*	Stereo	DGG, AP	Deutsche Grammophon Gesellschaft, Archiv Produktion	OIS.	Oiseau-Lyre
ACAD.	Academy			O L	Orbis Lexikon. Klingende
ALLO	Allegro				Musikgeschichte, Amaltea
ALPHA	Alpha	DOV.	Dover		Schallplatten Gesellschaft,
AM C	American Columbia	DUCR. TH.	Ducretet Thomson		musical examples for the
AMAD.	Amadeo	EA	Expériences Anonymes		*Handbuch der Musik.*
AMS	Archives sonores de la musique sacrée	EMS	Elaine Music Shop	ORYX	Oryx
		EPIC	Epic	PAT.	Pathé
ARGO	Argo	ER.	Erato	PER.	Period
A S	Anthologie sonore	EV.	Everest	PHIL.	Philips
BAM	Boîte à musique	FEST.	Festival	POL.	Polydor
C	Columbia	G	H.M.V. (Gramophone Co.)	RSS.	(British) Record Society
CBS	CBS	GIO A	Gregorian Institute of America	SEL.	Selmer or Ducretet-Selmer
C E	Classic Editions			SEMS	Société de l'Edition de Musique Sacrée
CAM.	Camerata	H M	Harmonia mundi		
CANT.	Cantate	HÉB.	Hébertot	S M	Studio S.M.
CHR.	Christschall	JER.	Jericho	SUP.	Supraphon
CH. M.	Chant du Monde	KINGS.	Kingsway	T	Telefunken
CFD	Club français du disque	LUM.	Lumen	TEC.	Technichord
CID	Compagnie industrielle du disque	LYR.	Lyrichord	TURN.	Turnabout
		MG	Music Guild	VAL.	Valois
CND	Le club national du disque	MON.	Monitor	VAN.	Vanguard
CONTR.	Contrepoint	MUS	Musicraft	VE.	Vega
CPT	Counterpoint	NIXA	Nixa	VIC.	Victor
CRO.	Crossroads	NON.	Nonesuch	V	Vox
D	Decca	OD.	Odeon	WEST.	Westminster
D FR.	Discophiles français	ODY.	Odyssey	WS	(Philips) World Series

AGRICOLA, Alexander

CHANSONS :
De tous biens playne — D Fr. 330222
D'ung aultre amer — D Fr. 330222

ARCADELT, Jacques

CHANSONS :
Margot, labourez les vignes — Er. 42021
Quand je vous ayme — Sup. 20009

MADRIGALS :
Il bianco e dolce cigno — Mus. 213; Sup. SUF 20009; Vic. 10-004
O felici occhi miei — Brun. SXA 4538 * (D. DL 710103 *); Cam. 17034; Non. H-71097 *

Sapet'amanti — Cam. 17034; Non. H-71097 *
Voi mi ponest'in foco — Allo set AL 14; G. CLP 1847
Voi ve n'andate — Cam. 17034; Non H-71097 *

BASTON, Josquin

LIED :
Verheugt u nu — HM 25306

BERCHEM, Jachet

MOTET :
O Jesu Christe — Er. EJA 11; Pat. PDT 273; Per. SPL 597

BINCHOIS, Gilles

CHANSONS :
Adieu, adieu mon joieulx souvenir — AS 3012; Amad. 5028; G. HQS 1041 *; Van. BG 634
Amoreux suy — Amad. 5028; Van. BG 634
Amour merchi — Amad. 5028; Van. BG 634
De plus en plus — AS 39; Amad. 5028; CND 9; T. SAWT 9466 *; Van. BG 634
Deul angoisseux, rage desmurée — Non. H-71010 *
Filles à marier — Amad. 5028; G. HLP 6 (Vic. LM 6016); Non. H-71058 *; T. SAWT 9466 *

Je loe amours — Amad. 5028; Non. H-71058 *; Van. BG 634
Marguerite, fleur de valeur — D Fr. 330222
Mon cœur chante — D Fr. 330222
Mon seul et souverain desire — G. HQS 1041 *
Triste plaisir — Amad. 5028; Van. BG 634

HYMN :
Beata nobis gaudia — Amad. 5028; Van. BG 634

MAGNIFICAT :
Magnificat primi toni — Non. H-71058 *

MASS :
Mass — Ois. OL 50104
Agnus Dei — Amad. 5028; Van. BG 634

MOTET :
Ave verum corpus — SEMS 37

BRUMEL, Antoine

Bicinium (organ) — Sup. SUAST 50548 *
Mater patris et filia — Non. H-71012 *
Missa Beata Virgine — D Fr. 11
Noe noe (instr.) — DGG, AP 14823 (198323 *) (ARC 3223)
O Domine Jesu Christe — T. SAWT 9471 *
Tandernac (instr.) — DGG, AP 14823 (198323 *) (ARC 3223)

BUSNOIS, Antoine

CHANSONS :
  Bel acueil   *Non.* H-71058 *
  Pucelotte (instr.)   *Non.* H-71010 *
  Seule à par moy   *D Fr.* 330222

MOTET :
  In hydraulis   *Non.* H-71058 *

CICONIA, Johannes

ITALIAN SONGS :
  Cacciando un giorno   *G.* HN 1870
  I cani sono fuera   *EA* 83
  O rosa bella   *G.* HLP 6 (*Vic.* LM 6016)
  Una panthera in compagnia di Marte *Allo* ALG 3029

CLEMENS NON PAPA

CHANSONS :
  Aymer est ma vie   *Phil.* 432605; *A S* 36; *D Fr.* 330224
  Misericordia au martyr   *West.* XWN 18683
  Puisque voulez   *Per.* SPL 738; *West.* XWN 18683
  Une fillette bien gorrière   *D. Fr.* 330224

SOUTERLIEDEKENS :
  Als ik riep met verlangen (Ps. 4)   *Cant.* 1116
  Aanhoort, mijn volk (Ps. 78)
  Here, lieve Here (Ps. 60)
  Hoort myn gebed, o Here (Ps. 102)
  O God, aanhort mijn klagen (Ps. 54)

COMPERE, Loyset

  Che fa la Ramacina ?   *Non.* H-71010 *
  Ne doibt-on prendre   *Non.* H-71010 *
  Nous sommes de l'ordre de Saint Babouin *G.* HLPS 7 (*Vic.* LM 6016); *Non.* H-71012 *
  Un franc archer   *Non.* H-71012 *

CRECQUILLON, Thomas

CHANSONS :
  Alix avoit aux dents   *Per.* SPL 738
  L'Ardent amour   *Per.* SPL 738; *West.* XWN 18683
  A vous en est   *D Fr.* 330224; *West.* XWN 18683
  Cessez, mes yeux   *West.* XWN 18683
  Je suis aimé de la plus belle   *D Fr.* 330224; *Ducr. Th.* 270 C 115; *West.* XWN 18683
  Plaisir n'ay plus   *D Fr.* 330224
  Puisque malheur me tient   *West.* XWN 18683
  Quand me souvient   *Ducr. Th.* LAP 1021; *Ois.* OL 50104; *West.* WL 5085. *West.*
                 XWN 18682

MOTETS :
  Cæsaris auspiciis magni   *CFD* 148; *Non.* H-71051 *
  Erravi sicut ovis   *CFD* 148; *Non.* H-71051 *
  Quæ est ista   *Ve.,* C 30 S 261
  Salve crux sancta   *CFD* 148; *Non.* H-71051 *
  Verbum caro factum est   *SM* 33-60

DESPREZ, Josquin

MASSES :
  Ave Maris Stella : Kyrie, Agnus Dei *GIOA* set PM 1
  Da pacem : Et incarnatus est   *Amad.* AVRS 5008

De beata Virgine	*D Fr.* 730063
Hercules dux Ferrariæ	*Lum.* AMS 4; RSS 10* (*MG* MS-134*)
Hercules : Kyrie	AS 73
Hercules : Sanctus	C WSX 502
L'Homme armé	*Cro.* 22160094 *
L'Homme armé : Gloria	G. W 1514
L'Homme armé : Sanctus	G. HLP 6 (*Vic.* LM 6016)
Pange lingua	DGG, AP 14171 (AP 198171 *); DGG, AP 14659 (ARC 3159); D. DL 79410 *; Er. 42075
Pange lingua : Sanctus	*Chr.* 119
MOTETS :	
Alma Redemptoris Mater; Ave Regina Cœlorum	*T.* SAWT 9480 *
Ave Christe immolate	*Cam.* 17014; G. GY 213; *Non.* H-71084 *; *T.* SAWT 9480 *; *Vox* DL 580
Ave Maria	*Cro.* 22160094 *; *Nixa* CLP 47; *Per.* SPLP 535; *Per.* SPL 597; *Od.* EMS 48; *Phil.* N 00678 R (*Epic* LC 3045); S M 25.03; *T.* SAWT 9480 *
Ave Maria : Ave vera virginitas	C. LX 767 (*Am C.* 69693)
Benedicta es coelorum Regina	S M 25.03; *T.* SAWT 9480 *
De profundis	*Amad.* AVRS 5008; *Nixa* CLP 47
Dominus regnavit	*Vox* DL 580
Dulces exuviæ	D. DL 79410 * (*Brun.* SXA 4004 *)
Fama malum	D. DL 79410* (*Brun.* SXA 4004 *)
Misericordias Domini in æternum cantabo	CPT 5546; *Lum.* AMS 4
Miserere	A S 107/8; *Argo* RG 90; RS 29
O Domine Jesu Christe	C. RFX 73
O Jesu fili David	*Vox* DL 580
Planxit autum David	*T.* SAWT 9480 *
Præter rerum seriem	S M 25.03
Stabat Mater	A S 73; S M 25.03; *T.* SAWT 9480 *
Tribulatio et angustia	G. HLP 6 (*Vic.* LM 6016)
Tulerunt Dominum meum	*Vox* DL 580; *Cro.* 22160094 *
Tu pauperum refugium	C. RFX 71
Tu solus qui facis mirabilia	D. DL 79410 * (*Brun.* SXA 4004 *); *Per.* SPL 597
Veni Creator Spiritus	*Fest.* 70-202
Vultum tuum deprecabentur	*D Fr.* 84/7; *D. Fr.* set 19
CHANSONS :	
Adieu mes amours	*Ang.* S-36379 *; G. HQS 1045 *; *Non.* H-71012 *
Allégez-moy	*D Fr.* 31/4; EMS 213; *Non.* H-71012 *
Baisez-moy	*D Fr.* 31/4; DGG, AP 14171 (198171*); EMS 213; *Mus* 212
Bergerette savoyenne	DGG, AP 14171 (198171 *); DGG, AP 14659 (ARC 3159); EMS 213; *Vox* DL 580
Cœurs langoureulx	*D Fr.* 31/4
Cœurs désolez	C. ID 33007; *Allo,* AL 17; G. HQS 1041 *
Déploration de Johannes Okeghem	BAM 040; D Fr. 330022; DGG. AP 14171 (198171 *); DGG, AP 14659 (ARC 3159); EMS 213; *Ev.* SDBR 3174 *; *Van.* BG 70671 *
Douleur me bat	EMS 213
Faulte d'argent	DGG, AP 14171 (198171 *); DGG, AP 14659 (ARC 3159); EMS 213
Fortuna d'un gran tempo (instr.)	DGG, AP 14659 (ARC 3159); EMS 213
Incessament livré suis	*D Fr.* 31/4
Incessament mon povre cœur lamente	EMS 213
J'ay bien cause de lamenter	*D Fr.* 31/4; G. HQS 1045 *
Je me complains de mon ami	*D Fr.* 31/4; EMS 213
Je ne puis me tenir d'aymer	G. HLP 6 (*Vic.* LM 6016)
Mille regretz	*Acad.* 308; CPT 514; *Cro.* 22160094 *; Er. 42021; D. DL 9629; G. HQS 1041 *; *Héb.* 2046

N'esse pas ung grant desplaisir	DGG, AP 14171 (198171 *); DGG, AP 14659 (ARC 3159); D. Fr. 31/4; EMS 213
Parfons regretz	DGG, AP 14171 (198171 *); D Fr. 31/4; EMS 213; Van. BG 70671 *; Vox DL 580
Petite camusette	D Fr. 33022; EMS 213
Pleine de deuil	D Fr. 31/4
Plus nulz regretz	Ang. S-36379 *; G. HQS 1045 *
Pour souhaitter (instr.)	EMS 213
Si j'ay perdu mon ami	Non H-71012 *
Tenez-moy en vos bras	D Fr. 31/4

FROTTOLAS :

Il grillo	G. HLP 6 (Vic. LM 6016); Phil. N 00678 R (Epic LC 3263); Vic. VICS 1231 *
Scaramella	DGG, AP 14171 (19871 *); A S 2501 L D

INSTRUMENTAL WORKS :

La Bernardina	D. DL 79410 * (Brun. SXA 4004 *)
Canzone (organ)	Contr. MC 20069; Nixa PLP 239
Coment peult	DGG, AP 14823 (198823 *) (ARC 3223)
Fantasias	Allo ALG 14
Vive le roi	D. DL 79410 * (Brun. SXA 4004 *); Non. H-71012 *

DUFAY, Guillaume

MASSES :

Caput	Lyr. 7190 *; Ois. OL 50069
L'Homme armé	Lyr. 7150 *; Oryx 722
L'Homme armé : Kyrie	G. W 1513
Se la face ay pâle	Amad. AVRS 5026; HM HMSt 530683 *; Van. BG 70653 *
Se la face ay pâle : Kyrie	A S 35; Vox. STDL 500.990 *
Se la face ay pâle : Hosanna	Amad. AVRS 5028; Non. H-71058 *; Van. BG 634
Se la face ay pâle : Sanctus	Vox. STDL 500.990 *
Missa sine nomine	Er. LDE 3023
Missa sine nomine : Kyrie	Allo AL 14
Gloria ad modum tubæ	Amad. AVRS 6163; T. SAWT 9439 *; Van. BG 582
Kyrie paschale "lux et origo"	T. SAWT 9439 *
Sanctus papale	Amad. AVRS 6163; T. SAWT 9439 *; Van. BG 582
Alleluia veni sancte spiritus	Non. H-71171 *

ANTIPHON :

Alma Redemptoris Mater	A S 35; DGG, AP 14019; DGG, AP 14537 (ARC 3003); DGG, AP 37057; Non. H-71171 *
(organ)	Contr. MC 20069; Nixa PLP 239
(organ and viols)	Vox STDL 500.990 *

HYMNS :

Audi benigne	T. SAWT 9439 *
Aurea luce	Van. BG 582
Ave maris stella	T. SAWT 9439 *
Christe redemptor omnium	HM HMSt 530 683 *
Conditor alme siderum	HM HMSt 530 683 *; Non. H-71171 *
Hi sunt quos retinens	Vox STDL 500.990 *
Hostis Herodes	D. DL 9400; Van. BG 582
Iste confessor	Van. BG 582
Jesu corona virginum	Vox STDL 500.990 *
Nobis datus	Vox STDL 500.990 *
Nova veniens e cælo	Vox STDL 500.990 *
Pange lingua	Van. BG 582
Qui paraclitis diceris	Vox STDL 500.990 *
Respice clemens	Vox STDL 500.990 *
Urbs beata Jerusalem	Vox STDL 500.990 *

Veni Creator Spiritus	*DGG*, AP 14019; *DGG*, AP 14537 (ARC 3003); *O L* 1; *Non.* H-71171 *
Vexilla regis	*DGG*, AP 14019; *DGG*, AP 14537 (ARC 3003); *DGG*, AP 37057; *G.* CSD 3606 *; *Ev.* SDBR 3174 *

MOTETS :

Apostolo glorioso	*Lyr.* 7190 *
Ave Regina cœlorum	*G.* HLP 6 (*Vic.* VM 6016); *T.* SAWT 9439 *; *Turn.* TV 34058 *
(instr.)	*Vox* STDL 500.990 *
Flos florum	*DGG*, AP 14019; *DGG*, AP 14537 (ARC 3003); *O L* 1; *Vic* 13557
Fulgens iubar	*Lyr.* 7190 *
Lætabundus exultet	*Allo* AL 14
Lamentatio sanctæ matris ecclesiæ constantinopolitanæ	*G.* DB 5117; *Non.* H-71058 *
Nuper rosarum flores	*Lyr.* 7190 *
O beate Sebastiane	*Dov.* HCR-5261
Salve quæ fama	*A S* 121
Salve Regina	*Amad.* AVRS 6163; *T.* SAWT 9439 *; *Van.* BG 582
Salvete flores	*Argo* ZRG 5148 *
Spiritus Domini replevit	*Non.* H-71171 *
Supremum est mortalibus bonum	*Dov.* HCR-5261
Veni Sancte Spiritus	*Non.* H-71058 *; *Van.* BG 634
Viri mendaces	*A S* 121
Vos nunc	*A S* 121

CANZONA SACRA :

Vergine bella	*D.* DL 9400; *DGG*, AP 14019; *DGG*, AP 14537 (ARC 3003); *DGG*, AP 37057; *Dov.* HCR-5261; *Non.* H-71058 *; *Pol.* 10751; *Van.* BG 582; *Vox* STDL 500.990 *

CHANSONS :

Adieu m'amour	*A S* 43; *BAM* LD 025 (*EMS* 206); *Dov.* HCR-5261; *G.* HQS 1041 *; *Non.* H-71120 *; *Vox* STDL 500.990 *
Bon jour, bon mois	*Allo* AL 14; *Amad.* AVRS 6163; *BAM* LD 025 (*EMS* 206); *G.* DB 5117; *G.* HQS 1041 *; *Van.* BG 582; *Vox* STDL 500.990 *
Ce jour de l'an	*BAM* LD 025 (*EMS* 206); *Dov.* HCR-5261
Ce mois de may	*BAM* LD 025 (*EMS* 206)
Craindre vous vueil	*Vox* STDL 500.990 *
Donna, i ardenti ray	*Vox* STDL 500.990 *
Donnez l'assault à la forteresse (instr.)	*Non.* H-71010 *
Franc cueur gentil	*Dov.* HCR-5261; *G.* HQS 1041 *; *Turn.* TV 34058 *
Hé, compaignons	*Amad.* 5018; *BAM* LD 025 (*EMS* 206); *Dov.* HCR-5261; *Van.* BG 634
J'atendray tant qu'il vous playra	*Amad.* 5018; *BAM* LD 025 (*EMS* 206); *Van* BG 634
Je donne à tous les amoureux (instr.)	*BAM* LD 025 (*EMS* 206)
Je languis en piteux martire	*Amad.* AVRS 6163; *BAM* LD 025 (*EMS* 206); *Van.* BG 582
Je ne vis oncques la pareille (by Binchois ?)	*D Fr.* 330222; *Vox* STDL 500.990 *
La belle se siet au pied de la tour	*BAM* LD 025 (*EMS* 206); *Dov.* HCR-5261
Le jour s'endort	*A S* 3; *West.* XWN 18683
Les doleurs dont me sens tel somme	*Ch M* LDX-A-8180; *Non.* H-71010 *
Malheureux cueur	*A S* 3012; *Dov.* HCR-5261; *Vox* STDL 500.990 *
Mon chier amy	*Dov.* HCR-5261
Mon cueur me fait tousdis penser (instr.)	*BAM* LD 025 (*EMS* 206)
Par droit je puis bien complaindre et gémir	*BAM* LD 025 (*EMS* 206)
Pour l'amour de ma douce amye	*G.* HLP 6 (*Vic.* LM 6016); *Non.* H-71120 *
Pourrai-je avoir vostre mercy	*A S* 3; *BAM* LD 025 (*EMS* 206)
Quel fronte signorille	*Dov.* HCR-5261
(instr.)	*Vox* STDL 500.990 *

334

Resvelons-nous amoureux (instr.)	*BAM* LD 025 (*EMS* 206)
Vostre bruit	*Van.* BG 582; *Vox* STDL 500.990 *

GENET, Elzéar, called CARPENTRAS

Motet :
Plorans ploravit	*Jer.* 401

GOMBERT, Nicolas

Mass :
Je suis déshéritée	*CFD* 148; *Non.* H-71051 *

Motet :
Super flumina Babylonis	*Tec.* 25

Chansons :
Alleluya m'y fait chanter	*D Fr.* 330224
En aultre avoir	*Acad.* 308
Quant je suis auprez de ma mye	*Per.* SPL 738
Souffrir me convient	*Per.* SPL 738
Vostre beauté plaisante	*D Fr.* 330224

Villancico :
Dezilde al caballero	*D.* DL 79409 *

ISAAC, Heinrich

Masses :
Missa carminum	*Cam.* CM 25004; *Non.* H-71084 *; *West.* XWN 18633
Ein fröhlich Wesen	*Lum.* AMS 5008

Mass propers :
In Dominica Lætare (excerpts from "Choralis Constantinus I"	*DGG*, AP 37094
In festo nativitatis S. Joannis Baptistæ	*D.* DL 79428 * (*Brun.* SXA 4546 *)
Excerpts from "Choralis Constantinus III"	*CPT* 5546

Motets :
Christe, qui lux es et dies	*T.* SAWT 9431 *
Ecce virgo concipiet	*T.* SAWT 9431 *
Illumine oculos meos	*Ang.* S-36379 *; *G.* HQS 1045 *
Imperii proceres	*DGG*, AP 14823 (198823 *) (ARC 3223)
Jubilate	*West.* XWN 18633
Optime pastor	*Lum.* AMS 67
Quis dabit capiti meo aquam ?	*D.* DL 79413 *
Rorate cœli	*T.* SAWT 9431 *
Sancti spiritus adsit nobis gratia	*DGG*, AP 14823 (198823 *) (ARC 3223)
Virgo prudentissima	*Non.* HB-73016 *

Secular vocal works :
A la bataglia (instr.)	*D.* DL 79424 (*Brun.* SXA 4536 *); *DGG*, AP 14823 (198823 *) (ARC 3223)
All mein Mut	*Ang.* S-36379 *; *G.* HQS 1045 *
Ami souffrée	*West.* WL 5347
An buos (instr.)	*DGG*, AP 14823 (198823 *) (ARC 3223)
Carmen	*Non.* HB-73016 *
Carmen in fa (instr.)	*DGG*, AP 14823 (198823 *)(ARC 3223); *Non.* HB-73016 *
Chanson (DTO, XIV, 51)	*G.* HLPS 7 (*Vic.* LM 6016)
Donna di dentro	*D.* DL 79413 *
Es vollt ein Maedlein grasen gahn	*West.* WL 5347 o
Et ie boi d'autant (instr.)	*Non.* HB-73016 *
Et qui la dira	*DGG*, AP 14032 (ARC 3071)
Fortuna desperata (instr.)	*Allo* ALG 14

Fortuna in mi (organ)	*DGG*, AP 14823 (198823 *) (ARC 3223)
Greiner, Zancker, Schnoepfitzer	*West.* WL 5347
Herr Gort, lass dich erbarmen (organ)	*Contr.* MC 20069; *G.* CLP 1442; *Nixa* PLP 239
Der Hundt (instr.)	*Allo* ALG 14
Ich stand an einem Morgen	*West.* WL 5347
In meinem Sinn (instr.)	*D.* DL 79413 *
Innsbruck, ich muss dich lassen	*Ang.* S-36379 *; *A* S 2501 LD; *Alpha* PHA 3001; *DGG*, AP 14823 (199823 *) (ARC 3223); *G.* CLP 1877; *G.* HLPS 7 (*Vic.* LM 6016); *G.* HS 1045 *; *Non.* HB-73016 *; *West.* WL 5347; *West.* XWN 18633; *West.* XWN 18848
J'ay pris amours (instr.)	*DGG*, AP 14823 (199823 *) (ARC 3223); *Non.* HB-73016 *
La la hö hö (instr.)	*G.* HLPS 7 (*Vic.* LM 6016); *Non.* HB-73016 *
La mi la sol (instr.)	*D.* DL 79413 *
La Martinelle	*Ois.* OL 50104
La morra (instr.)	*DGG*, AP 14823 (198823*) (ARC 3223)
Lasso, que ch'altri fugge	*Non.* HB-73016 *
Le serviteur	*D Fr.* 330222; *Non.* HB-73016 *
Mein Freud allein	*Ang.* S-36379 *; *G.* HQS 1045 *; *West.* WL 5347
Mein Lieb war jung	*West.* WL 5347
Mon père m'a donne mari	*D Fr.* 330222
Morte che fai ?	*Non.* H-71010 *
O Venus bant (instr.)	*Non.* HB-73016 *
Questo mostrarsi adirata di fore	*G.* HQS 1045 *
Sempre giro piangendo	*G.* HQS 1045 *
Susser Vater, Herre Gott	*G.* HQS 1045 *
T'meiskin was jonck	*A* S 2501 LD
Tricinium (instr.)	*Non.* HB-73016 *
Vergangen ist mir Glück und Heil	*Acad.* 308
Zwichen Berg und tiefem Tal	*A* S 1; *West.* WL 5347
Various canti carnascialeschi	*C E* 1042

LANTINS, Arnold de

CHANSON :
Puisque je voy	*A* S 39; *Van* BG 634

LA RUE, Pierre de

CHANSONS :
Autant en emporte le vent (instr.)	*DGG*, AP 14032 (ARC 3071); *A* S 27; *G.* HQS 1041 *
Fors seulement (instr.)	*DGG*, AP 14823 (199823 *) (ARC 3223)
Pourquoy non	*D Fr.* 330222; *DGG*, AP 14032 (ARC 3071)

MASS :
Dolores gloriose recolentes	*WS* PHC 9021 *

MOTET :
O salutaris hostia	*C.* RFX 73

REQUIEM :
Requiem	*T.* SAWT 9471 *; *WS* PHC 9021 *
Requiem : Introit	*G.* HLP 6 (*Vic.* LM 6016)

LASSUS, Roland de

MASSES :
Bell'Amfitrit'altera	*Van.* BG 651
Bell'Amfitrit'altera : Kyrie, Sanctus	*Chr.* 116
Douce Mémoire : Benedictus	*G.* DB 4949; *Vic.* 13498
Ecce nunc benedicite Dominum	*Non.* H-71053 *
In die tribulationis	*Van.* BG 651
Le Berger et la Bergère : Sanctus, Agnus Dei	*A* S 104

336

Missa pro defunctis : Benedictus	Vic. 13560
Missa VIII. toni ad imitationem moduli	DGG, AP 14071 (ARC 3077)
Puisque j'ai perdu	DGG, AP 14071 (ARC 3077); Lyr. 113
Vinum bonum et suave	Lyr. 113

PASSION :
St. Matthew Passion	Vox PL 400

PSALMS :
Seven Penitential Psalms (Septem Psalmi Davidis pœnitentiales)	DGG, AP 14129/30 (ARC 3134/5); DGG, AP 198014/5 *
De profundis	Ev. SDBR 3174 *

MOTETS :
Adoramus te Christe	Phil. 12027 G
Auditui meo dabis gaudium	Fest. 70-202
Ave verum corpus	T. SAWT 9431 *
Cum essem parvulus	Non. H-71084 *
Domine convertere	DGG, AP 14071 (ARC 3077)
Domine, labia mea	T. SAWT 9431 *
Exaudi Deus orationem meam	T. SAWT 9431 *
Factus est Dominus	Non. H-71084 *
Gloria patri	T. SAWT 9431 *
Improprium expectavit	DGG, AP 14071 (ARC 3077)
Ipsa te cogat pietas	Fest. 70-202
Jubilate Deo	Chr. 327 A; Mon. MCS 2054 *
Justorum animæ	DGG, AP 14071 (ARC 3077); G. ASD 641 *; T. SAWT 9431 *
Miserere mei, Domine	DGG, AP 14071 (ARC 3077)
Non avertas faciem tuam a me	Fest. 70-202
Nos qui sumus in hoc mundo	S M 33-01
Nunc cognosco	Non. H-71084 *
Resonet in laudibus	Non. H-71026 *; Per. SPL 597
Salve Regina	Per. SPL 597
Scio enim	G. HLP 8
Spiritus tuus	Fest. 70-202
Super flumina Babylonis	DGG, AP 14071 (ARC 3077)
Tristis est anima mea	O L 1; DGG, AP 14071 (ARC 3077)
Tui sunt cœli	DGG, AP 14071 (ARC 3077)
Venite ad me omnes	DGG, AP 14071 (ARC 3077)
Prophetiæ Sibyllarum	D Fr. 530001; Non. H-71053 *

ITALIAN SONGS (MADRIGALS, VILLANELLAS, ETC.) :
Amor, che ved'ogni	Sup. SUAST 50434 *
Ardo, si, ma non t'amo	Cro. 22160024 *
Chi chili chi ? (instr.)	D. DL 79424 * (Brun. SXA 4536 *)
Chi non sa	Per. SPL 738
Come la notte	Cro. 22160024 *
Hor che la nuova (instr.)	D. DL 79424 * (Brun. SXA 4536 *)
Hor vi riconfortate	Cro. 22160024 *; DGG, AP 14055
Il grave de l'eta	Sup. SUAST 50434 *
Io ti vorria contar la pena mia	DGG, AP 14055; DGG, AP 37008
Matona mia cara	Cro. 22160024 *; CPT 514; DGG, AP 14055; DGG, AP 37008; Ducr. Th. LPG 8238; Epic LC 3045; Mus. 214; Sel. LPG 8238; Vic. 10-0002; Vic. VICS 1231 *
O occhi, manza mia	Per. SPL 738; Vic. VICS 1231 *
O là, o che bon eccho	CPT 514; DGG, AP 14055; DGG, AP 37008; G. B 10196; Pol. 11755; Vic. LM 136
Passan vostri triomphi (instr.)	D. DL 79424 * (Brun. SXA 4536 *)

Providebam Dominum (instr.)	*CBS* SBRG 73525 *
Saccio na cosa	*Per.* SPL 738
S'io ti vedess'una sol	*DGG,* AP 14055; *DGG,* AP 37008
S'io vo dico	*Per.* SPL 738
Un dubbio verno	*DGG,* AP 14055 (ARC 3076)
Valle profonde	*D.* SDD 163 *; *D. DL* 79424 * (*Brun.* SXA 4536 *)

FRENCH CHANSONS :

A ce matin	*D Fr.* 35/8
Amour donne moi paix	*D Fr.* 35/8
Bonjour, et puis quelle nouvelle	*D Fr.* 35/8; *C.* DF 144
Bonjour mon cœur	*Lum.* 2.04.018; *D. DL* 9629; *D.* SDD 163 *
Dessus le marché d'Arras	*D Fr.* 35/8
En espoir vis	*DGG,* AP 14055 (ARC 3076)
Et d'où venez-vous ma dame ?	*Per.* SPL 738
Fuyons tous d'amour le jeu	*Mus.* 214
Gallans qui par la terre	*Cro.* 22160024 *
Guérir ma douleur	*D Fr.* 35/8
Hélas ! quel jour	*DGG,* AP 14055 (ARC 3076); *D Fr.* 35/8
J'ai cherché la science	*D Fr.* 35/8
Je l'ayme bien	*DGG,* AP 14055 (ARC 3076)
La nuit froide et sombre	*D Fr.* 35/8; *Cro.* 22160024 *; *Sup.* SUAST 50434 *; *Van.* BG 70671 *
Le rossignol plaisant	*D Fr.* 35/8; *Per.* SPL 738
Le temps passé	*DGG,* AP 14055 (ARC 3076)
Margot, labourez les vignes	*D Fr.* 35/8; *C.* DF 144
Ne vous soit étrange	*Am C.* ML 4517
O faible esprit	*Sup.* SUAST 50434 *
O mère des amours	*D Fr.* 35/8
Or, sus, filles, que l'on me donne	*DGG,* AP 14055 (ARC 3076)
O vin en vigne	*D Fr.* 35/8; *Brun.* SXA 4518 * (*D. DL* 710073 *)
Quand mon mary vient de dehors	*Cro.* 22160024 *; *D. DL* 9649; *Sup.* SUAST 50434 *
Qui s'y frotte, s'y pique	CID 33007
Sçais-tu dire l'Avé	*DGG,* AP 14055 (ARC 3076); *D Fr.* 35/8
Suzanne un jour	*D Fr.* 35/8
Toutes les nuits	*D Fr.* 35/8
Un doux nenny	*DGG,* AP 14055 (ARC 3076)

LIEDER :

Audite nova ! Der Bawr von Eselzkirchen	*DGG,* AP 14055 (ARC 3076); *DGG,* AP 37008; *O L* 1; *Vic.* 10-0002
Baur, was trägst im Sacke	*DGG,* AP 14055 (ARC 3076)
Der Wein, der schmeckt	*DGG,* AP 14055 (ARC 3076)
Die Fasznacht	*DGG,* AP 14055 (ARC 3076)
Ein Meidlein zu dem Brunnen gieng	*DGG,* AP 14055 (ARC 3076)
Hört zu ein news Gedicht (Das grosse Nasenlied)	*DGG,* AP 14055 (ARC 3076); *DGG,* AP 37008
Ich waiss ir ein Meidlein	*Acad.* 308; *Alpha* PHA 3001
Im Lant zu Wirtenberg	*DGG,* AP 14055 (ARC 3076)
Im Mayen	*DGG,* AP 14055 (ARC 3076)
Ist keiner hie	*DGG,* AP 14055 (ARC 3076)
Tritt auf den Riegel vor der Thür	*DGG,* AP 14055 (ARC 3076)

MANCHICOURT, Pierre de

MASS :

Quo abiit dilectus tuus	BAM 022; *Argo* RG 90

MONTE, Philippe de

CANZONA (organ)	*Contr.* MC 20069; *Lum.* AMS 5; *Nixa* PLP 239

CHANSON :
  Que me servent mes vers   *Van.* BG 70655 *
  Que me servent mes vers (instr.)   *Van.* BG 70655 *
MADRIGALS :
  Deh fate homai, co'l suon   *Van.* BG 70655 *
  In qual parte del ciel (instr.)   *Van.* BG 70655 *
  Non fuggi febo si veloce   *Van.* BG 70655 *
  Reviens vers moy   *Van.* BG 70655 *
  Settile e dolce ladra   *C.* WCX 539
  Sola te cerco ogn'hor   *Van.* BG 70655 *
  Sola te cerco ogn'hor (instr.)   *Van.* BG 70655 *
MASSES :
  Benedicta es cœlorum Regina : Benedictus Agnus Dei   *G.* HLP 8
  Missa secunda sine nomine   *Lum.* AMS 5

MORTON, Robert

CHANSONS :
  La Perontina   *Non.* H-71058 *
  N'aray-je jamais mieulx   *D Fr.* 330222; *Van.* BG 634

NASCO, Giovanni

MOTETS :
  Ave Maria   *Vox* PL 8790
  Facti sunt hostes   *Vox* PL 8790
  Migravit Judas   *Vox* PL 8610
  O salutaris hostia   *Phil.* N 00624 R

OBRECHT, Jacob

MASSES :
  Fortuna desperata   *D.* DL 79413 *
  Malheur me bat : Agnus Dei & Dona nobis pacem   *Chr.* 112
  Maria Zart : Qui propter nos & Et incarnatus est   *A S* 80
  Salve Diva parens : Qui cum patre   *Vic.* 13557
  Sine nomine : Kyrie, Agnus Dei, Credo   *Vic.* 13558/9
  Sub tuum presidium   *Amad.* AVRS 5026; *DGG,* ARC 198406 *; *Van.* BG 653
MOTETS :
  Parce Domine   *Phil.* N 00678 R (*Epic* LC 3045)
  Si obitus fuero   *G.* HLP 6 (*Vic.* LM 6016)
FANTASIA :
  Salve Regina   *T.* SAWT 9498 *
CHANSONS :
  Ic draghe de mutse clutse (instr.)   *Non.* H-71120 *
  La tortorella   *Phil.* N 00678 R (*Epic* LC 3263)
  Rompeltier   *T.* AW 8008
  Ein fröhlich Wesen (organ)   *Contr.* MC 20069; *G.* CLP 1442; *Nixa* PLP 239; *Sup.* SUAST 50548 *
  Tsat een meskin   *Amad.* AVRS 5028; *Van.* BG 634
  Vavilment (instr.)   *DGG,* 14823 (198323 *) (ARC 3223)

OCKEGHEM, Johannes

MASSES :
  Fors seulement   *DGG,* ARC 198406 *; *Lyr.* LL 108
  Kyrie   *G.* HLP 6 (*Vic.* LM 6016)
  Ma maîtresse   *Val.* MB 409
  Mi mi   *DGG,* ARC 198406 *; *Lyr.* LL 108; *RSS* 10 *; *Val.* MB 409
  Missa prolationum   *Kings.* 221
  Missa sine nomine : Kyrie & Gloria   *Phil.* N 00678 R (*Epic* LC 3045)

339

CANON :
Fuga trium vocum (organ)   *Contr.* MC 20069; *Niva* PLP 239

CHANSONS :
D'ung aultre amer mon cueur s'abesseroit ?   *Amad.* AVRS 5018; *Van.* BG 634
Fors seulement   *DGG,* AP 14069 (ARC 3052)
L'autre d'antan   *DGG,* AP 14069 (ARC 3052)
Ma bouche rit, et ma pensée pleure   *DGG,* AP 14069 (ARC 3052)
Ma maistresse et ma plus grande amye   *DGG,* AP 14069 (ARC 3052)
Petite Camusette   *DGG,* AP 14069 (ARC 3052)
Prenez sur moi vostre exemple (instr.)   RSS 10 * (*M G* MS-134 *)

MOTETS :
Alma Redemptoris Mater   *T.* SAWT 9419 *
Intermerata dei mater   RSS 10 * (*M G* MS-134 *)
Ut heremita solus (instr.)   RSS 10 * (*M G* MS-134 *)

PIPELARE, Matthäus

MASS :
L'Homme armé : Credo   *G. W* 1515

RORE, Cipriano de

CHANSONS :
En vos adieux   *H M* 25306
Hélas comment   *H M* 25306
Réjouissons nous   *Per.* SPL 738

MADRIGALS :
Anchor che col partire   *H M* 25306
Beato me direi   *C E* 1042
De la belle contrade   *Non.* H 71097 *
Non è lasso martire   *Brun.* SXA 4538 * (*D.* DL 710103 *)
Vergine pura   *G.* CLP 1847

GAGLIARDA   *CPT* 514

STOCKEM, Johannes

CHANSON :
Ha traistre amours   *D Fr.* 330222

SUSATO, Tielman

DANCES :
Excerpts from "Het derde musyck boexken" *Brun.* SXA 4511 * (*D.* DL 79419 *); *DGG,* AP 14032;
                                       H M 30610

WAELRANT, Hubert

CHANSON :
Musiciens, qui chantez   *H M* 25306; *Non.* H-71026 *

WERT, Giaches

MADRIGALS :
Dunque basciar   *Van.* BG 565
Vezzosi augelli   *D.* DL 710103 * (*Brun.* SXA 4538 *)

WILLAERT, Adrian

CANTI CARNASCIALESCHI   *C E* 1042

CHANSONS :
A l'aventure   *Ody.* 32160202 *
Dessus le marché d'Arras   *D Fr.* 330224; *Ody.* 32160202 *
Un jour je m'en allai   *Acad.* 308

MADRIGALS :
  Con lagrime e sospiri
  O bene mio
  Quando nasceti, amor ?

MAGNIFICAT

MOTETS :
  Beata viscera Mariæ Virginis
  Domine Jesu
  Dulces exuviæ
  O crux splendor

RICERCARE :
  Instrumental ensemble
  Organ

VILLANESCAS :
  Madonn' io non lo so
  O dolce vita mia
  Zoia zentil

VILLOTTA :
  Un giorno mi prego

G. DB 5018
A S 2501 LD; *Brun.* SXA 4538 * (*D.* DL 710103 *)
Ody. 32160202 *

RSS 18 *

Ody. 32160202 *
CFD 147; *RSS* 18 *
Ody. 32160202 *
Ody. 32160202 *

G. HLP 9; *Allo* AL 14; *Ody.* 32160202 *
Contr. MC 20069; *D* 123407; *Nixa* PLP 239; *RSS* 18 *

A S 2501 LD
Ody. 32160202 *
Ody. 32160202 *

A S 2501 LD

Index of Names

A

ADAM DE LA HALLE : 59.
ADAM VON FULDA : 249, 273.
ADIMARI, Boccaccio : 164.
ADIMARI family : 164, 200.
ADRIAEN VAN WESEL : 205.
AFFLIGHEM, Johannes of : 23, 24, 27.
AGRICOLA, Alexander : 62, 69, 75, 103, 110, 128, 129, 131, 142, 225, 226, 228, 231, 250, 262, 269, 273.
AGRICOLA, Martin : 273.
ALBA, Duke of : 261.
ALAIRE : 131.
ALBERT II, Emperor : 268.
ALBERT V, Duke of Bavaria : 278.
ALBINUS : 19.
ALBORNOZ, Cardinal Gil Alvarez Carillo de : 221.
AL-FARABI : 27.
ALFONSO I of Ferrara : 233.
ALSLOOT, Denis van : 178.
AMBROS, August-Wilhelm : 10.
AMBROSE, Saint : 67.
AMPHION : 69.
ANCHIETA, Juan de : 262.
ANERIO, Felice : 246.
ANIMUCCIA, Giovanni : 100.
ANTICO, Andrea : 136, 228, 249, 250.
ANTONIO DE CAMBRAY : 225.
APOLLINAIRE, Guillaume : 65, 202.
APPENZELLER, Benedictus : 143.
ARBEAU, Thoinot : 156, 158, 167, 200.
ARCADELT, Jacques : 110, 131, 140, 238, 240, 242, 257, 258, 273.
ARIOSTO, Lodovico : 237, 240.

ARISTOTLE : 14, 27.
ARISTOXENUS of TARENTUM : 17, 27.
ARON, Pietro : 243.
ATTAINGNANT, Pierre : 132, 137, 138, 139, 164, 166, 217, 251, 255, 256.
AUGUSTINE, Saint : 20, 27, 67, 81, 82.
AUXERRE : 131.
AVERROËS : 27.
AYMON, the four sons : 164.

B

BACH, Johann Sebastian : 37, 54, 89, 185, 186, 191, 236, 290.
BAERD, Antonio : 225.
BAETHEN, Jacob : 143.
BAIF, Jean-Antoine de : 139, 140.
BAKFARK, Valentin : 267.
BALDINI, Vittorio : 257.
BALLARD, Robert : 139, 278.
BANCHIERI, Adriano : 246.
BARBE, Antoine : 143, 253.
BARBIER, Guillaume : 58.
BARBIREAU, Jacobus (called BARBINGANT) : 89, 92, 250.
BARTHOLOMIO DI FIANDRIA : 222.
BARTOLI, Cosimo : 69.
BASTON, Josquin : 143.
BATHEN, Jacob : 143.
BATTRE, Henri : 222.
BAULDEWIJN, Noël : 272.
BAUTIER-REGNIER, Anne-Marie : 228, 242.
BEATRICE OF ARAGON : 227, 267.
BEAUJOYEULX, Balthazar de : 155.
BEDFORD, John of Lancaster, Duke of : 73.
BEDINGHAM, Johannes : 268.
BEETHOVEN, Ludwig van : 88, 95, 185, 186, 187, 290.

BELDEMANDIS, Prosdocimus de : 47.
BELLE, Jean : 143.
BELLEAU, Remi : 140.
BELLERE, Jean : 143, 164, 166, 257.
BERCHEM, Jachet : 131, 132, 238, 242.
BERCHEM family : 132.
BERG, Johann vom (called MONTANUS : 217, 249, 273, 274.
BERMUDO, Juan : 267.
BESSELER, Heinrich : 10, 67, 72, 116, 117, 200, 214, 222.
BEZE, Théodore de : 145.
BINCHOIS, Gilles : 31, 48, 60, 62, 67, 70, 72, 73, 74, 89, 100, 107, 108, 116, 117, 121, 122, 151, 161, 249, 261, 267, 268.
BOETHIUS : 19, 20, 21, 22, 23, 27, 32, 47, 67, 89.
BONMARCHE, Jean : 264.
BORREN, Charles van den : 10, 77, 161, 250.
BOSCH, Hieronymus : 194, 210.
BOULEZ, Pierre : 191
BOURBON, Charles, Duke of : 74, 129.
BOURGEOIS, Louis : 145.
BOUTEILLER : 131.
BRABANT, Duke of : 58.
BRACONNIER, Jean (called LOURDAULT) : 258.
BRAKELE, Mathieu de : 60.
BRANTOME : 155, 168.
BRAQUE, Georges : 193.
BRASSART, Jean : 221, 268.
BREDEMERS, Herry : 62.
BREU, Jörg : 269.
BROUCK, Jacques de : 257.
BROUWER, Jehan de : 60.
BROWN, Howard Mayer : 130, 173.
BRUCK, Arnoldus von : 271.
BRUEGEL, Pieter : 10, 136, 168, 210.

BRUGES, Victor de : 225.
BRUMEL, Antoine : 69, 75, 78, 92, 107, 131, 142, 226, 227, 228, 233, 258, 273.
BUKOFZER, Manfred : 73, 86, 87, 161.
BURCKHARDT, Jakob : 10.
BURGKMAIR, Hans : 175.
BURMEISTER, Joachim : 281.
BURTIUS, Nicolaus : 227.
BUSET, Martin : 266.
BUSNOIS, Antoine : 31, 62, 68, 77, 101, 107, 110, 124, 126, 129, 142, 192, 223, 228, 249, 250, 261, 268, 273.
BUUS, Jacob : 203, 242, 272.
BUYOR : 131.
BYRD, William : 110, 267.

C

CACCINI, Giulio : 286.
CADEAC, Pierre : 131.
CALVIN, Jean: 145, 146, 274.
CAMBRAY, Antonio de : 225.
CAMELIN : 131.
CANIS, Corneille : 138, 256, 262.
CAPELLA, Martianus : 19.
CARA, Marco : 228, 230, 231, 238.
CARLIER : 31.
CARMEN, Johannes : 67, 70, 72.
CARON, Philippe : 31, 68, 126, 268.
CARPENTER, Nan Cooke : 28.
CARPENTRAS : 110, 131, 240, 268.
CASERTA, Antonello da : 65.
CASERTA, Filippo da : 65.
CASSIODORUS : 20, 21, 32.
CASTIGLIONE, Baldassare : 34, 121, 231.
CASTILETI : 138, 271.
CASTRO, Jean de : 139, 146, 257, 272.
CAULERY, Jean : 146.

343

344

346

Contents

PUBLISHED BY FREDERICK A. PRAEGER, INC., NEW YORK • WASHINGTON • LONDON /
THE PRINTING OF THE PRESENT VOLUME WAS COMPLETED ON JUNE 30, 1968 BY
THE PRESSES OF THE IMPRIMERIES AND ATELIERS D'ARTS GRAPHIQUES LEEMANS
AND LOISEAU, INC., OF BRUSSELS / THE PLATES FOR THE ILLUSTRATIONS WERE
EXECUTED IN THE WORKSHOPS OF PHOTOGRAVURE DE SCHUTTER, INC., OF ANTWERP
/ THE BOOK WAS DESIGNED BY FERNAND BAUDIN / THE TEXT WAS PRINTED ON
CLIMATIC SPECIAL 140 GR. PAPER MANUFACTURED BY PAPETERIES DE VIRGINAL,
INC. / THE COLOR PLATES WERE PRINTED ON DOUBLE-COATED ART PAPER ALFA-
TYPE MANUFACTURED BY COPA, TURNHOUT, INC. / THE BINDING WAS DONE
IN THE WORKSHOPS OF J. AUSTRAET, M.A.P., IN BRUSSELS / THIS VOLUME,
ORIGINALLY IN FRENCH, ALSO APPEARS IN FLEMISH, GERMAN AND ENGLISH
EDITIONS.